AUGUST STRINDBERG
THE BEDEVILED VIKING

Statue of Strindberg by Karl Eldh

AUGUST STRINDBERG

THE BEDEVILED VIKING

BY V. J. McGILL

NEW YORK
RUSSELL & RUSSELL · INC
1965

ACKNOWLEDGMENTS

The author wishes to express his gratitude to Alice I. Bryan for much help and criticism in the preparation of this book. He is also indebted to Esther M. McGill for assistance with the Naturalism chapter, and to Dr. Houston Peterson for many fruitful suggestions.

Anyone writing on Strindberg must find Nils Erdmann's learned study: *August Strindberg, Die Geschichte einer kämpfenden und leidenden Seele,* an invaluable mine of information, richly supplemented by the more recent volume of Erik Hedén: *Strindberg, Leben und Dichtung.* Much of the first-hand material, of course, is to be found in the life work of Strindberg himself, amounting in all to more than 40 volumes, of which nearly all are luridly autobiographical.

V. J. M.

New York, 1930

CONTENTS

CONTENTS

ILLUSTRATIONS

AUGUST STRINDBERG

1

THE QUEST OF THE ABSOLUTE

ON May 19, 1912, a great procession moved down the streets
of Stockholm toward the poor section of the New Church
Cemetery. It was eight o'clock in the morning, a time when the
streets are usually deserted, but here in sudden evidence were
thirty thousand people—students, laborers, artists, musicians, playwrights, cabinet members, foreign delegates, and a royal prince.
With banners, insignia, black suits—the full accoutrements of
mourning—they marched in silent order with the stiff and somewhat preposterous dignity of the Swede. Many who had known
the dead man well, their faces wan and tired at that early hour,
reviewed for the first time the meteoric career of that northern
Prometheus. With the detachment and perspective which death
alone confers, they saw him as a revengeful giant, striding three
generations with his wrath and judgment, scourging and destroy-
ing, laying bare what was ugly and evil, surprising himself and
others in those terrible, most private moments of weakness,
awakening the soul to distrust and to a knowledge of its own hell.

The man in the hearse had been a scourge to them all. He
had reviled them, betrayed their secrets, blasphemed their ideals.
He had attacked the family, marriage, love, with ruthless concentrated fury. He had satirized schools, universities, art, science,
business. No person or institution had escaped his hatred and his
evil tongue. Yet they paid homage to him, this enemy of society,

marching thirty thousand strong to his grave, in a demonstration
which has seldom been accorded to a private man. Like Hercules,
his infamies were forgiven. By a sudden change of sentiment,
the outcast had become a god. This procession which celebrated
his apotheosis was no less than a national event.

Long before eight o'clock, thousands had gathered at the home
of the old fighter and regarded silently the house whence had
come so much passionate though erratic intellection. Eight huge
laborers bore the coffin to the hearse and the long lines formed
in the street. First came the students with their white caps and
standards. They honored a man who had been a student, a rebel,
an iconoclast, a radical, one who had struggled as they had, and
suffered and doubted and drunk himself into forgetfulness. Behind the white caps were the red banners of the trade unions.
Socialists and Democrats paid tribute to an open enemy who
years before had cursed and reviled them but who lately had returned to be their friend and defender. Then came the others,
rank after rank.

Though the hour was early, the northern sun had risen high
and shed a blank light over the silent pageant with its banners
and its long sequence of somber faces, conferring to the scene a
sudden tragic reality but also something of the timelessness of
historical events. A younger brother of Odin had died but the
Swedish nation, after all his wars and sufferings, would not have
it so. They prepared his place among the immortals. With the
sadness of these obsequies was mixed a mystical sense of the unreality of death, the triumph of genius over the accidents of time.
This man who had burnt himself out with thought, whose very
soul had gone into his works, will be a contemporary of many
generations. He has become one of that company of minds which
hovers over time and history, menacing with his passions and invective, evoking his suspicion and despairs in other minds distant
from him, elevating them with his mad energy, causing them to
think and feel and breathe as he did. It was perhaps with a reali-

zation of this high destiny that he spoke his last words: "Now everything personal has been obliterated."

John August Strindberg, whose death this ritual commemorated, was Sweden's greatest poet. He had written fifty-six plays, nine novels, numerous autobiographical works, lyrical poems, historical and scientific treatises. He had given Sweden a literature, developed its language to artistic perfection, composed the sagas of its kings, celebrated its culture and natural beauty. No one before had written with such music and grace nor with such rapid brutal energy. Strindberg had made Swedish bold and swift and trenchant, the voice of the orator that spoke of kings, of Chinese pottery, of sulphur and the Swedenborgian heaven with equal application; yet he had made the language lyrical, too, full of music, subtle and elusive. In his style were many innovations, crudities and charms and some bad grammar—the consequence of his genius and rapid composition. He was not shy of ugly expressions, even in his poems. His language was but a symbol of his reckless courage, his nervous tension, and high-strung discontent. For him thought and action were never separated from words. If his phrases became coarse and offensive, it was because he inveighed and defamed. The words did not falter but sprang to life with the thought. This gave his language its force and vindictiveness.

In his fury and energy he resembled a natural force, striking institutions and men with desperate blows, careless of the odds or his own danger. Once, when all Sweden was ready to accept him, he wrote, as he admits, "a terrible book," a vicious and calculated attack on society. At one stroke his reputation was lost and his admirers turned away in aversion. For this book, *Black Flags,* and for *The Red Room,* he will probably never be forgiven; they were too convincing, too insulting to be borne.

Before Strindberg there had never been such a critic—never such humiliating delineations of society and man. Everything he touched turned to dross—all the cherished ideals. If there were circumstances in human life which were delicate and unapproachable, protected from scrutiny by accepted lies and pretexts, Strindberg was sure to uncover the deceit. Marriage and love were reputable and good, yet everyone knew that at the bottom there was something mysterious and evil that it wasn't decent to discuss. Strindberg discussed this thing which everyone had tried to forget. In his plays he made such brutal disclosures that people left the theatre with a sense of personal insult. His critical novels brought forth such bitter protests that Strindberg stopped reading the papers. In general, society could not endure these tasteless uncalled-for attacks, and the fact that they were persuasive in their realism and undeniably superior in their technique only made the matter worse.

In the early nineties, therefore, the rumor gained ground, to persist for many years, that Strindberg had gone mad. Even his peers were often unable to understand him or see the point of his wildness. The brothers Brandes, schooled in contemporary literature and inured to the worst of Ibsen and Zola, were yet quite unprepared for *The Father*. Its author, they said, must be a madman. Others of his contemporaries conceived him as a natural force to whom moral laws did not apply; they forgave him everything. Others, in the same spirit, emphasizing his Norse and perhaps Finnish blood, pronounced him a wild-man longing still for the solitary woods whence he came, distrustful of men, resentful of cities and crowded places, angry, eruptive, vicious, walled in by his brooding subjectivity beyond which laws and gods were only chimeras. These critics saw him moved by passions, not by reason, a savage in his measureless hate and abnormal sensitivity.

Strindberg himself sometimes took this view and resented a mild and amiable delineation, for he saw himself foremost as a *Machtmensch*, passionate and uncompromising. The Viking, he says in *By The Open Sea*, is always half philosopher, half marauder, and here perhaps he was thinking of himself. In any case, his

misanthropy and savage energy were not qualities to recommend
him to society. At times the hatred of his own countrymen was
so pronounced, even after his literary eminence had been
thoroughly established, that he left his dear Stockholm with
eagerness, refusing to return to be again misunderstood and condemned—and torn to bits by such unappeasable critics as Wirsén and Levertin.

But, if Strindberg was usually rejected in Sweden, his reception
in other countries was even less gracious. In Germany, to be sure,
he had a run and in France, too, for a briefer period, his plays were
performed. But the French and the Latin peoples in general
could never understand or regard as more than a foolish vagary
his violent hatred of women—that race of ravishing creatures put
here precisely to be adored. In Germany, to be sure, there had
been since Schopenhauer a tradition of misogyny. There, where
Neitzsche and Weiniger have been widely read, *The Father,
Miss Julia,* and other such blasphemies of women have been accepted and performed with a gradually increasing success. In
Spain, Portugal, and Italy, on the other hand, scarcely a Strindberg play was put on and very few of his works were translated,
for Strindberg was both savage and theologian with all the
compact and incorruptible energy of Savonarola or Brand, yet
inconsistent, unorganized, at war with himself; he was not apt
to make a wide appeal to the stage of these countries. In England
a certain niceness and prudery drove him out—critics thought
him too gloomy, too mad and vicious—and it is only recently
that he has made any headway among English-speaking people.

One principal cause of Strindberg's unacceptability in so many
places was his absolutism, his fanatical adherence to ideals and
causes to the neglect of those exceptions and compromises which,
though they sacrifice the sublime, yet preserve the amenities,
making the world human (though perhaps all too human),
social, and comfortable. At his death, Martin Anderson-Nexö,
while admitting his greatness, refuses to count him among those

whom we usually call the greatest minds—"for that he was and remains too young." It was precisely this inalienable youth in Strindberg which made him an extremist and a bigot. The most bitter disillusions could not sour him. Love, religion, ambition frustrated, might turn to poison, never to ashes. There was nothing in him of the amiable cynic. If his cause was false, he forswore it, suffered, fought another. When he lost faith he became a skeptic, but not a gentle Pyrrhonist with cautious language, rather, as in *The Red Room,* a two-handed swordsman hacking on every side. Thus, like young Siegfried, he was not destined to become an old god with the old tired ways, but to die fighting with the splendid, absurd devotion of youth. In his last days he wrote polemical articles for Socialists and Democrats, for whom he became a sort of god, though during this time he was tortured by disease and at the end a cancer.

The absolutism of Strindberg is a master key to his character and to his writings. It was because he sought *the* woman, the blessed virgin-mother, with all the virtues and perfections, however incompatible these might be, and could not content himself with less, that he suffered at the hands of women all his life and became through his art and violence the greatest woman-hater in literature. It was his extreme ideal of truth and his fanatical hatred of humbug and imposture which motivated those scathing attacks on his contemporaries—the social dramas and novels. It was his quest for the absolute again which made him sacrifice wife and child, finally himself, that he might continue his fantastic chemistry, transmuting the baser metals into gold. The last step in his absolutism is the mystical denial of science and the restitution of religion, which he had for a long time rejected. Strindberg's desperate and sometimes grandiose search for *the* woman, *the* truth, the goal of impossible ambition, God and perfection, approaches at its best to the sublime, at its worst to the pathetic.

Strindberg's absolutism was shifting and many-sided. His

Weltanschauung shows the changes and the contradictions of a man fighting desperately in a changing environment, with reverses and disillusions, for the one changeless truth. Under the influence of Buckle, Voltaire, Darwin and Nietzsche, he became an atheist, and few writers have cursed the Christian God more vehemently than Strindberg in *By the Open Sea*. But he was also, after his conversion, a fanatical Christian who came to regret, like Sir Thomas Browne, the simplicity and credibility of Protestant dogmas, for he would try his faith by far more difficult beliefs. When Strindberg returned to God he became, as was usual with him, an extremist. He would have Christianity imposed everywhere and made compulsory in schools. He was known all over Europe as a woman-hater, yet no one worshipped women with such prostrate adoration.

At times he was an aristocrat as rash and intemperate as Nietzsche. In 1889 he wrote Georg Brandes that there was one thing he knew about himself; he was an aristocrat and would remain so the rest of his life. This was not true. "The son of a maid-servant" returned to be a leader of the Socialists and Democrats, espousing the cause of labor and condemning in his swift, telling style the idle rich. Strindberg's waverings between the aristocrat and the people were numerous and often abrupt, for the issue was complex and elusive, and he, the arch rebel, could never compromise.

The economic motif in Strindberg plays a persistent role. At times he valued economic utility so highly that he condemned all literature as a worthless luxury of the idle rich; useful truth was to be found not in poetry but science. At other times he satirized business, made it out a sort of swindle, and the producers—they were louts and criminals. Under the influence of Rousseau, he bids us to return to nature and give up the falseness of an artificial culture. Again he reverses his position. Now, we are to cherish culture and combat nature. These reversals of doctrine, many more of which could be added, do not import a fickleness of mind, for Strindberg fought and suffered through every change, but rather a romantic inescapable urge for the truth.

It is interesting to observe that, however much Strindberg shocked his contemporaries by the violence and novelty of his views and their frequent reversals, his ideology follows closely the main streams of thought in Sweden and in Europe. For no one had a keener sense than Strindberg for the thoughts and feelings about him. No one divined better than he what his contemporaries were thinking or were about to think, for his eye was open to everything that happened in Europe, whether in literature, politics, economics, religion, or (to a certain extent) science.

In the 80's, when Europe was under the dominion of science and evolutionary naturalism, Strindberg obeyed the *Zeitgeist,* or rather he became the *Zeitgeist,* for he created almost single-handed the naturalistic play. But, the naturalistic play may be regarded as merely a dramatic proof of the tyranny of natural law over the actions of men and their secret thoughts. The naturalistic play and naturalistic literature in general, arose as a necessary consequence of a wide-spread authoritative movement of thought in the 19th century. This movement needed to understand itself, to see itself reflected in dramatic form, drastically free from all irrelevance.

Strindberg was one of its earliest spokesmen. Zola had written *Thérèse Raquin,* Ibsen, *Ghosts.* Naturalism was in the air and Strindberg took the scent. Turning from the photography of the de Goncourts and the usual realism of Ibsen, he developed the naturalistic drama after the pattern of Zola's *Experimental Novel* and Balzac's *Cousine Bette.* In such plays as *The Father, Miss Julia, The Dance of Death,* he displays an intensity of mood, a concentration of action, a subtlety of psychological analysis which has never been surpassed even by the great Norwegian. Here, also, which is not always the case in Ibsen, law and circumstances clearly govern the action, and the characters, for all their egoism and intensity, are shown powerless and pitiful. In these plays, Naturalism, with its iron laws binding the fate of men, reached its finished excellence. Here, the protracted horror of *Thérèse Raquin* is surpassed, *Ghosts* with its final anguish outdone. But, Strindberg's development of naturalistic drama with all its metaphysical presuppositions was largely a reflection of the spirit of European history in the 1880's.

When, a decade later, he turned to a new dramatic form, this too was but a reflex of the changing times. In 1892, in a famous drinking resort in Berlin, Strindberg made a vehement attack on Naturalism. His friend, the poet Dehmel, surprised and hurt by his violence, withdrew from the company. Strindberg hurried after his friend to reassure him but the outburst was significant. Naturalism, Strindberg now thought, had served its purpose, and a new form was needed. In various parts of Europe a reaction had set in against science, evolutionary philosophy, atheism. Such men as Verlaine, Huysmans, Bourget, Brunetière, Wilde, and Beardsley were converted. In 1896 Strindberg was also converted and learned theology from Swedenborg: out of this came a new dramatic form.

The new play was religious, treated of suffering, sin, punishment, expiation; it followed Strindberg through sin and misery to the cross. Strindberg's play-world was now quite changed. The laws of nature, of the omnipotence of which Buckle had long ago persuaded him, were now found powerless to explain his new experiences. The soul in its pilgrimage had seen many things on the long road to Damascus. The world now became alive with numbers, with secret unsuspected potencies. Common events had a significance beyond themselves. Surrounded by mysteries, crossed by the shadows of another world, the soul retired within itself to develop intuition and a secret knowledge, opposed to the aristocratic reason of the earlier period; it became at once more powerful and more humble.

In Strindberg's new plays intervened supernatural powers, both good and evil, and this expressed a common tendency of the times. (Buckle and Darwin and Haeckel had been modified to suit Swedenborg and his mystical conceptions.) Sorrow and suffering have, if anything, increased, but now there is grace and religious atonement. The plays of this period (1897-1909), *Toward Damascus, Advent, Easter, The Spook Sonata, The Dream Play,* etc., though symbolic and mystical in their pattern and mood, retain much of the convincing detail from everyday life and much of the tyranny of economic and other laws which distinguished in such an important way the plays of the earlier naturalistic period. In the new plays the laws of nature still operate but not consistently. They must share their government with the law of Karma and the higher powers.

This blending of naturalism with mysticism and symbolism, a form developed by Ibsen and Maeterlinck as well as Strindberg, is a dramatic invention of the first importance. In the last decade of the 19th century it became the dominant mode. Hauptmann, like Strindberg, though somewhat later, turned from naturalism to symbolism and mysticism, retaining, however, at the same time the life-giving substratum of natural law and homely circumstance. With Toller, Keyser, Werfel, Wedekind, and O'Neill this type of play was further developed and became known as expressionism. The influence of Strindberg on O'Neill is especially interesting and can be traced through many of his plays. In preparation for his writing O'Neill once read almost everything he could lay his hands on; "practically all the classics and of course all the moderns, Ibsen and Strindberg, especially Strindberg." The pervasive influence of Strindberg on the modern plays of Germany and America is undisputed. Yet Ibsen is more often credited. Shaw and other critics have declared Ibsen and Strindberg to be the two pillars of contemporary drama. But, if this is true, the honors are certainly unequally divided. Ibsen is often performed; Strindberg, at least in this country, almost never, yet he has written fifty-six plays, historical, naturalistic, symbolical, mystical, religious, even fairy plays—a variety to suit every taste.

The explanation of this neglect of Strindberg is to be found in his peculiar nature, his wild and undisciplined volition, his unwillingness to make concessions to popular taste, his predilection for dramatic conventions which had no precedent, and the autobiographical and hence special character of his themes. Edward Brandes once wrote him an admonishing letter complaining of his self-will and whimsicality: Were you to control yourself, write an Ibsen play for example, you might become the greatest dramatic figure of our time. You have it in your power to become a dictator, yet you choose to follow your whims. At Strindberg's death a critic wrote in much the same vein: "The earthly honors, which fell to Ibsen's lot—a wiser but much poorer genius—Strindberg's exuberant life and creative power could not secure." It is this strain of mad and heedless energy and self-will, a dionysiac recklessness, which made Strindberg a sort of epic hero, prodigal of his time and strength. While he wasted himself in spiritual dissipations, Ibsen worked, as far as outward circumstances were concerned, in peace. A passionate and irrepressible individuality in Strindberg has cut him off, up to now, from the larger audience to which Ibsen has appealed.

Ibsen, like most of his contemporaries, was impressed with the dauntless power of Strindberg and resented his slurring attacks. Strindberg had satirized *A Doll's House,* had ridiculed Nora and her ilk, blasphemed the new woman as a preposterous criminal with the brain of a child. He had referred to her defender as the great Norwegian blue-stocking. Ibsen felt keenly the opposition and rivalry of the younger playwright. In 1899, a man calling on Ibsen expressed his surprise at seeing a portrait of Strindberg above his writing desk. "Yes," said Ibsen, "that picture hangs there not because I am friendly toward Strindberg, for I am an enemy of his. . . . But, I cannot write a line except when this bold man with his mad eyes looks down on me." Evidently the subtle madness in Strindberg's eyes, like the viper he kept on his desk, held Ibsen fast and provided a necessary poison for his creations.

Ibsen, like Strindberg, fell under the spell of the great theologian Kierkegaard. Both were strengthened by him in their sensitiveness to lies and imposture and in their polemical intensity; both derived from him much of the motive power of their plays. It was Kierkegaard who taught both playwrights to draw out the impossible paradox of "all or nothing," God or the world, the ego or mankind, art or life. Both embodied this formula in dramatic form, and by espousing both sides of the antithesis produced a play of great vitality and decision. Brand, the absolutist, sacrificed everything for God; Peer Gynt, the opportunist, nothing for anything. In *Brand,* Ibsen accepts the paradox, in *Peer Gynt* he denies it. Both show the influence of Kierkegaard. But what Strindberg learned from Kierkegaard was much more than that. He came to a consciousness of his own deep sin, of the drastic momentous antithesis in the world about him—a hatred of compromise. He came to a knowledge of an invincible power within him to conquer all evil. All this he carried over into his own life, so that while Ibsen in Brand created a superman, Strindberg became one. Strindberg, the absolutist, is Brand, or rather he is many Brands, for his absolutism takes many forms—first a fanatical pietist, then a heaven-storming atheist, then an alchemist who will undo the world, then a magician with secret power, finally a saint.

In his novel *The Scapegoat,* a character changes his skin and character and face overnight—a parady, no doubt, of his own instability. But, throughout all his vicissitudes of doctrine, his transformations of taste and character, can be discerned the same identical man storming and fighting—whatever the cause—in quest of the Absolute. Like Tamburlaine, he besieged many towns and knew many moods. When Tamburlaine negotiated peacefully, his banners were white; when roused to anger, they became red; when determined upon war and destruction of the rebellious town, his banners turned black. Strindberg's bitterest attack on society was *The Red Room,* his most terrible one, *Black Flags.*

II

THE SON OF A SERVANT

STRINDBERG was born January 22, 1849, in a desolate
poverty-stricken flat in Stockholm. He came into a family
quite shattered by economic reverses, in which there were already
too many mouths to feed. He was unwelcome, the one born too
late. This he saw in people's eyes and in their manner toward him.
His mother already had a favorite and there was no one, neither
in the family nor in the world outside, who wanted or needed him.
His first feelings that he could remember were fear and hunger.

The time of his birth was also fateful in the western world. All
Europe was swept by disorders and revolutions—the clashing of
old ideals and alignments. In France the starving silk workers
raised the battle cry of "live working or die fighting." Workers,
students and bourgeoisie stormed the monarchy and the timid
king retired. The news of the fighting in Paris was a signal to revolt in other places. In Austria the old chief minister, Metternich,
long the symbol of firmness and absolute authority, was driven
from his powerful seat. In Italy the popular patriot, Garibaldi, defended valiantly but hopelessly the Roman Republic of Mazzini.
In 1849, also, modern socialism sounded its battle cry in the *Communist Manifesto* and Marx and Engles came forward as the
revolutionary exponents of a scientific socialism fated to sup-
plant the class war and all future capitalistic sovereignties. In Germany and Switzerland, too, there were warring factions and

divisions and over all Europe these hostilities reached a sudden height and vehemence in the year that Strindberg was born. It was the war of liberals and conservatives, republicans and monarchists, aristocrats and people, masters and slaves, which accumulated and came to a head in this special year and the conflict seemed almost universal.

The discord was also in Strindberg's soul. His father being an aristocrat and his mother a servant, he was both master and slave, or neither, and the consciousness of the division of his nature and sympathies between these two hostile factions, or the cancellation of the difference in nonentity and ostracism pursued him painfully through the agitated long years of his life. And it would seem that in some mystical way the rancours and conflicts of Europe had officiated the turmoils of this suffering soul and made Strindberg the tragic symbol of those factious times. In any case he was born in the midst of conflicts which continued thereafter to divide his mind, inclining him now one way, now the other, throughout his life.

While Strindberg was being born, his great rival, opposed to him by temperament and national antipathy, with twenty-one years head-start, was finishing his first play, *Catilina*. Henrik Ibsen who was at this time an apothecary's assistant in the Norwegian village of Grimstad had worked secretly through the nights to finish this work, much as Strindberg, nineteen years later, as a doctor's assistant and tutor, composed secretly his first play, *Hermione,*—also an historical drama. When Ibsen's friend failed to find him a publisher or a producer he waxed as angry and intemperate as any young playwright on such an occasion just as later Strindberg fumed and grew doubtful when his *Master Olaf* was rejected,—for in these matters there is much repetition. In October, 1849, Ibsen wrote to his friend Schulerud thanking him for the "trouser material" which was "very acceptable, for I must needs save as much as possible nowadays." While Strindberg was getting born Ibsen suffered the same adversities as were destined for him, for the poverty and humble beginnings of Ibsen are those of Strindberg.

But in Strindberg's case it is much easier than in Ibsen's to trace the development of genius out of a poor and inauspicious background, for the Swedish writer whose interest in himself amounted to an almost exclusive passion is the most autobiographical of authors—more even than Goethe and Tolstoi. A thorough psychologist and pupil of Rousseau, he has given us an accurate and circumstantial account of his beginnings and progress through life. The first work of a long series of confessions is *The Son of a Servant,* and John (Strindberg) is the hero.

John's mother was the daughter of a tailor and was a waitress when John's father met her. For years she lived with Mr. Strindberg as his mistress but finally became his wife just before John's birth. She was an ignorant and somewhat neurotic woman but venerated her husband who had raised her to a higher social level and loved her children when her many duties permitted her the time. In later years her constitution was terribly weakened by twelve child-births and she suffered much from consumption. At heart she always remained a democrat, sided with the servants even against her children and never turned a beggar away without something.

John's father on the other hand, though he had fallen pretty low in the world, married beneath him, and now maintained a very poor and insufficient establishment,—nine people in three rooms,—remained an aristocrat in habits and taste to the end. In appearance he was distinguished, in manner grave and reserved. He had a taste for elegant clothes and clean linen and required his servant to wear gloves when he cleaned his boots in order that he should not dirty them.

During the period preceding John's birth financial disasters had swept the whole family "and its scattered members had crept together like frightened poultry, friends and foes alike, for they felt that they needed one another for protection." An aristocratic aunt with two well-educated daughters came to live with them with all the appurtenances of gentility and the sad reminders of vanished greatness. The aunt wore a lace cap and the children kissed her hand. She taught little John and his brothers good manners and how to behave in polite company, while his mother bound up his wounds and solaced him in trouble. And what a contrast for John between this elegant lady and his own humble mother! Here already were the two opposite ideals between which he was to swing for so many years. But there was also a democratic grandmother on the mother's side who kept to herself and neither loved nor understood the aristocratic members of the household. She was a severe, religious old lady who "taught the ABC, rocked the cradle and pulled hair." When she saw that John was no one's favorite, she tried to comfort him but he was never contented with his grandmother's love; he wanted to win his mother—his pale, black-eyed little mother—but she already had a favorite, his eldest brother, and could give poor John but a hasty and somewhat perfunctory affection.

That John could not satisfy his deep longing for his mother's love was a grievance which he never outgrew nor forgot so that years afterward as a full-grown man he was haunted by strange desires, sought the mother in other women but fled too from the consanguinity and could nowhere find his love or avoid her, or escape from his ambiguous passion. Perhaps his failure to win a high place in his mother's heart imported to him a general inability to win women at all, and weighed more heavily on his spirits than he or anyone else suspected. In any case he developed a shy reserve toward women, whom he continued to regard with a sort of religious awe. In his imagination he raised them to unattainable heights, and his search for love and understanding was a futility.

From the first he felt with a sensitiveness as common in children as it is unsuspected, that he was unwanted, unwelcome. The overcrowding was terrible—three rooms for the mother and

father, five children and two servants—and only a few articles
of furniture remained. Food was scarce though it was carefully
divided and meat was served only once a week. John was almost
always hungry when he left the table. This was a special hardship for him. Like a nervous, high-strung colt he needed more
nourishment than the others. In later years he cherished rich food
and strong drinks which gave him strength and gusto and complained bitterly that the women fed him badly.

Like other children when they become aware of their ego, he
regarded it as a thing of overwhelming importance, but unlike
the rest he was too sensitive and drastic, and possessed too little
of the genial sloth of the spirit, to forget his birthright in the
amiable exchanges of social life. He was therefore dismayed that
this god within him, this unique and priceless self, should be so
frequently and so thoughtlessly injured and that in general it
should pass by without the slightest recognition. The sense of his
injuries and slights, and the total failure in others to recognize his
uniqueness made him cling more desperately than ever to his ego
and to retire more and more to its fateful, lonely spaces. If he
could not be a triumphant god with his world in homage he
must be a martyr god, counting his thorns and wounds a glory.
He would not learn the humble lesson that his upstart ego was
but a fraud and a fly-by-night. This was a thought which proved
always too much for him. Throughout his life he saw himself as
a martyr and when fifty-five years old he returned, in his novel,
The Scapegoat, to describe his early, gloriously unmerited sufferings. For he continued true to himself and never forgot nor completely disavowed the child's first feeling of unlimited power and
goodness.

Yet he *was* unwelcome, injured, and neglected. His parents,
he felt, did not want him. And this produced at the same time a
persistent doubt and a weakness of will. So Strindberg came to
believe. In *The Father,* he has the captain say: "My parents did
not want me and thus I came into the world without a will of

my own." The one person who might have helped John over these difficulties and smoothed out the contradictions forming in his character and outlook, was his father, but there were too many children for that and he was far too busy. The tired bread-winner of the family appeared only at meal times and then more as a hostile stranger than a friend. When John and the other children did anything wrong it was always the father's name that was mentioned. They were invariably threatened with his anger and punishment. As a consequence they came to regard him with great apprehension and were rendered speechless with fear by his sudden appearance. Though a hard man, the father was not as severe as he seemed. The role of justice and hangman to the children was not of his choosing but rather a duty which had de-volved upon him as the head of the family. Like the characters in Strindberg's plays, his harsh justice, his cruelty, his cold reserve, his stern countenance itself, were but obligations of his station in life. Like the pale-faced, harassed people in the plays, he was not a bad man nor self-willed, but a servant of those necessities from which there is no escape. Both he and the children were victims, for one thing, of the educational system advocated by Locke, according to which punishment should correct each fault and be administered at times for its own sake. The notion that our original nature is weak or vicious and must therefore be severely corrected at every step, gave a somber and threatening tone to the household, made the children, especially John, con-tinually fearful and apprehensive, and imposed an onerous duty on the father. Another influence on the family life was the prev-alent Pietism. This cast a melancholy shadow over the most inno-cent pleasures and in practice it made hypocrisy almost a neces-sity. At first when John's mother prayed at night, he was puzzled and could form no idea what God was like. Later his concep-tion developed through many phases and contradictions which it will be interesting to follow. One of his first insights was that God in any case must be higher than the king. Once he was shown "God's Eye" in a church but he could make nothing of it. Once the fire alarm rang in the middle of the night with a deep boom which made him shudder and weep with fear. But his mother comforted him saying, "Don't be afraid; God protects unfortunate people!" He had never thought that of God before. In the morning the servant-girl read in the papers that there had been a fire in Soder, and that two people had been killed. "It was God's will," said the mother.

From his earliest years Strindberg was keenly alive to improbabilities and contradictions in what he heard and he was especially sensitive to lies. He pondered over them and grew uneasy. Later he was to write volume after volume exposing these stupidities and lies. He felt all the more keenly about it because on several occasions he had been obliged to lie to escape punishment though as a matter of fact he didn't escape it even then. At other times he had been accused of lying when he was innocent. Once while the family were at the table the father discovered that a flask of wine had been emptied and demanded who was guilty. John blushed. "It was you, then," said his father. "I didn't drink the wine," sobbed the child. "So you lie, too. When dinner is over you will get something." He was then forced to admit his crime and ask his father for forgiveness. Then he was beaten. Later he confessed his innocence to a maid. It was overheard and he was beaten again. Experiences of this kind embittered John and sharpened his consciousness of lies and injustice in the world about him.

Throughout the story of *The Son of a Servant,* Strindberg introduces psychological remarks and explanations of great subtlety and interest. With regard to lies he maintains that children often lie, or seem to lie, because of their inattention and forgetfulness and should therefore not be unjustly punished. Punishment in general, he feels, is too often vindictive. In a great many families the feeling grows up among the children that every little mistake or offense requires a criminal, one who must suffer for it, so that the children are continually on edge for fear that some wrong has been done of which they will be accused. Punishment of course may be necessary in some cases. When a child like John is afflicted with moodiness and perversity so that he does exactly the opposite of what is expected or he himself wishes, is miserable and at the end of his nerves, he will actually beg for a whipping and be comforted and quieted when it is administered. "But there is another way of expelling the 'black dog.' One takes the child in one's arms so that it feels the magnetism of friendship and is quieted. That is the best way of all." Evidently this was a kind of treatment which Strindberg almost never enjoyed, for in his family there was little sentiment.

Strindberg is not only remarkable for his special insights; he is a pioneer of a new psychology, which has been greatly developed by modern writers. This is the psychology of the natural discords and discontinuities in the soul, whereby it fails to adjust its movements to those of the outer world. An example may be seen in the account of John's trip to see his old wet nurse. This woman, ridden by disease which has rendered her unrecognizable, is confined in a stinking, poor house. When she sees the child she has nursed she trembles violently and shows the greatest joy. But John himself is bored by the whole affair. He cannot recognize his nurse or experience any of the feelings he should. Similarly when his mother died he wept for a whole day so that when the funeral came he had no more tears to shed. He was horrified to find himself no longer heart-broken, his mind turning selfishly to other matters. But the fact was, his grief had spent itself for the time being and he could not even join his father in an appropriate sigh. Many of these cases of the dissonance of mind with the affective situations of the objective world are to be found in Strindberg's writings. This was a psychological insight which was very important to him and like Dostoevsky he continually returned to it.

The account of John's early education is also of some psychological interest. Among all of Strindberg's early experiences those at school were perhaps the most crucial and formative. At six o'clock in the morning the seven-year-old boy and his brothers awoke in the pitch dark, long before the family arose, and made their way through the snow and the cold to the school. As John approaches his destination, the fatal clock strikes the hour. "Fear lends wings to his feet, his satchel bangs against his back, his temple beats, his brain throbs. As he enters the churchyard gate he sees that the class-rooms are empty; it is too late!" Once in the school he is treated with the same callous indifference and brutality as the other late comers. He hears the shameful on-slaught on the other offenders in the next room and weeps for humiliation,—"to think that he should be fallen upon like an animal doomed to slaughter, or a criminal." For the rest it is Latin and the rod, from morning 'till night, a continual horror. One of his teachers used to send for the cane at the beginning of the lesson and then tried to find as many as he could who were unprepared. Forty-eight years later Strindberg had not yet for-gotten this man. The teacher he introduces in *The Scapegoat* is the same man. He has a passion for pulling the fine black hair of a certain boy (Strindberg) and cannot desist from this curi-ous sadism. In the end this character hangs himself like Strind-berg's real teacher at the Clara School. And yet this man had his good side which the pupils never saw. He was a good conscien-tious teacher and was continually hurt by the ingratitude of the world. His character was so complex that people held very differ-ent opinions about him. Like his pupils he was not free but a victim of the system.

One of the greatest trials of Strindberg's school life was that he was continually held back with duller pupils and made to repeat lessons which he had known for a long time. The natural conse-quence of this was that he became bored and indifferent and lost all interest in the work. Once when his teacher asked him what he knew about Gustav I, the complete futility and silliness of the question made him ashamed to answer. He knew all about

Gustav I, the teacher and everybody else knew. Then why should he ask such an unnecessary question? When he attempts to answer it, however, his repugnance produces a sort of aphasia and he says nothing. The other boys laugh and the teacher thinks him unprepared. This is only one instance. It seemed that Strindberg must always undergo the ghastly inanity of repetition; like the ridiculous Phoenix, he must forever do the same thing over again though he recoiled from the necessity with a metaphysical horror. He must repeat his lessons. He must take care of the younger children and so live over again his early years. The reaction to this continual return to earlier experiences is everywhere present in Strindberg's writings and repetition is one of the darker penances of the soul on its weary road to Damascus. In *The Dream Play* the Officer must return to school and learn arithmetic, for he is still (people tell him) quite ignorant of the fundamentals. The sophisticated intelligence of the Officer is, however, soon baffled by the simplicity of his lessons and he shows himself as much of a fool as the young Strindberg in his class-room. But the vein of repetition occurs elsewhere—in love, and marriage, in hope and despair,—always with a somber and disheartening effect. In *The Dream Play* the Pensioner has spent fifty-four years waiting for newspapers and meals and the Officer his whole life bringing flowers to the imaginary love of his youth—always with the same joy and disenchantment. In these delineations all humor is carefully suppressed. As an old man Strindberg was still tortured by his childhood experiences. Throughout his life he avoided in books all references to school life. His own recollections were too painful and humiliating to be borne.

Another of Strindberg's early impressions, acquired mainly at school, was the distinction between the classes of society. At first he formed only a dim idea of this. He knew of course that there were authorities above him, his brothers, the scolding maid, his father with his stick. And above his father he knew there was the deputy landlord who threatened him with the landlord. But above them all, at the very top of this hierarchy of authorities, there was the king. Later at school he noticed that some of the children were badly dressed and wore boots which had an unpleasant odor. He noticed too that the teachers hated these children and beat them much oftener than the others. As for himself he, too, sometimes hated these boys, sometimes sympathized with them and hated the young lordlings in their fine clothes. At times he felt he belonged to one class, at times to the other, but usually to neither.

A somber theme running through all these humiliations and miseries was the repeated deaths in his own family. Deaths followed births with a terrific frequency and one of his earliest recollections was of the black candy served at the funerals. Ibsen's earliest memories were of an arrest and a madhouse, a scaffold in the market place, a church tower with its black mystical dome and the shrieking of a sawmill that sounded like the cries of women, or the gnashing and crashing of a guillotine. Strindberg's first impressions were of death, and the booming and chiming of bells.

"His first awakening to consciousness was mixed with the pealing, chiming, and tolling of bells. All his first thoughts and impressions were accompanied by the ringing for funerals, and the first years of his life were counted out by strokes of the quarter. The effect on him was certainly not cheerful, even if it did not decidedly tell on his nervous system. But who can say? The first years are as important as the nine months which precede them." (*The Son of a Servant,* 1886.)

III

YOUNG ŒDIPUS

WHEN Strindberg was only eight years old he already pondered and criticized and found no good reason for many things which his elders took for granted. For one thing, he could not understand why he was made to study Latin grammar or what connection it had with real life. At the Clara School noth-ing was explained except Latin declensions, and no attempt was made to show the reason or the consequence of all the discipline, and drudgery, and repression he was made to endure. John there-fore came gradually to regard his school life as a mysterious and painful ritual which was necessary to be undergone, for some in-comprehensible reason. Later in life when he himself had taught school and considered the matter from different points of view, he saw no reason to alter his opinion. It remained in his mind a sad hocus-pocus, full of crosses and humiliations,—good for the soul only as a penance or a purgatory. Most people are inclined to forget these early trials or are ashamed to mention them be-cause in retrospect they appear somewhat laughable. But Strind-berg, the pupil of Rousseau, could not forget what he had suffered as a child and in his plays and novels continually returns to the theme. One of the reasons for this was that his childhood meant more to Strindberg than is the case with other men so that he probably never outgrew it or made the normal adult adjustments.

In the midst of the mystery and unreality of his school life came the nine-year-old daughter of the headmaster, and then everything was changed. She sat at the back of the class and the boys were not allowed to turn around to look at her, though they felt her presence none the less and vied with one another in brilliant recitations. John fell in love with her at once and spent his time in hopeless longing, though what it was he desired from her he would have been unable to say. To hold her or kiss her? Certainly not. Such things were not done in his family. The truth was, he didn't know what he wanted. She provided, nevertheless, an object for his black mood of melancholy and for this he had a continual need. Like "Father Time" in Hardy's *Jude the Obscure* he was perhaps too early conscious of the misery and vanity of life. He did not, to be sure, like Father Time, go to the length of hanging himself and the other children, but his melancholy was often serious and once or twice reached the breaking-point at which everything commenced to shift and give way. One day in the midst of his infatuation he seized a knife and threatened to cut his throat. His mother was alarmed but John could not tell her what was the matter. No, he would have been ashamed to tell her. This was the first but not the last time that Strindberg was brought to the point of suicide by the love of women. The dear, unfathomable, unconquerable creatures he continued to seek out, woo, and long for, and they prepared many crises in his life from which he scarcely recovered. In each of them lurked his sweet dark-eyed mother but beside her, too, a hostile stranger in whose blood crept an unappeasable hatred. She lured him to death and dishonor. At times, even the mother turned on him with revulsion and then his thoughts became too poisonous to express, too revolting even for him.

About this time John's father decided to send the three elder boys away for the summer to a boarding school in the country. It was the first time Strindberg had been away from home. As the night falls on the steamer and the setting sun stretches long shadows and gives an unusual aspect to the world, John begins to miss something. "He has a feeling of emptiness, of being deserted, broken off. He wants to go home, but the consciousness that he cannot do so at once fills him with terror and despair and he weeps. When his brothers ask him why, he says he wants to go home to his mother. They laugh at him, but her image recurs to his mind, serious, mild, and smiling. . . . Her image seems glorified, and draws him with unbreakable cords of longing. This feeling of loneliness and longing after his mother followed him all through his life. Had he come perhaps too early into the world? What held him so closely bound to his mother?" To these questions Strindberg could find no answer. Had he later in life read Freud or Adler the whole matter might have been cleared up for him, but this apparently he never did. As it is, however, he has analyzed his own case with such thoroughness and judgment, that the work of the psycho-analyst is very much simplified. His confessions themselves constitute a rough analysis and a remarkable anticipation of the psycho-analytic theories.

Strindberg, as he himself recognized, "never became himself, was never liberated, never a complete individuality," though he struggled and later in life made furious and grandiose attempts. "He remained, as it were, a mistletoe, which could not grow except upon a tree; he was a climbing plant which must seek a support." His first feelings that he can remember were fear and hunger. "He seems to have been born frightened, and lived in continual fear of life and men." [1] This early fear persisted through his life, only changing its object from time to time. It was a fear of his father and other authorities, a fear of his brother's fists— later of women and witches, Doppelgänger, strange hostile men, his friends, vampires and demons. But why this fear? Was it a sense of guilt? In *The Confession of a Fool,* he himself raises this question. His first wife whom he regards as both woman and mother fondled and caressed him like a little child, softly and

---

[1] Persistent morbid fears during childhood are frequently taken as a sign of repressed incestuous desires.

tenderly, on the first day of their love. Yet he desired her as a woman. "Am I then a product of a whim of nature?" he asks. "Are my feelings perverted because I want to possess my mother? Is that an unconscious incest of the heart?"

Once away from home he felt more than ever his solidarity with his brothers. He was, as he says, only a third part of a person. When his brother fights and gets the worst of it, John throws himself between the contestants, for he cannot bear to see one of his own flesh and blood beaten or hurt. Similarly when his brothers are reprimanded he suffers as if he were the culprit, for the blood-tie is too close to be overcome. As for himself, he avoided every occasion of reproach and tried to live quietly without offending anybody, but he defended himself when attacked by bullies. He desired to be neither the highest nor the lowest, neither to rule nor to be bullied. He did things which would cause him to be praised, not to be superior to others but to escape scorn and contempt. At times he longed for his mother. At times, exuberant, he reveled in freakish amusements, for his mood was variable and uncertain, and neither the outdoor life nor the manual labor which his father had enjoined upon him, was capable of calming his nerves.

After his return from the country, his moodiness and craving for self-esteem resulted in very curious behavior. His father one day brought home a peach (a rare fruit), which he divided among the children, but John was forgotten. And in this oversight he took a special pleasure, for it showed that somehow he was exceptional and really more deserving than the rest. The same feeling visited him on another occasion when after picking berries with other children, his shyness held him back when they were distributed, so that he received none. On still another occasion he went out of his way to suffer martyrdom. When his brother Gustav, whom he idolized at this time, went away, John bought a bouquet of flowers and gave them to his mother as from Gustav. The brother was praised for his kindness and John thought cold. Still he felt no bitterness. "His youthful, enthusiastic love of sacrifice had found vent, the struggle against injustice had made him a self-tormentor, and he kept silence." Other experiences of the kind strengthened Strindberg's feeling that he was one chosen for special sufferings. It prepared the way for his early pietism and later when, as he felt, the whole world had turned against him and even his own mind could not be trusted, it was this exultant martyrdom which saved him.

The next summer was a very important one for John. Now, for the first time he was separated from all of his kin and this meant that he had therefore no "intermediary bond of flesh and blood with his mother." Though the experience was a good one for John, made him more independent and more of a separate individual, he had intermittent fits of longing for his mother. At such times her image "rose up in his mind in its usual ideal shape of protectiveness and mildness, as the source of warmth and the preserver." It was perhaps on account of these longings for the unobtainable mother that he fell in love this same summer with an equally unobtainable young lady of twenty, though it was not so much love as a distant madonna worship. This type of worship, which Strindberg later thought very pernicious for boys, especially in its effect on their subsequent attitude toward women, is the result, he thinks, of the very unnatural way in which boys are educated, their isolation from girls, and the secrecy, and mystagogery with which the whole matter of sex is surrounded. John did not dare to approach his enchantress but spied on her during her walks, but his older brother Gustav who visited with him on his way to Paris, went up to her directly and spoke to her. For the timid John this feat was the pinnacle of courage. His brother rose in his estimation to the degree of a superman. Gustav's visit was another high point in the summer. John idolized this vigorous, robust, healthy-minded brother, and voluntarily took second place in everything. As a man, Strindberg continued in his admiration of full-blooded, exuberant men but he also

feared the encroachments of these robust souls on his own struggling individuality, grew worried and uneasy at their jovial
humor and was distressed with too much swagger of the flesh.

In these early years John was an indefatigable reader. Chiefly
he preferred natural science and read everything he could find on
the subject. His father, who in his youth had been interested in
electricity, loaned him books on physics and chemistry. Poetry
he could neither understand nor appreciate. Here he seemed to
be in a different world. But romances attracted him exceedingly
and he responded to the love episodes just as an adult would do.
Why then, he asks himself, was he still treated as a child, and so
painfully hindered in his normal development?

His parents admired John's learning, but his father was perhaps a bit jealous and felt himself inferior in this respect, while
his mother, when she had tired of listening to his erudition,
warned him against intellectual pride and told him always to
remain "simple." It was also during this period that John really
got acquainted with his mother. After twelve confinements she
was much weakened and that, together with the consumption
from which she suffered, finally obliged her to keep to her bed.
John became her constant companion and since the authority of
parent over child was now relaxed, they became really good
friends. John had many things to tell his mother, for he had read
widely, and the mother, in her turn, could instruct her son on
many matters of which he had no experience. Among other
things she warned him against the besetting sin of boyhood and
made him promise never to enter a brothel even out of curiosity,
for then no man can resist temptation. In the meantime the servants took advantage of their mistress' illness, kept their lovers
in the kitchen, drank the health of the boys, had their own way
with the household economy and almost undermined the home.
Finally one night during his fourteenth year John was awakened
by his father's voice: "Come to Mother's death bed." After hours
of weeping, he asks himself the question, "How will it be when

Mother is no longer here? Nothing but emptiness and desolation, without comfort or compensation—" Suddenly he thought of the ring his mother had promised him. That will be something to remember her by, and then—"a gold ring looks fine after all." He found himself at his mother's death bed with this shameful thought! For years he was tortured by the memory. It became like a demon shadowing him along the long corridors of his mind, waiting until his resistance was weakened, that it might appear and make him suffer the shame once again. And yet he was quite innocent. Children are not responsible for their chance thoughts, which are very often, innocently, quite inappropriate. In *The Gothic Room* the children greet their adult sister quite cheerfully with "Mother is dead," their only feeling being the joy of being the first to deliver the news.

With his mother's death John was brought much closer to his father, whether this was because his unconscious rivalry was weakened or because the old man himself had changed his attitude. For a time a sort of understanding and friendship sprang up between them. Perhaps John could forgive his father, now that his mother was dead, for his long possession of the woman that John himself had loved and longed for. And the father may have felt, for his part, the relaxing of his son's resentment and secret rivalry. The boy grieved for his mother but—and here we have a typical Strindbergian turn—his "real sense of loss hardly lasted for a quarter of a year. He mourned for her indeed a long time, but that was more because he wished to continue in that mood, though it was only an expression of his natural melancholy, which had taken the special form of mourning for his mother."

His father in the meantime has grown sad and quiet. As he sits in the twilight with his little daughters playing at his feet, John feels sorry for the old man, who under the weight of his grief has become quite changed. Before long, however, the mourning is broken up by the return of John's lively brother from his Paris studies and the appearance of an old schoolmate of the father whose irresistible humor soon sets the whole house to laughing. In the midst of this recovery Oscar Strindberg announced unexpectedly that he had resolved upon making his housekeeper his wife. John's brothers are a little embarrassed because they have recently admired the young woman themselves, and John, because he has recently fallen out with her. And John, after considering the matter for a time, is violently opposed to the marriage and argues with his brothers that the father should not marry before the expiration of the year of mourning, nor impose a step-mother on the children. When the relatives of the housekeeper came to visit, John absented himself and went to his room miserable and hungry for the night. On other occasions he showed coldness and disapproval and was, in fact, for years quite unappeasable. This, of course, turned his father and the new wife against him and probably laid the foundations for much of his future suffering. His loyalty toward his mother and resent-ment toward the intruder were in fact a way of shunting off his melancholy and general dissatisfaction but they expressed also a strong half-conscious hatred of the woman who had dared to take his mother's place.

John's interest in his own origin and the relations between men and women had an early awakening. What knowledge he had of these matters was acquired haphazard by contacts with other boys and thus had an ugly and distorted aspect. Like many gifted children he was sexually precocious and the prevailing Pietism which pronounced damnation upon all sexual enjoyment made him ponder incoherently on this sin which, to his mind, seemed very terrible and inescapable. Moreover, the crowded quarters in which the family lived during his early years may have exposed him to scenes to which children are seldom witnesses. Quite possibly this also colored the boy's thoughts and gave them a morbid turn. About this time John came across a book which was to cost him terrible suffering and to cover with gloom and ugly forebodings a whole half-year of his life. The book was entitled: *Warning of a Friend of Youth against the most Dangerous Enemy of Youth*. This book, which was concerned with a common sin of boyhood, drew a very lurid picture of the consequences; John was aghast as he turned the pages. "His knees trembled, his face became bloodless, his pulses froze. He was, then, condemned to death or lunacy at the age of twenty-five! His spinal marrow and his brain would disappear, his hair would fall out.—And the only cure was—Christ." Even then, the body was lost. Christ could only cure the soul. John determined to give up the world since he had only a few years to live anyway and devote himself exclusively to saving his poor soul from damnation.

As it happened, his circumstances at this time were very favorable to mortifications and penances. His chief humiliation was the lack of money. He was the only boy in school who did not wear the traditional cap and was thus singled out as an object of ridicule. His clothes, as he grew, became too small for him but he had to wear them all the same, though his comrades jeered at his short trousers. Sometimes old clothes were made over for him with such a grotesque result that he was made constantly miserable and grew self-effacing by habit. When the students exercised, he could not remove his coat like the others and was put to great embarrassment. What was perhaps worse than all this,— his textbooks were hopelessly out of date so that he had difficulty in following the work. Moreover he suffered from hunger. His breakfast allowance was so ridiculously small that he gave up the idea of that meal altogether and spent the money for tobacco. Then again he was obliged to wake up early in the morning to do chores. All through the day in his free hours little services were required of him. He had no time to himself but must pay in work and humiliation for every day of education.

Yet the family were proud of the scholar they were raising and took some credit to themselves. The thing that made these duties and privations doubly hard to bear was that they were imposed not out of necessity, for the Strindberg finances were now in good shape, but out of cruelty and retaliation. His father had apparently determined to humble him, his step-mother he knew was his enemy, and so his tribulations continued. Once he accidentally broke the spring of his friend's pince-nez and promised to get it fixed but he had of course no money and as time went by his friend became pressing. Later he secured his father's permission to take lessons in mathematics with two of his schoolmates. When it came time to pay them his father felt sure that they were too rich to accept anything, so that John was again in what was, for him, a terrible predicament.

Once it came to an open break with his step-mother. One day John determined to save his little brother from an unjustified whipping, for the child he knew to be innocent. When his father returned, John himself was whipped for interference, but he had frightened his step-mother at least, that was something, and after this if the children were punished it was done in his absence. Strindberg had no forgiveness in his heart for this woman who had usurped his mother's place and in his plays and stories, the sad plight of every deserving child follows the fairy-book form. It is the cruel step-mother who plays the witch and starves and tortures her charge. To have a step-mother is, he feels, the worst of misfortunes, but a loving mother is the greatest blessing. This pattern of human relations in which an impostor takes the place of the beloved was with Strindberg a continued obsession. In consequence, he takes great pleasure in *Hamlet* and values it above other plays, for was not the Danish hero in much the same situation as his? Did he not suffer the cruel tyranny of a step-father which is almost as bad as a step-mother? Did he not brood and hesitate out of regard for his mother whom he worshipped?

His step-mother continued a thorn in his side. She had to respect his learning but tried to humiliate him at every turn. To this end she employed one powerful weapon which made all his erudition seem vain and idle: her pietism, her first-hand authentic knowledge of God; and this she used to such good advantage that young Strindberg, finally aroused to his own defence, himself turned pietist and beat her at her own game. Another defence against this woman was to remind her ceaselessly that she was but an intruder and not his real mother.

But his too great loyalty and love of his mother was dangerous. When young Œdipus learned of his terrible destiny, how he would kill his father and marry his mother, he travelled far into foreign parts that he might there escape his doom. When Strindberg first fell in love, it was with a woman quite the opposite of his mother. She was masculine and with her he never felt any desire, as he did with other women, to put his head in her lap. Here then, he had escaped from his mother, but it was only momentary. Religion, too, became important in his life and this, as he says, "also helped him to cut the mental navel string which had previously bound him exclusively to his parents." But Pietism and strange loves were but a shadowy and illusory escape from a destiny which could not be put aside. Like Œdipus he must pay the penalty before the fates were appeased.

IV

PIETISM AND EROTICISM

TOWARD the end of the 17th century a new renovating movement arose in the Lutheran church which broke up the complacent settled ways of orthodoxy and gave a new impetus to religious life. "Pietists," a name first applied by enemies in ridicule of a pretentious sect, was finally accepted by them as a highly appropriate designation. The pietists insisted upon the inwardness of Christianity, the importance of inner purity, and were far more interested in the practical life of virtue than in the subtle disputations of the theologians. They stressed the importance of frequent reading and discussion of the Bible and reaffirmed Luther's almost forgotten principle of the prerogative of the individual conscience. The movement was thus democratic and individualistic since it made no distinction of persons and allowed to the most ignorant and untutored the possibility of theological insight and secret knowledge of God. Through its insistence on feeling as the guide in religion, it lent itself to sentimentalism and was thus often espoused by people naturally inclined this way. In its later developments it turned ecclesiastical and called for antecedent sin, conversion, and agonies of remorse. In Strindberg's youth this movement was very powerful in Sweden and exercised so great an influence on him that he never escaped from it—even when as a hardened naturalist he cursed the Christian God and applauded the Anti-Christ, Nietzsche.

Many motives inclined John to Pietism. "Bankrupt on earth, since he was doomed to die at 25 without spinal-marrow or a nose, he made heaven the object of his search. Melancholy by nature, but full of activity, he loved everything that was melancholy. Tired of textbooks, which contained no living matter because they did not come in contact with life, he found more nourishment in a religion which did so at every turn." Moreover, it was a way to spite his step-mother, who, jealous of his superiority in culture, "wished to climb above him on the Jacob's ladder of religion." Irritated by her spiritual pretensions and resentful of the air of humble superiority with which she mocked his learning and accomplishments, John determined to outdo her in her own province and to become himself a child of God. He therefore attended services assiduously and once copied out from memory a whole sermon, which he could not refrain from presenting to his step-mother who received it, as can be imagined, with little pleasure. Yet she contrived to make a capable retort: "God's word," she said, "should be written in the heart and not on paper." With that the battle was on and the question was which of the two could be more humble and pious. In this contest the step-mother was at a great disadvantage for she was inconsistent, loving the pleasures of the theatre and dance though these were condemned by her own pietism. One Sunday when the whole family was expected to go on an excursion, John stayed at home to consult with his soul and wait for the Savior whom he had been taught to believe might come to him gloriously in one swift moment of conversion. Putting all thought of pleasure aside he betook himself to the church, a weird depressing place. Later, in the park, his prayers were interrupted by playing children. "Is it possible that all these must go to hell?" he thought. His conscience assented but his reason revolted at the measureless absurdity of it. In the evening when the family returned, full of boisterous happiness, John envied his brothers and sisters, yet started with remorse at the sincerity of this unwelcome feeling. He had but one comfort. "His step-mother did not look at him, for she had broken the Sabbath."

Three young girls of the family and the grandmother strove to bring about a reconciliation between John and his step-mother and at times they were successful, for the boy was not a firebrand of hate but yielded quickly to kindness and understanding. But the smouldering causes of his animosity, though they might be diminished, could not be destroyed altogether.

When fifteen years old, John fell in love (or was it only a passionate friendship?) with a woman quite the opposite of his mother, whom his step-mother could not but fear, for she was at once more cultured and masterful and a more accomplished pietist than the ignorant ex-housekeeper could ever pretend to be. This woman was the thirty-year-old daughter of the landlord. She ruled the household, entertained skillfully, was surrounded by admiring men (including John's own brothers) who loved and courted her. John watched her from a distance for a long time until finally one night she discovered him, and, taking a special delight in the boy's brooding, sickly self-consciousness, they became great friends. Often, when she left a delighted company of accomplished males and sought him out in his shy retreat, John was put to great embarrassment and was at a loss to understand how she could prefer his conversation to the sallies and clutches of those dashing bucks she had deserted.

John's first words with her show the sentimental, soulful tone which was to be characteristic of their friendship. "Heavens! how tired I am," said she. "Are you so unhappy, although you are always laughing?" he asked. "You are certainly not as unhappy as I am." As their acquaintance grew and she spent more time in his company, the rumor went around that she was in love with him. This led to serious conversations between the fifte-year-old boy and the spinster of thirty as to whether friendship between the sexes is possible, but John assured her that it was, and that his love for her was entirely spiritual and ideal. For her part, she accepted this news without feminine resentment and at once turned mother, helped him with his French, in which language they conversed and corresponded, and labored for his conversion, for she was more advanced than he in the order of Pietism. Their French conversation annoyed John's father who could not follow it himself and regarded it as a reflection on the other members of the household.

The lively spinster, once the darling of the family, sank to a very low regard when she became friends with John, and was no longer tolerated in the house. When she moved away a secret correspondence began which lasted for a whole year. "They wrote about Christ, the battle against sin, about life, death and love, friendship and skepticism—John was alternately her stern preceptor and her reprimanded son." When she had been too gay and frivolous she came to the gloomy boy with his high sickly forehead to receive her scolding, for a rebuke from him was a sweet torment to her dainty conscience.

One of John's essays to his spiritual friend was entitled "Is Man's Life a Life of Sorrow?" It concludes that man is naturally discontented unless he is at peace with his conscience. With God's help John will be happy and contented. His friend was not overpleased with this deliverance, for she found too little gloom and too much complacency in it. One should remain discontented with life, she wrote. Thus corrected, John wrote another essay entitled "No Happiness without Virtue; no Virtue without Religion" in which he so faithfully recorded his friend's ideas that she was perfectly satisfied. "One can find no peace," it announced, "till one confesses that one is the chief of sinners, and flies to the Savior. How foolish of us to push such happiness away!" Self-righteousness is especially condemned, whereas sin, which prepares the way for repentance and conversion, is almost praised. Old sinners come to God but the virtuous man is full of pride.

But this evangelical excess could not long escape John's inner criticism. At times he was beset with doubt. Thus, in one essay his whole tower of faith collapses and he is willing to believe that "Egotism is the Mainspring of all our Actions." This alternation between the extremes of faith and doubt and disbelief, the consequence of a feverish honesty and continual self-criticism, is to be traced throughout the long fantastic journey of the Swedish poet.

One of the main effects of John's soulful affair was that his pietism was much deepened and intensified and, in fact, so quickly exaggerated that the fantastic bubble of his faiths and torments was soon ripe for the breaking. At his confirmation, for which he had waited so long and painfully because he was "still too young," John did not attain the spiritual elevation he had expected, and was quite unmoved by the solemn initiation which reduced the boys and girls around him to tears and hysteria. No, the matter had been carried too far. It was becoming ridiculous. John suddenly decided that the best thing he could do would be to become a petty officer in the cavalry. He had sickened of his humiliations at school and hoped for little from a career as a scholar, while in the cavalry he would at least have an independent maintenance, and live in the out-of-doors, where, if any place, surely, he could escape the death at twenty-five to which he had been, as he believed, so sadly foredoomed. His spinster friend, however, was strongly opposed and dwelt on the immorality of soldiers. But John, more self-confident than ever in his declining faith, held fast, "his faith in Christ would preserve him from all moral contagion, yes! he would preach Christ to the soldiers and purify them all." But John never carried out this bit of evangelism. New experiences were to turn his thoughts in quite a different direction.

One of the principal causes of his backsliding from Pietism was his friend with the pince-nez. This energetic, opportunistic young fellow had had a sort of good-natured admiration for John's asceticism, but now took him in hand, and for better or worse, determined to make a man of him. First, he must have a good

meal at a restaurant. John experienced for the first time the ravish-
ment of excellent food and drink—beeksteak, cheese, brandy,
beer—in the company of a youthful friend, and the adventure was
a turning point in his life. He felt his muscles stir and his will-
power, long repressed, come to life. The room grew rosy with his
hopes and ambitions, vain though they were. Like a young stallion
he fairly snorted with joy at the good cheer and this awakening of
the flesh. His friend with the pince-nez urged him to give lessons
in order that he might have money to go out a bit and enjoy himself. Though John had never hoped for such good fortune, he
soon found himself a teacher in a girls' school with the means in
his power to attend parties and drink with his friends in the café.
Having no particular interest in Latin, and no longer sustained
by his pietist resignation, he began to read French, German, and
English novels during the recitations. And in other respects he
became a man of the world, learned to dance and play forfeits,
to kiss and to flirt a little with the waitresses. In the meantime, his
lady friend grew jealous and warned him against his new friend
and the girls with whom he consorted, reminding him of Christ,
his Savior. But John was too strong in the flesh to return to his
fasts and devotions. Though he continued his prayers out of
habit, his heart was not in it, and at times he marveled at the
slightness of the wind which had so easily blown down that
strong ivory tower of his gloomy faith. Under the influence of
his friend, the young engineer, "the doctrine of Christ the Judge,
the election of grace, the punishment of the last day, all went by
the board, and later even the divinity of Christ and the freedom
of the will tottered and sank under criticism." In the next year,
when he was asked to deliver a sermon, he had nothing to offer
but new interpretations and radical departures and only a shadow
of his old pious credulity remained. John was particularly worried
by the doctrine of freedom, for it seemed that according to the
pietists the will was both free and determined, free because it
could choose between good and evil, yet not free because his sal-

vation depended on God alone. "Thus he was not free and at the same time was responsible!"

This was Strindberg's first introduction to a problem which never ceased to perplex and trouble him, turning him now with hatred, now with mild extenuation toward the weaknesses and wickedness of men. When he could regard men as free, he vituperated their folly and deformities; when he saw them in bondage he felt only pity and sad kinship, for without freedom there is no moral responsibility and no one can be blamed. In *The Dream Play* the refrain of "Men are to be pitied," "Men are to be pitied," sounds the death-knell of freedom, for here is a land in which wrong-doing is a necessity, and no one can remember how to laugh. Throughout Strindberg's novels and plays the theological puzzle of freedom and necessity plays a deep antiphonal where hatred of wickedness and pity of man's bondage form the alternate measures.

John's defection from Pietism made him thoughtful about his father and step-mother. They expected him to be grateful for having educated him, yet they had done little to help him and had subjected him to humiliations and unnecessary hardships. Should John be grateful to his father because he had been instrumental to his birth? No! the event had been an accident, he had not been wanted. In educating him, his father had only done his duty and that not very well. In general, John had come to feel that the man who expects gratitude in return for services is the worst of criminals, for it is a debt that can never be paid. "It is a mortgage on a man's soul—which stretches over the whole subsequent life. Accept a service from your friend, and he will expect you to falsify your opinion of him and to praise his own evil deeds and those of his wife and children."

John's release from the restraints of Pietism, in consequence of the influence of his two friends, the engineer with his materialistic deism, and Fritz of the pince-nez with his buoyant love of life, gave a freer course to his awakening sexuality, permitted him the pleasures of cafés and parties with girls, and made him hate those writers who flatter human nature. Yes, and he enjoyed those parties and loved to look at the girls and dance with them, but to talk with them was another matter. His long seclusion and pre-occupation with religion had put the little nothings of frivolous conversation beyond his power and made a tête-à-tête with a pretty girl the most fearful ordeal. When he attempted humor he heard his own voice and, startled with the thin and unnatural sound, stopped dead in fright. When he attempted declamation, the same thing happened. Though John rehearsed plays with his brothers, he was never good at the comic parts, but took nat-urally to the grandiose roles of high tragedy. The girls with whom he conversed were probably as ill at ease as he was and perhaps stood in awe of him. Two actresses with whom he danced made no reply at all to his conversation. His friend Fritz, on the other hand, was a master of the business and said such strange elegant things that the girls were delighted with him. John liked the pale, dark-eyed, fragile creatures best, for they reminded him of his mother whom he always thought of as a frail flower with black eyes.

But these contacts with girls were fleeting and superficial and did not satisfy; rather, they aggravated his precocious desires. Years later (1882) he gives a lurid account of his early struggles with the devil of desire in *Asra,* or *The Wages of Virtue,*[1] wherein it is seen that the paralyzing effect of Pietism and asceti-cism and the long continued repression of natural functions is much more apt to lead to disease, idiocy, and death than is the dreaded boyhood sin. Theodore, the chaste hero of this story, is dead at twenty-five, while John himself, whose celibacy did not continue as long, recovered, yet he, too, might have been de-stroyed, we may infer, had he not given up Pietism in time and made himself independent of his father. Like John, Theodore

---

[1] It is interesting to note that *Asra* was written a full decade before Wedekind's famous play *Spring's Awakening.*

was devoted to his mother, who made him promise on her death bed to live a pure life. Yet he was tortured with desires which, he had been made to feel, were monstrous and unnatural at the early age of sixteen. He, himself, could see there was something wrong, for he was in no position to get married and raise a family. Yet his unhappiness and cravings continued none the less. He finds himself in a swing with the gardener's daughter and the contact with her warm body sends an electric shock through his whole system. He realizes that something has happened. His blood rises, he feels like a young god. On his return home, the bare shoulders of the house-maid made everything reel before him and he attempts to kiss her. The maid resists and he is overwhelmed with shame. That night, after repeating the Lord's Prayer, he falls asleep, but awakes suddenly with the dream that he holds the gardener's daughter in his arms. Even in sleep he cannot escape his desires.

One evening the minister explained to Theodore and the other boys the terrible consequences of onanism and read them accounts of boys who had died at twenty-five from tuberculosis of the spine,—of a boy confined to an asylum at the age of twelve who died at fourteen. Theodore and the others were terrified by what they heard, "they collapsed in their seats, and felt as if the floor was giving away beneath them—they saw before their shrinking eyes a hundred corpses, washed and shrouded." "There is but one remedy against this evil," went on the minister, "the precious wounds of Christ." Then he requested the first five boys of the form to remain for a moment. They were petrified with fear as if they had been sentenced to death. When Theodore's turn comes, he is asked whether he has sinned and answers no. "Did he have dreams?" "Yes." He was thereupon warned against dreams "because they proved that the heart was wicked." He was told "to chasten the flesh and be strong in prayer. Go in the name of the Lord and sin no more." But Theodore was powerless against erotic dreams which stole over him often in moments of least resistance and all his prayers and cold baths and hunger could not protect him. That night he dreamed of a champagne supper with "sparkling glasses and frank and merry faces with candid eyes which met his own unabashed." Suddenly "a charming little face peeped through the red silk draperies" and he drew a beautiful figure to his heart. Waking up thereafter and feeling he has been worsted in this contest with the devil, he goes to sleep upon the bare frame of the bed. In the morning, with a high fever, he took to bed where he remained for six weeks. On his recovery his returning health merely gave new fuels to the fires. Finally, his father grew worried over Theodore's condition and arranged for Gustav, his exuberant, healthy, but none too virtuous brother, to take him out in the world and arouse him to its pleasures. Gustav accordingly took him off to a restaurant where he was known and ordered a magnificent supper. Theodore is asked to play the piano and the girls kiss the lieutenant (his brother) behind his back, for Theodore is timid and the girls are afraid of him and his melancholy music. When the lieutenant leaves, Theodore, forgetting his pietism, makes love to Rieke, one of the waitresses at the restaurant and she reciprocates, allows him to kiss her as much as he pleases, but permits nothing further. Theodore becomes soulful and they plan to marry. On the return of the lieutenant, however, he learns that his Rieke is his brother's mistress. Overwhelmed with grief, he returns to his devotions and the enforced celibacy has the most terrible consequences. The anything but virtuous lieutenant, on the other hand, marries and lives happily ever after. The treacherous Rieke who plays the sad part here is also a character in *The Red Room* and enjoys, in fact, many an avatar in the works of Strindberg. She is one of the most deadly of her sex, being so soulless, beautiful, and incomprehensible, that Strindberg's feeling for her is divided between love and horror. Yet she has an irresistible attraction for him. Again and again he returns to paint her wickedness, like a man who has a long account to settle or an infinite revenge to satisfy.

Young Strindberg did not go Theodore's way of madness and death at twenty-five, but was saved, as he doubtless thought, in the nick of time. But between fifteen and eighteen years he suffered, as he thought every boy suffered, and had no peace or rest until his relations with women began. Even then he enjoyed no real contentment until his marriage, for, as he usually held, marriage, in spite of everything, is the only proper relation between the sexes. Had he had his way when sixteen he would probably have found himself a pretty little wife, settled down at some modest occupation and worked for his home and children! But how long would it have lasted? Strindberg had at this time but a vague premonition of the devils of discord which were to send him raging and gyrating through three marriages and many affairs, nor could he foresee that when sixty years old, after all these loves and disillusions, he would still court a young girl with youthful ardor, as if she were the first.

V

AMONG THE ARISTOCRATS

IN the summer of 1867 when John was eighteen years old, he
secured a position as a tutor in a noble family and was tre-
mendously pleased, for he was to spend the whole summer in the
Stockholm archipelago—"on the most beautiful of all the islands,
Stotaskär." The occasion was particularly fateful for him, for
these rocky islands and fjords were to become the scene of many
of his best stories in which the pounding waves, the birds, the
endless northern nights, the marooned fishermen on their gray
rocks, received the finest portrayal in literature.

The prospect of spending the summer in such surroundings and
hobnobbing with aristocrats was simply fascinating. His step-
mother's abuse and the systematic policy of the family to humble
him by proving him arrogant and presuming, had offended
him outrageously and turned his heart against the jealous smugness and mean insincerity of the middle classes. The gracious,
confident, fair-minded style of the upper classes, on the other hand,
gratified his aesthetic sense, for he was in full career at this time
to become an aristocrat himself. His ambitions, so long stifled,
came to life before this bright future, his blood sang and the wild
horses in him stamped and neighed. Now he would live among
his own kind or climb to their height by virtue of his superior
intellect. It was the aristocrats, he reflected, not his own middle
class, who always patronized the arts and sciences. His friend

Fritz told him how to get along with them. One must be yielding, not cringing, indulge in graceful flattery, but take care to make it seem as sincere and occasional as possible. Above all, one must not dispute, for then one always got the worst of it. John was too proud to take kindly to this advice, but still, the odds were worth it. What if his noble patron should send him on a foreign tour with the children!

On his way to the castle John attempted a bit of amiability of the kind Fritz had suggested and asked his employers in friendly, confidential manner, how they were. But the Baron's answer was nothing but a snub and John became thoughtful again. After a few days in his new position, his sense of social inferiority and pressure from above had increased to such an extent that the son of a servant was full of revolt. Moreover, though he loved the children, as indeed he could hardly ever help doing, he resented being made their nursemaid, for this deprived him of his freedom every hour of the day and he was continually fearful lest some mishap befall them for which he could be held responsible. Whenever he was seen alone he would be pressed with the question: "But where are the children?" He was becoming a slave to these aristocrats.

Yet he enjoyed some consolations, rode horses like his masters and carried himself high, and he managed to make Fritz jealous, and his brother indignant, at the exaggerated accounts he wrote back of his new dignities. Moreover, his pride was considerably soothed by his visit with the Baron X, the Baroness' brother, for this old man, the model of good manners and amiability, admitted at once that he had long ago been a river-pilot and had known John's father. Moreover, he took a special pleasure in John's theatre gossip and recent news from Stockholm. Here then, thought John, is the real aristocrat, who needs no outward ritual nor any forms of social arrogance to support his rank. After his visit with the old Baron, John became somewhat more confident and easy in his mind. But soon the news that the Baron and

Oscar Strindberg had been friends in the old days was reported to his employers and then even the Baroness felt bound to speak ill of her brother. This amused John. He had thought of aristocrats as exalted beings far above his own class. Now he had his doubts.

Still another thing helped to make the son of a servant forget his ambiguous lineage and his subordinate position in the household. The assistant pastor asked him to deliver a sermon. John felt it his duty, however, to explain the extent of his unorthodoxy before accepting this honor. "Well," replied the busy man, "but you do believe in God, I suppose?"

"Yes, certainly, I do."

"Very well! Don't speak of Christ. Bishop Wallin never mentioned the name of Christ in his sermons. Don't bother me any more. I don't want to hear about it." So they had a glass of wine and the matter was settled. After this, if John were asked for about the house, he could answer proudly, "I am preparing my sermon." When the great day came, John read the text and then added: "Since the text of the day gives no further occasion for remark, we will, for a short time, consider what is of greater importance." And so he turned to an account of conversion and made an attack upon the snobbery of the pietist doctrines of election. Salvation, he said, is not the incomprehensible fortune of the few, but within the reach of all, for the light of grace will shine, not only on a few "children of God" but upon all mankind. What a pity his stepmother could not have been there to hear him, for then his revenge would have been complete! The girls at the Pastor's house complimented him on his sermon which they thought very fine, because so short. John was surprised at the whole affair. To be sure, he had for a long time intended to become a preacher, for this was the only way he saw of becoming economically independent. What worried him was that his spiritual development had carried him so far that he was now almost a freethinker.

After this temporary triumph John's troubles came fast and

thick. He made friends with a steward whom he looked upon as a victim of the Baron's arrogance, and they enjoyed themselves of an evening drinking punch and playing cards. This move of John's was very impolitic; he was warned against this unsuitable companion who, the Baroness said, had "no education at all." But he continued in this forbidden friendship and the boys came in and took a hand at cards. Another source of irritation was the little military company which John organized, in which the Baron's boys were put side by side with workmen's children. This the Baroness would not endure. "Each class should keep to itself," she said. One day the steward was unjustly accused of taking the Baron's gloves. John, who was standing by at the time, defended him so hotly that it came to a complete rupture and John told Mr. Secretary he could look for another tutor.

He had now made the step from which, as he thought, there was no withdrawal and there was nothing for it but to return to the hell of his home which would now be doubly painful inasmuch as he had foolishly praised his new situation and vaunted its advantages above those of his father's house. But before leaving his brilliant post, now the grave of his aristocratic aspirations, he consented to an interview with the gentle Baroness, who seemed "like a portrait of a Medieval lady," and who met him now with such calm and soft entreaty that he consented to continue his lessons gratis until she could secure another tutor. When Fritz heard of this arrangement he was amazed at the simplicity of his friend and determined to take him in hand. You must write them at once, said Fritz, and withdraw your offer. When John had complied, he felt ashamed of his impoliteness. "Rubbish," cried his friend. "Waitress, bring half a punch."

The son of a servant returned to Stockholm fairly cured of his love of aristocrats, and began to study for the examinations, which, if he passed them successfully, would admit him to the University at Upsala. But his studies were hampered by his ever troubled conscience, though this time it was not the conscience of the pietist, but that of the free-thinker. About this time the free-thought fad was in its ascendancy and John considered it his duty to defend the new movement, tooth and nail. When his father asked him why he went to church no more, he replied: "I can make sermons myself." The father had no answer to this argument and so let the matter rest. John also refused to take part in the prayers and psalm singing at school and when the infuriated headmaster attempted to force him to conformity, the young enthusiast insisted that "his religion forbade him to take part in an alien form of worship," and hinted that he and others of his opinion could very well be excused from prayers, just as the Jews were. The headmaster was beside himself and devised new punishments and humiliations for the offenders, but John retaliated by organizing all the rebels in a band, who henceforth came to school late, filing in just as the prayers were finished. John knew that he was playing a dangerous game, for the headmaster could fail him in the examinations if he chose to, but yet, whatever the odds, he must follow his conscience. When his teacher at the theological lesson asked him how many persons there were in the Godhead, John answered: "One," whereupon his patient teacher, who had finally tired of arguing, admonished him to answer according to the book.

The fact was that John was gaining stature and his character was forming into that shifting and tumultous life-pattern in which rebellions, apostacies and quixotic allegiances formed almost the only constancy. The role of conformist proved always too small for John. When he had played it for a while, he grew doubtful and frantic and impious, and then he craved a big part from high tragedy to restore the equilibrium.

When John passed his examinations his father preserved his Icelandic calm and there was not one word of congratulation from his family, so he hurried off quickly to celebrate with his comrades in the café. It was the eve, he thought, of his greatest adventure, for in the autumn he would go to Upsala as a student at the University. What would be his destiny at that old institution of learning? His companions at the café that night had no doubt they would become rich and famous.

In more sober moods John doubted his character and therefore his success. "A man's character is his destiny," and John thought he had but to examine the one to discover the other, for he naïvely assumed that his character was already fully cast and could be read like a horoscope. But when he considered the matter a little more closely he was much saddened to find that his character was only a humbug. He was neither consistent, since he changed his mind over-night and was subject to strange fits of irrationality, nor original, since his peculiarities had been stolen from his father, his friends and his teachers. Sometimes it seemed to him he had no character at all.

At other times he thought himself cruel. On one occasion when a boy told him that his father had once stood in the pillory, John's revenge went so far that even the innocent brother of the slanderer was punished. He could be cruel and revengeful at times, yet for the most part he was soft as a lamb and suffered for the faults of others with the same intensity as if he himself were the guilty one. "If he had lived in the Middle Ages, he would have been marked with the stigmata." Whenever anyone did anything stupid or ridiculous he was overwhelmed with vicarious shame and in later years this sensitiveness increased until he came to regard himself as one chosen to suffer innocently and thus to bear the guilt of other men.

But what then was John's character? One way he could answer this absorbing question was to collect the judgments of others, but everyone, he found, had a different opinion. "His father considered him hard; his step-mother malicious; his brothers eccentric. Every servant-maid in the house had a different opinion of him . . . his lady friend thought him emotional; the engineer regarded him as an amiable child, and Fritz considered him melancholy and self-willed."

No two people agreed. On examination only two characteristics in his nature stood out as fateful and distinctive: doubt and sensitiveness to pressure, but these were enough to make his career in life a strange and exceptional one.

VI

UPSALA

IN the autumn of 1867 John took the short journey over the
water to Upsala, where he arrived with high hopes and ambitions which were not in the least dimmed by the fact, which he
must from time to time have recognized, that they were utterly
indefinite and unfounded. John's father, it is true, had given him
a box of cigars and earnestly exhorted him to help himself, and
Old Margaret, the housekeeper, who packed his box, had obliged
him to borrow fifteen kronas of her, but this was all the help or
encouragement he received from anyone. Eighty kronas he had
saved from the lessons he had given and these must pay for his
lodgings and meals, his books, and all other expenses for the
whole term at the University. If he succeeded in his career and
made a place for himself, it was clear that he would be beholden
to no one, and the gratitude with which he had been obliged to
acknowledge his father's occasional and somewhat reluctant generosity would not be required in this case. His father and his step-
mother would, no doubt, feel that he owed his education and his
honors to them and would have only himself to blame for his
failure, yet it was some consolation to know that this was by no
means the case.

Upsala had been, for centuries, the rallying point of Swedish
aristocracy where they idled and conversed, drank and grew proud
of their learning. Here, also, light-hearted joyous comradeship

prevailed, careers were spun, honor gained, and names went up like rockets. As a student, one shared the lustre of Linnæus, Rudbeck, and many other great men who had gone before and whose statues dominated the grounds. The University, which had been founded in the fifteenth century, was certainly a great institution with a long tradition of distinguished men, and the student life was a romantic ideal which all the drunkenness, and debauchery, and idleness had left undimmed. The student was the knight of ancient culture and the new civilization, the preserver of aristocracy, an ornament to his country. Moreover, he lived like a prince, proud, careless and brilliant, and no one could drink or laugh or sing as he could. Once, when John was quite young, his mother said to him: "Some day you may be a student and wear a white cap," and the woman who had been a servant was transported by the thought of this glimmering future which seemed to her almost the pinnacle of ambition.

But John was not pleased with the University, and its reputation and authority seemed only to increase his opposition. Later, when he came to relate his experiences and observations at Upsala (in *The Growth of a Soul,* 1886, and in other writings), he took exception to almost every feature of the institution, ridiculed the incapacity of the professors and the idle vicious life of the students, challenged the whole system of instruction, and laid about him with such good effect that the long-cherished ideal was almost in tatters. Ibsen had criticized the clergy. The army, the government, had been subject to continual abuse. Of all institutions, the University alone had escaped inviolate. It was left to Strindberg to lead the attack on this last fortress of aristocracy and privilege, and he did it in the vicious, thorough style which always characterized his offensive. In *The Gothic Room* (1904) one of his spokesmen suggests that, "With a well organized book dealer and a suitable commission of examiners the University, where one wastes one's time and ruins one's nerves with drink, could be closed down. The University is a combination of cloister, tavern and brothel; the University is a school—a school of pride, oppression, frivolity, envy, and toadyism."

The University is situated in the small town of Upsala which is old in traditions, being the seat of the archbishop, the place where the kings were chosen. Above the University buildings, stands the castle and the cathedral. Two miles north of the town is the site of the old Upsala where once stood a pagan temple. The town, which has no industries, seems to exist for the sake of the students and fairly falls to sleep in the vacation period. This was an ideal environment for study but John found everything wrong. The flat country around Upsala depressed him and made him long for the varied scene, the hills and waterways, of Stockholm. The town itself he liked no better. It was shabby and absolutely uncultured and it had the remarkably bad taste to imitate a great city, whereby it became a miserable caricature. John was vexed and discomforted by many things and shortly came to hate the whole place, part and parcel.

John and his friend, Fritz of the pince-nez, had rented a room with two beds, two tables, two chairs and a cupboard, which came to fifteen kronas a term for each. At noontime a meal was brought them, but for breakfast and supper John had to content himself with milk, bread and butter. As a consequence he went hungry most of the time and craved the meat and the strong drinks of the restaurants.

For his chief subjects of study he chose Æsthetics (including Architecture, Sculpture, Painting, Literary History and the systems of Æsthetics) and Modern Languages (French, German, English, Italian, Spanish and Comparative Grammar). This, he felt, was work enough for a life-time and yet it was a customary course of study. What made this program particularly grandiose and impossible for John was that he had no books, and no money to buy them, and could not pay for private lessons, though these were necessary if he was to pass the examinations. Everything at the University, he felt, was left very indefinite and he was not at all clear what he was supposed to do. To pass the time, he dropped into a few free lectures on the history of philosophy, but here the progress was so slow that he computed it would take him forty years to get through the subject and John concluded he could not give it the time. In another course of free lectures he had a like experience and estimated that it would take ten years to finish *Henry VIII.*

So far, his career as a student seemed pretty hopeless. He did manage to borrow the works of Swedenborg and Thorild, the two reigning heroes of Swedish literature, but was astonished at what he read and frankly concluded they must be mad. "They were two arrogant Swedes, who living in great retirement, had fallen prey to megalomania, the special disease of solitary people. It is remarkable how often outbreaks of this hallucination occur in Sweden, owing probably to the isolated position of the country and to the fact that a sparse population is scattered over enormous distances." John, much later, became a follower of Swedenborg but he was too honest to simulate an appreciation for authors, however famous they might be, before the sufferings of life had prepared him to understand them. Geiger, the great historian, he also found wearisome and uninspiring. Boström, who had just died, was the great philosopher of the day, but John had no sympathy for his absolute idealism. Boström's Platonic conception of a world of supersensible realities could make no very great appeal to John's essentially practical nature. The boy who was to become a great naturalist in literature and was already turning toward Rousseau, could never admit that the multiform evils of the world could be conjured away by a dialectical argument, however subtle and ingenious it might be. No, such a philosophy would be too smug, and too complacently optimistic for him. It was a state philosophy, a creation of the aristocrats who could afford to be optimistic because they wanted things to remain as they were. Thus did John dispute the glory of Upsala's dead and set his mind against his masters.

He found no inspiration in the preceptors of Upsala and more than once asked himself why he had ever come there. He had no prospects since he could not come up for the examination, his eighty kronas being scarcely sufficient to put him through a term, and he had no hope of receiving any more. Nor could he pay court to the professors, as the custom was at Upsala, because he had no frock coat. His friend Fritz, who went to them every morning, urged John to borrow his coat and discharge a duty which was both innocent and politic, but John was too proud to "toady" to the professors, and wished to shine by his own merits unassisted. "The way to the degree examination," he concluded, "was not easy; one was obliged to seek out secret ways, bribe door-keepers, creep through holes, run into debt for books, be seen at lectures, and much more besides." He preferred a gloomy hopeless retreat to an ambitious servility, but since he would not wait upon the authorities, he got no assistance from them and since he no longer went to lectures he was almost isolated. He saw his friend Fritz, of course, and had his meals with him. Although different from him in almost every respect, Fritz was a fine companion, and John's vexations and uncertainties were much lightened by his company. On Sundays when they could afford beer, they sat for hours recounting old stories and almost befuddled themselves, so unused were they to drinking. Fritz, who was an ambitious fellow and determined to get on in the world, kept company with aristocrats, and urged John to do the same. But John's "slave-blood" revolted at the imagined arrogance of a young noble and he withdrew from a society in which, as he felt, though Fritz certainly did not share his opinion, one might be thought forward and presuming. John preferred the company of poor students in the same deplorable fix as himself and when his loneliness and boredom became too oppressive, he made the rounds, discovering those who were even worse off than himself. Two young fellows he found who had only a prayer book between them and spent all day playing chess and wondering why they were there. Others lived in great seclusion in garrets, playing cards to pass the time, starving themselves slowly, watching their young ambitions dwindle as they waited for the end of the term. Like these other students, who were cut off from books, papers, and social intercourse, he lived a pale unreal existence. He knew nothing of what was going on in the world outside and cared less. Law and politics—he was frightened at the idea of having to study such things—had no interest for him. "Let everyone mind his own business," he thought. "There are enough to look after those things." All the avenues of sensation being closed, all the chances of fresh stimulation circumvented, he was thrown back on himself and could but continue the weary infinite study of his own inner life, reviewing old injuries, conjuring up new fears, foreboding fresh misfortunes, tracing the winding, doubtful continuity of the self. Like the characters in the plays he was to write, he performed mechanically his monotonous, hopeless tasks and sat for hours in a small room brooding and examining himself.

John, in reacting to the crosses and vexations in the outer world and in his own sensitive and passionate nature, was fast becoming an introvert. "The habit of self-criticism derived from his religious training had accustomed him to occupy himself with his ego, to fondle and cherish it, as though it were a separate and beloved personality. So cherished, the ego expanded and kept continually looking within instead of without upon the world. It was an interesting personal acquaintance, a friend who must be flattered, who must also hear the truth and be corrected. It was the mental malady of the time, reduced to a system by Fichte, who taught that everything took place in the ego and through the ego, without which there was no reality. It was a formula for romanticism and subjective idealism." Fichte's system, which said: The ego exists and therefore must produce its non-ego (the world) as an obstacle necessary for the moral life, was only one example of the subjective trend of the times. The ego was turning back on itself and retiring from a world which had grown too complex and baffling to cope with. This absorption in the self, of which Stendahl and others had already given such famous descriptions, is characteristic of all men, thinks Strindberg, who have worked with their brains rather than their bodies. "When the brain does not act to bring the muscles into play, there results a disturbance of equilibrium. The brain begins to dream; too full of juices which cannot be absorbed by muscular activity, it converts them involuntarily into systems, into thought-combinations, into hallucinations, which haunt painters, sculptors and poets. If no outlet can be found, there follows stagnation, violent outbreaks, depression and at last madness. Schools, which are often vestibules for asylums, have recourse to gymnastics," but the unhappy consequence is that muscular work and cerebral activity are introduced, there, out of all relation. This passage, which is rather remarkable for its description of the introverted self and the expressionistic theory in æsthetics, also shows the pass to which John had been brought by his idle and artificial life at Upsala; he had lost himself in his own ego and had ceased to be himself because he thought of nothing else.

His isolation and melancholy grew even worse when he fell out with Fritz, for his old friend had been a great comfort to him. The occasion for the break was John's refusal to associate with Fritz's friends and the storm which had been quietly simmering for a long while at last broke loose. For six weeks neither spoke and they ate their common meals in silence, though each desired at times, in a wistful and tragic way, to renew the comfort of their long friendship.

John's loneliness having increased and the various evils of his life accumulated, he naturally set about to find the cause. Could it not be that he was a victim of the educational system, that the University was nothing but a glorious long-perpetuated swindle? What is learning, after all? "Today you know nothing of Roman Law but tomorrow you buy a little book at the book seller's on Roman Law and over-night you learn what Roman Law is. That is the learning of which we are so proud." (*The Gothic Room.*) Perhaps too, thought John, scientists and artists are overrated, for after all they produce nothing, but only render life more and more complex. From time to time, he thought, there must be a return to simplicity; where the strain of rising civilization strings the nerves to the breaking point, men must flee from the cities, returning to the land and their old ways. "In spite of the accommodation to new circumstances there is always a tendency to go back. Civilization means a continual strain and struggle to combat this backward tendency. Education winds up the clock, but when the mainspring is not strong enough, it snaps and the works run down, till quiet ensues. As civilization advances, the strain is ever greater and the statistics of insanity show a perpetual increase." The only hope is an escape to the land. In the centers of civilization everything grows worse, competition becomes madder every year and toil and luxuries increase, for it seems that the individual must remain miserable to maintain a worthless and unhealthy society.

John craved at this time to return to the simplicities of the land and if he could not triumph over civilization or be free from the authorities above him, he would be a lord in some quiet, humble place. Moreover, since he had no other course than to leave the University, and so to sink in the social scale, he preferred to do so in the obscurity of some distant village, rather than in the city, where everything would remind him of his fall. He thought, too, that the pleasure of the onlookers might be much curtailed if he left the city, for then the step might appear quite voluntary. He, therefore, for these several reasons, applied for a teacher's post in the country.

The longing for nature and the hatred of the artificialities of a blind and preposterous civilization formed a persistent strain in the Strindberg character. His Rousseauistic rebellion against the forms and restraints of society, its deceits, illusions and decencies, led many of his contemporaries to regard him as a sort of wild-man longing for his native woods. He himself often held this opinion. He relates how sudden despair or shame drives him to the woods for cover and protection. And there is no doubt that he looked upon himself as a noble savage. Certainly he resented a mild delineation. When in the course of his life the pressure of cultured discipline became unbearable, he discarded his plays and other labors, and denounced the civilization on the building of which he had long been at work,—and again and again his cry is: Back to nature! The craving for a return to the primitive often reveals itself in literary form, as in the story *The Unwelcome One*. Here Strindberg lives again in his hero, Christian, who as a "noble savage" suffers the malice and stupidity of society, but also in the end triumphs over it, accomplishing a just and fitting revenge. The story is an allegory of Strindberg's early life, all his own sufferings at the hands of society are the lot of Christian, but, unlike Christian, Strindberg did not enjoy the noble revenge, which therefore occurs in the story rather as a wish-fulfillment.

Christian was born too late. His parents had not expected him and were very disappointed at his appearance. Everything he did seemed to annoy them and when he cried, as all children do, they were beside themselves. Fed nothing but the crumbs from the family table, he grew marvellously hungry and gradually took to the woods where he spent whole days in wild search for birds and birds' eggs with which to nourish himself. As time passed he became more and more independent of his parents and sometimes he remained away for months, sailing in his self-made boat in search of food. But he had a dream of becoming altogether independent and perhaps of marrying when the time came. This, however, seemed impossible for everything had to be paid for. One had to pay taxes, one had to pay to go to church, to the justice. One had to pay for a place to be buried. Everything had its price. Christian determined to accumulate a little capital and thus worked patiently and skilfully for a long time, and in the end had quite a collection of skins and down and eggs. As he climbs to the top of his little island, observes the boundless sea and the birds above his head, he feels like the lord of a lonely castle and continues to hoard his treasure. Finally his father and brother storm the island and demand to know where he has stolen his store. After a long and futile resistance, he is forced to lie, to admit he has stolen, and to explain how and where. The lie which made his whole family happy, left Christian in despair and he is not heard of for many years. When he does return it is from a dazzling adventure; he is rich and beside him is a pretty wife. Christian's first step is to build a high and costly house beside his brother's. But the brother becomes so jealous of Christian's splendour that he ruins himself in a vain attempt to equal it. This is all that Christian wanted, and having accomplished his purpose, he sails away again in his boat with Venetian sails.

This was the revenge of the noble savage which Strindberg himself could never enjoy.

VII

STURM UND DRANG

POOR John was compounded of the most opposite principles. He was a skeptic and an absolutist, an atheist and a zealot, a savage in his brutality yet weak and feminine in his yielding, cowardly and foolhardy, with a capacity for complete transformation, a worshipper of women and their deadly enemy, a stormy advocate of contrary courses. He was the son of confusion and, like the Hydra, put forth more equal heads than was either suitable or becoming. In his veins the "slave blood" contended with an aristocratic strain and in the faintly lighted passages of that labyrinth of his consciousness he heard at times strange voices which were new to him. Nature, who takes such care to separate her contraries in most men and compose them out of compatible parts, had made a scandal of her old discords and united all her opposites in one man.

John's face bore out his unequal composition and expounded his soul. His mouth was small and soft like that of the child's, or the serpent's, his forehead was high and intrepid and his hair bristled and stormed like the mane of a lion, but perhaps in too theatrical a way to express all the strength and confidence intended. His eyes were bold and strong with a glint in them which recalled the attention in a disquieting way, as of objects but half searched or understood. But though his eyes stared boldly and outfaced others, they themselves evaded scrutiny and could never be seized. His body, again, was strong and active but his shoulders sloped in the manner of a woman's.

It was natural that John should be at variance with his environment and develop a distaste for almost every career he undertook, for his purposes and desires were so crossed and opposite that they contended, whatever the circumstances, like blood-enemies who fight on every ground they meet. At Upsala, where his circumstances were particularly unpropitious, and his sensitivity strung taut and keen, it was natural that his ambitions should end in a great fall—not a noble defeat, either, but the tragedy of a clown. When he returned to Stockholm, people asked him whether he had now learned everything there was to be known, and what made John's humiliation hard to bear was that, sooner or later, they would learn that he was not to return to the University but would become a teacher in an elementary school, for he hated to see them exult in his downfall. If he could only secure a quiet post in the country, he might escape the comments of his family and friends, and their malicious delight. Moreover, the city had become unbearable to him, and he longed for the simple goodness of nature, which (he wrote) is like the longing of all northerners for the south who, chafing under civilization, strive always to return to their first home "in a sunnier land, to the bank of the Ganges, where the cradle stands." But the position he wanted did not develop and he was obliged to take a similar one, just where he did not want it, in the city.

One morning, therefore, he rose early and went off with many misgivings and a sad heart, just as eleven years before as a child of eight he had hurried along dreadfully, to the Clara School. In the school itself almost nothing had changed and every detail of the wretched, preposterous institution reminded him of the horrors of his childhood. There were the same "ugly, dwarfed, pale, swollen, sickly children with downcast looks, in coarse clothes and heavy boots." There was the same silence, and terror, and depression. Everything was repeated as before, a hymn was sung, then came the Lord's Prayer, for there had been little progress. The room in which John was to teach was almost identical with the one in which he had been tortured at the same school and the dreadful desk from which he was to preside was painted red as if stained with blood. John had suddenly become a hangman, despite himself, and seizing the stick under which he himself had so often innocently suffered he mounted the scaffold and faced his victims. They, in their turn, looked up at him curiously and wistfully, and the young student, so full of conflicts and ambiguities, began his career as a teacher.

"What is your lesson?" he asked.

"The first commandment," the whole class exclaimed.

John then admonished them to answer only one at a time.

"You, top boy, what is your name?"

"Hallberg," cried the whole class.

"No, only one at a time,—the one I ask."

A tittering went round the room, the fear and, perhaps too, the respect relaxed. The top boy repeated the first commandment. Whereupon, John had no course but to ask every child to do the same, but this used up but a small part of the period, and how he was to continue he was at a loss to know. He therefore inquired of his pupils what he should do next and they told him that an explanation was usually given. But John was almost an atheist. How could he tell them what he thought of the commandment: Thou shalt have no other gods before Me? No, it was quite impossible. "You need not do any more," he said, "but don't make a noise." For a moment master smiled at pupils and pupils smiled at master and John felt that there was a mutual understanding of the ridiculous farce they were both obliged to play. The next moment, however, realizing that they were laughing at him, he changed about, dropped his amiability and called for attention. In the course of the next few days he learned that his gentle, conciliatory method was not effective, that these children had been so trained that only harshness and brutal justice could correct them.

When the headmaster visited his class, the children were inattentive, though this (thought Strindberg, following Rousseau and Pestalozzi) was not their fault, or within their power to control, but was due rather to the failure of their lessons to interest them. The headmaster, when he saw how things were going, advised John to use a heavy hand, and apply the stick unsparingly, but though John knew this was the only way, it came hard to him to do it, and it seemed a sad and terrible thing. "The inattentive one was dragged by his hair or clothes and caned till he fell howling to the ground." John knew that he must play this part or give up his job. He must pounce upon these other personalities and hurt them, and humiliate them, and crush them as had been done to him years before, for that was his duty. He, therefore, put it to them squarely in the way of a bargain and said: "Either you must work or be flogged, for that is the law nor can you blame me for what happens." But John's conscience was not clear, for he knew that, since it was not in their power to attend to uninteresting things, he had not dealt squarely with them. He looked on it, nevertheless, as an obligation, and there was no remedy. So John returned to school to repeat his old sufferings, this time vicariously, no longer the innocent tormented one, but the tormentor of innocents, who himself suffered each pang that he caused. He was like the slave who has suffered the whip so long and patiently, that he is raised to the rank of foreman and obliged to beat his former comrades. At times, however, he saw the whole matter in the light of a comedy and then he was hard put to it not to laugh outright as he found himself beating a boy, with the utmost seriousness, for an offence in which he himself did not believe. If a boy became restless, inattentive, or noisy, John knew as well as Pestalozzi, that he was driven thereto by the irresistible promptings of his nature—like a savage longing for freedom—yet the ridiculous system of which he was an officer demanded that he fall upon the offender tooth and nail with all the fury, or all the cold self-righteousness, of outraged justice. At times, John found this tragi-comic role almost insupportable, for he was both criminal and clown and neither part pleased him. John, of course, could see (as he says in 1886) that at least one purpose was served by this beating and repression, it produced good citizens. It was a school for slaves who, with no will of their own, would suffer patiently the tyranny of their superiors and keep to their place. John remarked that in the schools which the upper-class children attended, there was little corporal punishment, and the patriotic songs which enforced a blind obedience in the poorer schools formed no part of the program. In John's own school the children were taught that Sweden was by far the finest country in Europe, though (as Strindberg remarks) for climate and natural resources it was certainly one of the worst, while its ideas, its culture, even its kings, had been imported from other countries.

Since John's school was one of the poorest he was brought into contact with the children of laborers, among whom were many pathetic instances of poverty and occupational disease and deformity. "Ibsen" (says Strindberg in *The Growth of a Soul*), "who does not believe in the aristocracy of birth or of wealth, has lately (1886) expressed the belief that the industrial class are the real nobility." John's observations taught him better. The children of the artisans were weak and sickly and stupid, were overdeveloped here and underdeveloped there, and in their wanness and anemia compared very poorly with the children of the upper classes. In his pupils he saw in miniature "the gas-worker's lungs and blood spoilt by sulphur fumes, the smith's shoulders and feet bent outwards, the painter's brain atrophied by varnishes and poisonous colors, the scrofulous eruption of the chimney sweeper, the contracted chest of the book-binder. . . . In truth this was no race to which the future belonged." It must be continually recruited from the fresh country stock.

In the sheerest contrast to these dour and sordid contacts which had brought him once more to the verge of a flight back to nature, he secured a situation in his spare hours as tutor in one of the richest houses of the city, and the association with the cultured free-minded people of the upper class reconciled him again to his urban life and the many miscarriages of civilization.

Schiller's *Robbers* with its bold rebellion against society had made a great impression on John and he had indeed felt himself so altogether similar to the bandit, Karl Moor, that there was no need to imitate him, but he now turned with even greater enthusiasm to the more aristocratic revolt of Byron's Manfred and was immensely pleased by this hero's fine discontent with Providence and the ways of God toward men. Here, he thought, is a bold fearless spirit like myself. A year or two later John commenced a play which was intended to bring an end to Christianity, by one fell stroke, but this play was never finished nor was the question of divine government ever settled in his mind.

As John became a little more reconciled to society and found a purgation for his discontent in the revolt of Karl Moor and Manfred, he began to take a little care to make a good appearance in the world. One of his worst humiliations had always been that he had been obliged to wear his brother's cast-off clothes and to dress in a shabby and often ridiculous fashion. But now his salary as a teacher, which seemed to him at first to put everything in his power, permitted him luxuries, and he began to wear fine clothes. (The inclination to finery became a part of his character and years later in the direst poverty he still remained something of a dandy.) As a young man with prospects and an eye to a fine carriage before girls, it was important for him to dress to advantage. As a tired over-worked teacher it was necessary for him to enjoy his drinks at the café and to entertain his friends. But in thus indulging and consoling himself, he so far overrated his salary that he ran deep into debt and became in fact so involved that he gave up all hope of ever paying, though the matter went very hard with him and became "a vulture gnawing at his heart."

One outlet for John's spirits as well as his purse, was cafés and restaurants, for there he could enjoy invigorating drinks, con verse with his friends and flirt with the waitresses. The strain of his life had greatly increased. All day long he taught at the public school or gave private lessons, while late into the night he read for his examinations. Strong liquors and flirtations seemed but a proper relief. "The desire for alcohol," he wrote, "seems to appear regularly in each adolescent. All northerners are born of genera- tions of drinkers from the early heathen times when beer and mead were drunk, and it was quite natural that the desire should be felt as a necessity."

Alcohol and women! These were two great fundaments of life and John could dispense with neither. Boccaccio, whom he discovered at this time, encouraged him in these inclinations, and the merry robust humor of the Renaissance poet quickened the pulse of his desire. He was accustomed, he said, to devote himself to three affairs at the same time, "one grand, sacred, pure, as he called it, out of contrast, with marriage plans in the background . . . a little intrigue with a servant-girl, and then the whole great free sisterhood, blond, brown, redhaired, black."

But Boccaccio also turned John's mind in another direction— to a criticism of society and the institution of the family. For the first time he saw the ridiculous position of the husband, obliged to support a wife who may not be faithful, and to care for chil- dren who may not be his. Here was the trap into which men had fallen through their infatuation and from it there was no escape. John had already hit upon a theme which was to occupy him with bitter attacks and relentless polemics throughout his life.

John's love life, to which he now devoted himself seriously, did not always run a smooth course. For some time he had formed the very agreeable custom of adjourning with a talented friend of his to the Stallmästergarden restaurant. While his friend played the piano he made love to Rieke, a waitress of the place. One day the girl asked him to write some verses for her birthday. John agreed but later repented his thoughtless promise, for poetry, he had discovered to his chagrin, was quite beyond him. From this predicament, however, he was saved by his friend, who agreed to write a few lines himself and give them to Rieke as from John. Thus the matter was settled, and Rieke got her verses in due course and was no doubt quite pleased with them until she learned that another servant-girl had received the same lines two years before. "For shame, John!" she cried. But John, detected in all his ugliness, turned deathly pale and ran headlong and mad, deep into the woods of the park. "The branches of the bushes flew into his face, stones rolled over his feet, and frightened birds rose up. He was quite wild with shame, and instinctively sought the woods in order to hide himself. It is a curious phenomenon that at the utmost pitch of despair a man runs into the wood before he plunges into the water. . . . The wood is the original home of the savage and the enemy of the plough, therefore of culture." Having made his retreat to his ancestral forest, John gave himself up to despair and horror, and burned with shame. He had lied, and cheated, he had deceived and insulted a girl who had really loved him. True, she was only a servant but so had his mother been. No, he could never forgive himself. After a long while he heard the voices of Rieke and his friend calling him, and for a moment he was tempted to have done with his flagellation and to return with them for a drink, for then she would laugh and forgive him. But no, he would not. He needed to suffer and so stayed on till the woods became dark and fearful. That night he had no supper and slept on the floor.

The summer of this year John spent in a settlement outside the city where he continued to give lessons. There the opportunities for social intercourse were more numerous and varied than he had yet experienced and he was subject to the most diverse influence from the different types with whom he consorted daily. Every individual, he learned, has a mystery, a uniqueness and a history of his own which it is profitable to study and understand. But though John collected impressions from morning till night, and like the bee made up his store from many places, there was little system in his gathering.

In this summer settlement to which so many types resorted, John had a splendid opportunity for comparisons. He was struck in particular with the contrast between the townsmen, who leaving their business behind them abandoned themselves to joy and frivolity, and the learned, the professors, who sat in cold, dour rumination and seemed to be slaves to their ceaseless gloomy thoughts. John deplored the cold sophistication and the bitter laughter of the professors and admired the light-hearted gaiety of the townsmen, for it showed that with all their lust for power and wealth, they had still a weakness in their hearts for nature and its bright parade, and could become children again if they chose.

But while John was observing the peculiarities of others, he also had occasion to watch himself, for the caprice and moodiness of his mind was becoming very striking. Sometimes when he was asked to dinner, he failed to appear, though he had no earthly reason and his irregularities were often subject to comment. Chiefly he suffered from a vague half-conscious desire to express himself in a grand way. Since he could find no outlet in literature, his mind being at this time far too chaotic to permit of composition, he turned to poetry and began when drunk to declaim in the high tragic style which had just then come into fashion. But at the height of his ecstasy "he heard his own voice, became nervous and embarrassed, found himself ridiculous, suddenly dropped into a prosaic and comic tone and ended with a grimace; he could be pathetic but only for a while, then came self-criticism and he laughed at his own overwrought feelings. The romantic was in his blood, but the realistic side of him was about to wake up." John's wildness and humors were out of order and this high declaiming when drunk looked suspicious. Things were

coming to a sorry pass, when suddenly everything was changed
by the odd proposal of his old friend, Dr. Lamm, a Jewish physician. This kind gentleman now took him in hand, and warned
him against his undisciplined fancies. "You must become a doctor," he said, and offered him a place in his own house as tutor.
John, who was himself a bit frightened by the disorder and independence of his mind, was at once attracted by this proposal,
for he desired more than anything else now to secure a station in
society in which neither superiors nor inferiors would plague him,
and he longed to walk through life alone bent on some praise-
worthy and unchallengeable business. The career of a doctor was
just the thing for him. But how could he forsake his pupils at
the public school? After a struggle between his conscience and
his rising ambition, he sent in his resignation, making a last bow
to the profession of teacher and torturer of children, for he would
never try it again, however pressed for money. Yet to forget was
impossible. His experience at school continued to shadow him
with a quiet vengeance. He was now bent for a new career, one of
wealth and independence, prestige and even fame. He would
now become a member of a cultured Jewish household and a
tutor to the boys of the family, he would discipline his outrageous
fancies and in the end, perhaps, win a place for himself in the
world.

VIII

MEDICINE AND THE THEATRE

JOHN now found himself in an altogether different environment, subject to many influences which were to have a great effect on his future, and he set forth on a new life. The household of the Jewish physician was in many respects quite the opposite from any he had yet observed and the family life was widely different from that in which he himself had lived. Instead of the parental tyranny, under which he had suffered so long, he found understanding and kindness. The children were not suppressed or required to feel grateful, but were rather treated as equals, and the respect they paid their parents was a free tribute. The servants, too, were regarded as equals and treated with so much generosity that they ceased to be servants. Throughout the house there reigned a freedom and light-heartedness which John had never known in his own home, or thought possible.

One of the curiosities of the family in which he now lived was that they could be classified neither as aristocrats nor democrats, but seemed to stand entirely above the distinction, living independently in their own professional and artistic circle. John noticed that though all their tastes were aristocratic, they cherished democratic ideas, and this duplicity was a decided surprise to him. John himself, though his feelings often agreed with theirs, since he hated the noises, smells, and the stupidity of the people, yet passionately sought their welfare, took the matter too much to heart and suffered too many conflicting emotions to view it in their considerate and disinterested fashion. No, his parentage and early experiences were too ambiguous to permit of that and so the conflict in his mind continued and had great issue in his succeeding history.

John could not help but admire these immensely civilized and disciplined people, nor to lament his own wild gloom and irresponsibility. These Jews, he concluded, are a great people. They have had no country of their own but perhaps that has been a certain advantage, for the struggle has sharpened their wits and developed all their potentialities. This judgment of John's is quite interesting when compared to his later pronouncements on Jews. At times he inveighed against them most bitterly, condemning them roundly as non-producers, and was known everywhere as an anti-semite, while in 1884 he wrote a pamphlet called *My Hatred of the Jews* in which he maintained that the Jews were the most civilized people of Europe. At the present time, however, he was quite enamoured of these very civilized people, for in the doctor's family he had his own way and enjoyed every privilege. For one thing, his work was very easy and pleasant and he became more a companion to the boys than their tutor. His obligations were in fact so light that his pietist conscience began to work and his high-strung nerves craved the discipline of disagreeable work. John's attitude toward his pupils was quite amusing. His public-school experience had convinced him that he was not a very successful teacher but now he fell into a greater doubt. He found that he could not treat the doctor's boys as younger than himself and he continually had the impression that they were "getting ahead of him" and "going on where he left off . . . When later in life he met grown-up pupils, he looked up to them as if they were older." One reason for this confusion may have been the fact that he himself was always being put back in school so that whether he was master or pupil or what not, was at times a perplexing question.

John was now to become a doctor and therefore found himself working away in the laboratories of the technological institute, boring himself to death with the dull rudiments of science, performing experiments which had been verified thousands of times and laboring for results which he would have gladly accepted on authority. At times, however, he attempted original experiments of his own, and then a sudden transformation occurred—a great idea stood up in his mind, his chemistry text became a set of magical formulae, retorts and test tubes took on power and fascination, the bunsen burner glowed quietly with a mysterious promise and the room about him swirled with the intensity of his great purpose. One of these individual studies of his, carried out at considerable danger to life, resulted in a few drops of prussic acid and it was a curious pleasure for him to feel that under the stopper of a little bottle he had imprisoned death. John indulged his curiosity and tried out his ideas in the laboratory, just as he had done as a child, and again glimpsed the wonders beneath the surface. He particularly enjoyed qualitative analysis, for there one was always making surprising discoveries and showing the presence of unsuspected substances in a clear solution. In addition to Chemistry, he studied Zoölogy, Anatomy, Botany, Physics and Latin,—"more Latin," for it seemed that he would never have done with that hateful tongue, which laid for him like vengeance in every career.

But here were too many subjects to be mastered and John's mind was already so burdened with a variety of things that he doubted his ability to learn any of them. He, nevertheless, continued his labors in the laboratory and poured over his textbooks for months together in the effort to make some headway on the long road toward his medical degree. His interests at this time, however, were fixed in quite a different direction, toward the beautiful world of art and imagination, and it was the voices of Goethe, Wieland and Lessing, Chateaubriand and George Sand, which sang in his heart, not the dull lessons of science. The dere-

liction of his interests was partly due to his intercourse with artists and writers and his increasing preoccupation with the doctor's
library, but art was also deep in his nature,—much deeper than
the official authority, the depressing discipline of science. Later in
his life when he turned to science with enthusiasm, it was as a
free-lance, a reformer who would sweep away all authorities by
dint of his great discoveries.

The dullness of John's medical studies also led him to a new
diversion—the theatre—and he fell into a great admiration for
the restraint, the balance and perfection of French comedy. What
a buoyant light-hearted race these Frenchmen were who could
fortify themselves against the blows of life in this graceful way!
John was so impressed with the Gallic temper as it displayed itself on the Brussel's carpet of the little theatre he attended that
he would have liked nothing better than to imitate it, but he
felt his German *Weltschmertz* like a dark cloud over the world
which he would have made graceful, witty, and *étincelant*. The
boy who loved the wild austerity of his native fjords and forests
was not likely to find himself at home in the artificial perfection
of the French theatre, and he never did. Though the ugliness of
reality with its "wounds and blood puddings" offended him, he
could not escape from it. Dreams and reality contended in his
mind in piercing disparity.

But the theatre, literature, and his other distractions were absorbing too much of John's time. The doctor thought it was high
time that his waning interests in medicine were resurrected by actual experience in the profession. He therefore made John his
assistant and they went thereafter together, making the rounds of
the patients, into the houses of the poor and the mansions of the
rich. Now they went down into a dark evil-smelling room where
the doctor bent over the shrunken breasts of some wretched
woman, then they were out in the street again bound for another
patient, stopping perhaps to see some old choice paintings along
the way. Their next call might be at a rich, magnificent bedroom

where a beautiful child was ailing. John learned to assist the doctor, and putting his feelings aside, would hold the struggling head of a patient while the doctor operated. Once he was called down before breakfast to assist at cauterizing a syphilitic sore, and to these disagreeable duties, as to the beating of children, he became accustomed after a while.

It was about this time that a series of events occurred that aroused John's class consciousness to a strange intensity and showed incidentally that there was the material in him for many explosions in the future. These were the riots brought about by the new statue of Karl XII and the conduct of its celebration. One night while the doctor was entertaining the Italian Opera Company, while the glasses were clinking gallantly and French and Italian phrases were flying about the room,—in the midst of this brilliant scene, there came an ominous roaring from the street. Several of the elegant guests turned pale. "What is it?" asked the prima donna. "The mob making a noise," answered the professor. But the word "mob" burned in John's heart and he hurried out in the street with a sense of guilt and betrayal. There he saw the mob in a dark mass and the charging police. In a moment he had become a great patriot who would crush the tyranny single-handed. In the name of freedom he stood in the way of the mounted officers. Luckily a hand seized his arm and he was brought back to the doctor's house. On the day when the statue was unveiled, however, John was not among the people but marched with the other student singers, a member of the privileged class—"among the elect, the upper ten thousand and had no reason to be discontented with his lot." After the ceremony, however, the people made an attack, and the police retaliated by beating some and arresting others. In a moment John forgot his upper-class allegiance and when he saw an officer trying to lay hold of a man, he forgot himself completely. Seizing the policeman by the collar and jerking him up, he shouted: "Let the fellow go." The officer regarded his assailant with amazement.

"Who are you?" he asked irresolutely. "I am Satan, and I will take you if you don't let him go!"John's effrontery was actually effective, for the man did get away, but then John himself was almost caught. He broke away just in time and joined a strange troupe of men who were running along behind the policemen, menacing them. The mob was retreating before the policemen but behind them came this band of well-dressed men determined on freeing the prisoners. Yet these men had no real sympathy with the people. They were well-to-do, conservative, with good positions and prospects. They were hazarding everything for the sake of an abstract principle of Justice which was not at all clear in their minds. Suddenly John felt someone take hold of his hand and looking around saw a middle-aged, very respectable looking man, staring straight ahead of him with glowing eyes and a sunken face. John returned the pressure, for he felt dimly that they were bound together now to right a great wrong. An hour later, this hysteria had completely subsided and John, over his beefsteak, could return to reality and laugh at his curious lapse. The man who had seized John's hand, he learned, was quite as conservative and respectable as he looked. John saw him several times after this but their eyes never met. Once this man passed him on a narrow pavement where he had to meet John's eyes but on this occasion his features were curiously fixed and he did not smile.

Later in the same year, 1878, John had another experience which aroused again all his bitter consciousness of class, but this time the pendulum turned the other way, and the son of a servant revolted against his own class. In the company of one of his pupils he made his first trip to Copenhagen, his first voyage out of Sweden, and it was not a happy one. His companions were bar-keepers, chimney sweeps, butchers, coachmen and pawn brokers who turned out on close acquaintance such shabby, disagreeable fellows that he soon wished them at the bottom of the sea and their arrogance and stupidity with them. The devil take them, he thought. The officers and officials would never be such tyrants as these democrats. If they ever got in power they would be as oppressive and selfish as the present rulers and much more ignorant besides. With a sudden insight he saw the inevitability of the war of the classes. Vivid memories awoke of the brutality of the charging police, the cowering, muttering resentment of the mob. "He had felt the feet of the future upper class on his heart." They were therefore his enemies. But society with its cruel and inviolable authority was also his enemy. He hated both classes, upper and lower, yet sympathized with each. Both were seeking selfishly their own ends and each in power would be a tyrant. Morally there was little choice between them. If anything, the lower class was more dangerous.

Though John had become an aristocrat, he did not long remain on the top of the world where aristocrats belong. An unforeseen event suddenly robbed him of his prospects and his future so that now, at twenty years of age, he had no other course, he felt, than to abandon his new career in disgrace. He had tried to become a student at the University and a teacher at a public school. He had failed at both. Then, under the eyes of a critical and unsympathetic audience of his friends and family, he had changed about, determined to rise in the world and become a doctor. Now, this new pretension collapsed and he was left helpless, without a foothold in society, his mind a chaos of uncertainties and inconsequences. The event which brought him so low was his failure at the chemistry examination at Upsala. Though he knew more chemistry, he tells us, than Dr. Lamm himself, had done his work faithfully at the Technological Institute, and received assurance that his knowledge was sufficient, he was plucked none the less.

He was advised to return next year better prepared. So, he must slave another year "in order to enter this dirty profession where one had to analyse urine, pick about in vomit, poke about in all the recesses of the body." It was not worth it. Besides, the prospect of spending another year at Upsala was too much for John. No, he had been cheated and betrayed. Knowledge was not sufficient at Upsala, one must toady and flatter the authorities, and this John would not do, for in his heart he had sickened of the learning and the hypocrisy of the small town and wished himself out of it at any cost. While in this mood it happened that he saw a band of actors stroll by, and, laughing, make droll comments on the towers of books which old Upsala had accumulated. Suddenly it struck John that their levity was completely justified, that their life on the stage was far more brilliant and profitable than the piddling provincial scholarship of Upsala. They lived, he saw it clearly now, a free, careless life above the distinctions of society and they enjoyed a privileged place. They were not in the power of provincial professors, but commanded the applause of large and free-minded audiences. John reflected for a moment and then his mind was made up—he would be an actor. This was the only way he saw to redeem himself and atone for his many failures.

On his return to Stockholm he addressed himself to the director of the Theatrical Academy and announced boldly that he had every intention of becoming an actor. But as he heard himself speaking he shuddered at his words, and his natural modesty revolted against his ambitious assurance. Now, for the first time he had taken away the veil which had hidden his presumption from the world. He felt naked and uncomfortable. The director seemed surprised that he should give up medicine to enter the worst of all professions and this strengthened John's determination. He loved to do surprising things and besides, if there was a presumption against his succceeding in such a hard career, the obligation was less, and his conscience would be easier if he failed. John hated to be put in a responsible position in which everyone could expect him to win. This weakness of his, the inability to accept responsibility, was doubtless occasioned by his self-distrust, and this in turn may have been due to his love and dependence on the pale, dark-eyed mother, for this yearning and incompleteness he never outgrew.

John also felt the fascination of the stage where great men come to life again, enacting their noblest parts, expressing their passions and resolves in the inspired transfigured language of the poet. As an actor John would escape from himself and his own responsibilities. He would become a great hero of the past and pour forth his soul from this elevation to a cheering audience. There would be no doubt of his identity. In the height of the action no one could think of him as John August Strindberg, the vacillating youth of twenty, who had failed so many times. He would convince the audience. He would convince himself. He would become Hamlet, Caesar, Napoleon, anyone he chose, and this escape from his own wretched self would not be madness. It would be a great and legitimate pretense—perhaps the highest of all the arts. The theatre, it occurred to him, is the great moralist and teacher of every period. It elevates and ennobles. It is the greatest illusion of all, for it fortifies us against life, by transforming the deaths of saints and heroes into spectacles of beauty. John felt that the lure of the theatre was deep in his blood. He remembered that his grandfather had turned to writing plays and that another relative had dropped a lucrative post and outfaced the whole family, to become an actor. And suddenly the roles of preacher, student, teacher, doctor, went up in smoke as he donned the mantle of Thespis.

To have more time to himself John dropped the two girls he had been tutoring and devoted himself to his art which he studied furiously in secret. At the doctor's house, where he remained to tutor the boys, he arranged a stage and there he practiced exits and entrances. He performed gymnastics every day, too, and fenced with his pupils. Moreover since carriage was important, he commenced to carry himself erect, with head back and his hands slightly clenched, as Goethe advised. To overcome his stage-fright and agoraphobia he accustomed himself to walk in open places where great throngs crowded. Also, fearing to be overheard if he declaimed at home, he formed the habit of going outside the city every day to a lonely plain where he held forth and laid about him in the high style in fashion at his time. In this barren place he had chosen, his voice died away so quickly that he was obliged to shout and so he thundered and imprecated, "and declaimed against heaven and earth; the town, whose church tower rose opposite, symbolized society, while he stood out there alone with Nature. He shook his fist at the castle, the churches, the barracks, and stormed at the troops who during their manoeuvers came too close to him. There was something fanatical in his work and he spared no pains in order to make his unwilling muscles obedient."

For all his drastic efforts, his progress was but slow and painful and he was continually advised to take a course at the Dramatic Academy as preparation. But this was more than John would do. He would not become a pupil again among children and uneducated louts. This much he was resolved upon, for he had already suffered too much from the enforced return to childhood. Even at the theatre it was bad enough. For all his knowledge and accomplishments he was treated like the youngest novice. Sometimes he was pushed into a dance which he did not know, often he was hectored and ridiculed until it seemed to him that his new glimmering career was a will-of-the-wisp like the rest. Yet he persisted in the "sacred art" and wrote his father that his mind was firm, that he would not return home until he had succeeded.

Finally he was given a role in Björnson's *Marie Stuart,* a play which he admired greatly. There were two parts in it which would have suited him admirably, that of Knox, "hard as a stone" with his moral fanaticism and "his terrible Norwegian Christianity," or Darnley, "the young man after the manner of Hamlet who must always burn with love of one certain woman in spite of everything: in spite of unfaithfulness, scorn, and wickedness." John could have taken one role as well as the other,

for Brand, the inflexible moralist, and Hamlet, the sensitive
doubter, were equal parts of his nature. Instead he was given the
part of a noble who spoke but eleven words through the whole
play. Thereafter he was obliged to remain for hours at the endless rehearsals, waiting to give his short speech, and what made
these delays particularly irksome was that he could not read for
fear of being thought indifferent to his art. Behind scenes the
stage appeared a great barn and all the trappings and trumpery of
dramatic pretense, the beards, the lights, the paints and mere-
tricious finery, were seen inside and so divulged their secret. It
was a scene of disenchantment as when the sleeper wakes from
a magnificent dream. Behind the scenes there was no illusion but
only fraud and downright imposture. For the audience the stage
glowed like a timeless picture. For the actors it was nothing but
shifts and open deceits. Everything had been done to invite dramatic illusion in the audience, nothing had been done for the
actor. John found the great actors quite disillusioned, and when
their acts were over he heard them complain of their lot and he
saw them sit alone in the gay habiliments of heroes, stroking their
false beards with a sad air. Was this his destiny, after all? Did
his lode-star point this way? John was commencing to have his
doubts. As an actor he was in fair way of becoming, like most
of those about him, a perfect nobody.

To crown all his reverses and humiliations came the final insult. He must return to school, he must take a course at the Dramatic Academy, for that was the only way, he was told, he could
ever succeed. Being afraid of ridicule should he drop his new career too abruptly, he soon found himself a pupil again, listening
to the recitation of poems which he had long since learned by
heart. Schiller, whom John had been reading, had ascribed the fall
of the theatre to the stupid actors who had come into favor and
had suggested that untrained men from the cultured class would
perform much better than the most finished fools. John believed
this at first and plucked up courage, but when he saw how read-

ily the raw boys in the Academy fell into form, and assimilated the manner of the greatest actors, he became doubtful, for it seemed that their ignorance was a positive advantage to them. When John had put up with the Academy as long as he could, he plucked up courage and asked for a leading role. After some time this was granted but John's performance at the rehearsal was so deficient that he was definitely discouraged and advised to take a long course of training. Was John's style too serious, too grandiose and declamatory? Was he self-conscious and too archaically grand? At any rate he had made a fiasco of his new career, and disgraced himself before the world. Returning home in the blackest despair, he took an opium tablet that he had long kept by him, for he had resolved to end his life. But John's last moments were disturbed by a friend who insisted that he go out with him on a carouse. John assented and, in the wild evening that followed, drowned his sorrows and all thought of the deadly narcotic. So ended John's histrionic ambitions. Was he a failure as an actor? If so, it is none the less true that he never in his life ceased to be one. It was characteristic of his type of mind that he felt himself always a lone player before a full house with every eye upon him, and his melodramatic career bears this out. If he was a bad actor on the stage, his many life-roles off of it produced a striking and wonderful effect, which brought great audiences to tears and rage.

After his great fall in the world John swallowed his humiliation with the best grace he could and continued half-heartedly his work at the Academy, for to stop in mid-course would only make his failure more evident and his family and acquaintances more triumphant. In the meantime the doctor, who had never given John up completely, attempted to draw his mind away from the theatre by an altogether new proposal. They would collaborate on articles for the journals. Their first publication was John's translation of one of Schiller's studies on the theatre, to which the doctor added an introduction. Next, John wrote an article for *Aftonbladet* on woman's emancipation, and as if the star which was to guide him through life already showed the way, before any experience had taught him, he turned upon the whole cherished movement in a downright attack. Every man withdrawn from industry by the encroachment of emancipated women means one less marriage, he wrote. If women do men's work they but rob him of his, to the neglect of their own, for their place is the home where they jolly well belong. *Aftonbladet,* however, so changed the article that it appeared a defence of woman's emancipation.

It was at this time that the most important event of his life occurred. On the day following the opium and the evening's carouse, a peculiar fever overcame him "and in a few days I had written a two-act play. In two months I had written a three-act play, a five-act drama (*Hermione*) in verse, and had begun a great drama concerning Christ, which however was burned before it was finished." John found the dramatic form surprisingly easy and loved to trace the exchanges and interweaving of the characters. As long as he wrote he was blessedly happy. Only then did he live. After a siege of writing he would collapse on the sofa and give way to a painful exhaustion. But again the fever would come and with it the glimmering irrepressible ideas. Once more he would return to his desk to write for hours. And this alternation between sofa and desk went on for months. It was a strange dream-like life that John had fallen into, full of exultation and despair, but through it all there ran a whisper of triumph. He had found his lost ego that had eluded him so long, and never again would he lose it. All the old confusions and diremptions which had torn his mind to a thousand wasted fractions, had gone. Out of chaos had come creation. When John had finished a two-act comedy in four days "he fetched a deep sigh as if he had outlived a year-long pain, or as if a tumor had just been removed. He was so happy that it seemed that someone sang within him, and he craved to send the piece off at once to the theatre. That was the salvation."

That same evening John made another crucial discovery which was to prove more important to him than an academic post, an inheritance, or any windfall conceivable. As he wrote to a relative on the circumstance of a wedding he was astonished to find that the lines were rhythmic and rhymed. With delightful ease he finished eight full pages and there before him lay a letter that was a poem. John was transfigured with the idea. He was a poet then. He had been blessed by the Holy Ghost—endowed with this priceless gift. Only a short time before he had asked a friend to help him with some verses and had met with a cold refusal. Now all this was changed, for the melody of words sang within him.

John's new powers appeared so suddenly and were altogether so unexpected that he distrusted them and thus determined to try them out on his learned friends. Would they prove captious and rob him of his treasure? John prepared his room for their coming and fixed the punch. It was the first entertaining he had ever done. When the reading was over there followed a blessed silence, for the friends found nothing to criticize. Was he a poet? There was no doubt of it. They congratulated him on leaving. Then John fell on his knees, and beside himself with pride and exultation, thanked God for his goodness and for the great miracle He had brought to pass.

Henceforth, whatever sorrows might come to him, he had but to objectify them, to pour them out in the flowing, sweet, absolving form of verse. When he had finished his lament a warmth would steal over his recumbent body and then it would seem that a woman, tender and gracious, spoke soft words to him and stroked his cheek till he cried. The solace of her tenderness, like a flower of heaven, would never die. It was at such times, at the height of his possession, that the little mother who had eluded him so long, crept quietly into his heart, and John in that moment became a man and a god.

IX

PLAYWRIGHT AND PROTÉGÉ OF THE KING

HAVING finished the play to his satisfaction John sent it off anonymously to the Academy, and waited with the apprehension and doubts of a young writer and the feverish self-distrust which was special to his nature, for a favorable return. When he had waited four months, however, his patience broke down, and throwing modesty to the winds, he declared himself the author. The consequence was that the play was praised but not accepted. John's instructor at the Dramatic Academy advised him to give up the career of an actor, in which he was not likely to distinguish himself for years, and return to Upsala, there to undergo a necessary preparation for the much finer profession of playwright. John, accordingly, gave a party, made a farewell speech, got drunk as usual and acted foolish. This was his formal exit from the Academy.

Most opportunely for him, John received word at this time that a small legacy was due him. He, therefore, returned home to the father who had beaten and humiliated him, whom he had feared and respected and admired, and assuming for the first time a bold style, demanded his rights—"not as a prodigal son but as a promising author and a creditor." There followed a violent dispute, but John was in the right and he knew it. The conference was a triumph; he had secured enough money for his first six months at the University.

At Upsala again, his mind turned upon the culture around him with the same acrimonious displeasure as before, for hatred of vested authority was becoming a settled feature of his character. Boström's philosophy, so highly celebrated at that time, did not impress him. All philosophies and all philosophers, he believed, were but spokesmen and the creations of their times. They originated nothing, but only accumulated and articulated the reigning ideas of the period. The poets were no better than the philosophers. They but reflected the ideas about them and often in a confused and contradictory fashion. "Bjorck and Snoilsky (for instance) sang of water and drank wine." Their lives were so out of spirit with their sentiments that there was no trusting them. "Why is a poet's life," he asks, "always at variance with his teaching? Does he want to escape from his personality and find a new one, or is it a modesty—a fear of exposure?"

Ibsen, however, was of stronger metal. In 1869 John saw *Brand* for the first time and was much struck with the power and gloom of the piece. The hero he particularly admired for the grandeur of his austerity, but he was also shocked and horrified at this man who scorned all compromise, sacrificing his dearest treasure to a fabulous faith. And John was the more shocked in that he recognized that this Brand with his monstrous, cruel austerity was a part of himself. Though he had ceased to believe the tenets of Pietism he was still governed to a great extent by its ascetic morality, retained his hair shirt and hated modern compromises, but he could not be as ruthless as Brand. Peer Gynt, on the other hand, the light-hearted, careless, opportunistic Peer Gynt, who forsook reality for his worldly dreams, was surely the hero of the times. John despised Peer's compromise and dishonesty, but he enjoyed the satire of the piece and the boldness and bitterness of Ibsen's attack on the proud Norwegians.

He had not been long at Upsala when, over a friendly glass of punch, he conceived the idea of a Runa (song) Club, which was to be devoted in a high way to the study and celebration of the

sagas and classics of the North. The membership was extended
to nine aspiring young poets, who, meeting together from time
to time, declaimed against contemporary movements and writers,
read their own compositions, confessed their hopes and ambitions,
and pledged the stars with many rounds of the insidious, almost
omnipotent Swedish punch. It was a joyous, exhilarating period
for John among these spirited young friends, and their contrasts
and exchanges were as stimulating for him as his contacts at the
doctor's house. Ancient lore and modern ideas seemed all to float
through the minds of this little group, to be reviewed and modified. They became critics and authorities on almost every subject for they were too young to be very modest.

At this time John was living in a wretched room, with an uncomfortable plank-bed and a ceiling which leaked, so that the
rain poured in. He was supposed to spend most of his time at
his chosen subjects of study, but as usual his program appeared
so hopelessly extended that he was quite paralyzed and lost all
hope of mastering it. From the tedium of imposed tasks, punch
and spirited disputes formed a welcome and recurrent escape.
John was now a poet disclaiming the discipline of scholarship, a
wit and a good fellow, and he carried matters so far that he
learned to play the guitar.

Suddenly he was aroused from this wordy and spirituous life
by an older friend. Why not write a one-act play for the Royal
Theater? John seized on the idea at once, and chose the subject
of Thorwaldsen (the great Danish sculptor) in Rome. In fourteen days he had finished the piece to such complete satisfaction
of his friends that they at once set about on a champagne dinner,
on the sure prospects of its being accepted. So high was their confidence that the affair became a sort of bacchanale. They drank
and drank till morning, and when the sun rose they went quietly
to sleep on the floor with their punch glasses beside them. After
a short but refreshing sleep they rose up, finished their punch,
and went out to continue the celebration. John's friends outdid

themselves to honor him and their admiration on this occasion was so sincere and unselfish that in memory it appeared a wonderful thing. In this roistering circle of downright friends, where all jealousy and self-interest were suppressed for the sake of good fellowship, the gloom of his pietism fell away, his star rose, and life appeared a shimmering, glorious affair. What inspired, besotten times they had together, with toasts and intellections, and fair hopes for the future! And now John had sent his play off to the Royal Theatre. What would come of that?

In Rome, as he named it, was certainly a light piece, and John's doubts of it were entirely justified. It represents Thorwaldsen, hard pressed in Rome and about to leave, when an English lord orders a statue, which happy circumstance permits him to remain. But as Thorwaldsen creates, he is beset with deep doubts of his capacity; so much so that in the end, at the height of the action, he takes a hammer to the great statue, and shatters it to pieces. John wrote this play for the Royal Theatre, but what a private satisfaction it must have given him! The great sculptor was in the same situation at Rome as he at Upsala; both were relieved from their distresses, both distrusted their abilities, both destroyed their masterpieces, which had grown dear to them through the labors and hopes of creation. John thus identified himself with Thorwaldsen, and the play turned out, as so many of his future works did, both a confession and a defence. But for all its limitations, *In Rome* was accepted and would be performed in the Royal Theatre in August! The news of this success was the occasion for further celebrations, in the course of which his great historical tragedy, *Erick XIV,* which he had begun the same year, was completely forgotten. This play was a much more ambitious effort, and though John worked a great deal on the third act and put out reams of verse, he could not finish it. Like Thorwaldsen, his doubts paralyzed him. But consolation was always to be had in friends and liquor. The month of May was spent in a perpetual carouse during which punch, ovations, pledges, songs, long controversies·on beauty, life and art, appreciations of the songs, recitations and criticisms of self-made poems, filled the days and nights. In June the brothers of the Runa Club went to Stockholm, the semester at Upsala having ended, and undertook a splendid picnic. They set out in the early morning through the lovely islands with high spirits and an abundant supply of food and drinks. John, who had studied archaeology for his play *Hermione,* arranged the meal in the old Greek fashion, so that the revellers reclined at their ease, and, crowned with wreaths, prepared for a long siege of drinking and feasting, ready for songs or poetry, or disgraceful stories, or whatever else might come. At a certain stage of these festivities John read his new play, *The Free-Thinker,* which was then criticized and celebrated. Thereafter followed songs which John accompanied on his guitar, a long argument about the poet, Bellman, and soulful discussions on the philosophy of life. But, returning to Stockholm on the bright June night in a high mood, their minds took a different course, and soon they found themselves with the girls in Apelbergsgata. The idealistic mood, which had prevailed on the journey home, now faded out, and the brothers of the Runa were soon seated at an open window feasting out of the lunch baskets, "and again sounded guitar and the flute, and now they cited the songs of Horace on Lydia and Chloe, and in white beds kindled the fire of love for Aphrodite Pandämos." But at the height of their conviviality came a sudden change and, as if they had all seen the fatal handwriting on the wall, each came to feel that he could bear it no longer, that he must get out into the open by himself, away from the voices and the faces which had suddenly grown so burdensome. They separated, shamefaced, with sickly excuses and departed with the greatest relief, the craving for loneliness being the conclusion of all of these protracted parties.

The Free-Thinker, like *In Rome,* is very revealing of the author's life and dreams, and much more autobiographical. The hero, Karl, is a young student like John, and like him, is a teacher in a public school. Oppressed with the formalism and dogmatism of theology, Karl has become a free-thinker who will fight for the truth against the tyranny of orthodoxy, awaking the youth of the country to new hopes and a new joy in religious life. As Jesus fought against the deadening forms of Judaism, so will Karl raise arms against the stifling orthodoxy of his time, preaching a rational life-giving faith, and if need be, he will sacrifice his life for the cause. After undergoing a religious crisis similar to John's, he finds the world such a splendid merry place filled with beautiful worthy people, that he has no higher desire than to continue at his post, spreading his joyous wisdom among all the youth of the land. But the people take unkindly to his teaching and Karl is made a martyr to his faith. His friends and family, even his beloved, turn from him and he wanders sadly out of the land, which would never understand him.—How prophetic this was of John's not distant future will be seen in what follows. *The Free-Thinker* was the first of his plays to be published. In this matter he was assisted by his faithful cousin, Oscar Strindberg, who helped him in a great many other ways besides.

During this time John continued to drink far more than was good for him and for long periods, as he himself says, was drunk every night. This account of the matter is, however, out of agreement with the report of his own friends. They found him on the whole industrious and sober, waking at four or five in the morning to do his work. According to them he drank but moderately, and when occasionally treated, could hold an unheard of quantity, so that he was almost never seen drunk. Habitually short of money, he was forced to forego the rich food which he always craved and content himself at supper with milk only. His love of fine raiments must also be sacrificed. His finely-turned figure was nevertheless always clothed with taste and care, though with worn-out clothes, and his bearing was distinguished. Thus he put a good face on his troubles and did not complain, though the poverty at Upsala was particularly hard to bear after the luxuries he had enjoyed at the doctor's house. John's friends knew very little of his inner conflicts and saw in him only a gay, erratic, impractical student, amiable and brilliant in company, sensitive, charming and lovable. They were happy to help him. Perhaps, too, they sensed something unusual in him, the awakening of genius, for he acquired the name of "the eagle" which he retained for a long time.

John was easily roused to skepticism and often at the height of an enthusiasm would suddenly come tumbling down with a great laugh at his own expense. His ardent love of freedom, which he was always quick to feel in any extended association, now made him skeptical of friendship. Were not his friends hemming him in, impeding his development, stifling his originality? Doubts and discords! John at his best, could not quite escape from them. He was also subject at times to strange outbreaks. A friend found him, on one occasion, cursing and kicking on the sofa, and was simply astounded at what he saw. "I am exercising myself in cursing," John explained. "I have never done it before, but there are so many beautiful alliterations in Swedish."

Though John complained of unhappy love affairs at this time, and wrote many sad elegies and lyrics expounding his sorrows and hopeless yearning, his friends regarded him as rather adroit and successful with women. And the truth is that he did possess a number of qualities which might well have recommended him to them. He was courteous, attentive, rather good looking, sensitive and spirited, and what is more perhaps, held them in the highest esteem. Being at heart quite shy, he seldom flirted, but allowed his charmer to take the first steps. This gave an impression of helplessness, which to some women at least, was extraordinarily pleasing. In the pension where John lived there were several girls and with one of them he fell in love again—for the eighth time. But, alas, this fifteen-year-old girl was unobtainable and his longings found no outlet save in a poem, in which he related how the youths gather garlands for their sweethearts, but one among them must throw his flowers away, since he alone has no girl to whom to give them.

A more serious passion was evoked by an older cousin, Maria, a sweet, tender, musical creature. In this case John gave way completely and allowed his erotic thoughts full play. That the beloved was engaged to another was a sad circumstance, but it did not prevent him from dreaming of her and despairing, and flying to her arms in phantasy. After she had sailed away, John continued unappeasable, and seeking quick distractions from his love, was haunted still by disquieting images of the black hair and blue eyes of his lost idol.

It was about this time that John made the acquaintance of several authors who were to have a surprising influence over him. Hugo's *Les Misérables, L'homme qui rit* and *Les travailleurs de la mer* quite entranced him. They were sublime works which he never forgot. Georg Brandes, whose modern critical studies he also read, gave him a new insight and helped to form the naturalistic outlook for which he was to be so noted a few years later. All at once he saw that the dramatist, the poet, must give up his dreams and devote himself to the actualities in the world around him, that the child's play of phantasy must give way to the vividness and strength of reality. Somewhat later, the idea occurred to him that this naturalism of Brandes and Taine and Zola would ultimately end in autobiography, since for an author who is convinced of the powerlessness of the will, and does not mind portraying himself as conditions have made him, he himself is the best possible object of study. Here, then, was the germ of Strindberg's rather distinctive, autobiographical naturalism. John's voracious reading distracted his mind from other matters and consoled him in the loss of his charming Maria.

In August, however, an event occurred of such importance, that for the moment, all the old doubts and sorrows were swept aside. John's little play, *In Rome,* was put on at the Royal Theatre and for the first time he saw the brilliant stage lit up for his honor and heard the gifted actors speaking his lines. It was this he had dreamed of through the days and weeks of feverish creation, and all his hopes and fears had related to such a happiness. Now, when the time had come, he was ill prepared to enjoy it, and fear and shame were his dominant emotions. As he listened to the performance from an inconspicuous place, his tears rose ceaselessly and his body trembled so violently that his friend took his hand to steady him. "Every stupidity which had inadvertently escaped him now jarred on his ear, and made him quiver; he felt so ashamed that his ears burned." Unable to bear it any longer, he rushed out into the street, and since there was no forest close at hand, hid himself in the dark market-place. Then he wandered about in despair and once it occurred to him to drown himself in Norrstrom, but the thought came to nothing, John's contemplated suicides never being very successful. He was finally hailed by his friends, congratulated on his brilliant début at the Royal Theatre, and shamed into a good countenance. Then, he was made to drink and eat and taken off with them handsomely to the solace of a group of girls. The next day he read a favorable review of the play and was a little comforted. When he returned to Upsala, however, he was greeted with a comment in the evening paper which was, as he thought, both damning and just. Not only was *In Rome* condemned, but the critic had gone out of his way to criticize his previously published play, *The Free-Thinker,* which last he thought so inferior as to deserve no real consideration. After this cruel rebuke, the justice of which he had to admit, John felt himself naked and unmasked in all his presumption and crept about like a criminal whose secret crime has been discovered. He had dared to identify himself with Thorwaldsen, the great sculptor, and to reveal his soul to the world. If only people would forget his stupidity! That was his only hope.

But instead of addressing himself to his studies for the doctorate and allowing people to forget his stupidity, John chose to redeem himself by a new play in a high style. He consequently set to work at *The Assistant at the Sacrifice* in which it was his intention to treat Christianity in an artistic way and to introduce as far as possible the atmosphere of the Icelandic Sagas. But this play, like his *Erick XIV,* was burnt in a fit of noble despair.

By the fall of 1870, John had tired of his drunken idle friends who spent their whole time in sleeping, smoking, drinking and bumming about. Such a life was sordid and spiritually deadening and his puritan heart turned away from it. Not that he disciplined himself to the extent of working for his degree. No, whatever good came from John would come from within. In his soul was the torment of a thousand half-finished thoughts, and, well,—scholarship in the mouth of a volcano is impossible. John labored on the ill-fated manuscript of his new play, and for the moment let his studies and his father's wishes go, if they would, to the devil. But his sensuous, warmth-loving nature had but a partial outlet in his creative work, and he longed for the inspiring, fragrant company of women. Once he was honored with a visit from Maria and a friend, and the contact was a quickening moment in his hermit's seclusion, for though he lived in a pension, he was quite alone. His guitar was ready and his heart was on fire, but there was no one to serenade. In this lack of a feminine environment there was a grave danger, he thought, for only by contrast does the male element disclose itself.

John's new play did not please him. His lonely thoughts weighed heavily, and his various miseries accumulated to such a point that his eyes turned more than once, with wistful hope, toward the poison on his desk. But cognac and burnt wine were easier to take, and so the matter ended in a carouse and long discussions concerning wisdom in the ways of the world.

The next important thing that happened to John was that he met, for the first time, "a genius." He had always had a curiosity about geniuses and had often deplored his own lack of this distinction. Now he was to meet one in flesh and blood. His friends had, of course, warned him of the peculiarities of this very clever and erudite man, but they had not prepared him for what he saw. There, in the doorway, was a sort of modest tramp who looked in at them shyly—as if afraid to enter. Could this shabby man be a student and a genius? When the shabby man came to talk, however, John was amazed and delighted as the rest. He discoursed on George Sand, Thackeray, Kant, Schopenhauer, or anything one pleased, with so much learning and command, that the Runa brothers were beside themselves to know how he could ever have learned so much.

"Is," for such was the name of this original, now entered into the life of the Runa Club, and for a time became its pride and lustre. John, who had been the founder, was now quite eclipsed, and the genius exerted on him such a bewitching effect that he hung on his words for hours and could scarcely call his soul his own. It was this sort of spiritual hypnosis that John later described in his story, *Vivisection,* and the encroachment of stronger minds was something that he feared, on and off, all his life. But the demonic Is faded out after a while and lost his power over the brothers of the Runa. They became bored with him and saw through his clever imposture. This shabby dress was simply a copy of a well-known Bohemian type, his dilapidated condition the fashion in Paris, his "hollow wisdom a web woven out of German metaphysics; his interesting air of hinting at uncommitted crimes and secret griefs was Byronic in origin."

John's nervous excitability, nourished by the confinement and discipline of the University, steadily increased and was brought to a head by a certain quite harrowing experience. A young student who sat opposite to him at the pension committed suicide. When John got word of it he hurried to his comrade's room, but seeing the blood on the floor, collapsed and reeled down the stairs. The event made the greater impression on John inasmuch as he had, a short time before, turned this same young man away as a disturbance. He had come to John, lonely and miserable, and asked if he intruded. John had answered honestly that he did, and so sent him away sad and without consolation. It almost seemed to John that he was the cause of the man's death. There are many ways of murdering and weapons are sometimes not needed. Tortured by his guilt, John could find no sleep at night unless a light burned beside him. In the daytime he fled to his friends for distraction. Finally, his melancholy reached such a point that he was afraid ever to leave his friends, for death made a ghostly play of his thoughts, and in his darker moments he felt the winding-up of a fearful resolution. Once his friend Wickstrom surprised him with a flask of prussic acid in his hand. Wickstrom seemed to approve of the suicide but insisted that John have a farewell drink with him. They therefore went out and ordered eight grogs which they drank down smartly on the spot, four each, with the result that John was drunk. When they returned home in a gay party, John's door was locked and not knowing anything better to do with him, especially in their condition, his friends threw John over a fence onto a snow drift. When he had recovered sufficiently he crawled home and got to bed.

Shortly after this John came into contact with a book in which his own life was so mirrored and interpreted that all his shifting and contradictions seemed philosophically explained and, in a measure, justified. This was *Either-or* by the famous Danish theologian, Kierkegaard. In this work, life is divided into stadia, at each of which a great and drastic decision must be made between two opposite alternatives: either art or life, religion or the world, God or the Devil. One should decide by a sort of leap and there must be no compromise. John did not care for the beginning: *The Confessions of an Æsthete.* It made him feel as though he were at a sick-bed. *The Diary of a Seducer,* another chapter, "he regarded as the fancies of an unclean imagination" for John was not a seducer and this was therefore no alternative for him. When he came to *The Discourse on Life as a Duty,* however, he was profoundly moved. There he found that he must choose between Ethics and Æsthetics. John had already felt this conflict. Now he learned that it must be one or the other, that there must be no compromise. But here his common sense, of which he sometimes had a good share, in spite of appearances, revolted, and he complained: "But why not both æsthetic and ethics, why not a synthesis?" At other times, however, John held to the extreme alternative and swung from one opposite to another in a fashion very disturbing to his contemporaries.

When John was 22 years old (1871) he wrote his doctor's thesis on the subject of *Hakon Jarl or Idealism and Realism*. But here as elsewhere his peculiar ambivalence and self-distrust played havoc with his achievement. After a bit of æsthetic analysis of Oehlenschlager's *Hakon Jarl,* he recoils from his task. His admiration for this work is too absolute to permit of criticism. He will not destroy its beauty with cold dissection. But this contempt of criticism in a critical treatise, though human and interesting, was very bad form at Upsala, and constituted in fact a bare-faced attack on the great traditions of that University. It was not apt to please the professor of æsthetics, who sent it back in May with the comment that it was excellently designed for the readers of a certain popular illustrated paper.

John was furious. He had unfolded his soul in that dissertation, with all its contradictions and weaknesses, and the rejection of it had the quality of a personal insult. He returned home in the spring and fell at once into a conflict with his father, with whom for some time he had been on the best of terms. "If you eat my bread," said the father, "you must ask my permission for what you do." "Nonsense," said John, and gathering together three of his friends of the Runa, retreated with them to an island where they boarded themselves out with fishermen. There followed a long hearty summer in the open air, full of friendship and strife and the most intimate acquaintance. So stimulating was this constant association that John started a novel which, unfortunately, was never finished.

In the fall he returned to Upsala, bursting with health, but absolutely penniless. Brother "Is" who had remained in Upsala all summer, becoming more of a shadow than ever, set him up for meals, and for a while he wandered from friend to friend, living on their mercy and generosity. It was a dog's life and John had an opportunity to discover that friendship is not made of steel, but gives way quickly when too much is demanded. But as a counterpoise to this humiliating poverty came the most shimmering success that John had ever had. In the fall his new play *The Outlaw* was performed at the Dramatic Theatre, Stockholm, and though it won little applause from the public, earned him the esteem and support of a man who stood far above the public and the press and beyond reach of John's fondest hopes. One day, after the performance of this play, he received a letter requesting him to report to the King! John was astounded, and, suspecting some practical joke, made careful inquiries before he could trust himself to believe such an impossibility. When the young dramatist walked clumsily into the elegant audience-chamber of the King, however, all doubts of his good fortune disappeared. The King praised the play, and undertook to pay the expenses of his University studies out of his own purse. As John understood it, he was to receive a stipend for the next two years, until such time as he had finished his studies and received his degree. It was in this manner that John was lifted from meanness and poverty to financial independence and high esteem. Suddenly his future appeared to him in bright colors, his ego expanded, his industry increased, but the friends who had fed and comforted this poor young dramatist—so brilliant and unrequited —were not altogether pleased at this sudden ascension.

X

THE RENEGADE

JOHN'S one-act play, *The Outlaw,* though much superior to his previous efforts of the kind, was not a success. Yet the King's recognition and, more particularly, his financial assistance, was highly encouraging to a young poet, who for so many days had slept on the floor or on borrowed couches, and had eked out his meals on the occasional generosity of indigent friends. He had frozen in his garret room, had read in his bed by candle-light, afraid to get up in the face of the accumulated coldness. He had borrowed money which he knew he could not repay, gone hungry, and begged for his bread. This had been very humiliating for John and what made it worse was that for these very inadequate favors, a meal here and a piece of money there, he incurred the endless debt of gratitude. The royal stipend, however, soon put a stop to all these crosses and privations, for John began to order the rich and complicated dishes and the strong drinks which had long been necessary to his health and spirits. His chest expanded, his back straightened and the joy of life returned. For a time he took up his University studies with great energy. But his new contentment did not last,—and John would not have been John if it had.

In his examination in Philology, Astronomy, and Government, he was unsuccessful, which circumstance he attributed to the aphasia with which he was often troubled. It was this, he thought, which hindered him in speaking and made foreign languages so difficult. The aphasia had been brought about, he said, by several wounds he had received above the left eye, one from an axe, the other from a stone. At any rate, he failed the examination, and in consequence lost all heart for further studies. Instead he became a rebel again and attacked the University, disclaimed its authorities, and worried its professors. In March, 1872, he wrote an article in a radical Stockholm paper, condemning the outmoded mediæval methods of Upsala and recommending a free university in Stockholm, the chief city of Sweden. It is the duty of professors to keep astride of their times, he wrote, and it is the duty of students to do something more than sleep and smoke and drink punch.

Often he opposed the professors in a most passionate manner, setting his own hasty, yet strikingly original conceptions against all their wisdom, and sometimes his spirit of contrariety went very far indeed. On one occasion in a student group he fell into a heated dispute with a professor, contending that Dante was far overrated and that his *Divine Comedy* was only a "wordy obsolete pamphlet." So excited was John that he verged upon actual rudeness and everyone at the time thought him shameful and half-crazy. Perhaps he was! Gradually he began to notice that his friends regarded him as strange. That was disquieting. Was he becoming a lunatic? John asked himself for the first time this sinister question which was to torture his mind for years. To be beforehand in the matter and learn the worst, John wrote to a private institute for the insane and received after a time, during which information was obtained from his companions at Upsala, a friendly comforting letter. He was given to understand that there are crises which all sensitive souls must undergo.

Mad or sane, John was sick to death of the University and it was therefore with a certain sense of deliverance that he learned that his royal stipend, which was supposed to have continued two years, would no longer be paid. Now his obligations were at an end and he was free to go where he chose. Naturally, he returned to Stockholm, the beautiful city among the islands, but not to the parental home. There he could expect no fattened calf or even a decent welcome. Too often his family had received him as the prodigal son and now their patience was at an end and their forgiveness, for in their eyes he was a changeling who would never settle down nor amount to anything.

There was nothing to do, then, but borrow some money, rent a room, and set out on the arduous, precarious, but fascinating career of literature. It was an important characteristic of John's writing, right from the beginning, that it concerned itself with problems in which he himself was passionately involved. Since he was a student he wrote about students and their troubles, since he had suffered poverty and hated Upsala, he recommended that the University be moved to Stockholm where students could earn a living and marry when the time was ripe, and having failed his examination he advised that they be discontinued. In all other matters he spoke from his heart in short jerky sentences. The editors found his style piquant and amusing, his subjects timely and journalese. For an illustrated paper for women he wrote biographies and novels and enjoyed his work. There was only one thing the matter. He earned less for his time than the lowest menial. In an article written at this period he undertook a defence of writers, learned men, and even clerks, for they were worse off by far than the farmers and laborers, though no one ever bestirs himself to improve their condition. Literary men were not only poorly paid, but little respected, so that John found himself socially underneath, below his brothers and friends who were merchants, below even the actors and public-school teachers. Yes, as far as social and economic position went, he might have done better had he remained an actor or a school teacher. In the eyes of the world John had taken a fall. Yet literary men wielded a great power and they were responsible to no one. Though they might starve in their garrets unknown, uncelebrated, they spoke like kings, using the royal "we," and society had no guarantee that they would use their power justly.

John now commenced to go about with a circle of artists who pleased him much better than the shallow journalists. He found them the most surprising people in the world. One of them had been a goose-boy, another, a blacksmith's apprentice. All of them ate and dressed in the shabbiest manner and lived in the worst of hovels, yet there was so much natural simplicity in them that they seemed scarcely to mind, and took their discomforts gracefully. Most of them could hardly read, yet they talked like educated men. They expressed their opinions freely, without fear, for they were quite without learning, and in consequence, their originality was often, as John thought, simply astounding. The world of the artists was quite the opposite of Upsala and this pleased him still more. Besides, John himself had commenced to paint and needed advice and help. His paintings of the sea with rocky islands and setting suns, though correct in a mathematical way, lacked reality and inspiration, and did not please him.

One friend that he had at this time was quite an original. Mons was his name, and he had first been a farmer's boy, then an artist, but had lately turned philosopher. Gifted with a sharp and tenacious understanding, and unencumbered by the opinions of others, Mons fell eagerly upon each new book, making a cold and ruthless analysis. Where John phantasied or grew passionate, Mons kept his head, and built syllogisms, and he could draw his conclusions calmly, though they were directly opposed to his interest. When John constructed a Utopia in the grand way which had become characteristic of him, Mons directed his attack upon John's premises and inferences. "You are so petty," John complained. Then Mons showed him that these petty errors invalidated all his conclusions. But John was always the poet, and though he derived great benefit from this logician, he could not cope with him in argument. Mons became one of the most famous characters of Strindberg's novel *The Red Room*.

Another friend John acquired during this time was an assistant telegrapher who acted as a literary adviser to him. This man
stood above all partisanship and special interest, enjoying the
free play of thought as a sort of game. Probably at bottom he regarded it all as illusion. It was through these two free-lances that
John made the acquaintance of an author whom he had never
heard of at Upsala, the English philosopher and historian, Buckle.
So much was he impressed that this author became his bible and
for many years his writings showed the dominant influence of
Buckle. John had been tormented by doubts. That was encouraging, said Buckle, for doubt means intellectual life and development. John had swung from thesis to antithesis, from one view to
its opposite in a most disconcerting fashion. According to the
English writer, this was only natural, for truth is relative to a
man's situation and presuppositions and there are, in a sense,
many truths. It was best to have no system at all. John had re-
acted against Idealistic Philosophy, which explained everything
in terms of the spirit, had fled from these festoons to the rock
bottom of natural science. Buckle taught that man is subject to
material laws as much as any other organism and all his spiritual
life has this foundation. John had longed for truth. It is the highest end and happiness of man, said his preceptor. In Buckle,
John found a self-defence and a weapon against the invincible
authorities who were always hemming him in and hampering
his natural development. Truth was relative. This was a very
powerful weapon against others and it helped John to keep patient and not explode as he had so often done in the past. Yet in
the end he found it a double-edged sword, so much so that when
his doubts subsided in the face of a passionate insight, there was
nothing to do but renounce this tolerant amiable principle, and
condemn it out of hand. At the present, however, John was
Buckle's complete disciple. When a friend told him to write, he
answered: "Yes, but what?" Buckle had already written everything. During a short trip back to Upsala, he noticed that his

friends, the Runa brothers, had not changed, while his development had carried him beyond them, and was bored in consequence.

In the meantime John's financial affairs were in a worse state than ever. The summer (1872) was coming on and his only resource was to retreat to the fishermen of the Stockholm islands with whom he could live the whole summer on credit. When June came he set to work on a historical drama, *Master Olaf*. The material for this play, which John had carefully accumulated at the library, concerned that spectacular period in the reign of Gustavus Vasa, in which Sweden became Protestant, the most important character being the apostate, Master Olaf, who, like Luther, led the revolt against the mother church and married against his vows. Encouraged by Goethe's *Götz von Berlichingen,* John determined to make a break with the traditional historical play. "Therefore no verse; no declamation; no unity of place. . . . The characters will speak the language of every-day life, . . . tragic and comic, great and small, will alternate just as in life." Though the action and the characters, for the most part, were dictated by the actual historical events, John saw nevertheless a wonderful opportunity for self-expression. "As an idealist, he was to be represented by Master Olaf; and as a communist by Girt," and as a shrewd opportunist by the King. "The King and his shadow, the shrewd Constable, represented him as he wished to be; Girt, as he was in moments of intense passion; and Olaf, as he had come to know himself after years of self-examination: ambitious and weak-willed; unscrupulous when something was at stake, and yielding at other times; possessed of great self-confidence, mixed with deep melancholy; balanced and irrational; hard and gentle."

The three main characters alternately combine and war against one another. The King and the revolutionist, Girt, are always enemies. Master Olaf, the idealist, sometimes sided with the King

and opposed Girt, sometimes with Girt against the King. Girt is
headlong and rash; the King, unpartisan, but calculating, makes
use of both Girt and Master Olaf. But these three characters were
John himself, and all their conflicts and shifting alignments were
events in his own soul. Which of the three was in the right? Each
of them, for truth is relative, as Buckle said. "All the chief characters are, relatively speaking, in the right. The Constable, from
the standpoint of his own day, is right in asking Olaf to keep
calm and go on preaching; Olaf is right in admitting that he had
gone too far; the scholar, Vilhelm, is right when, in the name of
youth, he demands the evolution of a new truth; and Girt is
right in calling Olaf a renegade. The individual must always
become a renegade—forced by the necessity of natural laws; . . ."
Master Olaf must prove false to Girt's cause of revolution and to
the King's cause of law and monarchy. The King must destroy
the church and execute the rebel Anabaptists; the fact that he is
King imposes obligations which dictate his opinions and actions,
uncontestably, whether he will or not, for no man is his own
master, least of all a monarch. Each character of the play is governed by laws and circumstance, and by his original character.
The King is a man of action, shrewd and discerning, Girt a revolutionist, passionate, half-mad, with only a vague apprehension
of the goal he aims at. Between these two opposite and incompatible poles of character, Master Olaf, the idealist, the man of
dreams, is torn and tortured, driven now one way, now another,
sympathizing with the revolutionists and their ideal of individual freedom, yet disclaiming the violence and madness which
attends it; respecting the political craftsmanship of the King and
the happiness and good order intended, yet detesting the oppor-
tunism and compromise. The King and his Constable urge Olaf
to put a rein on his passions, to keep his reform within the bounds
of reason; Girt condemns his faint-heartedness and goads him on
to a greater enterprise. Not only must the Pope be dethroned but

the Emperor as well, until freedom and equality reign throughout Europe and happiness smiles on the oppressed peoples of the earth.

In the third act, about the middle of the play, Olaf receives a letter from his enemy, the Bishop Brask, informing him that he has definitely won, that the old order is gone and the new faith triumphant. But this brilliant success has come too quickly to Master Olaf, he is too young for such a victory, for what should he do now with nothing more to fight for? No, he has been disturbed in his dreams to contest a great cause, his blood is aroused, his zeal runs high. It is too late to turn back. From this moment on he is an easy prey to the mad counsel of Girt, who soon persuades him to a rash attempt upon the life of the King. Olaf is apprehended and sentenced to death and the headsman stands waiting. To save his life he need only disavow his treasonable acts, but for a long time he struggles with his conscience. Finally, the Constable, who speaks in the name of the King, persuades him to forego a martyr's death and continue in his service to mankind. "The clergy of the young Church," he says, "demand that you live to finish what you have begun so splendidly.—The congregation demands its shepherd. The children of the congregation class demand their teacher. Those are your legal creditors. But there is one waiting outside, to whom you owe more than to all the rest, and who yet demands nothing at all—your young wife.— Let me open this door which will lead you back into the world. Discipline your heart before it hardens and thank God for granting you more time to work for mankind." Olaf breaks into tears. "I am lost!" he cries. Immediately the headsman removes his fetters and he is free. As he is leaving the church, however, he encounters his former pupil, Vilhelm, who had expected to bid him farewell before a glorious death. "Once," he says, "you told us how Huss was burned because he dared to tell the truth to those in power. You told us how he went to the stake and joyfully commended himself to the hands of God, and how he prophesied about the swan that should come singing new songs in praise of awakened freedom. That's the way I had thought you would meet your death—with your head thrown back, and your eyes toward the sky, and the people crying, 'So dies a witness!'" Olaf is prostrated by these words. From somewhere in the church he hears the voice of Girt who has also been condemned. "Renegade!" Olaf sinks down overwhelmed at the foot of the pillory and this is the end of the play.

Master Olaf, like John himself, was weakened by doubts and deep uncertainties. Even when his faith and ardor were at the burning point and all opposition fell before his stormy energy, his mind was darkened by that sickly strain of thought. Perhaps he had done better to remain true to the church and to work from within for its improvement. Perhaps the whole work of the Reformation was a cruel mistake. "Can I have lived and fought for a lie?" he cries. Olaf was not a strong man, but bold. His faith and skepticism, his passions and weaknesses, the whole mad congeries of his soul were John's. The play, though historically accurate, may be regarded as a phenomenology of a divided soul. The ground tone of John's nature is Master Olaf, while the King and Girt play the overtones. The conflict of these characters scarcely attains an Hegelian synthesis, for the conclusion of the play is doubt and despair. Nor was any conclusion reached in John's mind, nor any reconciliation of the conflicting principles and dispositions.

One subordinate theme of *Master Olaf* is especially important because of its bearing upon Strindberg's later writings. This is Olaf's relation to his wife Christine, whom he married against his vows, out of love, but also in repudiation of the Church. Although Olaf is not the knight of her dreams, she will marry him and thank God, she says, you were not that other one, for then you would have disappeared as in a dream. Christine, says Strindberg in speaking of the play, is a presumptuous hen, who attempts to understand the purposes of a great mind; and since she cannot do this, draws Olaf down to her level." The truth of the matter, says Strindberg, is that man and woman are incomparable magnitudes; man is superior as man, and woman as woman, and this opinion first expressed in 1872 was one of the few held to passionately all his life. It may be regarded, moreover, as the matrix of his whole philosophy of the sexes. From it followed the principle that women should not seek to rival men in their own province of bread-winning and intellectual achievement, just as men should not attempt to equal women in child-birth, cooking, and housekeeping.

Olaf loves Christine with the robust selfish love of a man, and she him, with the generous unselfish love of a woman. "Why are you always in the right?" she asks him. "Because I know it is your pleasure to have it so," he answers. Already at twenty-three and before cruel experience had taught him, John had arrived at a conception which he was to repeat and vary through volumes.

Master Olaf was written under the influence of Shakespeare's *Julius Cæsar,* Goethe's *Götz von Berlichingen,* and, in general, *Brand* and Kierkegaard. Ibsen's *The Pretenders,* though Strindberg does not mention it, must also have played a part, for the conflict between Haakon, the strong self-confident man, and Skule, the doubter, has much in common with the theme of the Strindberg play. It is so far superior to his earlier plays, so mature and finished, and so compact and complicated, that it is altogether remarkable that it should have been written at the age of twenty-three. It was John's first stroke of genius. Despite the multiplicity of themes, a sort of inspired unity pervades the whole and the various threads are woven into one; besides this dramatic unity, there is the coherence of reality itself, for, against the tradition of historical plays, speech and action take place as in real life. The play is also remarkable for the blending of the grotesque with the tragic, the juxtaposition of lofty pain and jocundry, a mixed mode inherited, of course, from the irrepressible vitality of the Renaissance and of Shakespeare.

The creation of this drama was a great event in John's life and he returned to Stockholm after the summer was over, unburdened and happy. But it was also a signal event for Sweden, for it was the first great play to be produced there. "Its completion was more epoch-making for Sweden," remarks Bjorkman, "than that of *Brand* was for Norway in 1865—since the coming of Ibsen's first real play was heralded by earlier works leading up to it, while *Master Olaf* appeared where nobody had any reason to expect it. This very fact," he continues, "militated against its success, of course; it was too unexpected, and also too startlingly original, both in spirit and form." When John turned his masterpiece in to the Royal Theatre, it was scornfully rejected, with the comment that any historical drama must naturally be written in verse, nor could John find a publisher. No one would have his play, and this double failure was a crushing defeat which paralyzed his efforts for years to come. For a time he thought of giving up writing altogether, and for eight years in fact wrote no new plays but busied himself with corrections and new versions of *Master Olaf*. But his efforts to adapt his form to the public taste were unsuccessful, the later versions being quite inferior to the original play.

When John had spent a lonely day at work he would betake himself to the café to meet his artists and philosophers, for the miseries of families, those prisons of the spirit, he could not endure. The establishment where John's circle consorted was called the Red Room, after the color of its furniture. Besides the artists and philosophers, were "the Post-Office assistant who was also a pianist and composer, and the great trump of the company, the Lieutenant of the Artillery." Other amiable and gifted men joined the group which, though somewhat heterogeneous, was still a famous company, ready music and steady drinking, arguments and disquisitions on every subject, sprees and mad adventures. Also a curious frankness and self-analysis prevailed. All sentimentality and self-deceit was quickly detected and rebuked.

If anyone complained of a toothache, he was answered: "That does not arouse my sympathy in the least, for I have never had a toothache, and it has no influence over my decision to give a drunken party tonight." When the Lieutenant departed for divine service with his company, he would be asked: "Where are you going?" Whereupon he would answer honestly: "I must go play the hypocrite."

About this time, too, John comforted himself somewhat by an unfavorable criticism of Shakespeare, for if *Master Olaf* had flaws, so had *King Lear* and *Hamlet,* the greatest works of the master. John's miserable disappointment still oppressed him. One evening his friends, from whom he had borrowed money, convened to hear a reading of his play, but unfortunately the work of the day had left them so tired that they all but fell asleep before the first act was finished.

Completely impoverished, living on the bounty of his friends, John was under the necessity of taking some decisive step to improve his condition. Suddenly he formed the decision of taking up his histrionic career again in Göteborg, borrowed the money for the journey, was given a farewell celebration, and set out. But this enterprise too ended in disappointment. John did not secure the success he wished and there was nothing for it then but to return to his patient friends in the Red Room. "So, another fiasco," he thought. And by this time his thoughts had reached a sad and desperate shift, for the whole world of human endeavor seemed to him only a ghastly swindle.

Fortunately he made the acquaintance at this time of an author who confirmed all his worst suspicions. This was von Hartmann, the great disciple of Schopenhauer, who weighed pleasures against pains and found them short in the balance, and so advised it as a social, enlightened duty that all mankind should one fine day gather together in a social way and shoot themselves. John learned from him that life is necessarily evil, for the unconscious Will which is the innermost reality, can never be satisfied, but continues to crave and to cling to the objects it can never have. The cruel exigency of this blind, insatiable Will increases on the higher levels, for when consciousness arises in the evolutionary process, conation becomes directed on myriads of specific things, for the desires of man are infinite, and it is sheer madness to attempt to gratify them. In superior minds the intensity of consciousness foredooms misery and anguish and there is no escape, for either the intellect presents too many objects to the Will or checks it in its gratifications. Moreover, those minds have seen through the illusion of the World and to them, as Schopenhauer says, the whole spectacle with all its "stars and milky ways is as nothing." John noticed that most geniuses have been pessimists, while optimism is found only among savages, children, and average men who, since they live only in the present, hoping always for some remedy of the evil which surrounds them and unaware of the hopelessness of their case, suffer less, and are almost happy. An inane hope spurs them on to live, in spite of everything. But great religions, such as Buddhism, have seen through the illusion and found a deeper meaning in life, and there is far more truth in their cult of resignation than in the contemporary doctrine of progress by evolution, or Utopia through education and the spread of culture. Philosophers who maintain this latter view are but reaching for a chimera, for evolution and increasing civilization does not remedy the wickedness of the Will, which is the very root of existence. How absurd it is of the Christians, thought John, to bewail the evil of the world. Evil is life itself. This tragic conclusion gave John much comfort, and peace settled once more on his ever-seeking, inveterate weary brain, for he had now generalized his own peculiar sufferings and reduced them to the necessity of a cosmic law.

XI

THE JOURNALIST

JOHN was now a complete pessimist, but he did not therefore choose to take his life, nor did von Hartmann end that way. No, pessimism is consistent with life and even striving. For one who knows how few pleasures are possible on this earth, the securing of what little there is will become more important than ever. From the level of every-day life, taught von Hartmann, there are certain small goods such as bread and butter, which are certainly worth while. But how, incidentally, was John to attain them? The fact that this is the worst of all possible worlds and life not worth the candle, did not make the problem of earning his living a bit less serious. The truth of the matter was that John, for all his pessimism, had what Nietzsche once ascribed to Schopenhauer, an intense and irrepressible love of life.

His affairs were now in a deplorable state. Confident of the success of his play, he had borrowed considerable money from his friends, and was thus deeply in debt, with no prospects. At the right time, or somewhat later, a friend urged him, oddly enough, to become the editor-in-chief of a new insurance publication. John replied that he knew nothing of the business, but the friend insisted so much that John agreed and set about to recall his mathematics and learn his new profession from top to bottom. Having acquired, as he thought, a thorough mastery of the subject, his old hatred of authority showed itself here as elsewhere. When a new insurance company was founded on a sort of profit-sharing basis, John attacked the plan roundly, for he saw in it not a democratic advance but a downright swindle, and boldly he contested the statisticians and noted authorities. This made him unpopular. The paper failed to receive the support promised by the insurance companies. John continued at his work, though he felt the ground sliding from under his feet. The paper was expensively published, but when his funds ran low he borrowed money at the bank, with the lieutenant and another friend as guarantees. As time went on, these loans increased beyond all reason, the illusion that one could repay keeping pace with each new demand. When the eleventh number appeared, the new insurance publication collapsed and the editor, his debts unpaid, and greatly oppressed with a new guilt, unwound a bitter reckoning in Kymendö. "Guilty!" he heard within himself and outside. Criminally indebted to the National Bank, he had misused the people's money and deceived their representatives. His conscience raved and stormed and then came fever and hallucinations. In vain he defended himself. "The creditors lay in wait for him night and day. They possessed a piece of his body for he had entertained himself with their money; they possessed a part of his soul, . . . why should they not put him in jail. He craved a real punishment; that would restore the equilibrium again; that would soften the pangs of conscience." In the meantime his friends laughed at his scruples and, while he lay in bed with fever, showed him little sympathy. John sank deeper in despair. Old memories of Ormuz and Ahriman rose up in his mind, for it seemed to him that this world, with all its lies and sufferings, was ruled by an evil God who conspired against him, while the good God sat by with folded hands.

Harassed day and night by creditors, and his life threatened by hunger, John now felt he had come to the end. One stormy day he set sail in his boat for Dalarö. On his return in the darkness and wind John played with the idea of death, and with a sudden impulse almost capsized his boat. As a storm approached, however, and real danger threatened, he strained every muscle to save himself. "The instinct of self-preservation proved stronger than the death impulse." Once on shore he felt again an ardent love of life, and finding the housekeeper alone, his comrades having gone to the city, made love to her, and for three days they lived together as married people, alone in the house. As shortly afterwards she went over to another, John was mad with jealousy, that hateful emotion which was to torture him for years to come, by anticipation and by retrospect—always. The following is his defence: "He had resigned a piece of his soul to the soul of this girl, had treated her like one of his own kind, interested himself in her fate, shown her gratitude for her kindness. That she spurned, and perhaps at this moment makes a jest of it. Besides, he had mixed his blood with hers, given her impulse, so accorded the fine strings of his nerves to hers that they already belonged to each other. Now came a stranger,—broke off his electrical current,—disturbed his work and brought disharmony into his soul, which he had improvidently resigned to a woman.

"Exclusively physical it cannot be, for with common girls, with whom only the body is involved, he was not jealous at all. What took place in him was a shattering of the whole complex of the self."

This woman had become a part of him and now he must cut that part away. As he walked into the forest to quiet himself, he noticed that nature had lost its beauty and seemed dead. And then, as his shame and humiliation increased, he felt his soul expand, and the sense that some hostile power strove against him aroused in his mind a strength of wild resistance. Breaking into the forest, he beat boughs of the fir trees, for now he would fight these dark giants to the death. Underfoot he crushed a thousand dwarfs. When trees stood in his way, he beat them with his stick as if he would fell them. Bushes crackled under his hand and rustled, their roots torn up, down the mountain; stones hurtled downward; he set his foot on young junipers and whipped them until they lay broken on the trampled grass. Thus he pressed upward and soon found himself on a mountain plateau. There lay the island and behind it the sea in a tremendous panorama. He breathed again, as if he had now for the first time enough air. But on the mountain stood a dilapidated fir tree, which was higher than he. With stick in hand he climbed aloft, and on the top, which made a sort of saddle, seated himself like a rider. "Now only the heaven was above him. But under him stood the fir trees, head on head like an army which stormed the mountain," and the sea, too, stormed his fortress and came wave on wave, like a cavalry of white currassier. John brandished his stick and threatened the enemy on all sides. And then the fir trees began to murmur and to plot among themselves, but they would not answer him when he called. "Jesus or Barrabas?" he roared. "Naturally, Barrabas," he answered himself. When the darkness came, however, John grew afraid, and descending from his saddle, went home. Was he insane? No, explains Strindberg, for he had had no hallucinations. He was merely a poet, who composed in this manner instead of on paper.

While John edited the insurance paper, the Red Room bloomed and prospered. The circle was now composed chiefly of business men and John loved these practical, hard-headed people. "They were free," he says, "without having read either Buckle or Hartmann." In fact they read nothing but the papers, yet could discuss everything. And these young merchants, like the artists, were a welcome contrast to the pedants of Upsala. John found them also quite talented in unexpected ways—some were musicians, others poets. One evening they performed a burlesque he had written before an audience of bank directors and big business men. The acting was good but the play contained far too much satire to please the directors, who were serious men, and they left before the curtain fell.

The Lieutenant of the Artillery was also a member of the group and a great drawing card. All the merchants felt honored to eat with a uniform and the artists, too, for then they were served as never before. Occasionally the Lieutenant's indigence gave rise to comic predicaments. The day before the coronation of Oscar II, at which affair he was supposed to parade, the Lieutenant had no money to retrieve his dress uniform. He therefore appealed to John, who about six o'clock at last met a bank clerk who gave him the amount. The friends were then so elated that they went off to dinner and drank deeply and thoughtfully. Finally John asked the Lieutenant for some of his money, which, he said, he would return early in the morning before the parade and the Lieutenant, too drunk to know better, let him have it. John entertained a girl that night, but in the same room reclined the Lieutenant in full uniform and read a novel. In the morning at five he was awakened harshly. "If you fail to get me that money, you are a dead man," roared the officer. John went out and luckily borrowed the money on time. But the Lieutenant's suit, when he got it, was terribly wrinkled. He put it on and went off, nevertheless, and when mounted on his charger, made a brave showing after all.

In *The Red Room,* which Strindberg wrote six years later (1879) many episodes of this sort occur, and many mad larks, financial scrapes, and inspired drunken parties, reminiscent of this period of his life, are described. The characters of this novel are in many cases drawn from real life with only a slight distortion. Thus Olle, the sculptor turned philosopher, who sleeps on other people's floors and eats, if he does, at the mercy of his friends, and Sellin, the true type of artist, and Dr. Borg, the hard-drinking, cynical scientist. Falk, the writer, is Strindberg himself. *The Red Room* is a portrayal of the Bohemian life of artists and students in the seventies, but though the subject is close to Strindberg's heart, there is no idealization or sentimentality to be found in it. The tone is hard and cynical throughout and no ideal is spared. There is considerable evidence to show that though John loved the Bohemian life he led at this time, and was in fact the center of the circle, he was not carried away with it, but kept his tongue in his cheek, while the old doubts and dissatisfactions of a born absolutist held him back from a warm uncritical appreciation, even of that which he liked best.

After his miserable failure as an editor, John returned home as a prodigal son, for the seventh time, and from there, having borrowed some money again, fled to Sandhamm, still tortured by the remembrance of the housekeeper's betrayal, and ever seeking to explain and justify his own jealousy. On arriving he rented a room and decided to write. But immediately he met an old friend at the customs' house, who advised him in a fatherly way to take some steps toward earning his own living. The consequence of this advice was that John began to study telegraphy and in a month sent off his first telegram. He had now found a remunerative job which allowed him much time to write, but it came hard to be a machine worker, after all his ambitions. When he had finished at the office, he hurried home to paint the sea which then had a great fascination for him.

John respected the sea captains, pilots and sailors with whom he now consorted. They were hard men who knew how to do their duty and bear their troubles. They knew nothing of romance or illusion, for all were contented with their lot and hoped for nothing beyond hard labor and the simplest gratifications. As time went on a shipwreck occurred and the pilots were threatened with prison. John sent in a letter of defence, which had at least this consequence, that he was offered an honorable position on the newspaper. He returned to the city with high hopes, and a craving to be once more in the midst of great events and play a part in them.

He was not long at this new work before he discovered that the newspaper was just the place for him. It was like "an observatory," he wrote, "from which one gazes out over the world, and sees the growth of the world-history." The proud University at

Upsala was by comparison a vestige of the Middle Ages, in which
men escaped from reality, burying themselves in the past. And
the beautiful part of journalism was that it was always new and
interesting.

It was at this time that John made the acquaintance of American humorists, who gave his skepticism, as he says, an unexpected
support. "The public took their jests as jests, but John took them
seriously, for they were serious. Here all was treated from the
standpoint of the present time and seen through, and in consequence everything proved empty and worthless. The American's
sense of reality has in the struggle for existence divined the true
meaning of life; freed from all hallucinations, all ideals and all
romanticism, he has intuited the relative nothingness of life and
the absolute nothingness of heaven, and now he laughs a broad
laugh at the whole of the old culture. Neither rank, greatness,
talent nor riches entitle him to admiration. . . . Napoleon and
Washington, Michelangelo and Beecher Stowe would be treated
as drinking companions." We learn here that Americans have no
sentimentality and no regard for private life. All laws are put to
naught and anarchy appears, with the end of the old world view.

This passage is quite interesting from several points of view.
It shows what Strindberg's idea of America must have been, or
at least his propensity to carry out an idea to the bitter end of absurdity. It also reveals the Strindberg conception of American
humor as a sort of robust pessimism which means all it says, and
is therefore in earnest. John was so impressed with this new type
of literature that he set about a few months later to translate
American writers, not Mark Twain, for that another had undertaken, but Bret Harte and others. When however he attempted to
apply this new *Weltanschauung* to his newspaper, he found it
quite out of keeping with the purposes of that organ.

As a reporter for the Reichstag John took the side of the farmers, for whom he had long had great sympathy. His articles on
art, literature, and the theatre were bold and original, but often

ill-conceived and hastily written. In one article he attacked the current Shakespeare worship and pointed out that the lack of good drama in Sweden was due to the undramatic character of its people. In another he held very unorthodox views concerning art. Once he attacked a Christian journal, suggesting that the publisher undertook a great responsibility in disseminating such an insane doctrine. When this editor called and demanded an explanation, he was told that the man who wrote the article in question certainly held the Christian doctrine to be false, and this was true. Again, he praised and defended a beautiful and accomplished actress whom strong influence opposed. On other occasions he attacked actors and plays and theatres in such a style that many complaints were heard. So unpopular had John become that other critics when they signed themselves anonymously took care to assure the public that their articles were not written by Strindberg.

John was warned at this time to adopt a more acceptable view of things, but there was too much combativeness in him and too little docility ever to conform. By his very nature, he must press forward toward novelty and progress. And by the spring of 1874 his position on the *Dagens Nyheter* had become unbearable. In a stormy scene with the editor over the style of his writing, John resigned, and so let himself out, on the street.

He had never been very fond of the Stockholm newspaper men. They gossiped for hours about petty events of the day, and though they held to actualities, forgot or disregarded the great problems and exigencies of the age. Moreover they were too aristocratically-minded to suit him. Yet John had a great deal in common with the journalists. He had their wide breadth of interest and alertness for all kinds of news. Though he had phantasied and expounded his own views more than journalists usually dare or can, there was a downright realism in his writing, a lack of sentimentality, which belonged to the Press. His language was never technical, tedious, stilted or pretentious, but popular, rapid and dramatic. Also his articles, like those of other journalists, were literature of the moment,—hasty and ephemeral.

John was now out of a job again and hunger and the dreary poverty returned. In desperation he took a position on a bi-weekly paper of the Farmer's Party. But here he remained only a month, in "dire need, sickness and humiliation." He could not, of course, return home for there he was damned. His friends on the daily papers pitied him his fall in the world, and his old friends mistrusted him as a debtor and fallen writer. His old consolation, the Red Room, had now broken up, the members having scattered far and wide. John as he himself expressed it, "was now completely bankrupt." He had attempted so many professions, tried so many roles, but always they had ended disastrously. Now he was weary of the struggle; his buoyancy and resistance weakened by hunger and disappointments, he sank into a hopeless dispirited state and perhaps would have ended in some quiet mediocre post, a bitter, moody man, had not his star suddenly risen again, a new and distinguished career opening up before him with fair presages of the future.

In the fall of 1874 John was appointed to the position of royal secretary and assistant in the Royal Library. He soon found himself wandering humbly through the armies of books which seemed at times to threaten him with their age-long memories. Yet at other times, too, he rebelled against the monstrous accumulation of wisdom for here were thousands of volumes, without one word of guidance through the perplexing problems of the day. He was not long in discovering that the other librarians held the same view and that among these learned men a quiet skepticism prevailed. One day a colleague suggested in a jesting way that he might classify the Chinese books, if he thought that would amuse him. This advice John took to heart quite seriously, for he had already been attracted by the golden bindings and the beautiful cryptic characters which expressed the thoughts and wisdom of this strange, far-distant, colorful people. After studying a year until his brain almost split, he had mastered Chinese sufficiently to compose the catalogue. He was now a sinologue and rightly proud of his accomplishment.

Thereafter Strindberg followed up these studies and, by discovering references to Sweden in Chinese literature and to China in Swedish literature, brought the two distant countries into relation. Following the publication of his monograph: *Sweden's Relations to China and to the Tartar Lands,* 1881, Strindberg was honored by the French Academy, received letters from sinologues all over the world, was presented with a medal, became a member of a learned society and secured a Russian order.

But these honors did not come till years later. At present, John buried himself in Chinese books, labored on a new version of his *Master Olaf,* and enjoyed the respectability and credit of being a royal secretary. But again the clouds hung low, the storm broke loose and John was precipitated into a new unhappiness. For a long time he had had a sweetheart, "a married woman," as she styled herself, whom he had met at an orgy. The affair began "without any sentimentality or idealism," the difference between their education and outlook being too great to permit of a real passion. She came to John's house often, demanding to be amused every day. John found that his work was suffering, and at last growing weary of the relation, resigned her to a friend. When he learned, however, that his friend had actually taken over his role according to the arrangement, he fell into a great despair and jealousy and once more it seemed to him he had lost a part of his soul. Seeking her out again he humbled himself before her, though he hated the necessity, while she, realizing her advantage, clamped down the chains which bound him in slavery. Determined upon revenge, John now wrote her a letter explaining that his affections had turned to another. She then came to him white and ill with jealousy, kneeled before him and kissed his hand and the result was a new reconciliation. But again she became so importunate that John determined to break away and tried, therefore, to fix his attentions on a girl whom he had known before and who was now a student at the Academy of Music. But his love for her was probably, as he wrote years later, more poetry than passion.

John had not seen his previous sweetheart for days when suddenly one evening he met her in a drunken noisy company of people, hanging on the arm of an officer. Seeing John she broke into a loud laugh but John went his way quietly. The next day he refused to admit her and she waited in the street for him. When he came down he turned his back to her and walked away while she followed, first entreating, then scolding like a woman of the streets. "There ended this love story," says Strindberg. "It had had many episodes, of which several were not very honorable for the lover."—But these unfortunate love affairs of the past few years were now to be overshadowed and forgotten with the coming of the one great passion of his life.

XII

MADONNA AND MISTRESS

IN the spring of 1875 Strindberg [1] commenced to brood again over his ill-starred drama *Master Olaf*. The ignominious rejection of a work into which he had put so much of his own conflicts and sorrows, had been a heavy blow to him. How was he to make it acceptable to the critics? In the first place he began to reduce it to verse, for it was inconceivable, he had been told, that a serious historical play should be written in prose. But it was a peculiarity of Strindberg's rapid style of composition, that it was seldom improved by corrections or rewriting. His pen moved swiftly while the inspiration lasted but would not bear the discipline of caution or revision. This boldness and haste did not make him a superior poet and *Master Olaf* was not improved by its poetical form.

Another reason for the rejection of his play had been its radicalism. In reworking it, Strindberg made Master Olaf much weaker and much more doubtful of his great enterprise. Like Strindberg, he has become infected by the skepticism of von Hartmann. Also, in the second version, love enters his life as a great power and he is afraid to love Christine, for fear that principles and reason itself will be put to naught. In the end his passion rises so high that he will sacrifice to his beloved his divine mission, his great dreams of spiritual freedom,—everything.

---

[1] John will be called Strindberg hereafter.

Girt in the new play is likewise milder and has given up his ideal of universal revolution. Gustavus Vasa also undergoes some change, and is treated in general much more sympathetically, for Strindberg, in the light of his new cynicism and pessimism, had now come to feel that only through wickedness does one rise in this world, or accomplish anything good.

In making these changes Strindberg was no doubt prompted by a desire to satisfy the critics, and so have his play performed, but also by a newly acquired world view. He himself had become weary and skeptical, and his creation, Master Olaf, changed with him, for the development of Strindberg's personality and views are faithfully reflected in the various versions.

At this time, Strindberg was obliged to give lessons and write for magazines to make up expenses. In *The Confession of a Fool,* in describing this period, he says: "Notwithstanding the fact that I was a member of a learned Bohemia, which had succeeded an older, artistic Bohemia, a contributor to important newspapers and excellent, but badly paying magazines, a partner in a society founded for the purpose of translating Hartmann's *Philosophy of the Unconscious,* the bearer of the empty title of a "royal secretary," and the author of two one-act plays which had been performed at the Royal Theatre, I had the greatest difficulty to make ends meet. I hated life, although the thought of relinquishing it had never crossed my mind; on the contrary, I had always done my best to continue not only my own existence but also that of the race."

While thus circumstanced, unhappy, longing for someone to adore, Strindberg received one day a strange letter from an unknown woman, demanding that he meet her at a certain house punctually at five that same afternoon. On arriving he found a superior, well dressed girl of good family. She introduced herself as the fiancée of an old friend of his, an opera singer, and explained confidently enough, that all she desired was that he show her about town during her stay. Strindberg at once recognized her as a dangerous woman and was on his guard. What irritated him particularly was that she professed at once to know all about him. "You're unhappy, that's all," she said. "You ought to be roused from your gloomy fancies." Strindberg was not pleased with her. The next day, however, perhaps realizing that she had not made a good impression, she appeared so cordial and charming, that Strindberg was delighted and a genuine sympathy rose up between them.

But Strindberg, who could never be contented with happiness, and wished to pay her off for the injuries he had suffered from other members of her sex, now explained that he was betrothed to another, and managed to arouse her jealousy to such an extent that their friendship cooled, and the role of guardian angel was dropped. After a week of theatres, concerts and social calls, however, her companionship had become a habit which he was loath to give up. "Conversation with a woman who is above the commonplace has an almost sensual charm," he wrote. "The souls touch, the spirits embrace each other." But suddenly it developed that Strindberg's friend, the opera singer, was jealous. The girl professed a detestation of that emotion but Strindberg defended it, as always, for was it not a certain proof of a sincere passion? This view of his did not prevent him, however, from falling in love with his friend's fiancée and communicating the fact by mail. The girl forwarded his letter to her fiancé, who thereupon wrote an insulting letter to Strindberg. In time he went so far as to offer to shoot the man who had robbed him of his future bride. But Strindberg replied that he could not have been robbed, for he had possessed nothing before, and eased his conscience with this sophism. He was in love with this plain, presumptuous, conceited woman, not so much because of her qualities, which mostly displeased him, as his own need of being in love with someone. She may have been, and he certainly believed she was, "a mangeuse a'homme, a chaste polyandrist," but she was not, at any rate, a servant or a woman of the streets, but a possible object of his tender emotions, always on the point of overflowing. Also, it is to be noticed that she was considerably older than he and no doubt understood very well how to play that role of mother or older sister, always, of course, an important factor in Strindberg's love life. Moreover, she was intelligent, a quality which, though Strindberg resented in women, he nevertheless demanded, and never, in fact, fell in love with anyone who did not possess precisely that rebellious flaunting feminism which he so much hated and condemned.

This guardian angel's fatal mistake, however, was to introduce Strindberg, without knowing it, to another guardian angel who in time took over her charge so completely that she herself had not a chance in the world of reclaiming him. This woman was the Baroness Wrangel, the wife of a captain of the Guards and mother of a girl of three, an extraordinarily charming woman. Strindberg agreed to call on her after his guardian angel's departure, for she was about to return to Finland and her jealous opera singer.

By a curious coincidence the Baron lived at 12 Nortullsgata, in the very same house in which Strindberg had spent so many troubled years of his youth. As he rang the bell he had a feeling that his father would open the door to him, and that his mother was somewhere within. The Baron turned out to be a large handsome man, strong, and sometimes arrogant, yet cursed with a weak constitution, friendly, self-willed, weak, extremely sad and gay by turns, loving his wife spiritually and other women sensually. But for all his sins and contradictions, he was always understood and forgiven. There was too much natural goodness in him and too many of the lovable weaknesses. On his first meeting Strindberg was struck by his "intensely sad blue eyes" and by "the smile on his lips, which was forever giving way to an expression of extraordinary bitterness, which spoke of disappointments, plans miscarried, illusions fled." Then the Baroness appeared, the slender beautiful Baroness with her "girlish appearance and her baby face—framed in roguish curls, golden as the cornfield on which the sun is shining; she had the shoulders of a princess and a supple willowy figure; the way in which she bowed her head expressed at the same time candor, respect and superiority."

Strindberg was immensely pleased with these new friends and they with him. A curious bond of sympathy sprang up between them and Strindberg became a frequent visitor at Nortullsgata. One day he confessed to them that he feared his affair with his friend, the guardian angel, had gone wrong and that it was love's labor lost. The Baroness thenceforth became his confidante, though Strindberg by this time was only half in earnest, and carried her sympathy so far that she offered to intercede for him, for she was sure, as she said, that the dear girl was fond of him and could be brought to see reason. For his part he had perhaps never loved the girl and would soon have forgotten her, had not she furnished such a permanent and interesting subject of conversation in the company of his friends. Besides, the role of rejected lover was a sad romantic one that Strindberg enjoyed. To appeal to the sympathy of attractive women had become an irresistible temptation.

Strindberg had not known the Baron and his wife long before he realized that beneath the calm surface of their happiness and mutual affection, there was some hidden trouble. Their occasional fits of sadness and wistfulness, a certain break or ominous tone of the conversation, convinced him, in spite of all the evidence to the contrary. But their trouble, whatever it was, drew him closer to them, especially to the romantic Baroness. Once when Strindberg came to bid her goodby before her trip to Finland, he was suddenly completely bewildered by her supreme beauty. "I was shaken," he wrote, "utterly confused, as if I were gazing at a vision." The God which he had dethroned and ridiculed now returned in the form of a woman who was both virgin and mother. "When I looked at the little girl by her side, I could not under-

stand how that birth had been possible, for the relationship between her and her husband seemed to put all sexual intercourse
out of the question; their union appeared essentially spiritual.
... I worshipped her just as she was, as she appeared to me at
that moment, as mother and wife, wife of a particular husband,
mother of a particular child. Without her husband my longing to
worship could not have been satisfied, for I said to myself, she
would then be a widow, and should I worship her still as such?
Perhaps if she were mine—my wife?—No! the thought was un-
thinkable. And, moreover, married to me, she would no longer
be the wife of this particular man, the mother of this particular
child, the mistress of this particular house. Such as she was, I
adored her, I would not have her otherwise."

Was it the memories of the old house in which he had lived so
long, he asks himself, or was it the veneration of the commoner
for the upper class which made him deify the slender, stately,
exquisite woman who stood before him? Or was it not that his
religious sense, long suppressed, now yearned for an object of
worship? Certainly there was much in the Baroness to remind
him of his "pale dark-eyed mother." As she stood in the garden
(he wrote) "the broad green leaves threw death-like hues on her
pale face, with its shining coal black eyes." Like his mother, also,
she was married and so out of reach. He adores her but the
thought that she should ever be his wife is strangely repugnant.
He wishes to worship her hopelessly from afar as he had worshipped his own mother, or rather the ideal "mother," whom he
regards as essentially pure and virginal. In the Baroness, Strindberg loved his mother again. His feelings toward the Baron were
mixed. The jealousy and resentment for the father, a feeling very
pronounced in many individuals, had persisted in Strindberg's
case beyond that childhood period in which it is normal or at least
very common. He had feared and respected his father and sometimes loved him, but there had been other feelings as well, feelings which would not bear the light of day. In order to escape

from them, he had persuaded himself subconsciously that there was nothing sexual in his parents' relation, and that he was, after all, closest to his mother's heart,—her chosen darling. That Strindberg was not in fact his mother's favorite, but somewhat neglected, may have increased the half-unconscious craving for her warmth and love. In any case he remained throughout his life dependent and consciously incomplete, longing like those original men described by Aristophanes for their other half, which the jealous gods had split off and taken away. But in Strindberg's case, the missing half is always the little mother who comforts and caresses him as though he were a child. He himself is aware of his propensity to regard his mistress as his mother. "Is this an unconscious incest of the heart?" he asks and trembles at his monstrous thoughts. Thus Strindberg in analyzing his own case, as he does so indefatigably in various plays and autobiographical novels, has anticipated Freud and particularly his doctrine of the Œdipus complex, for Strindberg's foreshadowings of that theory date back as far as 1886, about fifteen years before Freud's work began.

If it is true, and it certainly seems very likely, that Strindberg never outgrew the family situation, it is easy to understand how, in the house where he had lived as a youth, the friendly aristocratic Baron should come to represent his father, and the sympathetic motherly Baroness, though here in a disguised form, should come to stand for his mother. The fact that the Baroness is aristocratic, enlightened, with intellectual pretensions and in many respects quite the opposite of his mother, does not prevent her from being a substitute. Indeed, Strindberg's revolt against his unconscious incestuous feelings would naturally lead him to select a woman in whom the motherly qualities were united with others not possessed by his own mother, for in this way he could disguise his desire to cohabit with her and clear his conscience in the love of a woman, outwardly at least, widely different. In the light of such a view, the Baron's role becomes clear. He is the father who safeguards the virgin mother and saves her from the ardent love of her son. For this the son (Strindberg) is properly grateful. He values the Baron as an obstacle to his desires, for he will keep his goddess pure and undefiled and preserve her from the network of his passions. His fear and horror of incest has the consequence that he becomes a man of honor, to the point of militancy, and insists upon this quality on many occasions quite needlessly,—both to the Baron and his wife. And so, like Œdipus, he flies from the truth and from his own destiny.

It is perfectly obvious that many of Strindberg's characteristics and subsequent misadventures could be explained on a Freudian basis. His persistent fear and persecution mania, his pathological sense of shame and guilt, even his notion of being the divine scapegoat can be traced to incestuous desires of an unconscious order. Indeed, so powerful is this theory to interpret his life and character, that Strindberg's case may be regarded as a textbook example of the Œdipus complex. Yet, it must be added, there are many explanations of one life-pattern and all are not equally important. Strindberg may have been "a little Œdipus who would like to see his father out of the way in order to be alone with his handsome mother and to sleep with her," and this disposition may have carried over to his relations with the Baroness. But, when it is understood that the same principle of explanation applies to many men, it is at once clear that it cannot explain Strindberg's case specifically, or in so far as it differs from these others. A principle which applies to many men indifferently cannot explain any one of them in particular, but it is a specific explanation that is especially interesting in Strindberg's case.

Strindberg himself was one of the first to insist upon the multiplicity of causes determining the character and actions of men. Though he intuited, with an insight truly remarkable for his time, that his early infatuation for his mother had a dominating influence over his career, he also saw clearly that neither this nor any other particular theory could ever account for all the complexity and all the wild depths of contradiction and perversity he found within him. In his relation to the Baron and the Baroness, Strindberg was no doubt governed by an inveterate, morbid longing for his mother, but also as he himself says, by a long-repressed need for some object of worship, by his veneration for the upper class and the ambition of the son of a servant to rise to their level. These and many other factors are involved in any explanation of the particular intricacy of his thoughts and actions.

On the eve of her departure for Finland, the Baroness asked Strindberg whether he loved his guardian angel with all his heart. "Can you ask?" he replied, for he had determined to save her from his criminal passions, which but for this lie, might soon overpower him. She promised to intercede for him, and the Baron and he accompanied her a part of the way on the steamer. In the course of a sleepless night the three friends were drawn together in the closest sympathy and turning sentimental, vowed eternal friendship. Strindberg, who had been weakened by a long siege of fever, became quite ill, and in his over-excited condition, gave free rein to his poetical fancy. For hours he phantasied and raved without interruption; the hallucinations of a sleepless night transformed by the artistry of the poet, became mystical visions. Meanwhile, this flow of words bewitched his friends, who could not keep their eyes from the animated, feverish face. They encompassed him with affection, that of a mother and an older brother.

When the Baroness had bidden them a tender farewell and urged them to comfort one another during her absence, the two men were left alone and presently their sympathy and understanding fell away. Then Strindberg saw that it had been merely an illusion accomplished by the stronger will of the Baroness. This impression was strengthened when a few days later, the Baron called for him at the library, for then he saw clearly how fictitious was any friendship between him and this aristocratic captain of the artillery. Dismayed by the splendor of his uniform, Strindberg attempted to compensate by a display of his knowledge, but the captain could not understand and so the matter rested. Later, when Strindberg called at the barracks where the captain held forth in power, and witnessed the respect of the men and officers, his old class feelings rose up in rebellion against this show of authorized tyranny, for the captain and the army in general was a sworn enemy of the people from whom he had sprung. And, it fell out, as they talked, that the captain had once been anxious to fire on a group of rioters, of whom Strindberg had been a member. No, there could be no real sympathy between them. He, a member of the rising aristocracy of intellect, was a natural enemy of the old aristocracy based on birth and wealth. The only bond between them was the Baroness, but their love of her brought life into their eyes and good-fellowship.

The Baron hurried to Strindberg to read his wife's letters and besought him to write her. But Strindberg could not say what was in his heart and found himself, between honor and love, in the greatest perplexity. When he had finished his letter he turned it over to the Baron, it being a principle of his, he said, never to write to another man's wife without his full knowledge of the correspondence. Disarmed by such assurances the Baron felt no need to be jealous, and though he probably suspected his friend's passion, relied on him as an honorable man. Indeed it seemed at times that he even welcomed Strindberg's love, his own being revived thereby. Certainly it was their mutual love for the Baroness and that alone which held them together. But the Baron had another reason for conniving at Strindberg's evident devotion to his wife. He himself had become immensely interested in the Baroness' cousin, a pretty, intriguing creature whom he called Baby. This young woman he treated in every way like a capricious, innocent, helpless child, thinking in this way to prevent suspicion and to veil his passion under the cover of parental solicitude, but neither his wife nor his friend was deceived as to the character of his emotion. Besides this attachment, the Baron had fallen into the habit of pursuing various loose affairs. At the height of intoxication he assured the now quite angelic Strindberg that during his wife's absence she allowed him full license, and became so shameless as to discuss the intimate details of their married life. Finally he proposed that they call on some of his female friends. Strindberg was horrified that the Baroness should be so lacking in sensitiveness and jealousy, but he put it down to her natural coldness, to which the Baron himself had testified. And in the depth of his mind he was gratified for this discovery. The Baroness was after all the blessed madonna he yearned for, aloof, virginal, never once touched with passion.

And then the Baroness returned from Finland, radiant and happy, bringing him word from his supposed sweetheart, a presumptuous letter full of "the effusions of a heartless blue-stocking." "She doesn't know what love is," exclaimed Strindberg. Love, he said, is "a passion stronger than all others, a force of nature absolutely irresistible, something akin to thunder, to rising floods, a waterfall, a storm—" The Baroness listened fascinated, as well she might.

In the meantime Strindberg's pretended love affair with his guardian angel resulted in a very grotesque situation. The girl's father suddenly appeared in Stockholm, inquired concerning Strindberg's income and family and treated him in every way like a prospective son-in-law. The sham lover, pursued by the father of a woman whom he now regarded as the most odious bluestocking and a witch into the bargain, was thoroughly frightened. As he saw it, there was no way on earth to save himself except by avoiding the appointments of the troublesome old man and showing his worst side when they met. This method was fortunately quite successful, for after a time the zealous father departed, and Strindberg fell back on his old romantic role, so necessary in his present relation with the Baroness, of a sad and inconsolable lover.

Suddenly Strindberg had a terrible presentiment that the Baroness regarded him as more than a friend and after rebuking her harshly retired to the loneliness and safety of his library and his attic rooms. He did not want an affair with this madonna of his dreams. Her child and her husband were death to his passion. Yet now, alone, his mind turned again and again to the physical charms, the arts and temptations of this beautiful woman cursed by an unhappy marriage. As in a vision she appeared to him, lifting her dress to show her feet and ankles which were, incidentally, fatally small and well-shaped, beckoning, luring him to the betrayal of her husband. The apparition aroused all his sensuality. "Now," he says, "all the passion which burnt in me concentrated itself on a single object. I desired her. My imagination painted for me the exquisite beauty of her white limbs." Suddenly he searched through art books for her archetype among the august beauties of mythology. Was she the full-bosomed wanton Venus? No. The fertile, faithful Juno? The flat-breasted old-maid Minerva? By no means. Was she the chaste, exquisite Diana, now yearning for the intoxication of blood and strange flesh? Yes, so it must be. The melancholy lover continued his search, but in the evening he joined his riotous, drunken friends at the club. Drinking a deep and authoritative half-pint, he became as they were; the room swirling about him was like an ancient temple of monstrous orgies, in which all innocence and purity were vilified, and soon he led them in the cynical song of the ne'er-do-wells. But this was only the beginning of his madness. The vulgarity, the profanation flung across the room, the lemon-smell and the variety of color stimulation confounded his brain, producing a strange, discordant intellection. And suddenly in the midst of this orgy, inflamed by his long repression, he fell to insulting and betraying the secrets of his madonna. This was his vengeance. At a certain stage of this affair there was a unanimous cry of: "To the women!" and the night ended, as he says, in the din and uproar of wild indulgence.

The next morning Strindberg felt no remorse. On the contrary, he was quite pleased with himself, for he had now so far mastered his emotions that he was well content to regard the affair with the

Baroness as ended. The Baron, however, soon persuaded him to come to them again and soon he found himself once more in the presence of the sweet fragile madonna who now arouses his sympathies more than ever. "This woman a coquette?" he thought. "She was a saint, a martyr, bearing undeserved sorrow." While Strindberg and the Baroness talked, the Baron and the cousin carry on with such freedom that Strindberg remonstrated, but his madonna is not jealous. When the play they attended begins, the unhappy playwright cannot bear the memory of his previous failures and abruptly leaves the theatre. Later, at the restaurant, he redeems himself by offering to fight a whole troop of troublesome revelers and the Baroness betrayed her feelings for him, on this occasion, far more than she intended. Another time she flung herself at him desperately to put out a match which she feared would burn him. Such events gradually put their friendship on a little difficult basis and double entendre and the repartee of meaningful glances began, Strindberg remaining however still on the defensive. Then came a fateful walk with the Baroness in which her lover divined all the gorgeous, dainty curves and articulations of her body. So frightened was he by the growth of his forbidden passion that he determined upon a flight to Paris.

But first, he thought, he must give a farewell party for his dear friends in his bachelor attic. They had been very kind to him and, besides, it would be fine to have the Baroness there in that lonely room where he had so long worshipped and longed for her. He, accordingly, arranged his poor household with the utmost taste and elegance and served his guests a several-course dinner consisting chiefly of oysters. With the warm furtherance of wine, the hours passed pleasantly enough. At their departure, the Baron presented Strindberg with a ring, for he was a true friend, so he affirmed, one he had come to love as a brother and respect as a man of honor. He even went so far as to abuse the heartless guardian angel whom he innocently believed the cause of his friend's unhappy flight and the Baroness joined in with damaging gossip. "The Baron, slightly intoxicated, made sentimental speeches, took me into his confidence, overwhelmed me with brotherly love, attacked me with endless toasts, which seemed to lose themselves in infinity. His swollen face beamed benevolently. He looked at me with his caressing, melancholy eyes; their glance dissipated every shadow of doubt of the sincerity of his friendship which I might have entertained. Surely he was nothing but a big, good-natured child, of unquestionable integrity; and I made a vow to behave honorably toward him, even if it should kill me." Then the Baroness kissed Strindberg in the presence of her husband, and he was left alone. In the morning, contrary to all expectations, he met the Baron who had risen early to bid him goodby. "Take care of yourself, old man," he said, "you are not looking well."

As Strindberg saw the rugged shores recede, a great melancholy overwhelmed him and he was tempted by a mad desire to throw himself in the water, to swim back to the beloved woman he had so senselessly forsaken. Like a caged animal, he paced the deck with not a single passenger to comfort him. In leaving the shelter of his home he felt a vague terror of the unknown. As a defenceless crab seeks protection under a stone, so he sought a stronger personality to support him, for he was, as he often said, a child who had been born too early and no doubt was not wanted. Finally, he met an old lady who put him to bed, sick and feverish, and watched by his side like a mother. In a few moments he fell asleep, with dreams of the Baroness, for the mother was what he needed. Suddenly he awoke in great dread and seeing that they were alongside of a summer resort rich with memories of the Baroness, shouted to the captain, "Have me put ashore at once —or I shall go mad!" Safely landed, he ordered a cigar and a glass of absinthe and considered quietly and seriously whether he had, in fact, gone insane. Certainly his friends would think so when the news reached them, and perhaps insanity, for this and other reasons, was the only way out—that or suicide. To escape from his melancholy reflections he wandered along the damp shore seeking the footprints left by his beloved Siri [1] the summer before. As he clambered over the rocks and gazed about at the thousand fir-clad islands, snatches of lore and poetry fled through his mind, like a shimmering of hope in that black desolation. Memories of Swedish folk-songs, of love-lorn maidens who waste away, till their mothers, despairing, prepare their death-beds, gave poetic elevation to his despair. But the woods were always his retreat from a great humiliation and soon he raged and wept and stormed against the trees and, like Ajax, challenged nature with sad titanic fury. No, life without her was impossible, yet he must see her again before he died. Cunningly, he contrived a death delayed by illness, for then she would come again, with tears, to his sick bed. Hearing the loud tumult of the breakers, he made for the beach and throwing himself into the ice-cold water, determined to contract pneumonia and so die in the course of a few days. Swimming back to the cliff again, he dragged himself out amid the derisive calls of the sea birds and climbed up an alder tree where the freezing air could have full sweep of his naked body. "The icy air," he says, "scorched my skin like a red-hot iron." When he felt his purpose was accomplished, he dressed and made a shift to find his way back to the village through the dark woods, which now wore a weird and menacing aspect. On arriving home, he sent a telegram to the Baron, describing his condition. Since there was no doctor in the town, he sent for a clergyman, and was soon lulled to sleep by the pious exposition of a doctrine he had long ceased to believe in.

In the morning, after twelve hours' sleep, he found to his dismay that his condition was almost normal, and if anything his brain was more composed and orderly than before. To his mortification, however, a telegram was handed him announcing that his friends would soon be with him, so that there was nothing to do but face the matter out, though how he was to explain his sud-

[1] Siri von Essen, Baroness Wrangel.

den madness and the suspicious visit of the clergyman, and how avoid the sneering curiosity of the people, he was at a loss to know. But when his friends came they pampered and consoled him in every way. The Baroness, who was especially beautiful that day, petted and served him as though he were an ailing child. "And how sweetly she played the part of a mother!"—so sweetly in fact that he felt for a moment like the wolf who lies in bed waiting for little Red Riding Hood, that he may devour her. One look at the good and kindly Baron was enough. He promptly steeled his heart, treating Siri's attentions with the most callous indifference. Once more the angelic Strindberg!

Throughout this episode Strindberg seemed to have no idea what a ridiculous part he was playing and in self-condemnation, as was so often the case with him, forewent self-ridicule. Humor would have been too terrible to be borne. He could endure to be a monster, but never a clown.

When his friends had departed, the landlady inquired if the lady was not his sister. Strindberg was astonished. "Had my constant association with the Baroness affected the expression of her features? Or had the expression of her face influenced mine during this six months' union of our souls?" Yes, he concluded, the desperate desire to please one another had made each imitate the other to such an extent that even their faces took on a resemblance, bespeaking the irreparable union of their souls. And this is, incidentally, one of the ground notes of Strindberg's metaphysics of the sexes. It is especially important, since only through an appreciation of the spiritual consanguinity of lovers in Strindberg's scheme, is it possible to understand the fearfulness of their strife.

Back in Stockholm Strindberg was all gaiety and detachment though he continued the ruse of a broken heart, lamenting his guardian angel's cruelty. A constant companion of his friends, a brother to the Baron, a solace and confidant to the Baroness, sometimes the angel in him was dominant, sometimes the devil. Once under the table he "beheld the finely shaped calf (of the

Siri von Essen, Strindberg's First Wife

Baroness) clothed in a white stocking, a gaily embroidered garter belted that charming muscle which turns a man's brain because it stimulates his imagination and tempts him to the construction of the whole of the remaining form." Then the devil put it into him to think that his madonna was deliberately tempting him, for every woman under such circumstances knows when she is being observed. Strindberg left abruptly, returned to the library, to his play, and for some time he did not miss his friends. Then the Baron appeared as usual and, directed by the stronger will of his wife, begged him to return to them. And now for the first time Strindberg saw an abhorrent thing—the common bedroom of his madonna and her husband. It was a profanation of the sacred and Strindberg found everything there unclean and disgusting.

The Baroness at this time was growing more and more restless in her unhappy marriage, and lamented with bitterness that her husband's station should require her to sacrifice the career of an actress, to which she felt especially called. Her husband's affairs and particularly his manifest love for her little cousin, though she made light of it, did not contribute to her ease of mind. This dissatisfaction expressed itself in warm but ambiguous appeals to Strindberg (who, however, was usually man enough to repulse her), and in flippant, daring conversations with interested young men at the parties they attended. On such occasions her adorer was beside himself with jealousy, and with the great pity that the madonna he worshipped should go wrong.

When the little cousin returned again, a curious quadrangle was formed. Strindberg out of revenge made love to the cousin whereupon both the Baron and Baroness were jealous. Whenever the Baron could, he captured his sweetheart in a corner, whereupon Strindberg and the Baroness began a conversation, which made him very jealous. The cousin, though she of course had her eye on the Baron, played freely with everyone's feelings and was probably the only one to enjoy the situation.

Strindberg had for a long time avoided the obvious danger of being alone with the Baroness but one evening there was no help for it. The Baron, insisting on seeing "Baby" home, left them to themselves. "Why do you hate me?" began the Baroness. But Strindberg was so nervous that he became quite rude in his replies, whereby he unfortunately betrayed his secret. "You wanted to run away from me," she said. And so it came out. He had tried to run away from her and she from him. Each had been fearful of this forbidden love. Their passion was now discovered. What was to be done? Nothing. The lover made an eloquent ovation to honor and virtue and the sweetheart, responding to his exalted love, agreed that they should continue to walk the high road of propriety.

At this point their conversation was interrupted by two old gentlemen with a dark lantern. Strindberg here makes an æsthetic comment of great subtlety and interest. "Notice," he said to the Baroness, "how reality differs from fiction. Could I dare draw a scene like this in a novel or a drama without being accused of being humdrum? Just think—a confession of love without kisses, genuflections, or protestations, terminated by the appearance of two old men throwing the light of a dark lantern on the lovers! And yet therein lies the secret of Shakespeare's greatness, who shows us Julius Cæsar in dressing gown and slippers, starting from his sleep at night, frightened by childish dreams."

This declaration of love is followed by an intimate correspondence which reveals a deep communion and reciprocation of two related souls. The Baroness writes that she loves her husband in spite of his faithlessness. But she loves Strindberg, too. She cannot live without either. One moment her double devotion rends her conscience, the next, she feels only a calm happiness in the tender love of two men. But Strindberg comforted himself with the thought that since she admired his person and was jealous of it, while she had ceased to regard her husband in this way, she must be in love with him and him alone. In the course of time the inevitable happened. The Baroness gave the first kiss and Strindberg reciprocated as, indeed, he felt that his honor required, giving many more in return. But having gone so far, his old principles vanished in the air and now he would possess her as a woman. Eloquently he urged her to leave her "polluted house," and to begin under his guidance and help a brilliant career on the stage. And now the angel turned to a devil in good earnest. "Now," he says, "I want to kiss your throat and the dimples on your shoulders; I will smother you with my kisses, strangle you between my arms as with a necklet. My love for you fills me with the strength of a god. Did you think me delicate? Beware of the sick lion! Don't come near his den or he will kill you with caresses! Down with the dishonest mask. I want you and I will have you!"

The Baroness, half resisting, complained of her husband. When Strindberg learned that the Baron kept two mistresses, his blood boiled at the thought that this nobody should be so well provided, while he, the man of genius, must suffer unsatisfied.

But there were moments of modesty as extreme as those of sensuality. At times he worshipped her as before, embraced her with tears and wonder, kissed her shoes, blackening his lips, and then she became a goddess for him once more, pure and virginal. But this mood, too, changed. At Strindberg's urgent request the Baroness told the whole story of their love to her husband, who very much impressed her by forgiving them both out of hand— for he loved them still, he assured her—on condition that they preserved his good name. But Strindberg was not touched by this show of tolerance. The idea that they could live together like brother and sister was "an insult to my manhood; henceforth he had ceased to exist for me." In spite of this resolution, he was obliged to return to the old house, the Baron having written that his wife was dying. On arriving at her sick bed, Strindberg felt no anxiety or pity, but suspecting some ruse, soon departed, miserable and desperate. But the Baroness, who had commenced to call on Strindberg in his attic, continued her visits, until finally the day passed in which "the son of the people had carried off the white skin . . . the swineherd had mated with the princess." He trembled at his new responsibilities.

And now the divorce was in readiness and the Baroness about to leave for Copenhagen to conclude the matter. In order to give the lie to malicious gossip, she persuaded the Baron to receive Strindberg at their house and accompany them to the station. The poor, generous, childlike Baron. No, Strindberg could not bear that he should be disgraced, but the tears of the Baroness finally persuaded him and once more he returned to the old house, once more gazed into the intensely melancholy eyes of the Baron, the man who had been his closest friend. At supper their old triangular friendship seemed to revive and the glasses clinked just as in the old days and nobody was to blame for what had happened—only chance and circumstance. When the Baron failed to appear at the station, however, the Baroness lost her head completely and insisted that Strindberg accompany her on her journey, in defiance, so he thought, of every caution. Oppressed by the thought that now her reputation was irretrievably ruined, but persuaded by the sorcery of her entreaty, he boarded the train, whereupon a lovers' quarrel began, in which the passionate reproaches and illogic of the Baroness played the principal part. Not until she displayed her tiny feet, however, did she win the argument, since these for Strindberg were stronger than any syllogism. At last he managed to leave the train and was free, but again his ardent love arose and left him no peace in her absence.

"The first stage in the downfall of man had been reached;" he wrote, "the others were sure to follow—to utter degradation, to the verge of insanity."

XIII

FORTUNE SMILES—BUT TEARFULLY

THE day after their departure, says Strindberg, the whole town knew that Baroness Wrangel had eloped with one of the secretaries of the Royal Library. This was a bad beginning but he did his best to put an end to the furious gossip which was spreading insidiously in every quarter. There came sad complaints from the Baroness which involved him in an angry altercation with the Baron. Then the tone of her letters changed, she now spent her time in assembly rooms surrounded by flattering young men, had found a young adorer, and seemed as a consequence, quite calm and happy. Strindberg wrote an abusive letter comparing her to Madame Bovary and warned her "to break the spell which was leading her to a precipice." In reply she mailed him the love letters the young adorer had sent her, but in these he found only the customary poetic preliminaries of "criminal passion." Was his madonna a wanton at heart? He vowed to save her from her vanity and lusts.

When she returned rejuvenated from her stay in Copenhagen, and with the divorce concluded, the varied pattern of their love life began again. The fear of scandal and public opinion made their meetings precarious and humiliating, her reviving love for the Baron, her caprice, and despair at what she had lost, made Strindberg storm with jealousy; they suffered much from the infringement of their excitable, erotic, idealistic natures, poverty oppressed them and many adversities, but there were times when the bright heaven-storming sensual passion of Strindberg drove all shadows away. Then he swore that with her love he would become the greatest writer in Sweden—and all things within his power. His madonna fascinated him in strange ways. When she appeared in black silk stockings he was reminded of the legs of a she-devil. But one bar to his passion, which particularly irritated him, was her constant fear of motherhood, though this, to be sure, was quite natural under the circumstances. In order to put her mind at ease, he explained to her that there was nothing to fear—that he could cheat nature, and in the end he believed this himself. Strindberg's failure to understand his mistress' reluctance, was no doubt due to his prior conviction that every woman must naturally be eager to bear a child, under any circumstances, this being the biological end of her being. His deception he never attempts to justify or excuse, though he took complete responsibility later on when the child came.

Poverty, and the hostility of all respectable people made their life a misery. When they approached their old friends, they were shown the door; when they appealed to a theatrical manager to arrange for Siri's début in the theatrical world, he would have nothing to do with "a runaway wife." Piqued by these reverses, Strindberg determined to cure the Baroness' dissatisfactions and avenge her for the wrongs of a vicious hypocritical society, all at one stroke. She must become a writer. He therefore devoted himself to her new career, and wore himself out in the effort to find her suitable work. When she had finished one act of a play, he found it perfect, but suspected that his judgment was somewhat biased by her charms. But this play was never finished and Siri's career as a writer came to nothing. Suddenly her chance came to become an actress and this put everything else out of mind. Her public appearance was postponed, however, by the death of her little daughter, which sad event had also the consequence that Strindberg was once more brought into friendly contact with the

Baron. Once more they drank and played cards just as in the old days and the inconsolable Baron was much comforted by the comradeship of his former friend. The Baroness, for her part, was also pleased with the renewal of the old triangle and so fond of her previous husband that she spent much time in his company. Strindberg was all the while quite jealous and once had the horrible suspicion that she had betrayed him, yielding herself to the Baron out of old habit and indolence.

When the Baroness made her first appearance before the foot-lights she was a great, unqualified success, which was due, as Strindberg was so fond of saying, to a multiplicity of causes, which all followed, however, from her spectacular divorce. "The bachelors, the sexless, the enemies of matrimonial slavery" flocked to see her. The possible talents of the débutante, Strindberg does not mention. She herself attributed her success to her own merits alone and became arrogant and unbearable in consequence. It irritated Strindberg that she should accept the advice of the ignorant Baron and prize his own accomplished judgment so little. As he had predicted, her second appearance was a complete fiasco but unfortunately his prophetic gift was not appreciated, and like all Cassandras, he was made the cause of the evil he had only fore-seen. In spite of her failure the Baroness received a contract en-tailing a salary several times as great as Strindberg's at the Royal Library. This must have been highly gratifying to her and very deadly for him, for he himself had once been an actor and accord-ing to his own account, a bad one, with never a salary like hers. Moreover in later times he had condemned women's emancipa-tion, women's independence. It was a heavy blow, and now his madonna's self-sufficiency was insupportable. "I, the man of let-ters, the playwright, the dramatic critic, at home in all the litera-tures, through my work and position at the library in correspond-ence with the finest intellects of the world, I was cast aside like a worn-out garment, treated like an idiot, considered of no more importance than a footman or a dog." Strindberg's indignation at the rivalry of his wife was soon to pour itself out in the vicious play, *Comrades*.

It turned out that the Baroness was no great actress. She was given smaller and smaller parts, until finally she spent all her time making dresses or waiting behind the scenes for the most trivial entries. To retrieve Siri's honor, Strindberg now founded a literary magazine in which she was to appear as a critic and a writer of feuilletons, but this project, through her carelessness and lack of business experience, also ended in disaster. And the Baroness, under these reverses, continued to deteriorate. What would become of his idol, the aristocrat and saintly mother, now? She made the acquaintance of an evil meddlesome old woman and one day informed him in cold blood, that a woman had a right to expect money from her lover. "Prostitution," muttered Strindberg, as he wandered through the streets. Her rapid disintegration (as he saw it) was a kind of character transformation which occurred frequently in his later plays and novels. With all hope gone of recalling his former goddess to worthiness and dignity he spent days alone in the library mourning for "my love, my splendid, foolish, divine love."

Then, suddenly, came a welcome deliverance from the whole affair. A Bohemian friend who had just been left some money, offered to take him to Paris. And so they set out together, Strindberg rejoicing at his escape from the misery and shame,—and the whole tragedy of the divorce which seemed to him "like a repulsive heap of offal." Although it was his first trip to Paris he was not marvelously impressed but rather reveled in the discovery that "the great masters of Art and Literature were not as great as he had believed." He is surprised at the fact that oil paintings which were produced shortly after the invention of this style of painting, are priceless, as no later ones are, for that contradicted evolution and progress. French actors, as could have been predicted, did not please him, but he made allowance for different national tastes. For two weeks he delighted in theatres, museums and libraries and wandered, a barbarian from the north with his wild shock of hair like a storm-cloud above his elusive searching eyes, through this cultured Latin city, which was later to be the scene of the most terrible years of his life.

After a time, the image of "the white woman, the Fata Morgana of the virginal mother," returned to his mind with the old lustre and when the Baroness wrote that she was about to become a mother and implored him to return to her, he obeyed without a moment's reflection, for now she had risen purified and resplendent again, and not a trace of the fallen woman remained. On his return to Stockholm he prepared for the responsibilities of marriage by increasing his income. He was appointed assistant librarian, became a reviewer on the staff of various magazines. Then his stories appeared,—sketches of life at Upsala, based on personal experiences,—and they were a great success; he was acclaimed as the pioneer of Swedish realism. These were splendid days. Strindberg beamed on the helpless Baroness and gloried in his prospective fatherhood and his sudden notable capacity for bread-winning.

Then came the marriage, a modern marriage; three rooms, one for Strindberg, one for the Baroness and one in common. "We realized the dream of freedom in marriage," he wrote. "No double-bed, no common bedroom, no common dressing-room; nothing unseemly degraded the sanctity of our union. . . . The tender good-nights, repeated again and again; the joy of wishing each other good-morning. . . . How delightful were the stolen visits to each other, the courtesy and tenderness which we never forgot." Strindberg, beside his dear wife, accomplished an incredible amount of work. Then, long before it was seemly, the child arrived—a girl—and was immediately placed in the keeping of a nurse, where it died two days later. This death was, oddly enough, a great advantage for the parents, for social prejudice would never have allowed them to keep it with them. But though they were in no way responsible for its death, the suspicion of a crime weighed on Strindberg's conscience for many years. More than twenty years later, he wrote a play in which the secret desire of a father brings about, or at least seems to occasion, the death of his child.

The new ménage was now free from every encumbrance; good comradeship and a bright future seemed to promise, when suddenly a terrible, unforeseen intruder appeared. Strindberg had always hated dogs, the defenders of cowards, the enemies of society. Now, one appeared in his own house and bid fair to turn him out. It was a "blear-eyed little monster," who, taking him for a burglar, barked, yelped and even showed a certain willingness to tear him to pieces every time he entered his home. But this was not all; it dirtied the house and carpets, received the best part of the meat, was given hot chops while Strindberg, the master of the house, made a shift with a cold collation, and it made a pig-sty of the Holy of Holies, his wife's bedroom. When Strindberg attempted to correct it and train it to civilized life, or complained of its disgusting manners, his wife gave way to hysterics. At last, his patience overtried by this scurvy intruder, he commenced a program of cold withdrawal and for weeks never went near his wife's bedroom where the privileged monster held forth. In the end this method was successful, and the Baroness capitulated. She admitted that the creature must be destroyed, but Strindberg generously gave it its life, even consented to tragic mummeries at its departure. Anything, to be quit of the monster which had turned his home into a pig-sty or a lunatic asylum for over three months. . . . How deep and harrowing this experience was is indicated by the fact that his horror and hatred of dogs, if anything, increased as he grew older. In *Black Flags* (1904) he condemned the morals and manners of dogs more bitterly than ever before.

Strindberg also suffered from another interloper at this time, —an old maid of forty, who had so insinuated herself into the heart of Siri, that the two women became inseparable. So con-

stantly were they together that he sometimes imagined himself
as a bigamist, living with two wives, both of whom were hostile
and wished him out of the way. When Strindberg complained
of the dog or of any other household matter, his wife consoled
herself in the arms of her friend, who encouraged her in all kinds
of impudence and idleness. At night while he worked, they
closeted themselves in a distant room, smoking cigarettes and
drinking wine for hours. Also, Siri's friend, being poor, borrowed money. Once Strindberg caught her taking the silverware
to the pawn shop in order to raise money for her own needs.
Another time he was sent a bill for a coat which Siri had bought
for herself and turned over to her friend. One day he came home
for a week-end, after days of hard work and longing for Siri,
but on arriving, the two women ran away to swim, and left him
lonely and hungry for hours. These were small matters, to be
sure, but the cumulative effect was bitterness and hatred. His
only solace was to bury himself in his literary work and his
esoteric researches in Chinese pottery and literature. One evening, however, his eyes were opened to the vicious character of his
wife's new friendship. Siri and the old maid, who had drunk
more champagne than was good for them, were suddenly discovered kissing each other passionately on the lips. A famous
actor present called others to see the sight. "D'you see?" he said, as
if confirming a general rumor. Strindberg had already caught her
kissing her maid's neck and had warned her that she was verging upon the perversion of Lesbianism, but she had only abused
him and cursed his "evil imagination." He now begged her to
break that vicious infatuation, which was certain to end in disgrace. In reply she admitted that she delighted in kissing attractive women but saw no reason for denying herself such an innocent pleasure.

But his wife's sensual whims, according to Strindberg's own
account, were not all homosexual. On one occasion he saw her
cast lustful eyes on a young fisherman and later, he found her

drinking liqueurs with a friend of his, long after they had said good-night. When he reproached her for her thoughtless or vicious conduct, she flew into tears and hysterics, or asked him slyly whether he was jealous and he, consumed with that emotion, was driven to its defence. "And what is jealousy? . . ." he asks. "The fear of losing one's most precious possession. . . . The jealous husband? A ridiculous individual because of his absurd objection to losing his most precious possession." At other times he justified himself on evolutionary grounds. The jealousy of the male, which is found so frequently in higher animals, is nature's device for ensuring the parentage of the superior individuals. The stronger animal wins his mate and by fighting off rivals, becomes the indubitable father. Again, if women are allowed complete freedom in the marriage relation, the husband must slave for other men's children. This horrible possibility was a nightmare for Strindberg throughout his life. Many years later, while brooding over his first marriage and the sordid ambiguities which preceded it, he came to the conclusion that his first child, the one which lived only two days, was not his but the Baron's. Under the pressure of these painful experiences, he developed a sincere sympathy for all duped and doting husbands. M. Bovary was, after all, a worthy honorable man and certainly the superior of his foolish, vicious wife. The noble Othello was brave, temperate and slow to jealousy, but the evidence against the faithless Desdemona was plain as day, and her sudden death entirely justified.

While Strindberg labored as never before and created a literature for Sweden, all with an idea of ensuring the future of his family, his wife indulged her caprices. Mixed with her Lesbian and promiscuous inclinations, was a frequent abhorrence of relations with her husband. Now she behaved like a cocotte, now abandoned herself so completely as to suggest "perverse and licentious desires." This is what had become of his saintly madonna. At times they discussed marriage and Strindberg tried to recall her to her responsibilities as a mother and housewife, but Siri hated both these roles and neglected them. Her notion that complete freedom should obtain in marriage was the cult of the period. Emancipation, however, was the peculiar right of poor down-trodden wives, their husbands were only the tedious tyrannical, but indispensable bread-winners. To his expostulations, she sometimes replied that she was certainly free to do as she pleased, whereupon Strindberg would have to explain, perhaps for the hundredth time, that no one who lives in society is free from duties and obligations. But she insisted "that she was at liberty, if she felt so inclined, to ruin my reputation; that her freedom was, in fact, absolute. She was a savage; freedom, as she interpreted it, was the rule of an autocrat who trampled the honor and happiness of her fellow creatures into the dust."

To know who is most at fault in this stormy marriage is extremely difficult. If the Baroness had finished her novel (commenced 1879) vituperating a tyrannical husband, the task might have been easier. Also, if Strindberg had carried out the plan he once had of writing *The Confessions of a Foolish Woman,* his honest realism could have been trusted to give a fair exposition of his wife's case against him. But this project he abandoned, "because, after all, it goes too much against common sense to allow a criminal to give evidence against her victim." This much is clear, that however vicious and unbearable the Baroness may have been, Strindberg himself, as his own story shows, was far from perfect in the marriage relation. His madonna worship, devolving from his childish love of his mother and encouraged by Pietism and the long suppression of his desires, he himself sometimes recognized as a misfortune and perhaps a sort of vice. It elevated the beloved to deity and denounced with abhorrence every departure from perfection. The Baroness was at first quite delighted with this role of goddess, and naturally believed it quite becoming to her, but in the long run she neither would, nor could, keep it up. The lure and comfort of human weakness was too strong.

But when Strindberg found the *Erdgeist,* or the malicious witch, where he had sought the blessed madonna, he raged with jealousy and wild despair. When the sacred is defiled it turns to vileness and abomination. The old horrors of the blood crept into Strindberg's soul. Leprosy, incest, bestiality, could not have been worse than this self-profanation of his idol. But these extremes of adoration and abomination were not calculated to make the life of the Baroness an easy one, and soon she wearied of excess, of his jealousy and of his passion. They were cast too high and too low. There was too little carelessness and uncertainty in his love. He only complained of her, he said, because he desired her to be perfect, but she, for her part, preferred freedom. He became her slave, grovelling at her feet, sacrificed everything for her happiness (as he saw it), scorned other women, but she would have preferred at times at least a more ambiguous, less dependable passion.

One curious feature of Strindberg's love life was a certain distrust of his own powers to please. He seemed surprised to learn that the Baron, a giant, should almost never have given the Baroness happiness in their married life. When jealous of the Baron, he fears that the Baroness will return to him, for the nervous intellectual is no match for the athlete. In his plays and novels, women accuse their husbands of being too old, and the latter defend themselves by a reference to their offspring. Once the Baroness herself told Strindberg that, though not too old, he was unsatisfactory in the marriage relation. He was horrified and brooded over the insult for years, but refuted her charge (as in the plays) by a reference to his paternity. In *Black Flags,* the most brutal and outspoken of all his writings, he condemns those modern women who demand a man's pleasure in the erotic embrace. A woman's true pleasure is the child when it comes. Prolonged caressing, he says, is not an expression of love but only a "massage." It reminds him of two frogs who lie in a swamp together. These instances suggest, what of course is by no means certain, that some of Strindberg's matrimonial difficulties were due to his own peculiar nature alone. Yet, in spite of the frictions and jealousies of these first years of marriage, Strindberg refers to them as "the good times and the beautiful years of my life." It was during this period that he suddenly achieved his old ambition of becoming a famous writer and even a superman.

In 1879 a great financial crisis occurred and, Strindberg's bank failing, he was left a heavy debtor. By prodigious efforts, however, by filling newspapers and periodicals with profitable but ephemeral articles, he finally extricated himself and came out with a good balance. Recognition, applause, money, poured in from all sides. Debts were paid, a prosperous household established, distinguished friendships formed. Nothing seemed lacking to the dignity and happiness of a new, good life. In the summer of 1879 Siri was again to become a mother. This was a new responsibility and Strindberg, though at first shocked and frightened by the idea of supporting this intruder, ended by regarding him as a beloved guest whom he would love and cherish when he came and strained every nerve to provide for "the little chap" as they called it before its birth, and this time Siri was happy and exultant in her condition. "The period of waiting was more beautiful than the period of the betrothal and the honeymoon, and as the child came, the most beautiful of his life."

"As he held his newly born daughter in his arms he felt that the soul, through passing over into a younger body, can become immortal; and that life without children is a beast of prey that feeds only on other lives, without permitting itself to be eaten. But he had also the strange feeling that he had put forth seeds. He had become a child again in his child, yet believed himself to have grown old. This feeling of age and responsibility seemed to strengthen his literary powers so much that he worked from morning till night, with undreamed-of success." With the birth of the child, which contrary to expectations was a girl, came a reconciliation with Strindberg's family. "The good time, the spring time of my life had arrived," he wrote. "There was bread in the house and even wine. The mother, the adored, was taking new pleasure in life, and had regained all her former beauty."

In 1879 Strindberg's novel, *The Red Room* appeared, and was a tremendous success. It was acclaimed as the pioneer of Swedish realism. The author was praised for his originality and talent, for his unsentimental portrayal of the Bohemian life of artists and students, for his brutal uncompromising criticism of society. The acclamation came especially from the discontented groups, so that it was not long before Strindberg from his corner of the Royal Library became the hero and the leader of a sort of revolution. From Denmark came a letter full of warm appreciation from Edward Brandes. "You are the man," he wrote, "who will awaken Swedish literature and become the leader of the future. Your strength, your will, is not less than that of Björnson's or Ibsen's, your cultivation much greater. In a short time your name will be counted among the best that Northern literature possesses." Other critics praised Strindberg for his boldness and defiance, for his courage in portraying the lies and hypocrisy in society, his honest description of the miseries of those disinherited ones who suffer quietly without hope, for beside the world-pessimism of *The Red Room* was a world-pity. Many critics thought he had exaggerated frightfully, others that his whole world of Bohemians was phantastic and unreal. Another critic who knew something of the company at the Red Room denounced it as "shameless reality." A certain professor complained that he had marred his characters by giving them false masks. This last criticism, as Strindberg explained, was quite justified; he had purposely distorted his characters in order not to give offence to any private person. Most of the characters were built upon real men, his associates in the Red Room, yet they had been revised in various ways, and usually, as Strindberg explains, for their improvement. The novel was therefore phantasy, but it was also realism, for realism is something more than mere photography.

The intense realism of *The Red Room* was greeted with very mixed feelings by Strindberg's public. Some admitted the plausibility of the characters and events and were full of admiration; others condemned it on the same account and found it an immoral and dangerous book. Still others denied the realism. According to a very common judgment he was a follower of Zola, "the Swedish Zola," yet at this time he had not yet read the great French naturalist and knew nothing of his method. As he, however, came to read Zola, he was so struck with "the intensive power of delineation" and the undaunted way in which this writer grasped his motif, that he felt himself now quite superfluous. His method had already been carried out. There was nothing for him to do but return to his oriental studies, for this was a province in which he had not, he felt, been superseded.

In the meantime, he made little account of these criticisms of his novel. Buckle had taught him that a man's opinions are determined by his circumstances and position in society, and therefore relative to these, predictable, and unimportant. The public was even less disturbed than Strindberg by the unfavorable criticisms. They read it eagerly. In the year of its publication, 1879, a new edition appeared, and two more followed in a short period. This brought money to Strindberg, and distinction, it was his first great literary success. Also, at this time, he was honored by several foreign scientific societies, the Imperial Russian Geographical Society conferred its medal upon him, and his treatise on *Sweden's Relations to China and to the Tartar Lands* was read at the French Institute. Thus, at the age of thirty, conquering all his defeats and reverses, he had won fame in both the literary and the scientific world.

Only one thing was lacking, the humiliating rejection of *Master Olaf* had discouraged him from writing any further plays. But now he determined to write one for his wife's sake, and by giving her the principal role, revive her career as an actress. This was the occasion of *The Secret of the Guild* (1880), a play built largely on Strindberg's own personal experiences (particularly his love life) but also concerned with certain crucial problems of the time. As this was the happiest period of Strindberg's life, the play reflects his optimism, his confidence in the future, and his faith in the driving force of life. Altogether it is one of the gentlest, and most propitiatory of his writings. Those who had been wounded by the heartless revelations, the bitterness and the hopelessness of *The Red Room,* were delighted to see the terrible iconoclast recant and take a proper view of things. The liberals, on the other hand, growled in displeasure. But neither the conservatives nor the liberals understood, as he explained years later, that faith in the goodness of the world had been forced on him as the only means of recommending himself to the public which demanded conformity to a certain standard. The necessity of appeasing the critics and so making his way in the world, no doubt did play a part, but the religious faith and hopefulness of the play was also a direct expression of his mood at the time. Though *The Secret of the Guild* was no very great success itself, it seemed to lessen the brutality of *The Red Room* and thus promoted the success of the novel. Unfortunately, however, the play failed of its chief object, for Siri, as Strindberg said, ruined the part he had written for her, and losing her position at the threatre heaped reproaches on her benefactor, making him responsible for all her troubles.

Strindberg's energies were inexhaustible, fantastic. In addition to his office at the Royal Library, his numerous articles, plays and novels, he now undertook a great cultural historical work called *The Old Stockholm.* It was a new and radical type of history, subjective, intimate, impressionistic, at times polemical, treating of trees and plants, furniture, buildings, slang and jargon, old sayings and superstitions, poetry, music, morality and usages, clubs and police, laying great weight on isolated details, amusing episodes and curiosities. It began with a chapter *A Walk in Stockholm in 1730.* The strain of his various activities, however, proved beyond his strength and, threatened with serious illness, he finished the book with the help of a collaborator.

He now asked himself the question: What is history? Is it a rational process in which the indwelling Will gradually unfolds its purpose? Strindberg was too much of a naturalist to accept this Hegelian theory, nor could he any longer accept the materialistic interpretation of Buckle according to which the human soul is completely dominated by such external factors as climate, economic conditions, etc. His close examination of the past had driven him to the conclusion that human beings are creatures of a transcendent World Will, which governs the fate of peoples from above, directing their lives—to an end unknown to them. This conception, while emphasizing a transcendent world-purpose, admitted also the importance of material determinations—economic, hereditary factors, etc., and therefore satisfied the naturalist in part. Yet this view was a far cry from the materialism of Buckle and it speaks much for the plasticity of Strindberg's mind, if not for his consistency, that while an atheist and skeptic he was able to make this decisive step toward the conception of Divine Providence. In *Mysticism and World History* (1903) this doctrine is further developed, fates and demons come to govern the lives of men, intruding mysteriously and often with sinister import into the lawful passage of nature. In the later plays such as *Advent, Toward Damascus,* etc., the World Will is seen in action.

In 1881 a publisher asked Strindberg to write a popular cultural history of Sweden. After a few months of research among the materials at the library and the archives, he was very much discouraged, for it seemed to him that history was, after all, but a jangling helter-skelter of facts, without connection or reason, and the sad pageant of armies, religions, kings and peoples was but a weary hocus-pocus that went on forever. Just as he was about to give up the work, a principle occurred to him which threw his task into an altogether different light and invested the dull centuries with a new meaning. History had, previously, too often been written from an exclusively political point of view. Kings, diplomacy and military campaigns formed the subject matter, great personalities were made the moving causes, while the substratum of the whole political show, the underlying power of the laws, the necessities of natural development and the varied colorful life of the people, were quite forgotten. Against patriotic rhetoric, and national pride, and wasteful wars, he is a ruthless critic. Away from the palaces of kings and nobles, he cries. Back to the laborers, the fishers, the beggars!

When the first volume of this work was published under the title of *The Swedish People on Holidays and Weekdays, in War and Peace, at Home and Abroad or a Thousand Years of Swedish Cultural and Moral History,* a great cry was raised by the critics who, as Strindberg explained, knew nothing of *Kulturgeschichte* but judged his work by their own out-moded standards. But the truth of the matter is that Strindberg was often careless and inaccurate in his descriptions and at times mixes phantasy with fact in a surprising fashion. These mistakes, as well as the new method he employed, his iconoclasm and disrespect for authorities, were responsible for the resentment and enmity which the book aroused. Undaunted by the storm of criticism, Strindberg fell upon the great authorities with desperate, reckless abuse, and denounced them as petty copiers of third-hand sources or antiquated triflers,—according to his pleasure. During these years, 1881-2, he also wrote two more dramas, various articles, a satire, *The New Realm,* and commenced a book of poems and a set of historical stories. They were years of unheard-of production and Strindberg was happy in this creation, happy to lay these trophies at the feet of his Siri. Yet, again and again, the bright scenery shifted and fear and terror held him.

XIV

REALISM AND ROMANTICISM

THE triumphant, many-sided genius of Strindberg made its
first appearance during the years 1879–82 and it is little wonder that his contemporaries were astounded and dismayed at the
violence and doubts and bitter passions of this young upstart,
who stormed against society and men, against heaven and the
moral law, with such reckless and unpredictable daring. Had he
confined his attacks to one class of society or one set of principles,
his countrymen could never have hated and feared him, nor
cursed him as they did. He might then have become the leader of
a party or a program and lived honored and happy. But the versatility of Strindberg's discontent, the swift many-sidedness and
uncertainty of his attack put all partisanship out of the question.
He became a scourge to the whole nation; he became a horror to
himself.

During these three years he was a dramatist, a novelist, a short-
story writer, Royal librarian, an ethnographist, a sinologist, a
voluminous contributor to magazines and newspapers, a savage satirist, an historian, but in all of these roles his part was the
same. He was the idealist who despairs of reality because it falls
so far short of his dreams. Gifted on the one hand with an extraordinary sense of leading detail and significance in actual life,
he was also a man of high unattainable ideals. And the Platonic
contrast between the world of divine archetypes and the shadowy

makeshift world of actual existence was always more than he could bear. In his dramas and novels, where ideals and realities are blended like light and dark, good and evil, man and woman, their sad disparity becomes the principal theme. As a sinologist he fled from reality and its shortcomings, burying himself in the distant past. So, also, as a romantic dramatist. But this escape was only temporary and partial. As a satirist he returned to reality to denounce the pettiness, vice, and hypocrisy of the leading figures of his own city. But whether he defamed the life about him or fled from it, there was never peace between his dreams and his realizations; imperfection never became perfection, lies remained lies, the world full of evils, and his own self a hopeless mystery. The drastic opposition in Strindberg's mind between the ideal and the real, and his violent hatred of this contrast, was doubtless encouraged by his pietism and early experiences, by Kierkegaard and Brand, and many other influences. It distinguished him from other writers. It made him a blasphemer, full of hatred and insults and self-contempt, strident, irresponsible, contemptuous of compromise where reality was concerned, but tender and lyrical when momentarily he escaped from it. In some of his works, such as *The Red Room,* realism predominated, in others, such as *The Secret of the Guild, Sir Bengt's Marriage,* and *Lucky Pehr,* romanticism is ascendant.

The Red Room, though it is largely a compilation of Strindberg's own experiences and impressions, is nevertheless the first broad intimate delineation of the life in Stockholm. The fact is that his career in that city had been so colorful and diversified, that he had no need to go beyond his own memories. He himself had mixed with students, journalists, painters, actors, publishers, writers, officers, doctors, business men, insurance people, had been a spectator of family life and transient love affairs. Of laborers he knew nothing, but admits the fact and does not speak of them. The characters of the novel are mostly vivid, individualistic and yet representative types. Falk, who most resembles Strindberg, is the writer. Olle, the impractical philosopher, Sellin, the artist, Rehnbjelm, the handsome unsophisticated youth, Dr. Borg, the cynic materialist, Smith, the publisher, Falander, the famous actor, and so on. Falk, who like Strindberg has been educated at Upsala, gives up his career as an official to become a writer, but Smith, the publisher, who turns out to be a stupid tyrant, discourages his talented efforts and puts him to work at the most humiliating hack jobs. Sellin, though an excellent painter of the French school, is unable to sell his pictures and lives with his friend Olle in the utmost poverty. Rehnhjelm, who aspires to be an actor, is given silent parts for two years with no hope of success, while Falander, who has achieved a great reputation, is completely disillusioned. Everything seems to him old and weary and worthless and he sees the world sadly through the green of his absinthe. Both Rehnhjelm and Falk suffer the faithlessness of Agnes, an ignorant, pretentious, heartless actress. Her power over men is due to her distinguished appearance, her fine intelligent face, the soft modest lines of her body and her appealing beautiful eyes, always turned upward a little, toward heaven. We first see her as an actress playing the dangerous double part of mistress to Falander and the innocent beloved of Rehnhjelm. Then she reappears as Beda, a waitress, and Falk falls into a hopeless madonna worship, while she in her turn simulates a deep love for him. Yet her only interest is to secure him within her power. Once she has done this, she turns to others for distraction and deceives him as she had Rehnhjelm before. Like Strindberg when betrayed by the housekeeper, Falk runs mad through the woods and is presently restored and calm again. His recovery is also assisted by his sophisticated friend, the artist Sellin, who regrets that Falk should take the girl so seriously. In order to escape from the treachery of women the friends withdraw to a retreat, the cloister, where the intellectual comradeship of men strengthens their nerves again and prepares them to return to the struggles and desperations of the world. But the cloister is only the last resort. Their usual escape from the customary hunger and cold, the humiliations and the falseness of women, is a drunken party at the Red Room. The descriptions of such celebrations with an account of all the emotional and intellectual stages in the history of an all-night spree, are among the best in the book and throw much light on the Bohemian distractions which were often a solace and rejuvenation to Strindberg himself.

In ugly contrast to these gay, spirited, if somewhat cynical affairs, are the dinner parties given by Nicolaus Falk (the writer's brother) for his starving and therefore, servile, friends. Nicolaus Falk is a wealthy man who must at all odds feel superior to his companions. He therefore seeks out a group of poverty-stricken contemptible men and buys their praise and affection by food and wine, and frequent loans of money. As they eat, he insults them in the best of humor, commanding them to feed themselves like the hogs that they are, for the bill will be paid. Before they have eaten and drunk, they are completely humble and subservient, but as the dinner warms them, their spirit and independence begins to appear. One of the group, a perfect snake in the grass, recounts a bit of gossip which makes Falk, the host, falter and turn pale. The obsequious debtor now grows bold and presses his advantage. Finally, however, a poem is read in Falk's honor in praise of the great man, their benefactor. Falk rises to make a speech but finds he has nothing suitable to say. In his confusion he takes out his watch and immediately all eyes are fixed upon it. It is a ridiculous predicament, the only escape being to present it to some member of the poverty-stricken company. At a later stage of the carouse, Falk embraces the friends he had so despised but a short time before, communes with them on deep religious and metaphysical matters, and toasts them like brothers. When they depart in the morning, however, he is nauseated with the whole affair. To restore purity at once, he cleans up the room with his own hands. This episode with its pitiful ineffectuality and sordid incoherences of the spirit re-

minds one very much of some of the famous scenes of Dostoevsky.
Nicolaus Falk is a detestable man on this occasion and when he
cheats his younger brother out of his patrimony, but in his relations to his wife he arouses our sympathy. Madam Falk neglects
her household, sleeping till almost noon, is frightfully extravagant, and yet complains of her hard lot. Having a great deal
of time on her hands she organizes a society for the defence of
women's rights and so the oppressed ones gather to complain of
their husbands and men in general. Strindberg is no doubt mind-
ful here of certain sad aspects of his own marriage. But the happy
perspective is evidently foremost in Strindberg's mind since he
has his hero, Arvid Falk, marry a worthy girl against the will of
her parents and, like himself, set up an establishment in which
justice and freedom prevail. It is significant that, despite Strindberg's many complaints of his married life, his novel and plays
at this period end in happiness and a glorification of love.

Strindberg's passion for the gruesome was never quenched. A
tragic event at the end of *The Red Room* sounds the ground
tone of the whole novel—which is Vanity, Vanity, all is Vanity.
And this universal pessimism outweighs the momentary good
fortune of Falk. One night Sellin and Falk went through the
snow in a cynical mood to the hospital. There Dr. Borg led them
into a room in which three naked corpses lay flat on their backs
and one of them was their old comrade, the priceless Olle. Hunger
and disillusion had finally led him to suicide. In the pitiful torn
fragments of his clothes they found a farewell note which was
anything but sentimental, yet his friends Sellin and Dr. Borg,
react to it with cynicism and heartless unconcern. "It could have
been a little wittier," said Sellin. "It is, of course, the usual cry.
. . . Shall we go now?" And Dr. Borg wondered what a certain
butler, whom Olle owed for food, would think when he heard of
what had happened. Falk cannot bear the heartlessness of his
friends and tears himself away cursing the modern youth. Here
Strindberg's cynicism is expressed by Sellin and Dr. Borg, his

pity and kindliness by Falk. Falander usually speaks forth his disillusion and pessimism, and Rehnhjelm, his youthful hopes and despairs. In these characters Strindberg embodies his multiple soul and so frees himself momentarily from its conflicts.

It is interesting to note that *The Red Room* shows many traces of the influence of Dickens and the American humorists. Strindberg had recently returned to *David Copperfield,* which he had discarded as worthless in his youth, to find there a kindly English humor, social criticism, and "the philosophy of development." It was natural that the tense, drastic Strindberg should fix upon the serious aspects and miss, perhaps, the genial play of the grotesque. What he loved in Dickens was the praise and pity for the simple poor, the criticism of officialdom and the ruthless rich, and the plans for reform. What he admired in Mark Twain, Bret Harte, and other American humorists was the ultimate skepticism they expressed and the foreshadowing of the coming anarchy. It was the part of his nature to overlook humor, to treat it as dead earnest, or to fear it as a sneer of triumph or revenge. Besides these influences was the constant stimulation of Kierkegaard and Buckle. The one bid him separate good and evil and choose between them drastically without compromise, the other spread a great veil of doubt over everything and persuaded him that good and evil are only relative to the individual and his situation. Torn by the doubts and disillusions of Master Olaf, Strindberg turned sadly from the philosophy of conflict to the philosophy of skepticism and from there to the pessimism of Von Hartmann.

In *The Secret of the Guild* he renews the conflict between two opposite personalities. The strife between Master Olaf and Gustavus Vasa, between Hakon and Skule in Ibsen's *Pretenders,* reappears with a different pattern. Jaques and Sten, the rival masterbuilders of the mediaeval tower, are also effluxes of Strindberg's manifold nature. For one hundred and fifty years the Cathedral at Upsala had been in process of building but with little progress. Finally Jaques is unwisely elected master-builder though he knows nothing of construction. Though a weak character, he is possessed of a reckless egoism. Determined to succeed, he swears falsely that he knows the secret of the guild, degrades his rival Sten who should really have been chosen in his place, and rules with a high hand. Sten determines to leave the country but is restrained by his beloved, Cäcilie. In time, as was to be expected, Jaques falls into grievous difficulties but is comforted by his loyal wife. Finally the tower is finished, but evil rumors spread about and Jaques is afraid to ring the great bell. He is brought to do it however, by his good wife who cannot bear to see her husband shamed. When the bell rings the tower collapses and everyone rages at Jaques. In his great need, condemned by everyone, detested by his father and best friend, his wife alone stands true and loves him as ever. For the first time he begins to feel her priceless worth. After Jaques' disgrace, Sten is chosen masterbuilder and his love for Cäcilie has also a happy issue. Thus the play ends with a triumph for love and marriage and yet it is hardly a comedy, as Strindberg calls it, for the dark tragedy of Jaques' disgrace is scarcely removed by his wife's loyal devotion. There are, of course, a great many similarities between this play and Ibsen's *The Master Builder*—the vaulting ambition of the architect, Solness, the episode of climbing the tower, the attitude of the wives in both cases. That Ibsen was influenced by *The Secret of the Guild* is very likely.

The motivation of *Dame Margit,* or *Sir Bengt's Marriage* (1883) is to be found in the appearance of Sweden (1879) of Ibsen's *A Doll's House.* Immediately, says Strindberg, everyone went quite mad, pretending to find oppressed wives everywhere imprisoned in their dolls' houses and suffering under the tyranny of their husbands. The discovery was made that many women who neglected their duties as mother and housewife were longing for freedom and brilliant careers, "and all the young gentlemen wept over Nora's tragic fate." "But," complains Strindberg, "the play is sick like its author." In unsentimental Berlin it was laughed off the stage. But in the North,—well "even such a penetrating man as Georg Brandes was blinded by it. Unconscious or conscious sex impulses operate gradually in such a way that Nora, the tyrant of the house, the forger, was absolved from all blame, while Helmer, the loving and honorable man, was condemned."

To dispute the injustice of Ibsen's (and also incidentally Björnson's) demands upon the husband, and to deride the freakish idea of women that married life should be one long pleasure, he set himself to work on *Sir Bengt's Marriage.* But he had another motive in writing the play, which was curiously at variance with his polemic against *A Doll's House:*—He wished to reestablish his wife's career as an actress. After her last failure she had not been reappointed, but Strindberg determined to give her another good role and revenge himself on the world for rejecting her talent.

The new play, which like *The Secret of the Guild* has a mediaeval setting, opens with a scene in a cloister in which Margit, a nun, is about to be beaten for carrying on a secret correspondence. At the proper moment, however, Sir Bengt, her knight, enters the cell, announces that the cloisters in Sweden are to be closed, and carries her away as his bride. Their married life passes in hunting, pleasure-seeking, love and gladness. But the knight is oppressed with heavy debts to the Constable which he conceals from Margit in order not to mar her happinesss. When Margit, however, learns that her husband has concealed his true state of affairs for so long a time, she falls into a violent quarrel with him and finally forsakes him, declaring that she loves the Constable. When the latter, however, begins to woo her she will have nothing to do with him. Rather, she falls into a deep melancholy and is only saved from suicide by the intervention of the knight's father. Her love for the knight now declares itself again and she returns to him to begin a new life, with the full awareness that the world is not a paradise but full of crosses. They will teach their children, they decide, that there is a heaven above but here below is the earth. This is Strindberg's first answer to *A Doll's House*. Another one appeared in 1884 in the marriage stories.

Sir Bengt's Marriage is far more autobiographical than *The Secret of the Guild,* the chivalrous, doting Sir Bengt being much closer to Strindberg than Jaques with his weak, rash egoism. Similarly, Dame Margit, the capricious pleasure-loving independent wife of the knight, is much closer to Siri than the patient ever-loyal wife of Jaques. Indeed, this play is largely an elucidation of Strindberg's marriage as he saw it in 1883, transformed and elevated, of course, by its mediaeval setting and the happy conclusion, the returning love of Dame Margit expresses the author's hopes of a similar happy conclusion of his own affairs. If Siri would only give up her desperate whims, her craze for independence, and take a sensible view of marriage, he would (like the knight) move heaven and earth, leaving nothing undone to make her happy. Strindberg wrote this play to please his wife and avenge himself on the world for its sorry reception of her talents as an actress. But, in a sense, he also avenged himself on her— to be sure with the kindest intention—since he has her repeat just the lines, and play just the part, he wished. He has her return to her husband, the faithful Sir Bengt (Strindberg), full of love, admitting thereby that he is right, that her own notions of marriage are fantastic and impossible. By giving her the part of Dame Margit, he compels her to display publicly her own faults and then publicly recant. This histrionic confession and promise to reform on the part of his dear wife must have given Strindberg much private satisfaction, especially when he reflected, as he no doubt did, that this role of an erring wife returning to her honorable, loving husband was the only means by which her credit as an actress would be restored. It was a pretty revenge and a subtle method of bringing a wife to her senses.

But if Strindberg disclosed his wife's faults in *Sir Bengt's Marriage* he did not hide his own. The knight turns out too weak and scrupulous, too honorable and devoted, to please the awakened

sensuality and caprice of Dame Margit. She turns with preference
to a stronger man, the Constable. When the knight falls on his
knees and promises to be her servant, his wife answers bitterly,
"Do you think my soul could love a servant? It would please me
better if you struck me." There is in her blood a yearning for
suffering and hardness. Once on seeing a crucifix she weeps for
the pains of the Savior. When, however, she experiences the
selfish egoism of a stronger man, the Constable, she turns from
him with hatred and presently her old love for the knight (Strindberg) is restored.

The root of the trouble in this marriage, as in many others, as
Strindberg sees it, is the sentimental education of women, of the
consequences of which Madame Bovary is a good example. Women
are taught to believe that married life is nothing but romance
and chivalry and consequently regard their husbands as betray-
ers when financial difficulties and the prosaic circumstance of
ordinary life intrudes upon their paradise. But there is another
reason for the shipwreck of marriages. That is the husband's worship of the woman. It is the nature of such men as Strindberg and
Sir Bengt to idealize a woman beyond any possibility of attain-
ment, and then to curse her because she falls short of his expectations, but Strindberg himself is quite aware of this danger. In
spite of the final reconciliation of Sir Bengt and his wife, their
tragic differences and despairs, the occasional deep consciousness
of sin on the part of Sir Bengt and his father, give the whole play
a solemn tone which is altogether lacking in *Lucky Pehr,* the light-
est of all Strindberg's dramas.

Two years after the appearance of *The Red Room* and while
the noise of it was still in the air, the father of Swedish Realism
wrote a fairy play, describing the adventures of the famous hero,
Lucky Pehr. The first scene opens in a tower where the young
Pehr is imprisoned by his father, who is determined to shield him
from the world. When Christmas comes, however, Pehr's good
fairy gives him a magic ring which makes everything his for

the wishing and sends him out in the broad world to make a man of himself. As he enjoys himself in the woods throwing snow-balls, a young girl, Lisa, appears and henceforth follows his adventures, reappearing in times of need. When Pehr has tired of nature, it occurs to him that wealth might be a fine thing to have, and immediately, he has all the money he could desire. But in his mansion he suffers hunger and irritating conventions, until he curses wealth and will have it no more. We next see him in a town where he takes the role of reformer but this adventure ends in ridicule and humiliation. Pehr is condemned to two hours in the pillory but is freed by Lisa, who warns him against the dangerous power of the ring. In the next scene Pehr appears in the role of an Oriental prince but soon finds that his new dignity is only a sham. He is surrounded by lies and intrigue and is himself but a tool of scheming courtiers. When he is required at last to select a harem from a train of hateful creatures, he curses the falseness of the court and makes his escape. Later he is advised that if he will be happy he must cease to love himself. The boy who, having had his will in all things, has now become an egoist, takes council with himself and is overwhelmed with despair. On entering a church his own ghost suddenly confronts him and, leaning over the pulpit, warns him against his selfish ways. His adventures have all led to disillusion and sorrow, but now his playfellow and guardian, little Lisa, whom he had met at the beginning of his travels, shows herself to be the one real end and happiness of his life. As in *The Secret of the Guild* and *Sir Bengt's Marriage,* love is the sovereign solution, the one salvation. "Do you believe in good fairies?" says Lisa. "You see, when a little boy comes into the world, then in another place a little girl also comes into the world and they seek until they find one another! Sometimes they fail to get the right one and then it goes very bad with them; sometimes they never find one another and then there is much grief and affliction; but when they do meet, then joy reigns, and that is the greatest pleasure which life affords."

Like a great many fairy stories, *Lucky Pehr* is also an allegory with a deeper meaning for adults. The magical ring, which has the power to make all wishes come true, but also the power to turn them into dust and disillusion again, is the poetic gift and Strindberg, if one likes, is Lucky Pehr. The triumph of money and power have been his, he has played the part of the reformer, but these roles have brought him no satisfaction and the dear objects of his desire have proved specious and false. Only in love does Strindberg find the happiness he has sought so long and in so many places. His poetic imagination, like Pehr's ring, means a retreat to selfish dreams, from which only love can rouse him.

Lucky Pehr has thus a great deal in common with the much greater play of Ibsen. Peer Gynt is also the perfect egoist who avoids all the decisions and responsibilities of the world, seeking instead a glorious gratification in his own artistic dreams, and in the end, too, it is a woman's love that saves him. As the button-moulder waits to melt him down into firmer, better stuff he buries his head in Solveg's lap crying: "Mother and wife! You stainless woman! Oh, hide me, hide me in your love!"

Though Strindberg never took this fairy play very seriously and once insisted that it was only meant for children, the public were of a different opinion, for it has proved one of the most popular of his plays. There is a fascination in the sudden shiftings of colorful scenes and the theme makes a deep appeal to the dreaming hearts of both children and adults. It was soon performed in Paris with great success. On the other hand, neither *The Secret of the Guild* nor *Sir Bengt's Marriage* was very popular on the stage, though they went well in book form. To balance this disappointment, however, Strindberg had the pleasure in 1881, for which he had waited nine years, of seeing his *Master Olaf* (prose version) put on at the Dramatic Theatre. There it scored a great victory, was universally acclaimed and ran for forty-seven nights.

Lucky Pehr, for all its being a fairy play, is not altogether free from social criticism. The lives of the wealthy, the government of cities, the monarchy, are all ridiculed in a light satirical way, for the motivation of Strindberg's writings, even the most innocent, was nearly always a burning disapproval of conditions about him. By 1882, however, the public had forgiven him his vicious attacks in *The Red Room* and *The Swedish People* and were ready to accept him as one of their own. After the great success of *Master Olaf,* he was spoken of as a young writer of great promise who would be honored in many ways no doubt, perhaps later on with a place in the Academy. He had reaped the harvest of his scientific studies, had won fame as a novelist, dramatist, and historian. He had made money to support his family. Fortune had clearly chosen him as one of her favorites.

This was the time, if ever, to make a few concessions to society and to profit by his success. Instead, he wrote a lampoon, *The New Realm,* satirizing the institutions of Stockholm and ridiculing personally many of his most important contemporaries, with the result that his bright new reputation was ruined over-night. What had possessed him to reject the brilliant future that society had offered him? Did he wish to end as a pamphleteer, a scandalmonger? At one time, Strindberg explains (in 1886) that he might have laid his hand on his heart and testified that his conscience required him to expose that elaborate system of lies in which he and his contemporaries were enmeshed, that whatever came of it, he must remain true to his banners. But the truth of the matter was, he continues, that he could not do otherwise. It was not a virtue but a natural necessity which drove him to this fanatical and perhaps somewhat dishonorable attack. It was the divine nemesis which had already begun to govern his destiny, luring him on to vengeance, and new sins to atone for the old.

Partly, *The New Realm* was a work of vengeance. Strindberg could not forget the past, his luckless career at Upsala, his desperate struggle with poverty, his various misadventures as an actor, a journalist, a writer, the rejection of *Master Olaf,* his wife's ruined career on the stage and, more than all, perhaps, his "slave blood" and the old hatred of aristocrats. Naturally he attacks officialdom and the army, and ridicules the examinations at Upsala, which serve no other purpose, he says, than to separate the classes. Naturally he derides the Swedish Academy, a most inviolate institution, and scorns its heroes and masters with the best humor in the world. They are the hated powers and authorities which have oppressed him. But his satire, which shows the influence of Grenville Murray's *Men of the Second Empire* and Dickens' *Pickwick Papers,* is not confined to institutions and the celebrated dead. It extends to his contemporaries and their private lives, it being his purpose to show how little these correspond with their public lives and professions. Everywhere he finds hypocrisy and lies, and the public characters he had in mind are clearly indicated by his choice of names. Was this disclosure of living persons justified? he asks himself (1886). Yes, however unwise, it was. He had but told the truth and others were free to expose him in the same way. (Others, as a matter of fact, were soon to do this very thing, to Strindberg's despair.) Besides, personal satire, he says, has always been regarded as a fair weapon in ancient times and modern. The value of the book, moreover, does not depend upon its exposure of particular persons, since in Finland, where these individuals are not known, it was accounted "the best satiric literature of Sweden."

Motivated partly by a desire for vengeance, the lampoon was also an expression of Strindberg's old hatred for agreeable lies, his craze for disrupting truths. Kierkegaard's drastic lessons were still deep in his heart and Brand, his hero. All or nothing! He would not draw a compromise or a truce with the powers which had so lately honored him. No, not for all the comforts and decorations they could offer, and yet he is tortured by the thought of his wife and child whom he has no right to sacrifice. So fanatical has grown his hatred of lies that he is now almost a caricature of Ibsen. Brand, like Gregors Werle in *The Wild Duck,* was intended as an exaggeration, a caricature of the truth-seeker, a

reductio ad absurdum of the uncompromising man. But Strindberg had taken Brand seriously, would now himself drag every
lie to the light and kill it without mercy. He will expose the
treacherous deceptions and pretensions in the school, the church,
the business world, public and private life, and he is well aware
of the great power he wields. Truth is a tinder-box which at the
right moment could blow up the kingdom. He is aware that this
foolhardy book will cost him his reputation, yet he is convinced
that someone should die for the people. It was clear to him
that the bony finger of fate had singled him out unmistakably.
He was prepared. He would sacrifice his calling as a writer, even
his social position and future if need be, and die for the truth.

Yet, however fabulous his own pretension, however high he
rides on his Quixotic journey, he is subject as ever to self-criticism.
What is truth, after all? Perhaps it is a relative matter. Perhaps the
gods laugh over their cups at their poor truths which are too
weak to enforce themselves, lies being useful where they fail.
Sympathetically understood a lie is not a sin but an illusion, and
illusions are the air we breathe, a part of our original nature from
which it is impossible to escape. Nor does Strindberg feel that
lies are all external to himself. Indeed, he finds them first in himself and then in others. Throughout his life he defends his vicious
attacks on strangers and friends with the explanation that he is
even harder on himself than on them.

The New Realm when it appeared was a great sensation, and
critics vied with one another with praise and reproof. One compared it to the satire of Swift, others rated it as a mean, libellous
pamphlet, written merely for vengeance on those who had dared
to criticize the author, subversive, unfair; in short, a hanging
matter. It was not long before an answer appeared, a pamphlet
called *The Newest Realm* picturing the shamelessness of contemporary writers who stoop to personal attacks on living people.
The author took occasion, incidentally, to say a few unpleasant
things about Strindberg's marriage with the Baroness. But then

a defender appeared in the field who justified Strindberg's delineations from private life, yet felt he had gone too far. Though
opinions differed very widely, the wind blowing hot and cold on
this curious, exciting book, the usual judgment seemed to be that,
though a satirist of great talent, he had made an unjustifiable
and unmerited attack on his contemporaries. Certainly, he made
many enemies, particularly among those people on whom his
future depended, turning a number of critics against him who
had otherwise been neutral or favorable. Foremost among his
critics was his own wife. She lamented that she was married to a
scandal-monger who had brought disgrace and ruin on her and
her unhappy children, and posed as a saint and a martyr. One
day a notice appeared in the paper announcing that he was
mad and describing the martydom of his wife. "She had won
the game," says Strindberg (in *The Confession of a Fool*). "And
as she saw me go down before my enemies, she assumed the role
of the tender mother, weeping over the prodigal son."

But Strindberg, though he loved to imagine himself surrounded by enemies, a victim to their rage, perhaps a scapegoat
doomed to suffer, was not the man to go under so easily. With
his glorious capacity for sudden surprises he now abandoned his
scandal-mongery, and began a set of short stories, portraying the
stages and crises in Swedish history, a work which was so well
received that it almost obliterated the impression of his terrible
satire. At the same time, however, he had become a lyric poet
again and in the year following (1883) published a volume of
verse which proved in its way as radical and intemperate as *The
New Realm* and inflamed the critics quite as much.

Swedish Destinies and Adventures begins with a story of a
young nobleman, Sten, who, being left an orphan with nothing
but debts, is obliged to set forth in the world to earn his own
living. For this, however, he is entirely unprepared, his education having taught him nothing useful. As he rides along the
road, tormented by hunger, it occurs to him to eat a few apples,

but he is immediately accused of theft. Sten replies that he had supposed this was "God's free nature," but the man denies there is any such place and threatens to retain his horse on account of the theft. Then Sten explains that it was only a jest, that he has an estate of his own; whereupon the Constable changes face altogether and sends him on his way with great respect. This is a repeated experience of his. As a nobleman he is treated with great respect, as an adventurer, who will live by other men's labor, he is shown only contempt. Finally he decides to become a blacksmith but his inheritance and lack of early training prevent him from succeeding in this trade, or in any other, and gradually he realizes that there is no place for him in the whole world. Then a dangerous illness confines him in a hospital where he is told that he is unfit for heavy work. He could perhaps become a tailor or a clerk and contract an occupational disease like the rest. Alas, he is unfitted for anything. His last resort is a monastery where he is freely admitted as a nobleman but thereafter quickly rejected as a tramp. He is told that the culture and refinement he represents is a backsliding in nature. With no place in the world to lay his head, alone among the creatures of nature, the young nobleman has no course but to drown himself.

This story, which is representative of the whole series, shows the trend of Strindberg's thoughts at this time. It is away from nobility and a false culture and back to nature. Already he is a follower of Rousseau, giving judgment against cities, civilizations, wars, oppressions, and praising the simple productive life of farmers and artisans. But this is only the beginning. In the next few years he was carried so far by this nature cult that he condemned fine arts and literature as the extravagant luxuries of the rich, and so denied and neglected his own profession.

In the first story Strindberg's persistent feeling of being a stranger in the world in which no place has been left for him, and the subsequent death-impulse as a release and a return, are beautifully expressed. In the second story *The Unwelcome One,* which has already been described, a boy is forced to return to nature, where after a long struggle he is completely victorious, avenging himself on the society which has wronged him. *Higher Purposes* treats of the tragic consequences of the celibacy imposed on the Catholic priests, and describes how one happy marriage was shattered with the greatest misery for the priest and his wife, for the sake of the "higher purposes" of the Church. When the messenger from Rome imparts the sad command that he must give up his wife, it being unsuitable that a servant of the church should enjoy earthly love, the simple priest is broken-hearted. "Whom God has brought together, let no man put asunder," he objects. That applies only to the community, replies the deacon, and besides it is God himself who will annul the priestly marriages. The priest has a long struggle with himself but finally falls from virtue. The deacon reappears later on and explains that though he cannot keep a wife, he may, if he likes, have a housekeeper. But when the priest suggests that he will then take his wife as a mistress, the deacon says no,—anyone but her,—and warns him to remember the purposes of the Church. But the priest has borne too much. He flees with his family to a distant settlement, beyond the jurisdiction of the Church, perhaps to return in the end to the old nature-worship of his forefathers.

In another story, *New Weapons,* Strindberg pictures the oppression of the farmers in the reign of Gustavus Vasa. Deprived of their weapons, their fields converted into hunting grounds for the nobles, with no means of livelihood or defence, they retort by wandering out of the country, leaving it thereby defenceless against the enemy. Flight! That was a new weapon against oppression. The farmers could seek other fields in a new fatherland.

While Strindberg was dashing off these stirring tales of Swedish life, which won him more praise than any of his previous works, he often complained of his sterility and the paltry progress he was making though, to be sure, his composition at this period was incredibly swift. At times he forsook the Swedish adventures to work on another set of stories (*Married*). At times, he could do neither the one nor the other. All creative power seemed to be at an end, and only verses ran through his head, good ones and bad. It is a curious circumstance that just as Strindberg had almost convinced himself that poetry is a useless luxury and much overrated, his own lyrical gift returned, and the rhymes began to flow. It accords beautifully with Strindberg's own theory of the disharmony and inconsecutiveness of the mind.

In 1883 he published *Poems in Verse and Prose,* a set of poems intermixed with prose, with free verse forms; a radical departure from anything that had yet been seen in lyrical poetry. The principle of utility which had held Strindberg fast in his recent writings, now governed him in this new field. Beauty, like everything else, must meet the demands of Truth and Utility; if it is but sham and illusion, it is not Beauty. Truth comes before Beauty. Ethics is superior to Æsthetics. Not art for art's sake but art for the sake of enlightenment and the good of mankind. Phantasy is justified in part but pure invention should not be tolerated. The poet should merely rearrange the data of reality, not create them. Strindberg feels that the new age will demand Realism of a different sort; not the old Realism which satisfied itself with abstract general impressions of the world, but a new mode which will render the concrete circumstances and the leading details of life, vividly, in their full reality. As Strindberg watches from his window, he sees the people pass on the street below, observes closely their faces and manner, he sees a mother wrench the hand of a little child, and reads tragedies in the casual gestures of humanity. He is full of pity. These trivialities are the material of his poems.

The principles of Realism which Strindberg had laid down in *The New Realm,* he attempts to carry out in his poems, but with little success. His imagination, always insurgent, was not to be suppressed now. Almost none of the poems are realistic, consisting rather of vivid impressions linked by phantasy. The de Goncourt notebook has been used, but too few entries have been made. The various poems which make up the collection show quite a range of spirit and form. Some, which date back as far as 1869, are quite formal and proper, others written in the middle of the seventies show the marked influence of Heine.

But there were bizarre innovations in both form and content for which no one was in the least prepared. Many of Strindberg's verse forms are quite free and pass over easily into prose, a manner which he himself defends and consigns to the future. Some of the poems employ technical terms from chemistry and other sciences, to portray various sense experiences. Others are vicious and polemical. Hard, ugly words occur which perhaps had never appeared in lyric poetry before. One poem mentions syphilis. On the other hand, classical names and references, though Strindberg was now an enemy of classical culture, have a frequent occurrence. The worst of all, perhaps, was that Strindberg made use of poetry to pay back his old enemy Wirsén, the conservative critic who had lately shown himself so implacable.

The public received the poems with horror and dismay. Though perhaps brilliant and hair-raising, they were too radical and crude for any general approval. The Realist of *The Red Room,* the pamphleteer, had dared to carry over his invectives and crudity into the sanctuary of lyrical poetry. Yes, the crude Realist had invaded this pure idyllic realm, as well as the others, but how romantically, how many dreams and principles and phantasies he had brought with him!

XV

AMBITIONS IN THE ALPS

IN the meantime Strindberg's marriage, according to his own
account in *The Confession of a Fool,* was anything but happy.
He was appalled at the tremendous amount paid out for household expenses and when he considered their wretched cellar, their
parsimonious table, and the continual privations which he, in
particular, was made to suffer, he was at a loss to see where the
money went. He had an income equal to that of the highest
officials in the kingdom, yet he lived like a laborer. Perhaps Siri
had private expenses of which he knew nothing. He continued to
suspect her, rightly or wrongly, of the worst. When he learned
that she had undressed privately before a doctor, a "notorious
voluptuary," without even mentioning it to him, he was once
more aghast at this modest, aristocratic mother. Off his guard in
a moment of anger, he called her a prostitute, but immediately
repented as he saw the children. To make amends for the insult
he arranged a theatrical tour in Finland and sent her off to enjoy
the purple of patriotic triumphs. It transpired later, however, that
on the boat she met an engineer who charmed her exceedingly by
his doctrine "that there was no such thing as sin in the abstract,
and that circumstances alone were responsible for all happenings."
Unfortunately Strindberg's atheism at this time obliged him to
accept the engineer's doctrine, but, he added, there are still crimes
toward one another, and will be as long as society or law exists.

But Siri had been convinced, says Strindberg, that Fate alone guides our actions. "True," replied Strindberg, "but Fate also guides the dagger of the avenger." From various indications he was convinced that she had been unfaithful to him.

To add to his miseries, his wife had begun to isolate him from his friends, to draw them all over to her side, true and false alike. "Isolated, in the power of a vampire, I abandoned all attempt at defence." Exhausted by overwork and tortured by domestic miseries, his health gave way, and he longed for the release of death. In the meantime Siri, abandoning her duties as mother and wife, led a gay life among the artistic circles, and often came home noisy and intoxicated in the early morning. She seemed, as he thought, to long for his death and to do everything in her power to hasten it. What was he to do? "In love," he quotes Napoleon, "one only wins by flight." In order to escape from the terrible net which his wife and her friends had thrown about him, and free himself from the evil rumors touching the shady parts of her life, he wrote a cunning letter to a physician confessing a fear of insanity. The physician fell in with the suggestion and advised a trip abroad, and Siri had to submit.

On the way to Paris, Strindberg found his wife absent-minded and slovenly and she was equally displeased with him. It was scarcely the pleasure trip he had planned. On arriving in the great city—too great by far and too indifferent to be borne—he was more struck with the miseries of poverty than with the glorious trophies of culture, and presently, after a taste of the vanity and mediocrity about him, came to the conclusion that "the metropolis is not the heart of the body which drives the pulse but an ulcer which corrupts the blood and poisons the body." The glimpse of a poor old beggar who, unable to sell his vegetables, still pushes his heavy barrow along the Avenue de Neuilly, arouses him to speculate on the hopeless chasm between the rich and the poor, the impossibility of either ever understanding the other, and he spins a story (*The Confession of a Fool*) of the old beggar's fight with hunger and his final release through suicide. Paris affected Strindberg, in all, much as it had Rousseau over a hundred years before. Nor did the city please Siri. There her husband's genius was acknowledged, her own machinations penetrated, and her silly chatter stopped.

Among those who admired Strindberg so much and whose staunch friendship made all Siri's devices quite futile, was his rival the great Norwegian writer, Björnson. Strindberg, though he had never seen him, had been frightened and dismayed by his great reputation. Years before when he visited Stockholm, Strindberg "had heard a tumult as if a storm had gone over city and land, and he had the feeling that a magician had passed by,— John (Strindberg) felt that here was a powerful ego, which was stronger than his, and might lay strange seeds of life in his soul. He got out of the way as with a presentiment of the victor in the fight, and concealed himself." Björnson's portraits produced the same effect on him. They showed him "a great upright man, with a colossal head and a lion's mane, two beacon eyes which under great spectacles were ready to shoot, and eyebrows as large as the beard of a youth. His mouth had a firm strong set which indicated an extraordinary degree of manly strength."

Strindberg's fear of vigorous healthy minds and his horror of anything like "the swagger of the flesh" has already been witnessed to. His stronger brothers intimidated him. The Baron's animality disgusted him and later he fears that the Baroness will return to her husband, the poet being in the matter of women, no match for the athlete. In a story written the next year (1884) he relates how a stronger brother enjoys in careless pleasure a woman whom his weaker brother worships from a distance, with the very worst consequences for the latter. The exaggerated fear of stronger men, however friendly they may be, is a very important feature of Strindberg's character. In modern psychopathology such terms as "organ inferiority" or subconscious "fear of castration" might be used to describe the condition on which he was verging.

Björnson, however, would not allow him to escape, and one fine day when Strindberg came home he found the great man waiting for him, overflowing with kindness and fatherly solicitude. As they opened their hearts to each other, it developed that, despite their difference on the woman qustion, they had much in common. Strindberg had lost favor in Sweden by *The New Realm* and other writings, Björnson had lost his popularity and power by his *King* which had been damned as scandalous and treasonable. And Björnson had suffered other reverses. Strindberg felt himself in the presence of a fallen god, and though he feared his "sharper understanding" and wider knowledge, could not refrain from a feeling of tragic pity.

As an older man and a famous writer, Björnson naturally assumed the part of father, advising the bold young writer to confine himself for the future to belles lettres and leave persons and issues alone. At the same time, however, he betrayed his hatred against the King and made no secret of the fact that his play *Beyond Our Powers* was aimed at particular persons. One of Björnson's most delightful characteristics was his childishness, and Strindberg did not bother to point out his inconsistency. He was "as poet and man a complex of personalities. There was the priest (the paternal inheritance) who spoke to the congregation, without suffering contradiction; there was the farmer with a little trace of shyness; there was the theatre director who sought for effects; the tribune of the people who would be masterful. But behind all else was the good child. John (Strindberg) remembered later that when Björnson laughed he showed two rows of short worn-out teeth which were not at all dangerous, reminding him of the milk-teeth of a child." Björnson seemed to him at times to express the envy and hatred of Norway toward the more civilized but declining race of Swedes. The Norwegians were after all a close descent from the Vikings. It pained him to see Björnson, this son of the mountains, banished from his home, wandering the streets of a strange city unknown and unheralded. It reminded him of the great Sioux Indians on display for the pleasure of Parisian women.

Yet for all the friendliness and open-heartedness of Björnson, Strindberg woke up one morning to find himself in the power of this strong man whose great name with the mandate of the youth behind it, oppressed him. Presently he discovered great differences; Björnson was interested in politics, as he was, but would not make a study of modern conditions. Moreover Björnson was a staunch Christian quoting authoritatively from the Bible, and a woman worshipper, demanding moral purity of the man as well as the woman. Strindberg, on the other hand, had become so conscious of the hypocrisy of religious people that he was now all but an atheist. His hatred of women, and particularly emancipated ones, had also grown to such a point that he had no longer any tolerance for a simple veneration. Once when Björnson began to discuss the "woman question" Strindberg warned him to avoid a subject which threatened their friendship. Björnson was warm in his praise of his young rival. On one occasion he gave a dinner in which Strindberg was so generally applauded that Siri (according to *The Confession of a Fool*) was quite miserable. In order to comfort her he made himself as small as possible, and when his friend requested him to stay at least two years in Paris, deferred to his wife, whom, as he said, he always consulted on all important questions. Björnson gave him protection and fatherly advice, sympathized, and sought to remedy his poverty and ill health, and at first Strindberg was very grateful. Then he became frightened and saw a vampire in this stronger man.

Of perhaps greater influence on Strindberg at this time was Jonas Lie, whose "lively phosphorescent mind," and mild tractable nature "was more calculated to betray than to persuade.—Lie was a magnetizer and when he and John came together, it was a

question who could hypnotize the other, and give him suggestions in the hypnotic sleep. It was flint and steel which met, and
how it flashed and sparkled! But this debauchery of the soul
galled. They left each other feeble and were at a loss to know
what was mine and yours, in these children of the imagination,
which they had produced together, in these thoughts which had
two fathers. It was prodigality, debauchery." Strindberg saw that
the material for many books was being thrown away, that the
full play of his thoughts was turned awry, his ego hemmed in,
and presently he longed for solitude. Friendship, one of the
sweetest treasures of life, the public man must renounce.

In Lie's opinion Strindberg was a very learned man who suffered at heart, however, from a secret pietism, martyrdom, and
fanatical suspicion. He and Björnson tried to instill in him a little
of the bright gay Northern culture, and the latter warned him
against the role of a reformer and the nervous life of the moment. You, "whom I account the greatest dramatist of the north,"
with, "your colossal artistic capacity," can become great if you
seize the time and opportunity. But Strindberg already in 1883
had grown contemptuous of fine arts and literature. It was his
pleasure to reform the world, to preach and declaim, sound the
alarm, arouse the people, overthrow the old order, and build up
a new one on the ruins. Thus in every drama, novel or story he
grinds an axe. Ibsen who would "lay a torpedo under the arch"
and blow up the whole existing society,—Ibsen was in the right,
thought Strindberg. But Björnson replied that his was pure nonsense, for neither Ibsen nor you, he said, would sacrifice his skin
in such a business.

Closely connected with Strindberg's zeal as a reformer, was the
poverty he suffered, and the furious hatred of his own countrymen. One day when he received a considerable check unexpectedly, sufficient to defray his immediate expenses, he was full of
wonder and avowed a belief in God. Lack of money had become
a torture again. When the conversation would turn to Sweden

and his evil reputation there, he showed extreme excitement and anger. These adverse circumstances naturally made him discontented with the status quo. As he came to read Max Nordau's *Conventional Lies,* which pictured society as an elaborate structure of flams and deceptions, he found himself in complete agreement. He had moreover the pleasant realization that he now no longer stood alone,—an isolated crochet-monger. This gave him confidence. For once in his life he could allow a writer to go his way without criticism.

Strindberg's residence in Paris had great consequences in his development, for here he transcended the narrow limits of Sweden and buried himself in the culture of France which was henceforth to exercise a greater influence on him than that of any other foreign nation. With great difficulty he learned to write in French and became a collaborator on an international review which appeared in French. Later he was a frequent contributor to Parisian papers and once boasted to Nietzsche of his modish "boulevard" French, though to be sure, it was far from perfect. The idea of writing on an international review and thus controlling the taste and judgment of the world, was curiously exciting and gratifying to Strindberg. He had suffered hunger, humiliation, neglect and many other evils. The little country of Sweden had dared to denounce his writings. Now his field of action was the world where he might judge and dispose as he pleased. Grandiose dreams of power swept across his brain, overtried with troubles and exhausted by his incredible production. His satires had turned Stockholm topsy-turvy. Now he was in Paris, the pivot of the world, with his hand on an engine of great power. What if he were to write a satire on Paris, ridiculing the supposed greatness of that city, making the much envied Parisians the laughing-stock of other countries! This would be to play a great hand and there would be many to laugh. He was tempted by the sin of disrupting society, for that would balance his feeling of guilt or his many punishments. As a reformer he was inspired with the idea of remodeling the world to a happier place, but there were also Faustian dreams of sovereignty, which, as with the characters of Balzac, rose like a fantastic crescendo in the great moments of loneliness.

Strindberg was also requested to give a French lecture on Swedish Literature before an international institute. This was a great opportunity with prestige and wealth within his reach. Yet he declined. He would not speak ill of his colleagues. In later years, in calmer moments, he realized that had he played his cards deftly, everything might have been his. Why did he refuse? Because, however much he craved power, he also sought continuously the sweet comfort of martyrdom.

In Paris, Strindberg had been protected from his wife's cruelty by Björnson and Lie, but when early in 1884 he left for Switzerland he was again in her power and suffered now more than ever. In *The Confession of a Fool* he gives a dour picture of his life in the pension where they lived. "All I loved, she detested; she was disappointed with the Alps because I admired them; she scorned the beautiful walks; she avoided being alone with me; she made a practice of anticipating my wishes so as to thwart them; she said Yes whenever I said No, and vice versa; there was no doubt that she hated me. . . . My brain, keen and refined by study and culture, was thrown into confusion by contact with a coarser brain; every attempt to bring it into harmony with my wife's caused me to have convulsions. I tried to get in touch with strangers, but they treated me with the forbearance which a sane person usually shows a lunatic." For three months he scarcely opened his lips and was horrified to find he could no longer speak. Letters from Sweden betrayed so much sympathy as to arouse all his suspicion. His wife had persuaded everyone he was mad. And now she triumphed. "I was on the verge of insanity, and the first symptoms of persecutional mania showed themselves. Mania? Did I say mania? I *was* being persecuted, there was nothing irrational in the thought."

"It was just as if I had become a child again. Extremely feeble, I lay for hours on the sofa, my head on her knees, my arms around her waist, like Michelangelo's Pieta. I buried my face in her lap and she called me her child. 'Your child, yes,' I stammered. I forgot my sex in the arms of the mother, who was no longer female, but sexless. Now she regarded me with the eyes of a conqueror, now she looked at me kindly; seized with the sudden tenderness which a hangman is said to feel sometimes for his victim. She was like the female spider which devours her mate immediately after the hymenal embrace." This situation in which a wife drives her husband insane and forces him back to the role of a helpless child furnishes the theme of *The Father* and *Creditors* and plays an important part in other Strindberg plays.

But this whole picture of his life in Switzerland in *The Confession of a Fool* is at variance with his other accounts and the reports of friends. Helene Welinder described him as (Hedén p. 120) "fine and modest, in general quiet, full of courtesy, immersed in his work; but full of ardor and imagination when he received ideas toward an alluring enterprise, and volcanically angry when he thought of the enmity which reached him now and again over land and sea from Sweden. The marriage with his wife was always, in spite of discords, ruled by the bright happiness of the first years of marriage. When he met a guest of the pension in which they lived, he had almost always the same question on his lips: Where is Siri? Haven't you seen Siri? He seemed unable to dispense with her a single hour. She, for her part, gave expression to her feelings when in 1884 they celebrated her birthday, for then she drank to her husband with the words: 'Thanks for seven happy years.'" Toward children, and especially his own, Strindberg also showed himself very interested and devoted, sometimes playing with them for hours until Siri called them all in for supper, her big child and her little children. Strindberg's happiness was also increased at this time by the birth of his only son, Hans, which now made four children in all.

Nothing of all this appears in *The Confession of a Fool* or if it does, it is blackened by suspicions and miseries. There he is reduced to infantilism, on the verge of madness, through the malicious artifices of his wife. In *The Growth of a Soul* written one year before the French version of *The Confession of a Fool* he describes the peace and glamour of the mountains, the quieting effect of his lonely walks, the simple joys of nature, all beautified by the omission of the conventions, lies, and envy of society, and free from the reminders of his heavy destiny, and the hatred in Sweden. The frenzied life in Paris was forgotten. The long nights of good sleep, the simple diet without strong drinks, the lack of disturbing conversations, quickened his powers until it seemed to him that his mind was like a glowing volcano seething with new productions.

The discrepancy between these various accounts of Strindberg's life in Switzerland do not point necessarily to a contradiction or a distortion of the facts, but rather to a selection of various strands of the life-process. In writing *The Confession of a Fool* Strindberg set about to select those facts which would incriminate his wife and justify himself (the Fool) and he naturally omitted a great deal that was irrelevant. In *The Growth of a Soul,* he is more concerned with his intellectual development and therefore neglects the terrible circumstances of his marriage. Besides, in 1886 when this book was written, he would never have dared to expose his wife or seek revenge. She was still, in spite of all the horrors she put upon him, his madonna, his dear wife, the mother of his children. Many more horrors were needed before he could be brought to the point of publishing this "my most terrible book." The complexity of Strindberg's life (or indeed of any life), on which he lays so much weight throughout his autobiography, permits a certain validity to each discrepant account, but it must nevertheless be admitted that Strindberg was not always accurate even in the gross matters of fact. He wrote from memory alone and scorned revision or correction. Errors were unavoidable.

In Switzerland Strindberg continued his solitary walks in the mountains and by the Geneva sea, and like Rousseau who first discovered nature and taught the perversity of culture, brooded for days on the errancy of mankind with its cities and armies and its towers of Babel. Milder and more forgiving as a consequence of his recent successes, he determined to find an explanation of "the causes of the Universal Dissatisfaction," which would excuse men from all blame. His answer is the usual one. It is the social and economic organization which is at fault. With William Morris, he maintains that the specialization of labor in every department of human activity is responsible for the general unhappiness and the decline of the race. As in *Peter and Paul* (one of the stories in Swedish Destinies and Adventures) he contrasts the idyllic, independent ever-varied life of the farmer with the stilted unnatural ways of the city dweller. The one is producing the means to life and happiness, the other is occupied with bargaining, exchanging moneys and goods, producing and consuming luxuries. Toward non-producers and manufacturers of luxuries, Strindberg turns his usual battery of ridicule and reproach. His father and brothers were merchants, but this did not prevent him from reproving and subordinating this class to farmers and even laborers. Of all the classes in society the laborers are the most unfortunate, suffering most the undermining effects of the division of labor and the narrow oppression and poverty of the city. But the whole civil society must endure the tense, frantic stifling of the city, that "ulcerous" parasitic growth in the midst of the green lands and waters of the earth. In modern society, according to Strindberg, no one is so pitiful as the noble and the priest. Both believe that they are superior to the people and necessary to their happiness and salvation, a conviction they cherish in spite of all evidence to the contrary. Priests and nobles are superfluous in the modern world and artists, writers, and scientists are greatly overrated. Scientists work for science, not for humanity. Artists and writers are luxuries of the rich. They conjure forth expensive baubles while the people starve. The great figures of history,—artists, poets, philosophers,— men like Goethe, Raphael, Michelangelo, Shakespeare, are likewise overestimated, for their greatness is in part an illusion of historians, unacquainted with the teachings of Buckle. Yes, culture, our precious civilization itself, is nothing but vanity and luxury, and like the pride of the pyramids, blind, cruel, monstrous, built upon the miseries of the people. Then back to nature! Away from the lies and confections of man. Yet Strindberg is too much of a realist to think nature an idyll, to join the Eighteenth Century in a praise of the noble savage, or like Chateaubriand, to chase a nymph through the untrodden paths of a benevolent nature. He had heard the lessons of Darwin and Schopenhauer and knew that nature, beneath her beauty and her majestic repose, conceals a bloody, desperate struggle for existence, in which all living creatures die or triumph. Nor is it always the strong who survive, nor is it desirable that they should. Strindberg's writings are full of praises of the selective process of Darwinian evolution, and sympathy with its victims, the noble over-refined weaklings and the isolated strong. At times he defends himself and others on evolutionary grounds, at times he condemns the ruthless process which destroys its highest creations. In *By the Open Sea* he praises evolution as development, later in life he condemned it roundly as a most detestable, pernicious doctrine. Hereby he betrays his uncertainty and his honesty, his willingness to shift the whole floor of his world-view, the moment new reasons declare themselves.

In the midst of the mountains, surrounded by the peaceful, freedom-loving Swiss, he became a great enemy of wars and tyranny. In *Torments of Conscience* he portrays the hard case of an officer during the Franco-Prussian War when ordered to shoot down civilians. Tortured by conscience his only resource was madness. Another story, *The Island of the Happy,* opens in a tropical island where excellent food was to be had without labor. Naturally there was no need for a king, or laws, private property, police, or churches. But suddenly the same men are shifted to a barren land where they must earn their bread by the greatest pains. Immediately a king appears, and laws, officials, a state church and class distinction oppress the poor laborers, while confused but pompous scientists divide mankind according to how many indentations they have on their heads, or how many they haven't. Here is a wonderful opportunity for Strindberg's satirical gift and his nature worship. The story also discloses the fact that Strindberg has come to regard labor as a curse, and useless labor or idleness, a crime. In this year also he condemned private property, sovereignities and wars, and advocated, following Fourier's and Saint Simon's system, "the United States of Europe." He was fast becoming a socialist.

In espousing these new doctrines of democracy, "naturalism" and socialism, Strindberg displayed the same recklessness, and intemperance, and the same subsequent doubts as in other cases. Kierkegaard had taught him an extreme, unswerving advocacy, had warned him against compromising and paltering with ideas, but Buckle had taught him to doubt everything. Rousseau had said that men were originally good, that it is society that corrupts them. Strindberg maintained with his usual exaggeration that men are angels, but hardly had the paper dried before he reversed his view, for in the consequence of Rousseau's doctrine, the Reign of Terror, he saw its refutation. The wild beast with blood-soaked mouth peered out from the white garments of the angel. Other doubts came. Did he really believe that electricity and steam were of no use to mankind? Certainly not. Yet he had set out to test these teachings of Rousseau, to examine them in the light of their most extreme implications, and so for a time he would continue to expound them and drive them to the limit. If too many contradictions or absurdities developed there would of course be a revulsion of belief. This is what happened. When Strindberg had preached democracy, socialism and Rousseauism and pushed them to their limit of absurdity and falsity, he turned at once to the opposite doctrine of the Superman, and he advocated this principle as violently as the previous ones, and played as many wild variations as possible. But these, too, were largely experiments as he once explained to Georg Brandes. Strindberg's method of testing the truth of an idea was to advocate it with violence, and trace out all its implications and practical effects; in a word, to experiment with it. Like an efficient scientist, he forsook a theory the moment the experiment turned out badly. His many surprising shifts of doctrine are to be explained in this way. His biography was strewn with the sad shimmer of false dreams, with great hypotheses built up in pride and confidence, to be discarded painfully for a rival system further on along the long road toward Damascus. His great contentions and disillusions did not matter. They were simply the Kirkegaardian stadia on the path of self-unfolding.

XVI

INDICTED FOR BLASPHEMY

IN the spring of 1884 Strindberg left for Italy, to which he
felt irresistibly drawn, though of all countries it was the least
calculated to please him at this particular time. The marble palaces,
the paintings and sculpture were trophies of a decayed civilization; the temples and the wreckage of past splendor were carions
around which swarms of idle tourists hovered and fed. All beauty
was standardized, the guides pointing the way, indicating the
proper taste and judgment. The simple effects of nature were
everywhere suppressed or adorned. For the young Rousseauist it
was a model of all perversity. He longed for the great free vistas
of Sweden, the rugged hills shaggy with pines, and the wild fjords
with their noisy waters, and the air of the Icelandic Sagas about
them. The canals of Venice he found much inferior to the waterways of Stockholm and as for the blue of the Mediterranean, he
had seen bluer water. He had seen a better land, broken by hills
and visual variations. Here was only a dreary flat plain soaked
in sun. What nature there was in Italy had been walled up in
private reserves and guarded from the public view. With Strindberg's childhood memories of grass that could not be trodden
and flowers that could not be picked, this was a special vexation.
Before everything else, however, he was aware of the miseries of
the poor. They lived in squalid huts oppressed by the shadow of
the great civilizations that had drained their strength. The splen-

dor of Rome and the Renaissance were gone, but poverty and tyranny remained.

Strindberg's letters recording these impressions naturally shocked his contemporaries and gave them a new occasion for suspicion and resentment. This Strindberg, they thought, is decidedly original, no doubt, but has sacrificed everything for the reputation. For a poet to condemn Italy, the Mecca of cultured men, was an insult to tradition and decency. That he dared to oppose the taste of centuries of accomplished judgment was but another indication that he was, after all, a mighty disturbing and unpleasant fellow. For it is one thing to attack an abstract conception such as Religion or Monarchy, or a group of public men, or a particular government or institution, but quite a different thing to condemn the cherished foible of great men and artists—Italy, the eternal archetypal home of culture. This at least should be spared. Other institutions and interests, since they are active or militant in the world, can be fairly criticized, but Italy with its sad passionless pictures from the past should be held inviolable, a sanctuary and retreat from the distastefulness of the present.

But Strindberg in his present mood was an enemy of idleness and wasteful splendors and obsessed with socialism and grandiose dreams of reform, he could have little sympathy with a retreat from present realities and exigencies. Judged by the utilitarian standard of J. S. Mill, to which he was now a convert, Italian art was a monstrous extravagance and its admirers, parasites. Absorption in the past and worship of its great men was an idle dream from which the sleeper is afraid to awaken. Strindberg, who had dared to condemn the University at Upsala and the great figures of Swedish literature, did not hesitate to speak his mind on the subject of Italy. And soon he fled from that land of presumption and artifice back to Switzerland and the Alps and the simple ways of nature. The poet had now become a reformer. If he should return to literature it would be for special reasons—to support his family or to drive home his social arguments.

The motivation of Strindberg's next creation was his violent dissatisfaction with the prevalent movement for the emancipation of women and the increasing doubts and irritations of his own marriage, while the material was close at hand in the pension where he lived. There he found himself under the hostile surveillance of thirty women, of all types and descriptions; learned women, authoresses, invalids, slothful women, young women, beautiful ones,—all "idle, unoccupied, prattling, pretentious, pleasure-seeking." Naturally he asked himself how they managed to live in this idleness, with their schools of children. On inquiry he discovered that their husbands, the bread-winners, were confined in London offices or had taken long arduous trips to provide for the needs of their families. Yet it seemed that the more the men slaved for them, the more they regarded themselves as slaves of men. This was a peculiar inference, but Strindberg had discovered that the mental processes of women do not follow the rules of Formal Logic, but resemble more the untutored, egoistic, lawless reasonings of children and savages. It came to him as a distinct surprise that the cry for women's rights and the protest against the tyranny of men was a movement of upper-class women, who were of all women the most pampered and privileged. From the lower-class women, who worked beside their husbands in the fields or kept house and tended children at all hours with not a moment to themselves, no protests were heard. It was the idle wives of the rich, and the pompous blue-stockings who raised the rebellion and called for arms against the oppression and selfishness of men. Yet it was precisely these women who profited most from the financial support of their husbands and the accumulated splendor of "men's" culture and civilization.

It was obvious to anyone, thought Strindberg, that the three men in the pension were much mistreated. One man was put in a hot garret room while his wife and daughter enjoyed a most attractive one on the first floor. Another older man, who could scarcely walk himself, waited on his invalid wife hand and foot and, in all, showed her so much veneration that, but for his age, he might have seemed her son. There was also old King Lear with his thankless daughter. Once he had been rich and honored, with a handsome establishment and eight children. Then came bankruptcy and humiliation. Everyone had deserted him but one daughter, who had been left a small legacy. With her he lived out his old age, tortured at every turn by the arrogance and ingratitude of this one remaining child, but bearing all with patience,—eating the bitter bread of charity. He was made to wear such terrible clothes that he was ashamed to go into company. While at table he was scolded like a schoolboy. The women, of course, sympathized with the poor girl who was obliged to support an old fellow who refused so ungenerously to die, but Strindberg befriended him publicly, sought out his company and found him a most intelligent and lovable man. "You know, now," he once said to King Lear's daughter, "what a burden it is to nourish a single man . . . consider what a burden the father of a family bears, when he must labor for twelve." But she refused to see that the man's lot was harder than hers, and continued to plague her father with all the meanness and malice of which women are capable. When a doctor came to the pension, Strindberg observed that in his periods of rest he was made to take care of the children, for why, his gifted wife asked, should men be excused from a duty which women continually perform.

These thirty obnoxious women made Strindberg's life a purgatory, so he said, yet they furnished him copy for his *Married* stories, the first volume of which was ready, after three months, for publication. But was he justified in generalizing from the cases of these thirty women, to the whole sex? Yes, replied Strindberg, for they were typical, as his observations in Paris and Stockholm proved. But to tell the truth about women and marriage proved a difficult task for him. "A very old-fashioned, superstitious reverence for the mother" held him back at the beginning, and if, in the course of writing, he overcame this feeling completely and spoke his mind freely and even brutally, in the end he was ashamed and felt the need of punishment. Naturally he went to his wife for a motherly reproof.

"What have you done that you look so unhappy?" she asked.

"I have written a book!"

"So? What is it about?"

"It is about women."

"Have you said handsome things about them?"

"No, I haven't, but you must not read it. I regret it very much."

"But why, then, do you write what you later regret, my child?"

Strindberg explained that he could not help it, he must do everything in his power to solve the pressing question on which so many good heads had cracked. She must bear in mind, however, that what he said in this book was largely "theoretical."

In the *Married* stories Strindberg maintained that "Woman is not a slave, for she and her children are supported by her husband's work. She is not oppressed, for nature has ordained that she should live under the protection of the man while she fulfills her mission in life as mother. Woman is not man's intellectual equal, the man, on the other hand, cannot bear children. She is not an essential factor in the great work of civilization. This is man's domain, for he is better able to grapple with spiritual problems than she. Evolution teaches us that the greater the difference between the sexes, the stronger and more fit will be the resulting offspring. Consequently, the aping of the masculine, the equality of the sexes, means retrogression and is utter folly, the last dream of romantic and idealistic socialism."

Against the prevalent craze of women to enter industry, become independent and rival men in their own field, Strindberg contended in various writings. In the first place, he reminded the "emancipation" enthusiasts that women already have a calling appointed by nature, that of housewife and mother, which is necessary for the continuance of the race and fully as important as any of the labors or provisions of men. If the race is to continue, some women must bear children and thus suffer the "humiliation" of being supported by their husbands. It is possible, however, as Strindberg suggests, that the female sex should in the future be divided into two classes, the fruitful and the sterile. The former could resign themselves to being "slaves," while the sexless, the sterile, could ape the men and compete with them in the labor market. The movement for the emancipation of women was, after all, the work of a small minority and had not touched the generality of women. Strindberg felt that the "equality of the sexes" or rather, as he sometimes preferred to put it, the tyranny of the weaker over the stronger, was a theory which should not be generalized.

He also reminded the feminists that "every time a woman wrests an appointment from a man, there is one more old-maid or prostitute." This was an obvious conclusion which they had overlooked. Also, they failed to see that it is a gross injustice to allow women to compete freely in the labor market without first freeing the husbands and fathers from a part of their duties as bread-winners. As it is, the whole burden is thrown on the man and, indeed, the folly has gone so far that a poor husband is expected to support a rich wife. If men and women are to be economically equal, great reforms must be carried out, the family must be scrapped, and love and the rearing of children given over to the management of the state. But the family, Strindberg maintained in spite of what he had suffered in his own ménage, is the fundament of civilization. With its disintegration, European culture would pass away like the greatness of Rome, leaving only echoes and ruins and the shrill laughter of women. Even when the utmost had been done to equalize the sexes and render them indistinguishable, and all the necessary reforms carried out to balance their rights, there would still remain the intellectual, moral and physical superiority of the male which his counterpart, his envious weaker mate, would strive in vain to remove.

Like Schopenhauer, Strindberg was convinced of the natural inferiority of woman. She stands midway between the child and the man, he believed, and as the child obeys its mother and looks to her for guidance, so the woman should defer to her husband and obey him, for that is the order of nature. Like Schopenhauer also, he ridiculed and condemned the transcendent, idealistic conception of love, with its deification of the woman, especially before the marriage. Platonic love, gallantry—the servile fantastic worship of sex-starved boys—was the most pernicious nonsense. Women's careers, women's rights, women's mysteries and caprices, were blague and delusion. Marriage is motivated by the sex impulse and has its deepest metaphysical ground in the production of offspring, the perpetuation of the race. In modern society, however, economic conditions and the keen struggle for existence make the maintenance of a family, in most cases, painful and precarious, yet the World Will, blind and heedless of consequences, continues to draw the unfortunate lovers into the vortex of its great purpose, so that children are born with a deadly frequency into a world in which there is no place for them, and the parents, powerless against circumstances or their own desires, fight with poverty and their increasing responsibilities, growing old and weary, losing love and friendship and their precious sense of humor, falling further in arrears every day in a hopeless contest, until old age, death or suicide, drops a faded curtain on a private tragedy, too protracted and inglorious for tears or cartharsis. When the sexual urge is voluntarily thwarted, the situation is of course temporarily relieved, but the ultimate consequences of celibacy, according to Strindberg, are ill health, disease, or madness. When Pietism, or the exalted notions of idle women, constrain a man to repress his desires, or when poverty enjoins celibacy on a married couple, the very worst consequences are to be expected. For this problem of celibacy in marriage or for the alternative Malthusian difficulty, Strindberg remarks, the state-supported scientists offer no solution.

In those marriages in which economic conditions are favorable to the rearing of children, "blue blood" sometimes renders childbirth or nursing difficult or impossible, or the wife may be too much occupied with her career to give it the time. When a man is so unfortunate as to choose a blue-stocking, an idle pretentious woman, for a wife, he is almost certain to come to grief. In *A Doll's House* (one of Strindberg's stories), the wife is cured of her platonic love and other such caprices, and Ibsen's Nora reproved and corrected. It is a curious fact that Strindberg, for all his wildness and bizarrie, takes quite a practical, matter-of-fact view of marriage, though it is none the less dear to him on that account. For a happy marriage, he maintained, husband and wife must be careful, good, and economical. Love and children, a clean orderly household with a well supplied table, does the rest. He thus opposes the idealistic, impossible demands of Ibsen and Björnson, giving us a picture of domestic bliss as sweet and smug and prosaic as Dickens himself could have imagined. The husband comes home from his work, kisses his wife, plays with the children, eats a hearty dinner, reads his paper, becomes absorbed in his work, then retires with his loyal loving wife. This was nuptial bliss, a type of quiet happiness which Strindberg himself (according to his own account) enjoyed too seldom to ever tire of. Like Strindberg, the heroes of his stories are always faithful and devoted and their love continues even when their wives become emancipated and torture them, or grow old and homely, falsifying the romantic image of the beloved. In *The Phoenix* the wife fades until her husband finds she bears no resemblance to the bright pretty girl he betrothed years before. As she grows older, bears children and works in the kitchen, she loses all trace of beauty, yet his love remains the same. After a while, she dies and he marries a girl who resembles his wife as she was in the first bloom of her youth. But this second marriage is not a happy one. He is haunted by the memories of the old mother and the fresh young girl he had betrothed in his youth. As death approached, he felt a great longing for her alone, for the old mother who had always been so full of kindness and forgiving, who had cooked and cared for him and the children, and in his last moments he realized that she had been the dearest of all. (It will be remembered that Strindberg himself, far from coldness or a change of heart, grew tender and generous when he observed his wife's fading charms.)

The picture of constancy, though, is not always so bright. When the object of the devotion is a fatuous blue-stocking or a coarse, pretentious, unfeeling woman, the result is a tragedy. In *The Breadwinner,* a story of the second series (1885) we see the hero, a writer like Strindberg, working day and night to complete his manuscripts for the publisher, his overspent brain spinning fancies and inventions—weary, exhausted, at the end of his strength. The purpose of all this labor is to provide luxuries for his wife, a vain pretentious fool of a woman of the sort that Strindberg loves to describe. Under the influence and encouragement of cognac, of her dear lady friend, and the numerous women about the place, she makes the poor writer as miserable as can be. Her lady friend encourages her to revolt from the tyranny of her husband, to demand more money, to have him confined in an asylum,—anything for vengeance on a man who will not crawl at the feet of women and admit their superiority. The wife's great lament is that her husband does not understand her, while his only offence is that he explains to her again and again that she is no such great matter to understand, and the wonder would be if she could really understand him. When the husband is publicly attacked by his wife's friends, he feels in honor bound to defend himself, yet it is no easy matter to maintain his self respect and the love of his wife. When the struggle becomes too great for him, he commits suicide, whereupon his wife faints and everyone rushes to give her assistance and commiseration. The reckless exaggeration and passionate emphasis of this story suggest that Strindberg is relating a phase of his own married life and the scene in a pension and other circumstances put it beyond doubt.

It is clear that, though, as Strindberg says, he based these stories largely on the married lives of various friends and the thirty women in the pension where he lived, much has also been drawn from his own personal experiences. Each story of the set portrays a situation reminiscent of some aspect or section of Strindberg's own married life, and the problems in almost every case are drawn from the rich vicissitudes of his own experience. The power and vindictive force of the delineations owes much to that circumstance. In portraying the luckless lives of his friends, he is expounding and defending himself. It is worth noticing that divorce, the natural solution of the marriage of "a worthy man" and an incorrigible blue-stocking, is never recommended and occurs only once in the book under special circumstances, while birth-control, the usual solution of the Malthusian difficulty of increasing families, is viewed with horror. When in *Corinna* (1885) the husband finds that his wife has made use of contraceptives, he is inexpressibly shocked that a woman of superior lineage should so contravene the intention of nature and refuse to reproduce her stock. Strindberg stood firm all his life in his opposition to anything so monstrous or unnatural, for a marriage without children was to his mind no marriage at all. That a man holding such practical and conservative views of marriage should be indicted for blasphemy will always appear somewhat strange. The explanation is to be found in his violent attacks on the upper class, his derisive, insulting remarks on religion, and the broad political radicalism of the book. Socialism, though he does not explicitly say so, is the one solution of the over-population problem. When economic goods are more equitably distributed, there will be room enough for all the children of men, who will then cover the earth and reproduce like the birds and beasts, without fear.

Strindberg had not intended to give offence in religious or political matters, but to throw down the gauntlet before the women's party. When, therefore, he received a telegram, in Switzerland, announcing that he had been indicted in Sweden for blasphemy and for scoffing at the scriptures and sacraments, it came, as he said, like a thunderbolt out of the blue. But Strindberg was not deceived by this preposterous charge. The outraged women were behind it and there was no doubt about it. "The fury of the feminists," he wrote, "and the formidable party which they formed, may be easily imagined when one remembers that they demanded the confiscation of my book and brought a lawsuit against me," cleverly, under the cover of religion. The fact that this charge was taken seriously and prosecuted proved without question the depravity of the times, in which religion and women were so egregiously confused. Men had forsaken religion to worship woman, not Astarte or Ishtar, not the principle of love and fertility, but the sexless, pretentious harpies, idle-wives and blue-stockings. He had spoken his mind on religion and morals and the upper classes, had shocked and dismayed his contemporaries. Still all had passed over. Everything had been forgiven but this exposal of women. This was too much, for women had replaced God and were now inviolable.

But though the first volume of *Married* was undoubtedly, as Hedén says, the most moralistic book that had ever been written in Sweden, the morals inculcated were not those of Pietism nor suitable to the times, and the scoffing satire on religion in the first story, *The Wages of Virtue* was horribly unprecedented. Though the feminists were unquestionably shocked at the bitter exposal of their position, and dismayed by the lack of anything like gallantry or special concessions to the weaker sex, the blasphemy was after all the ground of the indictment. In this story, *The Wages of Virtue,* confirmation and the communion are represented as impressive hocus-pocus designed by the aristocrats to obfuscate the lower class and keep them in their place. Of his hero Strindberg says: "His confirmation took place in the spring. The moving scene in which the lower class promise on oath never to interfere with those things which the upper classes consider their privilege, made a lasting impression on him. It didn't trouble him that the minister offered him wine bought from the wine merchant, Högsted, at sixty-five öre the pint, and wafers from Littstroem, the baker, at one crown the pound, as the flesh of that great agitator, Jesus of Nazareth, who was done to death nineteen hundred years ago. He didn't think about it, for one didn't think in those days, one had emotions." Such passages as this gave occasion to the unexpected charge of impiety. But the story occasioned the greatest horror on a different account. In its whole tendency it was highly erotic and unseemly. A boy's struggle with his sexual desires, the celibacy enjoined by Pietism, the temptation to the boyhood sin; then, the church's malediction against that sin, and its subversive consequences; the lure of women, Freudian dreams, mortifications of the flesh, the resulting invalidism and insanity (the wages of virtue), and the author's open defence of sexual intercourse in youth as a hygienic remedy, made up a picture which was frightfully unacceptable to his critics.

The question, now, was whether Strindberg should return to Stockholm to meet the charges or remain in Switzerland in lofty contempt of them. His friends, particularly Björnson, urged him to go, arguing that his failure to appear at court might be construed as cowardice, for the least penalty for his offence was two years of hard labor. It was not a purely personal affair, they said, but a matter which affected the general right of free speech. He had no right to stay away. On the other hand, his wife obstinately opposed his going and finally took to her bed, though the nature of her illness, as he says in *The Confession of a Fool,* he could make nothing of. Also, "she was secretly afraid that I might escape from her strict guardianship and, worse still, that my appearance in court before the public would give the lie to the rumors concerning my mental condition which she had so sedulously disseminated." So he speaks in his "most terrible book." In another place he explains that the doctor had told him that his wife had only a few years to live, at which he had declared that at her death he would shoot himself.

When Strindberg learned if he failed to appear at the trial, his publisher, Bonnier, would be held responsible, he hesitated no longer but set out on the fateful journey toward his accusers in Stockholm, his intense excitement lending a strange daylight reality and distinctness to all the common objects on the way, and his morbid conscience eased perhaps by the threats of punishments and the unknown dangers awaiting him in Sweden. At Hamburg, he broke into tears but at Kiel, discovering a good omen, his spirits went up and his courage. In Copenhagen, he received the warning that he would be arrested the moment he entered Swedish territory. But, on arriving in an outpost town, he was pleasantly surprised to find no policemen but only the most courteous officials. Presently, however, one of them exclaimed: "Here is a telegram for Mr. Strindberg which will prevent him from proceeding on his journey!" Strindberg threw back his head and straightened his back, ready for the blow. The warrant for my arrest? But no, it was a telegram from a theatre-director who wished to produce his drama, *Lucky Pehr* and begged to see Strindberg at once. He sighed, with an uneasy sense of triumph.

On arriving in Stockholm, he was surrounded by many friends and admirers and as he listened to their exclamations and hurrahs, which echoed through half the city, the prison seemed far off indeed. He breathed deeply the air of his beloved home-land and remarked that the poisonous atmosphere had apparently lifted. "Whatever comes of it," he said, "I will do my duty." Thereupon

he was conducted through the town which he had left so ig-
nominiously in a procession of triumph. The impeachment had
made him a man of the hour, a hero of the people. The socialists,
the radicals, forgot that he was a reactionary who had fought
tooth and nail their new cult of women, forgot his two-edged
vicious sword, and remembered only that he was now a martyr
to the precious cause of freedom. Strindberg was undoubtedly
flattered by these ovations, but repressed his ambition. The role
he was called on to play, he considered a false one. He was expected to be a reformer, a tribune of the people, a leader of a
party, everything but what he was—a poet. At one point of the
affair, he confessed, when the enemy threatened to become too
strong, he was tempted to play the demagogue in real earnest,
to open the sluice-gates and unloose the repressed passions and the
old Titan powers, to enact, in short, a dazzling dangerous part.
Yes, he was willing to be the grand sacrifice if need be, to deliver himself over as a scapegoat for the people. From the moment he received the fateful telegram, he had felt himself con-
secrated to some such purpose. He had already dreamed during
the summer, so he said, of healing mankind by "abstemiousness
and simplification," and now in the autumn, as a popular hero,
he turned to vegetarianism, sobriety, even temperance, cleansing
and purifying himself for the sacrifice, or perhaps, like the Hindu
sage, to ward off the threatening danger.

Strindberg's doubts and self-criticism, however, did not permit
him to carry out with pomp and inflexibility his grandiose, but
unaffected postures. For that, a stronger character was needed
or a simpler mind. Many times he forswore life with tragic
resolutions, many times he deserted his wife forever,—some absurd triviality detained him. No sooner had he swung himself
into the starlight and elevation of a heroic resolve, than some
friend haled him for a drink, or an unfinished manuscript caught
his eye. Many men are withheld from heroism and the grand
struttings of the spirit by a sense of humor. Strindberg was rarely

bothered in this way. When his sudden throwing off of the tragic mask did strike him as ludicrous and anticlimactic, he laughed a bitter laugh, as became him, only to fling himself more violently than ever into some new role of Judas, Paracelsus, or the Redeemer. This time, being indicted for blasphemy of religion, he became a religious ascetic. Nor was this an easy role for him when one considers the importance he attached to rich food, strong drinks, and particularly, absinthe. It did not last long. It occurred to him that since the archbishop condoned dancing and card playing, it was nonsense for "the Chief of Radicals" to drink water. Besides, his abstemiousness robbed him of his strength and courage so that the doctor advised him to return to his old ways.

On the evening of October 20, 1884, the day of his arrival in Stockholm, *Lucky Pehr* was performed as a celebration in the New Theatre and Strindberg attended in the company of a friend. The mood of the audience, from the beginning warm and appreciative, rose as the play proceeded to frenzied enthusiasm. During the episode in which Pehr becomes a reformer, the gentle satire of both conservatives and reformers aroused violent clapping before the open stage, which mounted in time to a perfect tornado of applause. When the lines of the play concerning religious freedom occurred, the audience rose to its feet, stamped on the floor and waved handkerchiefs, while the actors performed a sad dumb-show, and the hero of the occasion bowed his wild mane of hair many times, with mixed feelings of pride and foreboding. When the performance was over, Strindberg was called out five times, the enthusiasm running so high that many in the gallery threw their hats and coats into the orchestra below.

This extreme ovation! Was this the reward for blasphemy? His table at the hotel was heaped with telegrams of allegiance, with verses, flowers, petitions and proclamations. Hurrahs greeted him in the street and burnt-wine festivals celebrated the great man all over the city. But above everything, loomed the threat of two years' imprisonment. His laurel crown made him uneasy. He perhaps remembered that "the divine animal" in ancient times was fêted and pampered before the sacrifice and that the scapegoat was often treated as a king or a god before his glorious death,—the noble Aztec youths, for instance, reveling in every pleasure; the victims of the Saturnalia crowned and applauded, before they died in vicarious atonement for the people. Strindberg felt that his dazzling honors had perhaps a double meaning.

He felt like a man who has climbed to the highest peak of a mountain, from which he can see to a great distance, but so high that he knows there is no way down but to jump. When one climbs above on the heights, one must, like Brand, leave friends and all the dearest things behind. For that, one must be strong. Strindberg found himself weak. Yet, he would not falter on that account. "I know," he said, "that my book is a great cry from the breast of nature, . . ." a scourge to "the monstrosities of superculture. And still I struck my own wife, I myself. It was a personal sacrifice that was required of me. That I struck the unhappy ones was dismal enough, but it was perhaps the most necessary course. I regret it, now, and will beg for pardon in the next part, *Married II,* that comes out in February, but without recanting a single word." Yes, he regretted having laid hands on Ibsen, Björnson, and their followers, but it was unavoidable. They were principles of evil, as he saw it, which could not be allowed to stand uncontested.

Strindberg had already broken with Björnson as a result of a fatherly admonishing letter he had received, while in Switzerland, urging him to return to Sweden. Of all things, Strindberg could least endure protectiveness. He found the letter highly presumptuous and penned a reply which began: "Your Majesty, I have received your imperial command and have the honor to completely overlook it. Dear brother! Your shamelessness makes you petty. . . . If you prattled less and read more, you might have progressed as far as I have. Take, now, the counsel of a mind which is stronger than yours, a mind which has no need of the powerful support of the charming sex! Do not be old-fashioned, a romantic!" One sees that the close friendship of Strindberg and Björnson had been caught on the reef which threatened it all the time, the woman question. Neither Björnson nor Ibsen, continues Strindberg, has stood alone in the fight as he has, for they have always been surrounded by devoted enthusiastic women, while he is lonelier than any other man, even his wife being against him. Then, out unto the heights! he cries, to meet the great spirit of nature, and turn one's back, if one has a mind, to the whole race of women. He warns Björnson not to interfere with his books or his affairs and signs himself, "Your former friend—A. S."

This letter, which must have hurt the proud Norwegian not a little, did not apparently interfere with his friendship, for, as the trial was beginning, he wrote an article for a Stockholm paper describing the *Married* proceedings as a scandalous, immoral attempt to repress the freedom of the mind by brute force. Although, of course, he was utterly at variance with Strindberg's doctrine of women and was, in fact, one of the woman worshippers attacked in the *Married* stories, he stood firm on the ground of fair play and answered for his adversary's sincerity. He would cross swords with Strindberg in the open field but not have him stabbed in the back. Strindberg, on reading this article, was much heartened in his own affair and all softness and conciliance toward Björnson. "Pardon me my pettiness," he telegraphed. Yet he was not willing to reestablish their old friendship. They were too opposed on the woman-question to allow of any true understanding. Besides, Strindberg was still afraid of Björnson and did not dare to come under his influence again. His retaliation was an attempt to kill his adversary's pride and self-confidence, for it was that in particular which paralyzed him. But the great Norwegian writer was not to be vanquished in this way. Strindberg had, as he complained, thrown vitriol in the face of his faithful friend, yet he continued to advise him and reprove him like an older brother, and in a manner which set Strindberg's teeth on edge. When, for instance, Björnson intimated that Strindberg was perhaps not a fit judge of what was suitable for him to publish, this was too much. What Björnson suggested was that his wild Swedish friend might do well to publish nothing without the sanction of some good person such as his wife. This was the one way to maintain his credit and influence. Such advice was naturally intolerable to Strindberg. The frictions between the two friends accumulated bitterness, Strindberg suspecting that his "former friend" had stirred up ill feeling against him in Stockholm, and once he left a card for Björnson warning him to remain quiet and not to meddle, or else. . . . It was a threat delivered to a stronger man, whom he feared, and could only conquer by arousing fear in him.

Jonas Lie and others give a sad picture of Strindberg at this time, which goes far to excuse his ingratitude and bitter suspicions. A man in whom an inner conflict was continually raging, his hair disordered, falling over a damp sticky forehead, his body giving way under the terrific strain of the trial, the dimensions and dangers of which he saw greatly enlarged through the wide eyes of the child or the poet, his enemies closing in about him, his wife and child sick and helpless, irritated and exasperated by everyone, obliged to live alone, with no weapon against his enemies but his terrible pen which, however, he seemed to believe, could effect certain death. Besides, the conservative press had become quite vicious. He was regarded as a charlatan, a demagogue, a man who blasphemed and attacked public persons and institutions for the sake of private vengeance or for the brief popularity which always belongs to the libeller, the scandal-monger. *The New Realm* had not been forgotten, nor the poems, nor *The Red Room*. Strindberg was an old offender and little mercy was accorded.

In the trial, which began on October 21, 1884, Strindberg, acting as his own attorney, explained quite briefly that the objectionable statements in his story *The Wages of Virtue* should not be considered mockery since he had been dead in earnest. That he had blasphemed God was also an odd charge because he was a believer, a deist. While the court was in recess, Strindberg received many tributes and telegrams. Many great men defended him, even the faculty of Upsala. From labor circles he received the warmest allegiance, but he forbade public demonstrations. On October 17 came the verdict. Acquitted! Immediately the people swarmed and shouted, and celebrated their hero. Ironically enough it was only by help of the police that he avoided the press of his admirers and escaped by the back way from the courthouse. Before the Grand Hotel, he addressed the people, admonishing them to remember they were celebrating not a particular man but the triumph of freedom. The next day he left Sweden, exonerated, fêted, popular as never before. He left in time to avoid the reaction, which often overtakes a triumphant hero acquitted of a serious charge. Although he had come off a victor and for the moment had Sweden at his feet, the victory was not a joyous one and Strindberg, unstrung by the tension, the personal frictions, and the extremity of the protracted affair, was never the same man again. Instead of rejoicing at his escape from two years' hard labor, he perhaps regretted that lost consolation, which might have eased his taut nerves and smoothed away the hate and rancor. Instead of composing himself to work on a new masterpiece, which would instruct his accusers in their error, he brooded on a great revenge.

XVII

ATHEISM

WHEN Strindberg returned to Switzerland, he found his sick wife apparently quite well and happy but "absent-minded." The evening with her compensated him for all his sufferings during the six weeks in Sweden. But in the morning he found that his family were settled in a disreputable pension frequented by students and light women, in whose company his wife felt herself quite at home. When he remonstrated, she reminded him of their contract of mutual freedom, called him a jealous fool and a snob. It was her mania, as that of all weak and inferior brains, to reduce everything to one level. Nothing pleased her better than to force her famous husband into low company, for that was a refutation of his greatness. (*The Confession of a Fool*.) To these matrimonial frictions were added embarrassments of a financial kind. For three months after the trial, so he said, he was unable to work. Moreover, in Sweden, the publishers were determined against him, while the Paris papers paid next to nothing. Already he felt the sting of poverty and privation. In his imagination he saw himself marooned in Switzerland, confined to one room with his whole family, the children's shoes and clothes giving way, the winter approaching without wood to burn. What was to be done? He could become a blacksmith like his character Sten. Though he would probably have ended just as sadly, in sickness and suicide, yet his adherence to Rousseau and the utility principle made it seem a possible career and more than once he considered it as a solution. The role of a great man and reformer seemed a delusion and honest labor the only reality. But, alas, honest labor would not support his family. No, the famous writer, honored in Sweden, France, Switzerland, Germany, would be forced back to Paris to eke out a precarious living as a contributor to French periodicals. The contest with the upper class, however dear to his heart, now threatened his very existence and he felt himself too weak to persist in it. Had he a right to sacrifice wife and children for mankind or his capricious pride? He watched his children at play with sad prophecies and misgivings.

Strindberg's critics, even his friend Jonas Lie, often complained that in his preoccupation with the economic needs of mankind, he had forgotten the requirements of the spirit, attempting to solve all social questions by a better distribution of bread. If such a view was one-sided it is not to be wondered at, for there were times when the simple requirements of life appeared to Strindberg of immeasurable value and all else hypocrisy and waste.

Then came the inevitable reaction of the press. Strindberg had escaped justice; the laws were shown powerless against outrage and blasphemy, for the perpetrator had been honored as a hero. The role of martyr for the people, which in the eyes of his followers had placed him beside Jesus of Nazareth, was pure humbug. Fortunately, said one article, he had failed to win his martyr's crown. The idea that Strindberg had been persecuted was another piece of nonsense. No one had been pampered and honored so much. The great Swedish writer Snoilsky protested against the *Married* proceedings, not because he sympathized with Strindberg's polemic, which he thought monstrous, fanatical and swinish, but because the trial only called attention to the blasphemy, which otherwise might have been overlooked, aroused sympathy for the author and his views, since it made a martyr of him, and branded the opposing party as tyrants and oppressors. He was surprised to hear that Strindberg was personally quite mild and lovable. How were such qualities to be combined with the hatred and revengefulness in his writings? Certainly those who had rescued him from prison could demand better things of him in the future.

But no, Strindberg was determined upon vengeance. Instead of devoting himself to a worthy, unchallengeable work which would have silenced his enemies he wrote an account of his experiences in Sweden during the trial, which turned out such a bitter arraignment of the whole proceeding, and so back-handed and libelous, that Bonnier refused to publish it. *The Arrest Journey* was unworthy, he thought, and too many firebrands had already been thrown upon the public conscience. But his publisher's objection was, to Strindberg's way of thinking, nothing but undemocratic, romantic nonsense. By birth a democrat, he was not apt to cherish the upper-class notions of dignity and propriety. He would have his revenge and carry on the fight, let what come of it would, and soon he found another publisher. Abnormally sensitive to criticism, even as early as this, he had been much offended by the attitude of both friends and enemies. The socialists had been unable to see that his program was the only hope of socialism. Young Sweden had criticized his works and taunted him as a reactionary, he, whose name alone was a provocation, a fanfare of trumpets marshalling thousands to the fight. The moderns, the gyneolators, could not forgive Strindberg his "homely truths about women." They had dethroned him to make place for a blue-stocking, but he paid them back in *The Arrest Journey*, in the plays and novels, full measure. Strindberg, as he explained in *The Arrest Journey,* had continually attacked the upper class, ridiculed their pretensions, stormed against their privileges, and this "the son of a servant," of all others, had no right to do. Had he been a member of the upper class he might have been awarded a seat in the Swedish Academy, as a plebeian he was threatened with prison. He, a plebeian, had enjoyed the privilege of education in Upsala and a trip to Italy, but instead of dying with admiration and gratitude, he had expressed himself in caustic ridicule. To the powers this was unbearable. Then he had written a sympathetic history of the lower class, *The Swedish People,* and a hateful satire on society, *The New Realm.* Finally, as a crowning insult, he had written *Married,* an open attack upon "Women's emancipation," a movement having its whole origin and life in the upper class. Here he had shown his usual vindictiveness against the perversities of the aristocratic culture. There will come the time, he says, when the suckling children will die at the breast of the Kultur-mothers, the cows wander away, industries subside, merchants cease to bargain,—with silence, decay, and resolution. But the Russian nihilists are the people! They see clearly that civilization is decadence and therefore live simply, close to nature, awaiting the time when the strong shall come into their own. As they see the trend of the age, that men no longer wish to be men, women ashamed to be women, the collapse of the demoralizing culture seems close at hand.

Strindberg, according to his own account, is obliged to journey to Stockholm in order to lead the people to victory. He must leave his writing desk and his slippers behind, and his sense of humor, for the people demand a sacrifice. During his stay in Stockholm, so he relates, a curious visitor calls him Lucifer, for it is by no natural means, he intimates, that his bitterest enemies have died within so short a period. (This is one of the first indications of Strindberg's belief, later so open and apparent, that he was possessed of supernatural powers and could wound or kill at a distance by hatred and vengeful thoughts.)

But if Strindberg indulged himself for a moment with this delusion of grandeur, and believed himself Lucifer, with special powers for evil, he was but reflecting a view which had become quite general in Sweden. An Archbishop delivered a thundering reproach and a warning against Strindberg and his followers before the Swedish Academy. These realists, he affirmed, deal only with drunkards, fallen women, seducers, atheists, and such pestilence should be barred from every decent family. But the realists themselves disclaimed the excesses of their young leader. The deep guilt was Strindberg's and his alone. Even his friends were dead against him. Branting wondered whether he intended to throw dirt on his wife as well as other women. "The devil take the man who has set one half of mankind against the other," cried another. Some regarded Strindberg as a liar, a betrayer of the youth, the corrupter of their morals. Thus, in Liktor John Personnes' book *The Strindberg Literature and the Immorality of Students,* Strindberg is portrayed as the corrupter of youth and the author of all evil. He is made out a satanic trickster, a shameless liar. In the end the author calls upon the authorities to sue him for immorality. Strindberg's publisher (Bonnier) he compares to a receiver of stolen goods or the mistress of a brothel. Hedén makes the interesting comment that Personne's book "had the success that one would expect; the immorality remained the same, Mr. Bonnier became rich, Strindberg famous and beggarly poor, and Mr. Personnes was made a bishop." Somewhat later Strindberg's old enemy, Wirsén, also launched a diatribe against him, condemning each successive work with a scholarly, moralistic fury.

For Strindberg, it was like the Day of Judgment with every voice against him, every bony finger and every glaring eye, accusing. In *Toward Damascus* scenes occur in which the Stranger (Strindberg) is damned and cursed by everybody and once a long writ of excommunication is read in his presence which so terrifies him that he flees to his wife for protection. No doubt the avalanche of hatred and abuse at this time took deep root in Strindberg's mind, strengthening those morbid tendencies which were already present from the first and furnishing much material for the fire and religious frenzy of *Toward Damascus,* and other such passion plays and moral writings. No doubt, also, he enjoyed the glamour of sudden power, for, though he was the object of general abuse, no writer in Sweden had ever elicited such a general interest, and no one's name was heard more often than his. In a novel written at this time, *The Secret Way,* the hero (Strindberg) proudly refuses the gold and honors proffered by the upper class, declines to be a leader of the proletariat. Standing alone, he has something more desirable than any tribute of theirs,—he has power. Alone with his power, Strindberg will meet the stream of hate.

If Strindberg sometimes thought of himself as the scapegoat who must suffer vicariously for the people or sin to appease the fates and rescue mankind, his experiences are in large part responsible for the delusion. In Stockholm he was celebrated as a popular hero, a savior and leader of the people, and honored like a suffering god. On his return to Switzerland he continued his war against the upper class and the upper-class women. But gradually everyone turned against him, with curses and abuse, even his friends and his wife. He found himself alone, an enemy of society, penniless, without hope, paralyzed by the hate around him. The idea that he was a chosen sacrifice fated to suffer for others, was naturally very attractive to Strindberg, for it would have explained his tragic lot and the special degree of his suffering to perfection; but he was still quite unprepared for the acceptance of such an extreme religious notion; Darwin, Buckle, Hartmann, Rousseau, Spencer, J. S. Mill were still his teachers and their doctrines were widely at variance with any such notion, however alluring it might be. Suffering and the evils of life, according to Strindberg's present view, are to be explained by natural causes, by the world will or a degenerative civilization, never by divine appointment of a scapegoat to atone by his special sufferings for the sins of many. Thus, while he was tempted by the role of scapegoat, he could not bring himself to assume it nor approach the royal sacrificial stone quite seriously. The idea was out of accord with his world view and he was still too young in sin and suffering not to feel the bitter absurdity of it.

The effect of his journey and trial for blasphemy was, as a matter of fact, quite subversive of what little religious faith he had. The hypocrisy and compromise, the smugness and cruelty of religious people had always offended him, but now these qualities appeared to him in deeper colors. As he looked out over the sea and "saw a great blue nothing on which the eye sought in vain for an object, the ear in vain for a sound" he was seized with a feeling that "he had come to the end of his course and stood directly before death itself." As he reviewed his stormy career with its pain of love and burden of striving, torn with hate and disillusion, seeking for some reason in all those riddles and frustrations, which had taunted him along the way, he was seized with a special doubt of Providence. As he saw his children at play he asked himself how he could have risked their life and happiness by his reckless polemics. Yet with his education and temperament, could he have done otherwise? No, every action was determined, not by a wise all-seeing Providence, but by fates and furies unappeasable. During the *Married* proceedings, when he felt the whole world against him, he had climbed to the heights like Brand and given himself over to God. But, when he perceived how poorly he was repaid, how the furies raged against him, allowing injustice and self-seeking to triumph everywhere, "he came gradually to the notion that the world could be directed by quite other powers than a beneficent, personal God." Fate was the great engineer and Fate he no longer sought outside himself but within his own soul. "There lay his Fate, and in all the other selves rested the destiny of the world."

As he reconsidered his career as a reformer he saw how mad and useless it had been. He had preached universal freedom but the laborers "stoned him" when he went too far, for they thought only of themselves. As for the servants and lackeys, they preferred their slavery and its privileges to an onerous freedom. Every class in society was struggling selfishly for its own advantage. The labor party used its victory to promote its own affairs and, like the upper class, could not be brought to sacrifice a jot for the universal good. The law-suit and the contact with the people whose cause he was fighting had made Strindberg a skeptic, doubtful of human nature or of any remedy for social and economic evils. By 1886, he had lost all faith in Socialism and the people to whom he had given his energies and devotion. Human motivation, as he now saw it, is based upon egoism and that is the one mainspring of all striving, however it may adorn or conceal itself. Like Olaf (of the verse edition), Strindberg is now the disillusioned reformer, weary and disheartened, his great work turning to an illusion and a lie. There was truth in his assertion that that drama would be the tragedy of his life. For it seemed that every great undertaking of his would end in skepticism and apostasy. Followers of Strindberg would have a sad surprise to see him forswear his whole program. Knut Hamsun, who read Strindberg with the greatest enthusiasm, admired his fighting powers which overwhelmed his enemies and forced them to the wall, the richness of his gifts which gave a thousand answers for one, and swore by all the gods he was right, would now have to see Strindberg recant all his arguments and tear down the whole structure he had raised. This was a disturbing thing about Strindberg and probably no one ever forgave him for it. The moment he had convinced you, he turned face and argued with more violence and persuasiveness than ever, for an opposite view.

One of the principal reasons for Strindberg's backsliding from Socialism was that a more detailed and thorough study of the ramifications of economic questions and a reading of such authors as Marx, Lasalle, etc., had convinced him that the matter was far more complex than he had formerly supposed. In his investigations in Europe he observed many laborers, some poor but some rich. Occasionally a man from that class rose, by thrift and sobriety, to the role of capitalist, sold his products, paid his laborers, enriched the town and made money for himself. But in these cases the laborers after a time were more than likely to strike, declaring that the capitalist was a thief who lived parasitically on the profits of their work. Strindberg's sympathies here are with the capitalist. If the laborers were to take over the factory, profits would decline, the trade fall away and no good would ever come of it. Strindberg had a horror of this kind of Socialism. Marx, the great prophet of Socialism, was not the unbiased investigator that he is accounted. He was influenced by his milieu which was always, whether Berlin or Köln, an industrial center. It was natural for him to regard the world as a great industrial organization, and to make no special account of farm laborers, fishermen, servants, etc. Also, he was caught like everyone else in the irresistible world-streams of thought. Hegel, at first his master, though he gave him up, continued to exercise on him the greatest influence. As a Jew, Marx could never become an optimistic ideologist like the philosopher, Hegel. Rather, at heart he was a party agitator. Yet the system he built up was a rationalistic one, attempting to order and harmonize the manifold, ever-changing, bewildering appearances of life, and as such was more an expression of the ordering passion of the subjective Spirit, than a true account of the objective facts. But the chaotic, evanescent, germinal flux of reality, thinks Strindberg, has always resisted the world ordering of philosophers and the lawfulness of science, and with its teeming disorder, gone its own way elusively.

The classes in society, Strindberg now believed, and all the individuals which compose them, are selfish and shortsighted as they have always been. There is nowhere in history any sign of progress. Armies, kings, and empires cross the stage in futile sequence,—reformers, saints, kings and regicides rise in triumph, apply their medicaments and save the world. Everything remains as before with no solution of the riddles and miseries of the people. In all those fretful strivings and changing scenes of enterprise, no issue or advance. The old gods whisper sadly among themselves, lamenting the blindness and inconsequence below, infirm, powerless to change the course of history, with Telos dead and Fate triumphant. Everything is for the best, they say, and shudder at the thought. New dynasties appear with fanfares and rejoicing. A few years pass by and the people crave the old order. The Germans won the Franco-Prussian War. Did that mean that they were culturally superior? Was it music, art or science that led them to victory? Rather cannons and primitive brutality. The lower stage of evolution scored a victory over the higher, a thing which may happen again and again. Is European civilization, Strindberg asked himself, advance or decadence, but could find no answer. The truth was, as he saw it, that evolution brings forth new forms, mastodons, elephants, apes, and men, but there is little to choose between them, and in the long run, perhaps, no progress and man a decadent ape.

While Strindberg made this reckoning with life and the ways of Providence, hunger and want crept closer about the house. At night he heard the threatening danger, like a flood rising to engulf him, and could not sleep, for "in eight days (he knew that) death would be there. Famine in a civilized society for a man and his small family. The means to existence had come to an end, resources exhausted, the springs dried up, his labor-market ruined." This was his reward, at thirty-six, for having been more industrious than others, for having labored for society. It was intolerable. Perhaps, he thought, society had a right to starve him out since he had been its enemy? But no, he had only attacked the ruling class, "its prejudices, superstitions, dogmas and oppressions and the new sacrament of the female." Here he had been within his rights, yet an avenging, perverted justice sought him out like a criminal, confiscating food, hopes and life itself. The vindictiveness and the many miscarriages of justice, the smug happiness of the wicked and the miseries of the virtuous suggested anything but the wise government of Providence. As the winds of reality flung his ship about, on the precarious verge of sinking forever, Strindberg felt that his only hope was to lighten the ship. "God, heaven and Eternity must overboard." He must live henceforth for himself and his family, allowing causes and principles and mankind, to shift for themselves. Egoism is the only principle of action, all else is hypocrisy and imposition. To live for oneself and one's family, to enjoy in peace the dear necessities and the homliest desideratives. How wistfully sweet was life and its simple pleasures when threatened!

About this time Strindberg read Ingersoll, "an inspired atheist, full of faith and love and hope," and was much impressed. "Then he read Tolstoi who construed Christ, quite simply, as an atheist, and yet retained the kernel of Christianity, if to be sure there was a kernel there." The consequence of all Strindberg's reckonings and reflections was that presently he became an ardent atheist. Unable to prove his position he brought it forth as a categorical postulate: "It must be so, that there is no God, or we are lost." Better no God at all, he thought, than an evil one. The Zoroastrian alternative, that God exists but linked in battle with another, evil God, a view which appealed to him a few years before, does not occur to him now.

Having arrived at Atheism, Strindberg became, as his custom was in the matter of faith and advocacy, a perfect zealot. Christianity (and especially Protestantism) as a state religion is simply a powerful instrument in the hands of the upper class for the oppression of the poor. They are taught the vanity of the world, and the sinfulness of ambition or any attempt to rise or better their condition. When the people would have reforms or improvements, the church signs them back to their appointed place and warns them of the vanity of the world, and the impiety of disturbing God's order there. In a Catechism for the Lower Class, written at this time, Strindberg explained that religion is a need arising in a lower stage of development, which is employed by the upper class to oppress the lower. Yes, and the punishments of religion are damnation to the poor who dare to disobey their masters, and the reward of religion is eternal happiness in heaven for those who labor and suffer for the upper class. Such pronouncements, of frequent occurrence in Strindberg's works, show the direct, passionate, not to say callow nature which his polemic occasionally assumes. Often invective and hate got the better of reason altogether and emotion reigned alone, as in few authors besides.

Strindberg, having now become an atheist, was obliged to revise his whole world view and fit all the parts together. Atheism and Misogyny! How did they agree? It was no doubt a special pleasure for Strindberg to discover that they were as harmonious and interdependent as two views could well be. It was the women, after all, who sponsored this cult of the suffering god, whose weak brains were fed and comforted by superstition,—they who were seen at the churches, and it was a woman, the wife of Constantine, who had imposed "the terrible Christian religion" on Europe. Later, in his plays and novels, he was fond of representing women as religious but mean and wicked. Thus, the heroine of *By the Open Sea,* and the Mother in *Toward Damascus.* Women in general, thought Strindberg, are apt to feel their mental inferiority to men and to seek to overcome it by the superiorities and mystagogeries of religion. Strindberg had already suffered from the snobbery of Pietism and the fine airs of his mother and mother-in-law. Women, feeling their inferiority, will naturally be inclined to deny greatness and merit above their own. Christianity was the great leveler which answered their purposes precisely. They became pious. They could, moreover, be as false and stupid as they pleased, so long as they were pious. Mysticism and secret knowledge were the best defence against the rationality and honest worthiness of men.

It is interesting to observe that Strindberg's new-won Atheism was not proof against a sudden onslaught of good fortune. When, in Paris, he had received an unexpected sum of money, he was beside himself with astonishment and, then, he declared, he believed in God. The same thing happened at this time. He suddenly received one thousand francs and returned to deism, but the sum was soon exhausted by his expenses and he relapsed into atheism. These sudden vicissitudes of faith will seem a bit surprising until it is remembered that Strindberg's world view was always intensely personal. The world was, after all, a pilgrimage of the soul, and if God exists, he must declare himself, and beneficently. Perhaps, too, such deviations of faith are more common than is supposed, Strindberg being no exception in this respect but only in the degree of his confession. However this may be, Strindberg's violent shifts of doctrine were the cause of great astonishment to his contemporaries. A year or two later the brothers Brandes were immensely amused to see him one day a faithful deist, the next a heaven-storming atheist.

In 1886, however, Strindberg's atheism was put to a severe test and almost passed away, by an event in his own house. In Frankfurt am Main, he relates, there lived a wonder-healer who effected cures by the touch of his hand, just as Charcot did in Paris, but unlike Charcot he attributed his powers to God and muttered prayers during his ministrations. "Being a doctor," so he says, he was anxious to expose the charlatan, but refrained and kept his peace, knowing that his opposition to public opinion might bring him and his family to ruin. Yet, as he relates, his silence on this matter was itself dangerous since it could easily be interpreted as assent and inquisitors went about everywhere, "full of suspicion." Strindberg would have loved to denounce this type of therapy, for being an atheist he knew that no help could come from God, and "being a physician" he knew that nothing could occur which was at variance with science.

Then came the event of his daughter's illness and his own essay as a wonder-healer, the curious success of which silenced him quite effectually. He was awakened one night by his wife who announced in the greatest agitation that their seven-year-old daughter was having a severe attack. Strindberg diagnosed the case at once as "Epilepsia nocturna" and prescribed a medicine which reassured his wife, who in turn communicated her confidence to him. But as the prescription failed to take effect and the attack renewed itself with violence, he collapsed, for now death alone was all that could be expected. He felt as though a part of his body were being cut away and he had no power to stay the blow. On the floor by the bed he saw his wife on her knees praying. "Do something," she commanded. "Pray to God to help us," she insisted. But Kant had said that it was beyond the power of prayer to change God's will, "or the laws of nature," added Strindberg. Naturally he did not pray. "She is dying! Pray for her!" cried his wife, beside herself, and Strindberg prayed and laid his hands on the forehead of the child, at which she was marvelously quieted, the convulsions ceased and she breathed easily. As Strindberg prayed the words brought old thoughts to mind, old hopes and a new confidence. Now he felt himself possessed of the power to heal with his bare hands alone, and indeed the child seemed quite relieved as long as he continued the performance, but grew worse again the moment he left off. Toward morning she fell into a deep sleep and was saved; by God's intervention, thought his wife, but Strindberg, though he was much shaken by the whole affair, was not ready to admit this theory. That a stream of nervous energy could be communicated from his fingers to the child was incontestably proved by science (animal magnetism), but how could the stream be awakened by the prayer? To this question he found no answer but mysticism, i.e., secret, unscientific knowledge, and this, as an atheist and naturalist, he was unwilling to accept.

What he does know is that prayer was a solace and a secret resource to him as a boy and later a habit, that his first God was his mother, his recent God a philosophical formula, that in 1885 his miseries and sufferings made a sadistic demon the only possible deity. Prayer he knew to be the resource of all peoples, especially those at a low stage of development, where it appears as a pitiful dodge from the responsibilities and difficulties of life, and suspected it much on this account. Had he been a pantheist he might have explained the strange power of prayer as an out-streaming of the world will, but as an atheist he can only opine that it results from the psychological effect on the worshipper, the sudden enhancement of his powers through hope and confidence. The strange power of prayer is thus explained in a manner agreeable to science, as are the wonder cures of the quack. Strindberg attempts at this time to reduce all occult and disturbing transactions in nature to the solid basis of natural law; yet the very insistence of his explanations betrays an uncertainty in his mind, a sense of the strength of the opposition which was only partially suppressed and with great difficulty, by the assumed rigor and discipline of science. In 1886, however, his mood is that of a thorough naturalist and remains so despite the wonders in life, the evil witching of women, and the apparent curse which hung over him.

The divine Nemesis, the God of vengeance and retribution, had seemed to him in later years more plausible than any other. Some houses it appeared were cursed, an evil fate hanging over their tenants,—bankruptcy, death, lunacy, ruin, and some families likewise seemed to be blighted in every member, due to envious gods or their own past sins. But Nemesis, like other gods, says Strindberg, is a conception arising from fear. Having observed many crushing disasters overtake a single family, seeing them suffer in apparent innocence, we are quick to infer that past sins must have occasioned their steady misfortunes, for we thereby guard ourselves in a fashion from a similar fate and reconcile our conscience to the moral order. In observing instances of divine wrath, however, we frequently select the evil and overlook the good, for if we were to examine the vicissitudes of any family or house without preconception, and over a long enough period, we would find a variety of fortune of every kind.

Moreover, it is an oddity of our minds that we frequently confuse a temporal sequence with a causal and conclude that because a sin precedes a misfortune, it must have caused it. Here the primitive demand of blood for blood, a moral and consoling balance, blinds us to the possibility of any other agency. Again our evil conscience, with which of course Strindberg himself was more than equally proportioned, makes previous sin a plausible and even gratifying explanation of a sudden thronging of adversities. Strindberg himself, so he says, was once tempted by Nemesis. After a four-year literary-social-political quarrel of the most furious character, he was appalled on reviewing the battle-field, to find so many dead enemies. Some had been ruined, one went mad, another died in a tavern, another disappeared suddenly, etc. Strindberg's life had become mysterious and his great powers oppressed and frightened him. His enemies had gone under, one after another, as if by magic. This seemed a great argument for Nemesis. He was clearly under the protection of the powers. Yet, when he came to consider his *triumphant* enemies, he found quite at many of these, men who had won medals, advancement or fortune by opposing him and his writings. A more thorough examination of the battle-field showed some enemies dead but others strong and victorious. There was, after all, nothing to indicate that a partial god had befriended him or that any but natural agencies had been at work. The theory of divine intervention, he concludes, is only the illogic of inferior minds. He had been neither the darling of the gods nor a scapegoat for their wrath, inasmuch as natural causes are sufficient to explain all things,—yes, even his own unbearable miseries.

XVIII

"A CRIME HAD BEEN COMMITTED IN
SECRET,—OR ELSE I WAS MAD!"

CHIEF among Strindberg's vexations at this time and crucially linked with all the rest were the miseries and frictions of his marriage. He had lived through the trial for
blasphemy, had awakened shattered and frightened as from a
nightmare of power and shame. This was not enough. He had
borne the subsequent impact of public hate and resentment, endured poverty, financial anxiety, overwork, exhaustion, all the
while alone in the world, alienated from his friends. The fates
were not appeased. He tortured himself ingeniously, lived deep in
his suspicions, nourishing dangerous doubts and convictions,
tempted by death and the subtle allure of borderline insanity, but
was horrified at their approach. Yet "the powers," of which, in
spite of his occasional disavowals, he loved to imagine himself the
victim, would not cancel his debt. They prepared the finishing
strokes, the final punishment. Across a properly rounded stone
they stretched the body of the impious woman-hater, and, flour-
ishing the knife, prepared to tear out his heart as an offering to
the one woman he loved, his wife, who meanwhile stood by with
mixed feelings of pride, vindication, and pity.

For a long time the storms had shaken the house of Strindberg.
Interludes of intense happiness were broken suddenly by thunder and tension, with sulphur in the air and repressed hatred.

Now the rather melodramatic affair approached a climax and a real explosion threatened. The provocations and troubles were, of course, the old ones but intensified, now, by the incremental force of years of bitter exasperations, by Siri's new waywardness, and by Strindberg's increasing nervousness and morbid suspicions. Under the strain of these and his other adversities he succumbed at times to utter helplessness and despair, for it seemed to him that only suicide or an asylum could be the end of it. While at Ouchy he visited a hospital in the vicinity partly to get a judgment on his case, and partly, we may be sure, to secure evidence of his sanity.

While Strindberg was in Stockholm undergoing trial, his love for Siri quickened by absence, burst into full flame again and he wrote the most ardent letters declaring his passion. In his overwrought condition "everything that was base, ugly, evil, disappeared; the madonna of my first love dream reappeared," and he wove a new halo for her pretty face. "The influence of a good woman had made me more humble and pure-minded," he told an old friend, a reporter. Later he asks himself whether the unfaithful wife would laugh when she read that in the papers. But in response to the love letters and the halo Siri replied with coldness and clever reserve. The unhappiness of their marriage, as she saw it, was due to his inability to understand her, an idea which struck Strindberg as absolutely absurd. When a banquet was given in his honor a toast was proposed to Siri "because she had persuaded her husband to appear before his judges," a turn of events which irritated Strindberg because she had been almost the one person who had urged him to stay in Switzerland.

According to *The Confession of a Fool,* she was distressed by the recognition and admiration he received in the theatre, the street, and the court, and called his judges stupid when they acquitted him. When he returned to Geneva he found his wife and family ensconced in a house full of drunken students and loose women. When he realized that his children had lived in such an environment six weeks and that his wife had made a bosom friend of the worst of the women, he was lost between wonder and dismay. From then on, he says, it was war between them. Her neglect of the children, a fact attested to by Miss Thommesen, was a particular trial to him, for "the little ones were a great factor in my life, and in my darkest moments, when I was almost broken by my isolation, contact with them bound me afresh to life and their mother."

To add to his discomforts the feminists made a counter attack with the result that the Swiss press condemned him, the sale of his books was prohibited and he was obliged to flee, "hunted from town to town" (*The Confession of a Fool*). "Hemmed in like a wild beast" he changed the scene and finally ended in a colony of artists near Paris. Here he found himself in the most disagreeable company imaginable, consisting chiefly of women artists— emancipated, Lesbian, pretentious. Everywhere, these hateful bluestockings with their hermaphroditic literature and their equality mania. When, about this time, Strindberg learned that a woman, whose only claim to fame was her abuse of men, had been admired as a great writer in Sweden, he raged against the stupidity of the world which so misplaced its praise. Yes, the women were spreading a net everywhere and would soon be invincible. Already it was not safe to be a woman-hater, yet women were applauded for their hatred of men. Already people were beginning to think him insane, said Strindberg. There was certainly no fighting a machine like theirs. He determined upon suicide and bid adieu to life once more.

As he examined one day the hotel album with its caricatures of prominent Swedes he was dismayed to see that in his own a lock of hair had been so twisted that it looked like a horn. He demanded an explanation of the proprietor on the point, who, however, having been informed by Siri of Strindberg's condition, explained that the horn he saw was an illusion, for none appeared in the drawing.

One evening the conversation turned upon the doctor who had aroused Strindberg's jealousy in Sweden. When a friend hinted that this doctor enjoyed "a certain reputation"—Strindberg grew angry; "as a conceited fool," he added. Siri grew pale and her mouth gave a cynical twist. Later Strindberg pressed his friend to tell him the truth about the rumors he had heard, but the friend swore he knew nothing. "Moreover, my dear fellow," he said, "if you suspect one man you may be sure there are many." There follows in *The Confession of a Fool* a typical example of Strindberg's subtle analysis: "But from this day onward Marie (Siri), who had been so fond of telling tales, of mentioning the doctor's name in public, that it sometimes seemed as if she were trying to get accustomed to talk about him without blushing, never again alluded to him."

Strindberg now recollected that a play he had read sometime before threw further light on his suspicions. This was *The Wild Duck* by "the famous Norwegian blue-stocking (Ibsen), the promoter of the 'equality-mania'" and obviously, he thought, a veiled attack on his wife's good name and his own honor. The photographer in the play represented Strindberg, who was often so-called on account of the realism of his writings, while the photographer's wife is Siri. The wife in the play had been the mistress of a smelter before her marriage and the money she received from her former lover supported their establishment. The smelter was, of course, the Baron. Also, the wife makes money while her idle husband drinks and dreams. Siri likewise had made a little money from translations, but Ibsen and the publisher perhaps did not know that he, Strindberg, had edited and corrected her work and paid her the full amount. Again the photographer accepts a large sum from his wife's old lover in the way of damages. This was an allusion to Siri's loan which the Baron guaranteed. Everything agreed, though the facts were of course disguised! But the illegitimate child! Strindberg at first could find no remote parallel in his own life. Then he thought of their first child which had died. Yes, that poor baby must have been the Baron's. Strindberg determined upon revenge. "I intended (as he continues in *The Confession of a Fool*) to suggest that Marie should draw up an indictment, or rather a defence, which would clear us both, for both of us had been attacked by the feminists' man of straw; he, doubtless, had been bribed into undertaking the profitable job."

When, however, he broached this matter to his wife, and begged her to confess if her first baby was the Baron's, explaining that she was free at that time, and quite justified, not having accepted any money from him, she turned pale and silent and when he opined that the hero of Ibsen's play was a man of heart who would rather sacrifice his honor than the future of his wife and child, she admitted that the deceived husband was "a noble heart," and was tempted for a moment, says Strindberg, to confess everything. Yet in the end, she was not to be caught. When he returned to her after two hours he saw her sitting in exactly the same position. She had been brooding on her infidelity, thought Strindberg, but perhaps her immobility and excitement were due to consternation at the thought of what she and her children would do now that her husband had gone completely mad.

In a weak moment Siri confessed, according to Strindberg's account, that she had frustrated his attempt to pass her off on a friend and so be rid of her, by deceiving both husband and friend. So, she *had* deceived him. No, she hadn't. Prove it,—if you can. Strindberg is crushed by her treachery. "I bowed my head, I fell on my knees, I whined for mercy." How could she believe that he had tried to get rid of her, he who lived for her and regarded the women who tried to make love to him as evil witches? She relented, soothed and comforted him, burst into tears and praised his generosity which he extended, so she said, even to "the worst of sinners." Strindberg now lived through the darkest days of his whole life. After a long struggle between his delicacy and his jealousy, and unable to resist the basic instinct of the male, he became a spy on his wife's correspondence. The first letter he opened, one from Siri's bosom friend, was taken up with mocking references to his insanity and concluded with the hope that the asylum would soon deliver her "dear Marie" from such a husband. Strindberg watched his wife while she read this letter and observed with horror that she laughed loudly at the objectionable passages. She wanted her freedom, that was clear, and his life-insurance, was his sad conclusion. To find another husband or to remain a merry widow was her heart's desire and no secret to her friends.

At a party they gave during this time the wives did not appear and the men behaved scandalously at dinner. When Strindberg observed one of the officers repeatedly kissing his wife, he waved his billiard cue above their heads, demanded an explanation and would surely have committed murder, he assures us, had not the thought of leaving his children without parents withheld him. Afterwards he called her a prostitute, accused her of perverse inclinations toward her two women friends and forbade her to have anything more to do with them.

Siri had confessed to him that she was mad about one of them and afraid to be alone with her, and that the other was jealous on this account was open gossip. Yes, Strindberg admitted, "he did not believe in sin in the abstract but when individual interests were involved,"—that was another question. He learned from a friend that Siri's perverse tendencies were well known in Scandinavia and her two friends, notorious Lesbians. Happily these objectionable women offended the peasants and were obliged to leave. Strindberg relented and gave them a farewell party at which Siri sung a love song to her departing enamorata, full of passion and sorrow, and betraying so much candid feeling that Strindberg was both charmed and horrified. He plied the masculine "hideous" creature with drinks until she was intoxicated, when, her restraints gone, he saw her kiss his wife sensuously, full on the lips. The affair ended with a brawl in the streets. After her "hermaphroditic" friend had departed Siri was inconsolable and passed through a real love-crisis, fled into the woods to avoid her husband's embraces and be alone with her sorrow. He, for his part, was desperate at the loss of her love. Then, the evening came when he fought with her in the moonlight. "She bit my hands, I dragged her to the river to drown her like a kitten —when suddenly I saw a vision of my children. It brought me to my senses." But, now, he no longer cared to live and determined to shorten his life by liberal recourse to his beloved absinthe (though he admits that it destroyed his nerves) "and in the meantime play billiards to calm my excited brain."

It is interesting to observe that this account of Strindberg's life in the artists' resort near Paris, taken from *The Confession of a Fool,* is out of all accord with the reports of the same period in his letters to his friend Heidenstam. There he speaks of the love and the friendship of his dear Siri, which supports him in his darkest moments, of the complete confidence existing between them, and the perfect freedom they enjoy, of the vile, unfounded rumors about his innocent wife. His life at this period is painted in bright colors. Women, good food, billiards and credit. The party at which Strindberg found the officer kissing his wife is now described as a brilliant orgy, like a scene from *The Decameron,* with music, dance, girls, reckless drinking, and wild joyfulness. In comparing these divergent accounts it should be remembered that *The Confession of a Fool* was written partly as self-justification and partly for revenge upon Mrs. Strindberg and grinds an axe with fury. Nor should the letters, on the other hand, be accepted as unadulterated truth, for it is quite possible that Strindberg is, here, as anxious to defend his wife and put a good face on his married life as, there, to expose them. Moreover, for Strindberg, both in practice and theory, events are always marvelously complex, with different strata of analysis. If he at times separated these strata and gave conflicting accounts of the same circumstance, this was only natural, for he was an artist who demanded a certain unity, and a passionate man with many causes to contend. But never could he escape from reality altogether. He was as far from pure romance as from "seeing life whole."

Strindberg can now perceive only one aspect of the world: the pettiness, treachery and wickedness of women; and his approaching mental crisis lent a fury to his attack which was unprecedented. Woman, as he sees it, is a sham through and through; her sufferings, her virtue, her work, her pretension to vote without accepting the responsibilities involved, her curse of pregnancy, her mother-love, her scruples, delicacy, self-sacrifice, are all humbug and imposture, for she is born to be the parasite, a scorpion and the death of man. Cold, heartless, scheming, unscrupulous, with full leisure and strength for the execution of her purposes, she is more than a match for her honest, loving husband. Further, she possesses the tremendous advantage that motherhood can be proved but not fatherhood, and knows well how to make use of it. On being told that English husbands threw lighted lamps at their wives, he was aghast at the thought of what sort of women they must have in England.

When Strindberg learned that the two objectionable women, Siri's friends, were coming back, he packed up and left for German Switzerland. There, in a military land where men are still honored and women keep their place and their virtue, with a new diet of "golden beer and smoked sausages," Strindberg felt all his old energies return and his love of life, but Siri, cut off from her modern friends, ignorant of the language, oppressed by the reign of men, was anything but happy. Also, she was experiencing the approach of middle age and strove pitifully, as her husband says, to remove its traces. Next, she took it into her head to be jealous of him, though here, as he explains, she need have no fear since at heart he was a monogamist, and exclusively devoted to her though she should grow ever so much older. After a three months' trip he took her in his loving arms so masterfully that the poor woman was terrified at the thought of having such a wife-tamer for a husband. But when he discovered that she had formed a new attachment, that she kissed and walked and bathed with a young girl, there was nothing for it but to move again.

This time they took up their lodgings on the shores of Lake Lucerne, and Siri, rejuvenated, returned to her old ways. A young officer who took her fancy entertained her with solitary walks in the garden while Strindberg worked, but she could not hoodwink her husband, who continued to watch her with increasing disquiet. Once, in order to get rid of him, he relates, she pretended that she was going to bed, but later he heard her downstairs in the drawing-room. When, upon being reproved, she bowed to his authority, he exclaimed, "This candor, this sudden submission. . . . What had happened?" Siri's next offence was to admire and court the attention of a presumptuous porter who strutted like a Napoleon under her eyes. Then the village beau, a tobacconist, began to court her favor and "Marie's heart caught fire." At last he dared to offer her a cigarette in public and in the presence of her husband. "Was I a jealous fool or . . ." That night he discarded all his principles of freedom and spied on her through the keyhole. There he saw her kiss and caress the children's nurse, and lament the unfounded suspicions of her husband. "There is no doubt he is mad," he heard her say, and would, she feared, try to poison her before long unless she escaped to Finland. An evil conscience, thought Strindberg. That night he heard Siri moaning and hurried down to comfort her, an office which she greatly appreciated, yet she obstinately refused to clear up his doubts or give him peace.

In January, 1887, they left Switzerland and took up their residence in Germany on the shores of Lake Constance. Here, in a man's country, where women were womanly and young girls forbidden to attend the University lectures, Siri's prattle about women's rights found no listeners and Strindberg, his "manliness" and energy restored, lived in glory. In the company of the officers he felt strong and happy and to some extent took over their manners, for "after ten years of spiritual emasculation my manhood reasserted itself." When Siri attempted her shifts and machinations she was at once reproved by the worthy sensible women, among whom Strindberg found true friends and several admirers. But Siri was anything but pleased with his new manners, detested his confident masculinity. She had loved him, he now realized, as "the page, the lap dog, her child. The virago never loves virility in her own husband—" Siri was also jealous of Strindberg and suspected the girl who made his fire in the morning before he was up. No, his new airs were unbearable and Germany a wretched place.

In the meantime Strindberg was still tortured with doubts. The letters he had sent to Sweden imploring information concerning his wife's infidelity yielded no answer. None of his friends would betray a poor woman, he reflected, though they let her husband suffer without a thought. Isolated and helpless, unable to quiet or resolve his disturbing doubts, he was thrown back on his own powers and presently the brilliant idea occurred to him of making use of "the new science of psychology and thought-reading." He therefore chose a time when Siri was off her guard and ingeniously brought the subject round to gymnastics which under his guidance suggested "massage" and the pain of massage. This in turn suggested her own experiences, whereat she exclaimed, "Oh, yes, the treatment is certainly painful—I can feel the pain now when I think of—" At this she turned pale and silent and, after a moment of embarrassment, hurried out of the room. She had been caught. The concatenation of thoughts he had artfully "suggested" had moved on like an engine which she was powerless to stop, though the abyss, the memory of the affair with the doctor, lay directly before her. A little later she returned lovingly and stroked his head to show the soothing effect of massage, but he saw in the mirror that her face was drawn with terror and anxiety. "This sort of evidence would not satisfy a jury, but it was sufficient for me who knew her so well." He resolved never to return to his own country to live like a ridiculous cuckold, suspicious of everyone.

And now he made his first attempt to escape from his dear little fury—a precipitate flight to Vienna. But the loneliness of the unknown city, with its meaningless throngs of people, affected him with a weird melancholy for which the memories and longing for Siri were the one and sovereign remedy. He commenced a lively correspondence with her, reported the operas for her pleasure and drowned her with love and compliments. Thoughts of her infused life into the spectral city. He spent hours before the Venus in the Belvedere for it resembled so much his beautiful Siri. When he returned home he laid down his arms. He had tried to escape from her but she had been too strong. Her love meanwhile had been reawakened by his letters and the incontestable proofs of his devotion. She blushed like a young girl when they met and for six months they kissed and cooed and chirruped, played duets and backgammon. There was no limit to their happiness. But all good things come to an end and love philtres lose their power. Siri grew indifferent, neglected her appearance and was soon discovered kissing young girls and "devouring them with lascivious eyes" just as before. Strindberg was now frantic. In his imagination he saw "prison, penal servitude, a scandal that we could never live down." In the heated argument which followed and which lasted 'til daylight, both husband and wife lost their heads, she making dangerous confessions and he, incredible charges. "And this mysterious illness, these headaches from which I suffer—" exclaimed Strindberg. But did he blame her for that too, she replied. No, he had been merely referring to the symptoms of cyanide poisoning which he had shown for some time. But now that he thought of it, a new suspicion more terrible by far than the old fear of poison, crossed his mind. Years ago he had received an anonymous letter refer-

Bust of Strindberg by Agnes Kjellberg-Frumeri

ring to Siri as "the prostitute of Soedertelje." This set him to thinking. Siri had been engaged to a young officer in poor health before her engagement to the Baron. After her marriage to the Baron she had lived with him in curious retirement; later when he had become interested, the Baron had tried to get rid of her, but Siri had always been loyal to him, fearing he would expose her past and she had been afraid of her mother for the same reason. Siri's bitter hatred of her mother was now explained. By threatening to ruin her life by terrible exposure she had forced her daughter into all sorts of concessions. For one thing, Strindberg had been obliged to support the mother's sister. All this was quite clear and indisputable. The Prostitute of Soedertelje!

Strindberg determined upon divorce and set out for Copenhagen to make inquiries about his wife's early life, but there he was greeted by his old friends as a sort of jealous maniac. He returned home and fled again for the fourth time to Switzerland, but the bonds of his foolish love were still too strong. He was drawn back again as by a powerful magnet to the source of his being. It was about this time the accumulated bitterness of ten years rose in a sharp crescendo and he struck her, for the first time in his life,—struck her again and again in the face. Immediately everything went black, the children screamed with fear, and the criminal, realizing too late the horror of his act, staggered, faint and sick. Yet, afterwards, came calm and a sense of vindication. If he had struck her ten years before everything would have gone well. "Remember this, my brothers, if you are ever deceived by a woman!" Siri's retort was to confess that she had once, but only once, been unfaithful. She begged him for forgiveness. He granted it, but again he resolved upon divorce and again he fled, but this time ironically enough to revisit the scenes of their former bliss on Lake Geneva. Now he swore never to return to the adulteress, the murderess, who had robbed him of his peace forever, and now he wondered whether Siri's confession had not been a ruse to get rid of him in order to live with some lover. Finally, he decided to return to her long enough to write the story of their sad tangle, *The Confession of a Fool,* and make use of her, incidentally, for copy. When he returned to Siri, who was now quite broken and woe-begone, he proposed that they should be divorced but that she should continue to live in the house and be paid as a guardian for the children.

On his sixth homecoming, he fell sick and was long in bed in fever and despair and not a whit did he care for life, but first he must have his vengeance. In the meantime his pretty executor played the part of a little mother to him and her little hand, which had driven him to insanity and the verge of death, smoothed his feverish forehead and drove away all the devils which tormented him. When she brought him his elder tea she tasted it first herself. "You may drink it without fear," she said smilingly, "it contains no poison." Then he asked her attention and made a review of the events of their common life, right from the beginning. In the end he "grasped her little hand firmly and implored her to forgive me all the wrong I had done her." In the morning, however, his brain cleared and the stupor gone, he reviewed the very same facts in an altogether different light, for now under the scrutiny of cold reason he saw clearly that he had been the martyr all along and she a Delilah who had shorn her Samson's hair. "Truthful, unsuspicious, I had lost my honor, my manhood, the will to live, my intellect, my fine senses, and alas! much more even, in this ten years' sleep in the arms of the sorceress." He rose from bed and determined to settle accounts with her once and for all, but through the door of his wife's room he saw her lying in bed surrounded by her little ones, her lovely body only half concealed by the loose night-gown and coverlet. As he stooped to kiss the mother, the chaste perfection of her beauty exorcised all his black suspicions. That she could be a criminal was forever impossible, yet he stole away, as he says, convinced of the contrary. Again his deep suspicions tortured him. To be a deceived husband was not the worst, but to be in ignorance of it is horrible. He resolved to scruple at nothing to discover the truth. "Was this monomania, the paroxysm of rage of a lunatic; it is not for me to say."

Strindberg could not determine whether his jealousy was a delusion or a valid system, whether his sense of persecution was a mania or a legitimate feeling. Was he indeed mad, or the most crossed and tormented of men, the victim of whispered conspiracies, a sacrifice of the universal hatred, and the silent manifold vengeance? He could not say, but continued to waver with sad contrarieties of judgment, now terrified at the power of that lost engine which hurried his thoughts to such blackness and extremity, now triumphing bitterly in the shrewdness of his insight which had unriddled, so easily, the malicious plots and dangers which encompassed him. Sometimes, feeling the approach of insanity, he cursed "the sorceress" who had woven that evil spell; he cursed his parents, friends, society, and the world, for he was but a creature of these forces and it was they who destroyed him. Yet, at times, too, he flirted with this oncoming disorder, enjoyed the quickened, feverish intellection, the freedom, the heedlessness, the glamour of forbidden ways, of bold specious arguments and overreaching ambition, painted heaven white and hell black and sat between them full of power, and deep in the affective sources of his mind, he returned to that first dream as he lay in his mother's arms, the dream of omnipotence. Several times in his life, as he confesses, he courted insanity as an escape. His drastic dreams and enterprises, his deliberate recklessness in argument and speculation show how at times, resentful of all authority, he could throw down the entrenchments of reason and consciously release the clutch. Alone with his fabulous ego which stretched to the ends of the earth, laying judgment on all things, good and bad, playing before a great theatre with all the spotlights of Europe upon him, the pivot and vortex of all the swirling interests of Scandinavia, now Hamlet, now Othello or Tamburlaine, but always the central figure in the changing scene, it would scarcely be surprising if on occasion he felt certain wonderful obligations toward himself and toward the world, a duty to continue those splendid astonishments and that reckless originality which had signalled the beginning of his career. A short time before the writing of his maddest play, *The Father,* and his "most terrible book," *The Confession of a Fool,* he wrote to a friend a revealing letter declaring tersely "we must not be tedious" like some of our contemporaries, but meet the changing interests of the public almost at any cost. Certainly the powerful demands of the theatre play a part in determining the pathological picture. Hamlet's feigned madness had been a great trump. Strindberg could not let his audience weary. Yet an artifice of this sort need not imply insincerity. The man who plays a fabulous role becomes fabulous and posture swaggers into truth. Empedocles and Paracelsus played for great effects but perhaps ended by believing. As for Strindberg, in one story he ridicules hypnotism and magic, then has his hero (Dr. Borg) employ them to advance his ends, and finally practices it himself, in, it would seem, full sincerity.

Many judgments have been made on Strindberg's mental disturbance but, alas, the subtlety of his case, the changing symptoms, the sudden recoveries, the complexity and resources of his personality, carry their own vengeance. The experts do not agree. The fact is that there are so many currents and plots in the rich character pattern we have been considering and so many conflicting clinical pictures, that analysis becomes as baffling as Strindberg himself maintained, and differences of opinion among experts are to be found quite parallel to his own divergent judgments in the autobiography. Dr. Upvall, following students in Germany, has fixed upon the Œdipus complex as the most central source of Strindberg's derangement, an opinion which must be accepted, though it would be too much to say that it covers the whole picture or that all the morbid manifestations can be traced to this one spring. Indeed, so obvious is the Œdipus fac-

tor, that Strindberg himself all but expounded it, twelve or fourteen years before Freud startled the world with his first pronouncements. Yet the delusions of grandeur and persecution and
the jealousy mania which play such an important part in this life
history are but extraneously related to the Œdipus complex, in
many cases appear in its absence, and seem in general to arise
from a different source. The ground tone of Strindberg's consciousness was perhaps consequent upon his early morbid fixa-
tion on the "frail dark-eyed mother," the madonna who lured
him and betrayed him through life, but the symphony had many
lurid episodes, contrapuntal storms, many-voiced pyramids of
accent, crises of fear, jealousy and mad ambition, and sometimes
the ensemble fell out altogether, the symphony went wild, and
each separate string played its own sad monologue. These special
crises, though dependent in a general way upon the Œdipus
cast of character, owed their distinctiveness to other causes, chief
among which was a deep uncertainty of self, a persistent irrational sense of inferiority. That "organ inferiority" was an important factor in Strindberg's condition is without doubt and the
morbid jealousy and disgust of women, the fear of stronger,
more masculine men (such as Björnson), with the horror of pronounced sexuality in women, can be traced to this source. Strindberg once complained that his first wife accused him of impo-
tence or rather of a certain inability. This insult Strindberg never
forgave and raged for years against the pretentious, emancipated
women who insisted upon a man's pleasure, scorning their true
blessing, the child, and the theme returns again and again in
his writings.

Though the persistent feeling of inferiority is probably somewhat independent of the Œdipus motif, it is, nevertheless, related, the interplay being intricate and profound. Thus, the urgent sense of sin of which so many manifestations have already
been seen, arises from both sources, from the ground fear of
incest as well as the sense of inferiority. The same is true of the

antithetical worship and abhorrence of women, the detestation of their "emancipation" or rivalry, the passionate insistence on the male prerogative of initiative, command, and genius. Women must be womanly and men, manly, else the race will go under in gyneolatry and desolation—and Strindberg's own femininity, his felt weakness and dependence, materialize and come to the light of day. The primitive and sophisticated defence against a conscious defect, employed at all levels of spirit, is an exaggerated emphasis on the opposite, an assumption of the corresponding virtue or perfection. This is the vindication of the fighter, but there is besides a more humble resource—confession of sin and weakness, for this expiates the fault, and by exposing the strains and oppositions in the self, releases them, building a confident integration. This method, too, has its pride and affirmation. Strindberg made use of both expedients as his needs required.

In 1886-7 the rising fury of Strindberg's jealousy broke in a sharp crisis and the deep exasperations which had been preparing for many years grew up like a magic mountain and crumbled. After this explosion, though he was married twice again and had many affairs, he showed little or no signs of jealousy, for it would seem that he had worn out this emotion and killed it by exaggeration. But at the peak of his marital difficulties its force was unparalleled, breaking in upon work and good council, luring reason into false intricate ways of self-deception, countenancing the most terrible conclusions, so they served its purpose, promoting suspicion, counseling fear and despair, construing each casual gesture as guilt, and so insinuating itself into thought and feeling that the personality could no longer endure its unity, but split off into more or less independent selves, each with its own character and persuasions,—one rational, the other irrational, one disciplined and practical, the other mad and suspicious; each assuming command of the body by turns, each hostile toward the other, and quarreling visibly in print until in the years

1886-7 the jealous personality went much too far and died of its absurdity and excess.

Woman is the sweetest and bitterest thing in life, said Strindberg. She is abomination and the blessed manna. His extreme reverence and repugnance for woman was due to the fundamental Œdipus yearnings as well as the persistent sense of helpless dependence and inferiority, and the same is true of the jealousy mania. Strindberg was not jealous of the Baron while he and the Baroness were married and together, but rather delighted in the union of his two good friends. Moreover, as he says, he first loved the Baroness as the wife of a certain man and the mother of a certain child. There in the old house in which he and his parents had lived he felt himself at home again and was treated by them like a child. When on the other hand, the Baroness left her husband, Strindberg grew frightfully jealous, for now, according to the Freudian explanation, the Baron no longer represented his father but a libertine who would defile the saintly mother and destroy her honor, disturb his security as a child, and poison his mind forever. The excessive jealousy is also founded upon the sense of weakness and inferiority, a feeling which was perhaps somewhat justified. Strindberg once explained, when jealous of the Baron, that the intellectual in the matter of women is no match for the athlete. What women *really* want, he seems to have thought, is brutality and male domination. When a man is too "moral" or respectful, they lose all respect for him, turn to other men, and force him into the role of a lackey, a lap dog, a servant of their caprices. The sexual act is by nature, he thought, a device for the propagation of the race, a pleasure for the male and a blessing to the woman since it gives her the child. Such "wholesome" ideas, he believed, were quite out of accord with those of the emancipation enthusiasts. Hence he was persecuted at home and abroad. Knowing that his ideas did not agree with those of the up-to-date woman, yet feeling the utmost dependence on her, he was brought to feel more insecure and suspicious than ever, and in the end his jealousy went wild altogether.

The jealousy and the persecution mania, of course, show the closest affiliation. Embittered by jealousy and by the enmity of his wife, Strindberg's hatred for her became generalized to include all emancipated women,—even beyond this; irritated by his own reverses, he first struck back at this class of women, and in his writings disguised his personal vengeance under the cover of a general polemic. Then, of course, he believed himself persecuted by women. They had brought him to trial, had so managed that his books were censored and denounced. They had all but starved him out. In 1887 he believed that people would shoot him if he returned to Sweden. His manuscripts were censored, refused or lost in the mails, and the women were behind it, without doubt. Alone with his "great power" and wretchedness, he could indulge the most grandiose dreams and the utmost fear and despair. Thus, the delusions of grandeur and persecution were also bound up casually with jealousy, the sense of inferiority and the Œdipus feelings.

Strindberg's condition at the crisis of 1886-7 may best be defined as a borderline case of schizophrenia with paranoid trends (or states). Unlike most schizophrenia, however, there was no mental deterioration, even to the last, and one very decisive recovery; and, unlike most paranoiacs, the condition did not develop but remained the same or underwent improvement during long periods of his life. In general it is difficult to pronounce a man insane who has produced such a mine of literature, who was throughout life so active and many-sided, so fertile in his invention, so ceaseless, rapid and original in his composition. On the other hand, it is impossible to accept the verdict of some, that Strindberg was at all times social, lucid and rational, that his suspicions were in general only too well-founded. There is unfortunately too much evidence to the contrary, most of which appeared, however, later on in the crises of 1894 and 1904.

Heidenstam, Strindberg's one close friend during these crucial years of jealousy, found him one of the most excitable and pretentious gentlemen in the world. When Strindberg communicated to him his plan of blowing up Stockholm society by a very penetrating analysis, of taking all Europe by the ears with his lordly satires and proclamations, Heidenstam, though sincerely admiring his wild friend, was absolutely astounded at the lengths of his self-conceit. It was only matched, in Heidenstam's opinion, by his nervousness, his grumbling, and finical temper. Nothing was good enough for him, neither the society of Stockholm, nor the civilization of Europe, nor the menu at his hotel, and often the Son of a Servant complained bitterly of a beefsteak which the tourists and plutocrats would swallow in contentment. To these two qualities of grandiose conceit and finical irritability, Heidenstam attributed most of Strindberg's energy and genius. He deserves no special sympathy, however he bids for it, thought Heidenstam, since his troubles accrue from his own nature and the private peculiarities of his wife and children, for they are likewise afflicted with the same morbid nervousness and grumbling dishumor. When Heidenstam communicated these opinions to Strindberg, the latter was anything but speechless with anger. He complained profusely. His friend is now a shameless slanderer, a false noble, one of those who had plotted and discriminated against the plebeian Strindberg, jealous and fearful of his overriding genius. As for his sensitiveness and irritability, Strindberg defended himself in many writings. His nicety of sensibility is, he says, but the outward manifestation of a more subtle, ingenious, a more developed nervous system. He was, in short, like his character Dr. Borg (*By the Open Sea*) the last peak in evolutionary progress, Nature's most subtle and dangerous experiment, gifted with a delicate mechanism far beyond the crude ganglia of most men, receptive of the slightest wind or sigh in his environment, quick and orderly in his assimilation of these impressions, suffering keenly their disharmonies, bold in his judgment and original, construing and comparing all things synoptically in the long sweep of his extraordinary intellect, and fated therefore to be universally misunderstood, hated and persecuted by smaller minds.

Strindberg's break with his one friend, Heidenstam, to whom he was so much attached, shows, as will indeed many facts hereafter, how impossible it was for him to continue in amicable relations with anyone. Whether Mrs. Strindberg was any better off in this respect it is difficult to say, though her children when questioned gave of course a most favorable report.

Nowhere do Strindberg's morbid peculiarities show up more clearly than in his own outspoken and lavish confessions. There, in the midst of faithful records and ingenious, unbiased interpretations, we are confronted from time to time by a marvelous bitterness, rooted in the facts, of course, but frantic and overstriding, or by a sudden mad leap of judgment, non sequiturs or derelict imaginings. We are shocked to find in this admirably rational writer that disquieting twist of mind which marks the insane. Rationality is the bond which unites society in amiability and understanding. A violation, when serious and without humorous intent, affects us with a sort of horror as of something inhuman. It reminds us, perhaps, that we are but machines which may go wrong. We turn to our interlocutor in a quick glance of dismay, fearful, hoping we have misunderstood him or that he pursues a jest. In Strindberg's case, we continue our perusal, and suddenly the madness snaps, the ingenious knot in human reason untied by his own doubts and dissolving contentions.

In 1886, when Strindberg saw himself at the end of his liferope, sinking in the black absolving waters, alone, his strength gone, and the baubles of love and ambition floating away out of reach, he determined to make a reckoning with his past life, to review like a drowning man, the signal events in the origin and growth of his soul, to bring order into that disquieting confusion and to find his true self at last. He, therefore, set to work feverishly on an autobiography, beginning with his earliest years, tracing the combined effect of heredity, education, original temperament, and the impact of the spiritual movements of the historical epoch, seeking in the catacombs of causes for the lost self. Within a year the work which he called *The Son of a Servant* had grown to three volumes. It constitutes today a remarkable landmark in autobiography, its honesty and shameless circumstantiality being quite beyond anything in St. Augustine or Rousseau. Its originality, moreover, is to be seen in the insistence on the power of natural incidental causes and, above all, its emphasis on the plurality of influences and motivations. It is undoubtedly a decisive innovation in biographical style,—a contribution to psychology as well as literature. It was not his purpose in writing this autobiography, he assures us, to excuse his faults. Rather, he points them out and analyzes them on every occasion. Often in his recollections he came upon unwelcome episodes, displeasing to the public and unfavorable to himself, yet his realism would not permit him to leave them out. Life appeared to him as a dark road with many dangers and obscurities behind him which must be scrutinized and understood before he could dare to go on.

The reception of Strindberg's book was what would have been expected. "But where is the result, the unity, where the truth in all this medley of conflicts and opposing principles?" complained the public. "It lies here and there in a thousand printed places," said Strindberg, for the truth is not fixed and conventionalized as the orthodox have imagined, nor like the charmed Princess, scorning time in her tower. Truth, in time, changes in time and undergoes development. Young Strindberg was a strand in a segment of the changing stream. If the public complained of contradictions and mistakes, these, too, were but a part of the stream and could not be avoided. Also, there was an outcry against the social and economic criticisms for the book had attacked the upper class and the most fundamental and honored institutions of society. There was also a group who denounced the impiety of *The Son of a Servant*. That an author should dare to write a book criticizing his mother was horrible and unheard of. (No doubt Strindberg was somewhat unfair to his mother, but she was a woman after all and he was at war with women.) Strindberg's old enemy Wirsén denounced the book roundly and raged against its blasphemy and impiety with a vehemence reminiscent of Strindberg himself.

The three volumes of *The Son of a Servant* cover the first thirty-seven years of Strindberg's life (1849–1886), while *The Confession of a Fool* written in the next year, 1887–8, recounts the first ten years of matrimony, 1877–87. This book, which Strindberg himself thought so terrible that he regretted ever having written it, was far more scurrilous and repugnant to the public, when it was finally published, than *The Son of a Servant,* or any of his previous writings. Written originally in French with the title of *Le Plaidoyer d'un Fou,* it was first published in German translation as *The Confession of a Fool* (Berlin, 1893). An unauthorized Swedish translation appeared in 1893–4, in 1895 it was published in the original French, but not until Strindberg's death did it appear in an authorized Swedish translation. That Strindberg wrote this book to avenge himself on his dear wife, his "madonna," can scarcely be doubted, but the extent to which he incriminated himself and thereby excused Mrs. Strindberg should serve in part as a remission of sins. Even the title *The Confession of a Fool,* or in more literal translation *The Self-defense of a Lunatic,* shows his willingness to accept the responsibility for his unhappy marriage, if this should be the truth. At the end of the book he leaves it for the reader to decide whether he is a lunatic or his wife a monster of wickedness, and so concludes with a crucial alternative, so bold and daring as to leave no doubt of his moral courage, and so fair-minded and honest, that many readers have decided one way, and many another, and most have been racked by the same doubts as the author.

How did he come to write such a terrible book? asks Strindberg. "Because," he replies, in a preface to the first edition, "I felt under a powerful and justifiable compulsion to wash my corpse before it was laid in the coffin forever." Moreover, a friend of his, who knew some of the facts, had threatened to use them as copy for a novel of his own. In the second preface in 1894, about the time of the birth of the one child of the second marriage, his mood is bitter and cynical. "The sympathy which everyone felt for the heroine of the novel, absolves me. You may gauge from this fact the great depth of love I bore her, for not only did it survive so much brutality, but communicated itself to the reader. . . ." The "poor defenceless woman" rules over the four northern countries, there she has only friends with which to fight one lonely invalid, whom people desire to commit to an asylum because his superior intelligence could not but oppose gyneolatry, the last superstition of free-thinkers." (The picture Strindberg here gives of himself is incidentally a little out of keeping with other facts. He is married again at this time, the father of a little girl and according to report "looked ten years younger.") But the shameful confessions, rising from a bottomless reservoir of unbearable memories, of shames and infruitions, old doubts and despairs, and poisoned words never forgotten, whirred and rasped beneath the surface consciousness, gathered force when the attention relaxed, assumed complete authority when indulged, stood like morose and threatening shadows beside each bright thought or tender fancy, frightening out new hopes and inventions, guarding their horrors, and weaving again in ever-changing forms the whispered frenzied tale of one unhappy marriage.

In 1886–7, poisoned by his inadmissible, irrepressible memories, Strindberg found a new form for his confessions in the drama, and produced during these years, in addition to his biographies, novels, stories, and other works, two very remarkable plays, both portraying with rather ghastly variations in the style of Zola and the mood of the German *Schauerromane,* the story of modern marriage. In *The Father* which has been regarded as *The Confession of a Fool* on the stage, Strindberg follows rather closely the events of his own married life, distorting them, of course, through the mirrors and perspectives of his passion to redress his mad sense of injury, but holding throughout to the deeper significance. The theme is the war of sexes in which the Father is completely worsted by his cruel, determined, unscrupulous wife, losing the love of his child, his parenthood, his liberty and in the end perhaps his reason.

The other play, *Comrades,* though written in 1886, did not appear until 1888 and then in a revised form. This is a story of the modern marriage of two artists, of a tyrannous, stupid wife and a noble, long-suffering husband and again it is the war of the sexes, but this time it is the man who triumphs. Bertha, the heroine of the play, like Laura in *The Father,* is determined to humiliate and subjugate her husband and employs for the purpose the most dastardly weapons. Though not possessed of Laura's power to drive her husband insane, she manages to reduce him to despair and ineffectual weakness, and by her deceits and impositions, and her carefully contrived humiliations, to rise above him, and for a time accomplish her purpose. In this comradeship, for this is the basis of their marriage, there must be, she insists, complete equality; each will do his own work and earn his own living and both will be free. While claiming her rights, however, she exploits and deceives her husband at every turn, their comradeship becoming the tyranny of a vain, talentless woman over her gifted, but somewhat weak and gentlemanly husband. Bertha insists upon having a nude male model, expensive parties, fine clothes, all of which Axel, the husband, pays for, though he cannot afford a model himself or luxuries of any kind. Instead of being grateful to him for his goodness she complains of the humiliation of being obliged to live at his expense, and for that she will not forgive him. She implores him to help her to be equal to him and self-supporting and demands that he intercede on her behalf with a friend, one of the judges at an exhibit, in order that her picture will be accepted. Though such manœuvering is highly distasteful to the honorable Axel, he is obliged to do it all the same. When Axel's picture is refused and Bertha's accepted, she cannot conceal her pride and malice, which irritates her husband and leaves him thoughtful and shaken. Abel, the wife's woman friend, betrays Bertha's mercenary character, Axel for himself discovers that she has borrowed money from her admirer, and falsified the household accounts for money to pay for her luxuries. Finally it comes to a quarrel between them and Axel decides to leave his false comrade forever. But in the meantime Bertha and Abel have planned a great humiliation for him. His rejected picture is to be brought home during a party, which Axel has promised to attend. When the picture arrives, however, it turns out to be Bertha's. Axel, knowing that Bertha's picture has little chance of being accepted, has generously changed the numbers in order that his wife might win the award. In a previous scene Axel had bent Bertha's wrists and forced her to her knees, an action which had aroused her love, and now, witnessing his generosity, she feels what she had never felt before. He, on the other hand, has lost his love for her and this is the tragedy. As he turns his false comrade out of his house, the maid announces his new sweetheart. Axel's one fault, without which he would have been absolutely perfect, is the lack of a certain "brutality" and masculine dominance. While he was good Bertha mistreated him but when he crushes her wrists in one hand her love awakens for the first time. In explanation, she says, "Be a little evil, rather, but don't be weak." Was Strindberg here recalling a speech of Siri's? At any rate Axel is very much the character that Strindberg thought himself, the shipwreck of the comrades follows in spirit the course of his own unhappy tangle, and the triumph of the husband, the return of manliness and the escape from the little tyrant, is what he many times attempted and longed for in vain. Either escape from the beloved or be destroyed. These were the terrible alternatives between which Strindberg wavered and fretted, for he could settle upon neither. He has the Father suffer the penalty and Axel escape and planned another play to make up a triology. His own irresolution was painful but prodigiously fruitful in a literary way.

Strindberg's readiness to confess and his indifference to publishing his most intimate secrets is certainly surprising and not without its pathological import. In the middle of the eighties, in the midst of the storms and rancors of his marriage he made overtures for the publication of his and Siri's love letters, those ardent communications of their first love period. That they were not published was no fault of his, for though he prided himself on being an extremely tasteful and sensitive person, he saw nothing amiss in this exposure. Perhaps he thought they might complement *The Confession of a Fool* and other such revelations.

It is a glaring proof of his many-sidedness and energy that in this period so full of confession and self-revelation he could be much more objective when he chose. In August 1886 he made a tour of France with his family, in order to gather material for a monumental work on French peasants, which was to have been extended to the farmer population of Germany and other countries. Too many books had already been written on nobles and the wealthy dwellers in cities. It was time for a great work on rural life and Strindberg saw an opportunity for political power and heavens knows how many honors and distinctions in this enterprise. The first volume, when it appeared, showed the same repugnance for false culture, and the same love of farmers, as appeared in earlier works of this period. It is an intimate and captivating study of peasant life, but not altogether reliable in matters of fact. The great undertaking on which Strindberg had built such high hopes came to nothing, and only a fragment, the first volume, was accepted for publication.

A better instance of Strindberg's objectivity in a period of self-obsession is the excellent novel, *The People of Hemsö* (1887), an account of the life of fishermen in the lonely islands of the Baltic. At home in this bit of nature where he had spent so much of his youth, and uncannily knowing in the native psychology he created a genuine masterpiece which many still rank as one of the finest of its kind. It recounts the career of a farm laborer, Carlsson, who by his superior intelligence brings a dilapidated farm into prosperity, marries the widow, its owner, and thereby almost climbs through to a higher class, subdues the widow's son and all his other associates by his iron will and cleverness, but is finally corrupted by the luxuries of summer tourists, ruined by a rash investment and fails, on the death of his wife, to rise above his class, losing thereby his superiority and advantages, to become in the end an adventurer and a nobody. What a conclusion for Strindberg's second superman! The first, Master Olaf, had perjured himself. It seemed that it was not in Strindberg's power to create a quite admirable hero. Beside the amiability and capacity in Carlsson's nature, lies a deep strain of the untrue and the monstrous. It is the false culture which ruins him and this is the burden of the tale, some scenes of which, such as the loss of the widow's corpse in the ice-flow, are among Strindberg's best.

But with all this incredible production Strindberg was little satisfied. In 1887 he declared himself bankrupt for all his schemes had come to nothing. When a poet's stipend was proposed for him he protested sadly. Money given to him was thrown out of the window for, alas, he could no longer write. Yet when it came to the point he must write, if only for his children's sake. The untapped energies of his "plebeian blood" fortify him. New hopes come. Then disillusion and "revolver thoughts" again. So life spun out its pleasantries and the fates wagged their heads in approval.

XIX

NATURALISM

IN the early 19th century, Absolute Idealism enjoyed its long riot of rational speculation and there was scarcely a department of thought which was not affected by the width and power and urbanity of the great systems. For Idealism taught that reason is supreme over the forces of nature or rather that these forces are but the reflections of Spirit as it unfolds its logical stages in the course of world-history. The dialectic or the logical development of Spirit thus takes precedence over the laws of nature and their orderly manifestation. These are but a reflex or a lower stage in the necessary evolution of Spirit and here, in the rational unfolding of a world reason, their final explanation is to be found. Hegel and Fichte, daringly true to their spiritual monism, went so far as to deduce natural science from the laws of spirit, and though they admitted scientific truth to a modest place in a great system of truths, they allowed it but a partial validity and rather disparaged the blundering, empirical inductions of the experimental scientists.

Early in the 1830's, however, it was clear that a change had come and that the reign of German Absolutism had come to an end. Hegel complained that philosophical students were no longer interested in philosophy, but had turned to science. Feuerbach and Marx, making a complete reversal, became materialists and Marx "stood Hegel on his head" making Hegelian dialectic do service for materialism, economic determinism, and socialism, all of which were quite repugnant to Hegel. Schopenhauer, whose hatred for Hegel knew no limits, opened up his batteries of mordant ridicule and branded the whole movement as the most pernicious, the most unutterable nonsense. The reaction soon spread to all parts of Europe where German philosophy had been influential.

In Denmark Kierkegaard opposed with his powerful eloquence the dialectic of the Spirit. There is, he said, no dialectic which can transcend the contradictions of the spiritual life. At every stage we are presented with a sheer alternative and must decide by a sort of leap—all or nothing. The choice is subjective and depends upon the intrinsic power of will; each individual must make his own decision, must face the terrible antithesis alone as did Brand or Pastor Sang. The final antithesis is between the æsthetic life of pleasure and the religious life of loneliness and suffering, and any attempt to transcend this alternative is an unworthy compromise. We have in Kierkegaard, then, a break with Hegel and a return to Kant.

Ibsen and Strindberg both take part in the reaction to German Idealism. Thus, Peer Gynt is made to solve the riddle of the world. When asked who he is, he replies, "I am myself." This answer (approximately the first proposition of Fichte's philosophy) is acclaimed as the truth which has so long been sought in vain. Peer is applauded and taken to an insane asylum full of long-bearded professors of philosophy. Strindberg in *The Red Room* also ridicules Fichte and German philosophy, which throughout his life he continued to regard as jugglery and word-play.

The scientific trend of thought in Europe in the 19th century, as opposed to the grandiose speculative systems, was given a great impetus by the publication in 1859 of the *Origin of Species*. It was now no longer possible to ignore, or even subordinate, those material conditions on which human life depends, nor to treat man as free and unique in creation, nor to raise up reason to the old dignity of high arbiter and executive of the world. Henceforth, man must resign himself to being an animal with an animal's wants and gratifications. If he would investigate the stars or his own soul, he must do so with a brain specifically developed to knock down nuts and escape from larger animals. And the ironic consciousness of this dark uncertainty of his instrumentalities is to pursue him with troubled doubt and skepticism. However flaunting his pretensions and ambitions, he must remember that his brain, like the claw of a crab, may be incapable of reaching the stars or embracing the world. He must now submit consciously, with what grace he can, to the authority of chemical, biological, and psychological laws, and contrive by patient studies of nature to foresee, if he cannot control, his fate. This is the basis of Naturalism.

Naturalism arose as a movement in science and philosophy. It proposed to explain every event in nature by those mechanical laws which had already been found so excellent and sufficient in Physics and Chemistry. It thus implied the subjection of man, the impossibility of free will, and the inefficacy of human reason to change the order of the world. Occult and mysterious causes were excluded or relegated, as in Spencer, to the Unknowable, so that nothing remained of divine direction or the power of human purposes, but only the frictions and exchanges of the far-flung, wandering matter. A cry of human pain or desire was but a disturbance of the air like any other; an idealist, an absurd and mistaken martyr, an animal whose brain had turned parasite, preventing adaptation. Human values were but sports or accidents of evolution and they have no further significance.

Naturalism, thus, with its elevation of mechanical science to the single throne, became, or tended to become, indifferentism, and to regard human values, as nature itself might account them, as of no moment whatever. And this indifferentism was close to pessimism! Naturalism, like Stoicism and Rousseauism, bids us "back to nature," but not to submit to a rational and perfect order, nor to enjoy in simple nobility the handiwork of God. It was back to an enemy powerful and blind, unmindful of humanity, but fatuously obedient to its senseless uniformities. \

Though Naturalism began as a movement in science and philosophy, it soon spread to literature. In the novels of Balzac and in *Madame Bovary* it is in evidence; in Zola's *Experimental Novel* and in Taine's *Introduction to the History of English Literature* the program is laid down. Following Claude Bernard, a great French physiologist, whose *Introduction to Experimental Medicine* was a great inspiration, Zola makes his beginning: "We must admit nothing occult; there are but phenomena and the conditions of phenomena." These phenomena the novelist must study and he must conduct experiments just as the medic does. The novelist, Zola contends, must be a scientist, he must follow in his composition the methods of the physician and the chemist. "We naturalists, we men of science," is a favorite expression of his. "Heredity has its laws, like gravitation," and in the light of their heredity and environment, the characters of literature must be analyzed. The novelist "must possess a knowledge of the mechanism inherent in man, show the machinery of his intellectual and sensory manifestations, under the influence of heredity and environment, such as physiology shall give them to us, and then, finally to exhibit man living in social conditions, produced by himself, which he modifies daily and in the heart of which he is undergoing constant transformation."

This is the basis upon which Zola rests his *Rougon Maquart,* a series of novels which traces the progress of a family through several generations and shows how his characters are shaped by the milieu and biological heritage. *Germinal, L'Argent, Travail, Thérèsè Raquin,* etc., also profess to carry out, though we will see with how little success, the theory of Naturalism.

Flaubert, though he does not approve of Zola's frankness in giving away his secret and thinks that a thing no novelist has a right to do, is nevertheless in main agreement. "The farther art goes," he says, "the more scientific it becomes." In the end, like science, it should be wholly objective, so that "every work in which the author can be divined should be condemned" (Letters to George Sand). In *Madame Bovary,* Flaubert, in accordance with this principle, becomes a hard impartial scientist, describing the passionate yearnings, the invariable disillusions, the sins and sufferings of his beautiful, exceedingly attractive heroine without the slightest tenderness or pity. His business as he sees it is to trace the consequences of the sentimental education on a weak but pretty wife of a country doctor, not to sympathize like a sentimentalist, nor to condemn in the name of morality and reform. As a scientist he neither pities nor condemns. The moral life of his heroine is a phenomenon to be studied and explored, and he is as far from criticizing Emma's morals as Zola the repeated sins of Nana. "The natural consequences of determinism," says Pellisier, "is the abolition of morality." There are interests and appetites, but duty no longer exists. The naturalists with their determinism, their insistence on the omnipotence of natural law, have made human beings pathetic, inconsequent, and morally irresponsible, and have themselves risen to a height of objectivity from which good and evil appear the same. This, if not their practice, is certainly their profession.

If we were to sum up the various sayings of such writers as Flaubert, Zola, De Maupassant, Strindberg, selecting what is essential from each, we should arrive at the following definition of Naturalism. It is a type of literature, we might conclude, which presents a world in which human will and divine or occult agencies are alike powerless against the blind inexorable strength of natural laws or the equally blind dominion of chance (as in Hardy); in which, also, the author confines himself to an impartial description of the operation of these laws (usually with cruel, sordid, or pathetic effects, for these are the most illustrative of his point) and does not intrude either his personality or his moral persuasions.[1] Naturalism is thus easily distinguishable from Realism by its selection of those events which best exemplify the natural laws. Here lies the difference between Strindberg's *The Father* and Ibsen's *A Doll's House,* between a novel of Zola and one of Jane Austen, and it is a most important difference—yet, how often and with what an odd perversity these two types of literature are confused! Romanticism also is often confused with Naturalism and this, it is true, is only too often the naturalist's fault, but in principle the distinction is clear. The insistence on natural law, and the faithfulness to a bitter reality in the one is the very opposite of the capricious, wilful, imaginative character of the other and this difference can be easily seen in most cases.

With this definition of Naturalism before us, we shall be in a position to see how far Zola and other naturalists, especially Strindberg, lived up to it and whether, in the end, there was any good reason why they should.

Strindberg, like Zola, was early attracted by natural science. As a boy he had been tempted by the idea of perpetual motion and had in fact stolen the furniture to fabricate his machine. He had carried out chemical experiments in his room, though with more zeal than equipment, being moved more by personal curiosity than by any respect for the authorities. Like Ibsen, he was apprenticed to a doctor and learned much from the contact with this genial and cultured Jew. No doubt he would have gone much farther and learned much more of science in his brilliant and erratic way had not his rising interest in the theatre turned him aside and determined him upon a career as an actor. His scientific interests continued, however, and by 1874 were greatly strengthened by Darwinian evolution. In that year he wrote an article in defence of this system, in which he maintained that so far from being inimical to faith, the evolutionary doctrine is

---

[1] Some of these ideas on Naturalism in general were first worked out in collaboration with Esther M. McGill.

really a support to it and that it is no worse to have an amiable ape for an ancestor than a dwarfish bushman or cannibalistic New Zealander for a brother. Henceforth, though his wandering interests took many directions, he continued intermittently his studies of chemistry, botany and other sciences.

One factor which drove Strindberg into scientific studies was his reaction to his early pietism. When doubts first occurred he struggled painfully for a long time, but finally arrived, as was to be expected of him, at the opposite pole of Naturalism, for there was no middle ground which would satisfy him. Again it was a distrust and partly, too, a contempt of his own passions and explosions which made him covetous of the restraint of natural science. It was perhaps his sentimentality, self-pity, his intense subjectivity which made him crave the discipline of Naturalism in which these weaknesses of character would be concealed and forgotten. Perhaps Strindberg's predilection for the naturalistic mode was but a defence against a far too undisciplined imagination. This will appear in a study of the plays and novels of his naturalistic period.

It is interesting to observe that Strindberg's naturalism begins at a time when his matrimonial difficulties had grown unbearable and that his theme is invariably the same—the strife of the sexes and the horrors of marriage. *The Confession of a Fool* was written in the same years (1887–8) in which *The Father, Miss Julia, The Son of a Servant, The Red Room,* etc., appeared. And of course, as we will have occasion to see, almost all his naturalistic works are confessional and self-justificatory. But, why the naturalistic form? One reason for this is certainly the prestige of science and the scientific method, and Strindberg's desire to protect and reinforce his personal complaints with authority and established laws.

Strindberg's naturalism, though it had its tentative beginnings in *The Red Room* (1879), did not appear in a finished form until the collection of stories called *Married* published in 1884.

Here, however, the importance attached to economic necessities, heredity, the laws of sex-psychology, and environmental influences in general, confer a very special tone and character. In the first story, a sensitive and talented boy falls a victim to the teaching of Pietism, then current in Sweden. He is made to feel a deep sense of guilt, he is taught to repress all desires and to pray for strength. He reads a book in which those who are guilty of a very common boyhood sin are threatened with horrible disease and death in a few years. He is amazed and horrified at what he reads. Can it be true that he will lose his hair and teeth and die in so short a time? He determines to devote himself to God for the few remaining years, but is disturbed in his piety by a healthy spirited brother who takes him off to a gay party. There he meets a girl for whom he conceives a deep and tender regard so that, as he feels, there is only one woman for him in the world. He thereupon courts her with shy devotion and she reciprocates, modestly. But a cruel disillusion is prepared for him. As he walks down the dark hall of the girl's house, he sees through an open door his beloved and his brother—and what he sees there destroys all his hopes. He returns to his prayers and devotions, endeavoring to suppress all his evil desires, though his erotic dreams betray him. The result of this continued suppression is that his health is completely shattered and his sanity endangered. His ruin is finally accomplished by a strong and vigorous widow, who, marrying him in his physical and mental exhaustion, manages to kill him in a few years. The wages of virtue is death. The biological and psychological constitution of man makes continued continence a most dangerous thing. In this case, the measure is full, rather too full. The wages of virtue are disease, idiocy, and death. What Strindberg inveighs against is the social hypocrisy which prevents this truth from being generally known. Later in life he maintained that boys should be spared the years of torture between puberty and the marriageable age of thirty, and should be allowed to marry at fifteen. In fact, the spirit of

Strindberg's reform would be much in tune with certain recent theories and proposals with regard to marriage.

Love and Bread is an excellent little story of a couple who married on expectations. The allurement of love blinds the poor husband (a writer like Strindberg) to the economic necessities and his own incapacity. Suddenly the inevitable disaster occurs. They are thrown out of their extravagant apartment and their furniture and all the dear appurtenances of their love are returned to the dealers. Moreover, the young husband is dreadfully in debt. His wife must return to her parents who are themselves poor and unable to help. A child arrives and her parents must support it. And finally the poor husband is only allowed to see his wife and child once a week and then never alone. "He has calculated that it will take him twenty years to pay his debts. And then? Even then he cannot maintain a wife and child. And his prospects? He has none! If his father-in-law should die, his wife and child would be thrown on the street; he cannot venture to look forward to the death of their only support. Oh! How cruel it is of nature to provide food for all her creatures, leaving the children of men only to starve."

This theme of poverty, the dominance of economic factors in the lives of men returns again and again in these stories and plays a great part throughout Strindberg's writings, often where it is least expected, as in the symbolical and historical plays.

A variation of this economic theme is the desire of the emancipated wife to earn her own living, for if she is beholden to her husband for food and clothing, she feels, she will lose all self-respect and their marriage become a prostitution. This situation is also a persistent one in Strindberg. The outcome is either that the wife makes a farce of her bread-winning, or, what is more usual, the child when it comes, puts an end, once and for all, to such curious notions. A woman's true happiness as determined by biological laws, is the child. If she prefers a career as a second-rate writer or artist and refuses to bear children, nurse or bring them up, she is opposing the course of nature and the continuance of the race. At this point we see one of the most important differences between Strindberg and Ibsen. Strindberg not only condemns the modern woman who insists on living the life of a man, neglecting her own; he rests his case on the laws of biology and the predestined place of woman in nature. No woman, neither Nora nor Hedda Gabler, has a right to satisfy her whims at the expense of the race. It is her duty to bear children and make a home, that the race may be preserved. Here Strindberg takes the side of the race, Ibsen of the individual.

In the story *A Doll's House,* Strindberg makes an open break with Ibsen, ridicules his play by that name and defends the husband against the foolish Nora. The hero of the story has for some time had trouble with his wife who has come under the influence of a meddlesome blue-stocking. This old maid is full of ridiculous fancies. She persuades the wife to Platonic Love and any number of other absurdities, until the captain, her husband, is made miserable and his happy home-life destroyed. Finally the wife sends the captain a copy of Ibsen's *A Doll's House* to show him what is wrong with their relationship. The captain opens the book with great interest and asks himself: But, why not a doll's house? "His home had been a charming doll's house; his wife had been his charming doll and he had been her big doll. . . . What was wrong? He must read the book at once and find out." What he finds out is that Nora has been a fool as she herself admits and Helmer, too, had made mistakes. They have both been fools but he was anxious to turn over a new leaf and set everything to rights, so that there was no earthly reason for Nora's desertion of her home and children; there was really nothing wrong at all.

This criticism of Ibsen's play does not, however, solve the captain's own domestic difficulties. The meddling old maid continues to pervert his household. The captain appeals to the doctor: "What is the matter with those women? Isn't it bad for

them to remain unmarried? Doesn't it make them?—What?"
The doctor replies that it is too bad that there are not enough
men to go around. In the state of nature, he says, there is no
such thing as an unmated female, but among civilized people,
bread is so difficult to obtain that there must be many. And these
unmated females, it is Strindberg's view, are bound to cause
trouble.

In this story he has the captain conquer the old maid by making love to her. The blue-stocking, for all her spirituality, re-
sponds and becomes human again, while the wife grows jealous.
This sets matters to rights in no time, and their delightful little
doll's house is restored.

The emphasis in this story on biological, evolutionary, and
economic determinism is very noteworthy, and characteristic of
Strindberg. A comparison of Strindberg's story with Ibsen's play
shows in clear relief the naturalism of the one and the realism
of the other.

In another story of the same series, *Unnatural Selection or the
Origin of Race,* Strindberg shows how the sickly and degenerate
nobility would soon die off if nature had its way and that their
children were bound to perish unless they took the mother's milk
from the children of the lower class. This tragic theme of en-
feebled aristocracy and the effects of bad heredity returns in
Strindberg's *Miss Julia,* and has in fact a large place in naturalistic literature. In Balzac and Zola it is very important and in
Ibsen's *Ghosts* and *Hedda Gabler,* if there is anything naturalistic about these plays at all, it lies here, in the unfolding of the
dark unforeseen consequences of bad blood and hereditary
disease.

These stories of Strindberg's, while naturalistic in their emphasis upon heredity and environment have one grave defection
from Zola's ideal. They are all frankly partisan and polemical.
The choice of the story-form is itself but a means to his practical
purpose, providing a brief and powerful medium for his ideas.

This is not the first time that a naturalist has turned propagandist. The thing happens again and again and Zola himself is the worst offender.

But, in spite of the polemical nature of these stories, they make excellent reading. In their brevity, power, and simplicity of form, they are quite remarkable and deserve a place beside the best short stories of Chekhov and Sologub.

Soon after they appeared a court action was commenced against the publisher, the charge being that the book was impious. Strindberg was sure that this was not the real charge, but only a straw-man behind which the outraged women, the witches and emancipated blue-stockings, could hide their vengeance. Strindberg, who was living in Switzerland at this time, hurried back to Sweden to defend the book, and the charge was finally withdrawn. Strindberg thereupon set to work to finish the series and published the second part, containing other stories in the same naturalistic vein, though with a change of mood which has already been discussed, in the following year (1885).

The naturalistic play as opposed to the naturalistic novel or short story is to an amazing degree the creation of one man. Zola, it is true, had dramatized the terrible *Therésè Raquin* and this play with its mental tension and silent horror watching through the scenes, made so great an impression on Strindberg that he took it for his model. But, it was the Swedish writer who developed the technique of this new type of play, fabricated the characters against natural settings, pitting them hopelessly against the necessities of nature or the laws of their own souls. It was he who developed the rapid and brutal energy which later became so characteristic.

His first naturalistic play, *Marodeure,* comes in 1886, but the type suddenly reached its perfection in the next year with *The Father*. This play which is often regarded as Strindberg's finest performance, though intensely motivated by his own personal experiences and therefore subjective, is nevertheless a splendid example of Zola's naturalism, Zola's objections notwithstanding. Laura and the Captain, the two main characters, are bound irremediably by the laws of their own natures; however conscious of their fate, and desirous of life and happiness, they are helpless against the destructive movements of their own dark impulses. Laura, in particular, is bound by the laws of her own nature. She must hate the Captain, humble and destroy him. She must intercept his mail thereby preventing him from winning the fame and recognition which his scientific discoveries deserved. She must alienate the affections of his beloved daughter and raise doubts in his mind as to her paternity. And the Captain? He must retaliate with what powers he has against this deadly and versatile enemy. Yet he is no match for this little woman with her witchery and craft and shameful expedients. His own worthiness, his knowledge and courage prove quite unequal to her iron will and cunning savagery. He is at a great disadvantage. She can use the weapons and devices of both justice and injustice, he those only of justice. He is too civilized to use her weapons while she shames at nothing so it accomplish her purpose. Being a child, a savage, she is morally untrained, being a witch she will stoop to abominable measures. The particular device she hits upon is that of driving her husband insane, by instilling the doubt in his mind that he is the father of his child. Men in general, Strindberg feels, are at a great disadvantage in this matter for no man can know for certain who is the father of his children. For that reason a husband should not speak of *his* children but only of the children of his wife. This circumstance gives women a terrible weapon. Laura uses it to such advantage that the captain, under the terrible pressure of doubt, does lose his mind, at least his freedom and rights. Laura, cold and remorseless even in the midst of hysterical passion, is a complete victor. She has persuaded the Captain's friends and colleagues, even his daughter, that he is mad and has thereby won everything she desired—the Captain's humiliation or destruction, her own free way with his household and income, and the control of her daughter.

But Laura is not all evil. Many women who saw the play even came to sympathize with her, a fact which impressed Strindberg very much and convinced him that there are many Lauras and many crimes like hers on foot. Laura is not all evil. As a woman she destroys the Captain, as a mother she could be tender and cherish him. She is not cruel by principle but by instinct. The hatred of the opposite sex is as deep in her as love and love breeds the strife of the sexes. Laura is not free in her diabolic cruelty but forced by the exigency of nature itself.

At times she seems to realize this herself and to view the terrible part she is playing quite objectively—a curious spectator of her own cruel devices. At times she can talk to the captain quite reasonably, analyzing her animosity and its causes and then both contestants lay down their arms and play the philosopher, reflecting freely on their actions in which, as they divine, there is no freedom. These interludes of reasonable reflection occur frequently in Strindberg's works and particularly in a play very similar to *The Father, The Dance of Death.*

It is this philosophizing over their own situation which Zola condemns in *The Father.* The characters of the play, he says, are "creatures of reason." But this is a very doubtful objection. There is a certain elevation of the action which is, on the contrary, quite dependent upon the characters glimpsing momentarily, at least, their predicament and their fate. It is the foreknowledge of disaster in Greek plays such as *Œdipus,* and *Trojan Women* which produces the deep reverberations and the sense of the inescapable fates. If the hero does not foresee his fate, his death will be meaningless and accidental. But foreknowledge gives to death a general significance and a cosmic value. Let us consider Achilles raging at the height of his anger. He conquers a Trojan youth and is about to kill him when suddenly his mood changes to one of sadness. To each man death comes sooner or later. Some day I, too, shall meet my fate, whether by arrow or by the enemy's spear, etc. But again his rage begins and falling upon the youth with the utmost fury he cuts him to pieces, and throws the white body of his enemy to the river. This sudden change of mood—from rage to calm and tragic reflection—gives this scene a power and timelessness which could not otherwise be achieved. It is this effect which Strindberg and Hardy obtain when they make a creature of passion turn suddenly philosopher, and reveal a knowledge of his own bondage and the sad destiny prepared for him. This change of stride in the midst of the naturalistic reversal of human joys and ambitions is so far from being a defect that it is almost the only device by which the naturalistic action is raised to a proper plane, and changed from the brutal and sentimental slaughter of innocents, to the tragic defeat of a superior man, fighting vainly but knowingly against the fates and the forces of the earth. It is premonitory wisdom that makes a character a tragic hero who was before only pathetic. So *Tess of the D'Urbervilles* becomes a tragic figure for the first time when, out on the quiet heath, she turns a rational being, considers her crime, and knowing her fate, waits for the officers who must take her away to the scaffold.

In Hardy's characters the sense of their doom and the cosmic malice is sometimes, perhaps, too frequently apparent. In the *Dynasts* it is not enough that the human figures should fathom their doom but the ruling spirits must sing dirges from time to time on the purposeless but necessary transactions in the melancholy world. Thus the Spirit Ironic speaks from above explaining the dismal course of human affairs:

"It's only that life's queer mechanics chance to work out in this grotesque way, just now. The groping tentativeness of an Immanent Will cannot be asked to learn logic at this time of day." And the Spirit of the Years:

"O Immanence that reasonest not
In putting forth all things begot,
Thou buildest Thy house in Space—for what?"

Here the ironic consciousness of fate, which Aristotle first ascribed to the tragic hero, is transferred to the skies and the aerial spirits speak for the deep forebodings of men. Elsewhere in Hardy, throughout the novels, men speak for themselves.

In Strindberg's *The Father, The Dance of Death,* and to a much greater degree in the later plays, the characters reason and analyze their conflicts and passions and understand their place in the world. In *The Father,* the Captain, tortured by the suspicion that he is not Bertha's father, begins to cry and then attempts to justify his weakness. Laura immediately becomes the mother. "Cry then, my child," she says, "and you will have your mother again. Do you remember that it was as your second mother that I first entered your life? Your great strong body was without nerves. You were a giant child that had come too early into the world, or perhaps was not wanted." The Captain agrees and continues to analyze his nature and his relation to her. Yes, he was her child and as long as he remained so, they were happy but when he became the man, he became her enemy and her blood was ashamed. "And that was your mistake," says Laura. "The mother was your friend, you see, but the woman was your enemy, and love between the sexes is strife." This scene of mutual understanding and even sympathy is but an interlude to the deadly hostilities. The Captain realizes suddenly how cold and secretly determined his wife has become—one of them must go down in this struggle. Which one? The weaker! Laura will win because might is right. Suddenly she shows him her weapon—a letter from the Commissioners in Lunacy depriving him of all rights. The Captain, at this juncture, does what Strindberg was often tempted to do, he throws a lighted lamp at his wife. This frenzied climax is obviously much strengthened and deepened by the calm sympathy and understanding which went before. Zola's objection to this play, that the characters are "creatures of reason" would seem to be groundless. If the captain and Laura are philosophers in their way, the art is improved by it. "Metaphysical man," said Zola, "is dead," but how false this is may be seen from his own works and from those of his followers.

In the plays of Ibsen, Strindberg, Hauptmann, Wedekind, etc., metaphysics is not suppressed as Zola desired,—it enjoys a long riot. In *The Dance of Death* the artillery captain and his wife spend scene after scene psychoanalyzing each other and the plot is advanced thereby, for the action is within their souls. Similarly in the other plays, metaphysical speculation, which gives generality and depth to even the most unusual or pathological action, is never long silent. These are metaphysical plays which analyze the nature and consequences of love, sin, and religion in a general way without particular regard for individuals. And the motivation? In Strindberg's case it is the craving to body forth ideas which burned in his mind and allowed him no peace until they were expressed.

Ibsen and Strindberg do not use sex as an excuse for intrigue as did the French comedy before them. The question is not who Nora or Laura will marry in the end, but rather what they will do when they do marry and love, and what, under close analysis, is love and marriage in general. Thus the romantic play deals preferably with the unmarried couples and shows how accidents keep them apart or bring them together while the plays of Strindberg are concerned primarily with married people and devote themselves to an analysis of love, marriage, sin, suffering, religion, according to their essence, using the characters merely as illustrations of his metaphysical ideas.

This is particularly the case in the one-act play *Miss Julia,* a work in which the environmental and hereditary factors are much more complicated and numerous than in *The Father,* and developed with such clarity and economy as to leave no doubt that the philosophical ideas preceded and determined the creation. The multiform character of the motivation, the numerous causes assigned for Miss Julia's eccentric behavior, show that Strindberg had developed a new and more sophisticated Naturalism than Zola or any of his other followers had achieved. Miss Julia is not a pathological case or a very exceptional woman; she is a type of worn-out nobility, just as Jean, her seducer and executor, is a type of the crude and remorseless lower classes rising by dint of energy and superior will power to the higher places. In this play the souls of the characters have become so diffuse and complicated, and so contradictory and willy-nilly, borrowing their words and ideas from other men, that they properly have no characters at all, and it is only out of courtesy that we speak of them as individuals. This is a new departure in Naturalism and in Psychology in which Strindberg shares the honors with Dostoevsky. In the following passage from the author's preface to *Miss Julia* he defines the numerous influences, all of which are necessary to explain the curious wildness of Miss Julia. (See also Strindberg's letter to Georg Brandes, p. 291.) She was a martyr to the "discord which a mother's crime produces in a family and also a victim of the day's delusions, of the circumstances of her defective constitution. In explanation of (her) sad fate (are) her mother's fundamental instincts, her father's mistaken upbringing of the girl, her own nature, and the suggestive influence of her fiancé on a weak and degenerate brain; furthermore, and more directly, the festival mood of the Midsummer Eve; the absence of her father; her physical condition, her preoccupation with animals; the excitation of the dance—" Here the motivations are trivial but cumulative and the soul has become a congeries without unity. We have thus traveled as far from the formal simplicity of Classicism as from the villains and heroes of Romanticism. Art no longer renders life simpler, more noble and logical, but reproduces its seeming irrelevances, its disjointed meaningless determinations, so that the skeleton of the primitive confusion is revealed in nature and in the human soul. In the light of Strindberg's analysis the clear-cut moral conflict of Antigone or the romantic despair of Werther are alike unreal and improperly motivated. After Dostoevsky and Strindberg confusion of character and the accumulated force of trivial factors in nature and the mind formed a dominant motif in modern literature.

Miss Julia is also important in its emphasis on evolution and racial superiority. Miss Julia is racially and socially superior to Jean but her stock has degenerated. Hence the fresh and vigorous servant has the upperhand. He survives because he is, though to be sure, a low fellow, still the fittest in the struggle for existence. As a consequence there is mixed with our pity and misgiving at her sudden and terrific death, a fatalistic resignation to the way of nature.

The climax of the play and the calculated death of Miss Julia is one of the most horrible scenes ever attempted in literature. It was performed in many places unsuccessfully and was sometimes censored and withheld from the stage. In Denmark it was performed privately in a student union but even here it met with a reproof, for it was necessary to prepare the public very carefully for this play. Perhaps if Georg Brandes had prepared the way for Strindberg as he did for Ibsen matters might have taken quite a different course. As it was the play was censored and ill-received and the finale scarcely anyone could endure. Perhaps this was to be expected. It will be remembered that a somewhat similar scene in Dostoevsky's *The Possessed,* in which the terrible Stavrogin sits quietly while the child he has seduced hangs herself in the next room, was suppressed in Russia and has still never been published except in Germany.

During this same early period of Naturalism, Strindberg also wrote a novel, *By the Open Sea.* Here he is occupied as, in *Miss Julia,* with racial superiority and evolutionary survival. The hero

Dr. Borg, who is really Strindberg, with a slight disguise, considers himself with some reason to be one of the foremost figures in the progress of the race. Yet in the struggle against nature and the lower forms of nature,—women and savages,—he is completely worsted, and the evolutionary process which he has so frequently expounded and praised, is itself the cause of his defeat and death. By a common regression in the evolutionary advance, he, the highest in the series, is vanquished by lower forms. Like the noble lion, he is killed by a colony of parasites.

In *Pariah* and *Simoon,* (1889-90), two one-act plays, Strindberg is already subject to new influences which were to change his whole metaphysics and transform his naturalistic drama into morality plays and dream plays and pilgrimages of the soul. It was Edgar Allan Poe who inspired these plays, especially *Pariah,* and gave them their weirdness and infernal coloring. His hand is also seen in *Pariah* in the sudden probing of the secret past of the two criminals. Strindberg had also learned many things from Charcot and other psychologists of the abnormal mind. He had become interested, at first with only a skeptical curiosity, in hypnotism, mental telepathy, spirits, and supernatural influences in general. But his scientific curiosity was soon to change to an uncommon credulity. The time was to come when Strindberg's naturalistic world would be peopled with fairies and witches and vampires, and ruled by demons and powers and black-hooded spirits muttering below. There was also to be a world purpose, a moral destiny for man. The cruel demons and the suffering gods were to grow sad and spiteful, requiring new atonements, and new sins and sufferings, of the pale ghostly men in their peep-show world. This was the fate of Strindberg's naturalism.

With Zola the same thing happens though to a lesser degree. The forces of nature become demons and powers. In *Germinal,* for instance, a scene occurs in which the fields, filled with amorous couples, themselves stir and throb and come to life, responding to the movements of this solemn orgy. Here Zola's laws of nature are transcended and forgotten. It is rather the majesty of the earth-mother,—of Ishtar or Isis,—who presides and directs her own ritual. Across Zola's great canvasses a god often walks. His greatness, like that of Strindberg, is to be seen, not in his scientific rigor, however noteworthy this may be, but in the wealth and power of his imagination.

Though Strindberg in his wandering advance toward the truth admitted new principles and powers to the government of the earth, he retained the old laws of nature and left them their authority, and he blended mystery and science in a new play.

XX

STRINDBERG AND NIETZSCHE

"WHEN Zarathustra was thirty years old, he left his home and the lake of his home, and went into the mountains. There he enjoyed his spirit and his solitude, and for ten years did not weary of it. But at last his heart changed,— and rising one morning with the rosy dawn, he went before the sun, and spake thus unto it:

"Thou great star! What would be thy happiness if thou hadst not those for whom thou shinest! . . . . Therefore must I descend unto the deep as thou doest in the evening, when thou goest behind the sea and givest light to the nether-world, thou exuberant star!

"Like thee must I go down, as men say, to whom I shall descend. . . . Thus began Zarathustra's down-going. . . . And Zarathustra spake thus unto the people: *I teach you the Superman.* Man is something to be surpassed. What have you done to surpass man?" Just as the ape has been surpassed and is now a thing ridiculous and shameful, so man must be surpassed.

And so Zarathustra taught that the old gods are dead and the old values. Christianity, democracy, are cults of the weak and the ugly. They are programs of the humble to destroy the strong. The weak ones, with their whining and canting, with their pity and forgiveness, are the great Evil. With their principle of Equality they would kill the higher man. To put an end to their fears and envy they would destroy the one hope and justification of man. All evil springs from the weak just as all good springs from the strong. There is but one impulse in man, the will-to-power and but one value, power. Man must will power and he must will the power of a greater man. It is his one glory to surpass himself.

One of the first men whom Zarathustra met on his down-going was Strindberg. On him the new doctrine worked a great effect, for he was prepared for it. He had lived by strong passions, recklessly, fought against cowardice and lies and pettiness. He had lived dangerously to the length of his energies. He had craved power and raged at his weaknesses.

But it had not been easy for Strindberg to anticipate the joyous doctrine of Zarathustra, so complex was his nature and divided that he turned now to the aristocrats, now to the people. For he was himself half slave, half master. From the very first he had sensed the rancor and the conflict of the classes, felt painfully the oppression of each and his own divided allegiance. Throughout his life, he continued at intervals to feel the same bitter resentment at the presumption and stupid cruelty of the autocrats. But he had also suffered at the hands of the lower classes. Necessary contacts with inferior minds had dwarfed his heart, destroyed his fine-spun thoughts, forced him back to the commonplace. Petty scribblers, jealous of his genius, had ridiculed his plays and novels, taken away his peace, and robbed him of his livelihood. The public, i. e. the people, would not attend his plays or buy his books. He had been asked to adapt his thoughts to their meanness and inferiority. This was too much.

The conflict in Strindberg's soul between master and slave was violent and long contested and both sides won decisive victories. At times, the son of a servant stepped forth as a rebel against the tyranny of established order. At times, the aristocrat was dominant and condemned the rebellious slaves as criminals. Once, while watching the manœuvers of marching soldiers, he

fell into great admiration of their power and disciplined superiority, identified himself with the army. The next moment, he
thought of the arrogance of the officers and of the people whom
this army suppressed and enslaved. He then became the mad
revolutionary who would meet and crush this cruel, organized
tyranny single-handed.

In the historical dramas, such as *Gustavus Vasa,* Strindberg
shows the same shifting allegiance; his sympathies—now with the
king, now with his subjects, now with authority, now with freedom. In Strindberg's plays and novels, where the war of the
sexes unfolds its grief and horrors, it is usually the upright man
of culture who is pitted against the pretentious but ignorant
woman. The man is really the stronger, but the woman often
wins through her persistence, singleness of purpose, and unscrupulous choice of weapons. Strindberg, like Nietzsche, regrets that might should be right when the might is that of the
petty and unscrupulous, combining and plotting for their safety.
The superman in Strindberg's naturalistic period is really a creation to combat the fiendish cruelty of the "modern" woman. If
Laura kills the Father and the Father is a great man and a
scientist, like Strindberg himself, her crime is that much blacker.
If she kills the superman, Strindberg's own defeat and humiliations
are explained, and the cunning strength and the full wickedness of her type is made clear. But, though Strindberg's superman of the period 1886–92 is mainly an anti-type to the emancipated woman, it has a broader significance in his writings.
Strindberg, in keeping with the times and before his knowledge of Nietzsche, was enamored of culture and of great
men.

The "superman" was, of course, not an isolated phenomenon,
nor a creation of Nietzsche. For at least two generations a radical
glorified cult of individualism had been growing up independently in various parts of the western world, in reaction against
the leveling tendencies of democracy, industrialism, and "de-

generate Christianity." While Kierkegaard was creating the ideal of the priestly man in Denmark, Carlyle was exalting the role of the hero in history, and Emerson in America was praising what he called the representative man. In the midst of the revolutionary excitement of 1848, Stirner's *The Ego and Its Own* carried on the rising theme. In France, meanwhile, Flaubert with his venomous hatred of the bourgeoisie was finding solace in the saintly role of the artist, and Comte de Gobineau was elaborating his doctrine of the unequality of races which led later on to his exaltation of the Renaissance egotists. Dostoevsky's *Crime and Punishment,* an experimental study in the would-be superman, appeared, it is significant to notice, as early as 1856. And finally Ibsen, 1864, painted varied pictures of the superman in *The Pretenders* and *Brand.* All this, it should be noted, anticipated Nietzsche and was independent of Darwin. This is not to say that Nietzsche was influenced by all or any of these writers, but merely to indicate that his great theme had already been sounded throughout Europe before Zarathustra had started his down-going.

In 1886, Strindberg's sympathies had turned away definitely from the lower classes, women, and in fact, all the biologically inferior. In this year, he took the part of the Americans against the Chinese and in 1888 defended them zealously against the negroes, whom he said resembled very much the criminal type of Europe. In the years 1886–92 occur also his most drastic indictments of women. Personally, he had come to think of himself as an exceptional man who had a right as a genius to more than others could rightly desire. The sufferings of great men form a continuous motif in his writings at this time.

The superman doctrine had appealed to Strindberg long before his acquaintance with Nietzsche and had already made its appearance in his early play, *Master Olaf* (1876). Here, the main influences were Kierkegaard, Ibsen's *Brand,* and Goethe's *Götz von Berlichingen.* It was Kierkegaard who taught Strindberg the way of the saintly man, that man of indomitable will, who, ruthless of consequences, devoted recklessly to God, sacrifices all values on the altar of his faith. Brand but reinforced this lesson and showed him the dramatic possibilities of this lion become a saint.

Master Olaf, who brought the reformation to Sweden, is represented as a man of superior boldness and strength, passionate and resolute in his search for the truth. He is the idealist, just as Girt and Gustavus Vasa, the next two important characters in the play, are respectively the revolutionary and the opportunist. The action is the struggle between these three men, representing three irreconcilable principles in Strindberg's nature, and the victory does not fall to Master Olaf. At the end of the play he repents and bows his head before authority, both temporal and spiritual. He is forgiven, but neither he nor Strindberg would be apt to forgive himself the apostasy to self.

Master Olaf betrays a weakness which haunts all Strindberg's supermen, a complexity and an indecision of character, a proneness to understand and sympathize with the enemy, which renders his victory costly and marginal, and his defeat almost certain. Neither Dr. Borg, in *By the Open Sea,* nor the Magistrate in *Tschandala* has anything in him of the blond beast, of the joyous, ruthless warrior. Dr. Borg, for all his cultural discipline, falls victim to the primeval urge of sex, is overpowered by the malice of a solid majority, and finally sails out to sea under Hercules, cursing the Christian God in utter helplessness. The Magistrate, like Dr. Borg, is a quiet man and no warrior. Unable to conquer his enemy, the malicious gypsy, by main strength, he has recourse to his science. Like a sorcerer, he ensnares the gypsy with dreams and visions and, thus, playing upon his occult fears, conquers this wretched enemy. But the victory is not a glorious one. The Magistrate has none of that lofty contempt of the enemy which Zarathustra shows the hostile viper. When the viper had bitten Zarathustra, it turned sad and regretful and

Zarathustra said, full of proud confidence: "When did you hear that a viper's poison could kill a dragon?"

Neither the Magistrate, nor Dr. Borg, nor any of Strindberg's heroes, is a dragon. Gustavas Vasa approaches that degree, but he, too, is full of doubts and scruples, and in the end it is only a miracle that saves him his kingdom. Billgren, the hero in *The Secret Way,* 1887, engaged in a frantic and even fight with an hysterical, deceitful woman, and opposes his reason to spiritualism and a cult of Nirvana. He, too, is a superman but possessed, like the rest, with human weaknesses.

In his novel *The War of the Brain* (1887) the strong are given a new weapon against the weak. In the light of Charcot's teaching, Strindberg sees "that suggestion is only the hostile attack of the stronger brain and its victory over the weaker, and that this process goes on in daily life unperceived." Actors, writers, preachers, painters, thus carry out their will, imposing their moods and convictions on the inert and suggestible public. The hero of this novel, a socialist, engages in a sort of psychical or hypnotic duel in which he is defeated. This is also the defeat of Socialism. Strindberg now turns in high admiration of the nobles and the upper class.

By 1888 Strindberg had gone so far with his master-slave dichotomy, had become so enraged at women and socialists, and so enamored of supermen and nobles, that Georg Brandes felt it was high time he became acquainted with the man who had begun to stir all Europe with this theme. He, therefore, wrote to Nietzsche recommending Strindberg. He is a bit mad, said Brandes, like all geniuses (and non-geniuses). But he is a true genius and his views on women are quite close to your own.

Strindberg, at this time, was living in Holte near Copenhagen, where he had tarried in part to consult a specialist at the nerve clinic, for even at this time he feared that his wife and relatives were plotting against him and would commit him to an asylum.

He desired to secure a certificate of sanity and it was with some disappointment that he learned that this was impossible, unless he remained in the clinic some weeks for observation. Strindberg imparted this bit of information to Georg Brandes at the beginning of his first interview, which astonished that gentleman not a little. He became aware, he afterwards wrote, that in Strindberg he had to do with an original, of whom nothing common was to be expected.

Strindberg's residence in Holte consisted of four rooms in an old and dilapidated castle. Here, in these narrow quarters, he took up his life with his wife and three children, under conditions which were calculated to make him as miserable and mad and lonely as any that could be conceived. The estate was in great disorder, his rooms always upset and untidy and his wife or children usually sick. Dogs, whom Strindberg hated so bitterly, stalked uninvited through the rooms, and a malicious, evil-looking gypsy, supposedly the care-taker, lorded it over the place and pried into his secrets. Strindberg had but one shelter from these miseries: that was the island in the pond near the castle. Thither he could escape and drawing up the bridge after him, remove himself at one stroke from his ailing wife and children, the untidy rooms, the dogs, the malicious gypsy, and the persistent reproach of poverty. This was his one solace and here on the island he spent most of his time, reading and composing, his one horror being the thought of the approaching winter when, this escape being closed to him, he must needs spend day and night in that "witches' kitchen," however stifling and ominous it might be.

In Holte, actual events followed one another much as they are related in *Tschandala,* a novel which covers this period. Strindberg, whose marriage had become intolerable (a "laughable farce" as he himself expressed it), fell into a brief and regrettable attachment for the daughter of the gypsy and had his way with her. This gave the gypsy what he wanted, a weapon against

Strindberg. He proceeded to threaten the famous author with blackmail and demanded money which Strindberg, of course, could not pay. Thus, the scandal went the rounds, got into a newspaper, and there was danger of its going much farther, though the girl herself defended Strindberg. The Magistrate in *Tschandala* destroys the gypsy by a sort of magic; Strindberg, less heroic, thinks only of flight. Finally, the matter is put to rights by the gypsy's arrest for theft. But Strindberg did not so soon forget and later carried a gun everywhere in fear of the gypsy's revenge, should he be released from jail.

Such was the situation of the great woman-hater and aristocrat during his correspondence with Nietzsche, and such was his martyrdom.

Nietzsche's first letter shows the ominous wandering of a great mind in the paths of irrelevant egoism. It reads:

DEAR SIR:
A priceless letter from M. Taine, which I enclose, gives me the courage to ask your advice on a very serious matter. I am keenly anxious to obtain an audience in France; more than that, it is for me absolutely necessary. Such as I am, the most independent and perhaps the strongest mind who lives today, doomed to the fulfillment of a stupendous task, it is impossible that the absurd boundaries which an accursed dynastic national-politics has drawn between peoples, should hold me back and prevent me from greeting those few who have ears to hear me. The character of the intellectual world of France is nothing unknown to me; people say my style is essentially French although in the German language, especially in my Zarathustra, I have attained perfection in German, itself, so far unequalled by any German— My forefathers on my father's side were Polish noblemen while my grandmother on my mother's side lived in Goethe's period at Weimar: reason enough for (my) being today, to an almost incredible degree, the loneliest of Germans. But not a single word of recognition has reached me and frankly I have never sought it. . . . Now, I have readers everywhere, in Vienna, in St. Petersburg, in Stockholm, in New York, distinguished minds

who do me honor. . . . I had lived in the closest intimacy with Richard Wagner and his wife, who at that time resided at Lucerne and a more profitable association it would be difficult to conceive. At bottom, perhaps, I am an old musician.

Later, sickness tore me loose from these last relations and brought me to a condition of the deepest self-consciousness which perhaps has ever been attained. And since in my nature itself there is nothing sickly, I hardly regarded this loneliness as a hardship, but rather felt it as a priceless distinction and at the same time, a purification. Also, no one has complained of my wearing a gloomy face, I myself, never: I have come to know more terrible and more problematic realms of thought than anyone, but only because it lies in my nature to love the other side of things. I account the spirit of gaiety a proof of my philosophy. . . .

Perhaps I will prove this to you in the two books which I send you today.

YOUR FRIEDRICH NIETZSCHE.

To this, Strindberg replied:

DEAR SIR:

Without doubt you have given mankind the deepest book (*Thus Spake Zarathustra*) that it possesses, and what is more, you have had the courage and perhaps the urge, to spit these splendid sayings in the very face of the rabble. I thank you for that! Still, it seems to me, that with your fairness of mind you have somewhat flattered the criminal type. If you examine the hundreds of photographs which illustrate Lombroso's types of criminals, you will admit that the criminal is a lowly beast, a degenerate, a weakling, who does not possess the ability to get around the phrases of the law, which oppose to his will and strength too great an obstacle. . . . And you wish to be translated into our Greenland language! Why not into French or English? You can judge our intelligence from the fact that people want to confine me in an asylum on account of my tragedy and that so fine and rich a mind as Brandes has been brought to silence by this compact majority.

I close all my letters to friends: Read Nietzsche! That is my *Carthago est dilenda!*

In any case, your greatness from the moment you are known
and understood will also be lowered, when the sweet rabble grow
familiar with you and greet you as one of themselves. It is
better for you to preserve the noble seclusion while we, the other
ten thousand higher ones, put forth on a secret pilgrimage to
your shrine, there to gather according to the heart's desire. Let
us protect the esoteric doctrine, preserve it pure and unimpaired
and not permit it to become common property except through devoted disciples—in whose name I sign myself,

AUGUST STRINDBERG.

This letter pleased Nietzsche very particularly. It was the first
letter to reach him, he wrote, with a world-historical cadence. It
is interesting to notice that though Strindberg indulges in rather
extreme adulation, he does not fall in with the purpose of
Nietzsche, but rather discourages his dearest wish, that of winning the public and gaining recognition. Strindberg, for all his
praises, is no servile follower, but sets his will and judgment
against Nietzsche. He was not a man to own a master. Strindberg's advice with regard to the importance of translation and
the value of securing a public is perhaps in Nietzsche's case the
wisest counsel that could be given, and his prediction of the consequences of a general dissemination of Nietzsche's works has
proved only too prophetic. Few authors have suffered more from
the popularization of their doctrines than Nietzsche.

Nietzsche's next letter acknowledges his receipt of *The Father,*
and comments on Zola's criticism of this play.

DEAR SIR:
I fancy our books must have crossed each other! (The books
which crossed each other were *The Twilight of the Idols* and
The Father.) I read your tragedy twice over with deep emotion;
it has astonished me beyond all measure, to come to know a
work in which my own conception of love—with war as its
means and the deathly hate of the sexes as its fundamental law—
is expressed in such a splendid fashion. But this work is really destined to be presented by M. Antoine in Paris at the Théâtre

Libre! Simply demand this of Zola. At the moment he prizes it very highly when he attracts attention to himself.

I cannot but deplore, of course, the preface he has contributed, although I should have been sorry to miss it, for it contains countless naïvetés. That Zola disapproves "of abstraction" puts me in mind of a German translator of one of Dostoevsky's novels, who also cared nothing for "abstraction"—he simply left out recourses to analyses—they annoyed him! How odd, too, that Zola is unable to distinguish between types and creatures of reason! And that he should demand a complete social setting for your tragedy! And when he finally tried to make a question of race of the whole matter, I almost shook with laughter! As long as taste really existed in France, the whole instinct of the race showed itself opposed to all that he represented—it is precisely the Latin race which protests against Zola. In the final analysis, he is a modern Italian—he worships the verisimo. . . .

With expressions of my highest esteem,

Yours,
Nietzsche.

Torino, Via Carlo,
Nov. 27, 1888.

Zola's letter, on which Nietzsche comments, is as follows:

Paris 14, Dec. '87.

Monsieur and dear Colleague!

I must ask you to excuse me for my long silence. But if you knew what a life I have led, what work and fatigue! I didn't want to send your manuscript back to you without having read it, and finally I found the necessary time.

Your play [1] interests me very much. The philosophical idea is very daring, and the characters are boldly drawn. You have traced the doubt of paternity with a powerful and disquieting effect. Finally, your Laura is the true woman in the unconsciousness and the mystery of her qualities and faults. She will remain buried in my memory. In all, you have written a very curious and interesting work, in which there are, especially at the end, some very beautiful things. To be frank, however, the recourse to analysis there troubles me a little. You know that I

---

[1] *The Father,* for which Zola wrote a foreword.

am not much for abstraction. I like my characters to have a complete social setting, that we may elbow them and feel that they are soaked in our air. And your captain who has not even a name, your other characters who are almost creatures of reason, do not give me the complete sense of life which I require. But the question between you and me here is really one of race. Such as it is, I repeat, your piece is one of the few dramatic works which has moved me profoundly. Believe me your devoted and sympathetic colleague,

ÉMILE ZOLA.

The following is one of Strindberg's letters to the celebrated Georg Brandes, sometimes known as the Voltaire of Denmark. The subject is again Nietzsche and Nietzsche's doctrine.

Holte, December 4, 1888.

DEAR DOCTOR:

First, concerning Nietzsche, whose (enclosed) letter it will be a pleasure for you to read. I find it modern (in him) to speak those proud but true words, and we must remember that in our days, strong minds with increasing self-consciousness are not un-expected; when a great force like him finds by comparison with others, that his mind is the greatest and strongest, the discovery once made, the temptation to speak it out becomes irresistible. Nietzsche appears to me as the herald of the decline of Europe and Christendom, of the awakening and re-entry of the Orient to its rights, as of the eagle who displays the oldest nobility. Christianity is to me namely a barbarity which only gained ac-ceptance through the wandering of the people, since the bar-barians found in Christian superstition a substitute for their own. While the cultured Romans and Greeks would never permit themselves to be baptized, the Goths, Lombards, Germans, Sax-ons, and Normans accepted the husks of the degenerate Christ. Christianity is for me a set-back in development, the religion of the petty, the miserable, the castrates, women, children, and savages; therefore it stands in strict contradiction to our evolu-tion, which aims to protect the strong against the wretched, and the pressing forward of women at the present time seems to me simply a symptom of the regression of the race and a conse-quence of Christianity. Nietzsche consequently seems to me the one modern spirit who has dared to preach the right of the strong, the wise, against the blockheads and midgets (the democrats), and I can understand the suffering of this great mind in the power of the host of petty ones, for this is a period in which everything is dominated by women and stupidity. I recognize in him the deliverer and as a teacher of the catechism, I conclude my letters to literary friends in the following way: read Nietzsche.

And now *Miss Julia!* "The deathly hate of the sexes" which Nietzsche sees in *The Father* is also to be found here, but here also a conscious repugnance of the pernicious sort, generating itself, comes to play a part (compare Schopenhauer concerning pederasty), also, a weakness of the will-to-live, the dream of the fall of the column,[1] the disinclination of the mother to cohabitation, masculine education, etc. The suicide is properly motivated: the disinclination to live, the longing to extinguish the race in the last wretched individual, the noble feeling of shame over intercourse with one of a lower class, and more particularly the suggestion afforded by the blood of the bird, the nearness of the razor, the fear that the theft will be discovered and the command of a stronger will (first the will of the servant, then that of the Count). Notice that Miss Julia, left to herself, would have lacked the strength, but as it is she is driven and led on by various motives.

It is strange that through Nietzsche I am now prepared "to oppose to everything" my particular system of delusions. I reverse valuations and give old things new worth! That, no one understands. I hardly do myself! Thanks meanwhile for your letters and Auf Wiedersehen

YOUR AUGUST STRINDBERG.

Brandes who is in Copenhagen, only a short distance from Holte, answers the following day:

DEAR MR. STRINDBERG:

I return Nietzsche's letter with many thanks. I am delighted

[1] Miss Julia's dream that she is on the pillar and grows dizzy and is about to fall is an obvious piece of erotic symbolism, but Jean's reciprocal dream of lying in the grass and desiring to rob the nest is exceedingly neat and clever but scarcely in accord with dream analysis.

to have brought such important men as you and him together and made it possible for you to understand one another.

Your explanations with regard to Miss Julia interest me very much and almost persuade me. Only one little thing is wrong, but to go into that would take us too far.

You know how highly I value Nietzsche and likewise how keenly I feel the injustice of the fact that he has pined away almost unknown. Nevertheless his doctrine, in which there is so much that is admirable, contains also a great many things to which I personally object.

Much of his doctrine seems to me far less original than it appears to you and him. His opposition to Christianity, you will surely grant me, is not apt to make an especially deep impression on one who for twenty years and more—for a long time alone—has borne the odium of being the Anti-christ of the North.

It seems wise to me to leave any sort of praise of oneself to others—a man of the strongest self-consciousness would be too proud to praise himself and so indifferent to the judgments of other men, that he would keep silent and say nothing for himself.[1] But this sort of thing is really a matter of feeling and taste.

Nietzsche's judgment of Zola's letter is surprisingly fine and felicitous.   Your devoted G.B. (Georg Brandes.)

In his next letter, Nietzsche begs Strindberg to translate *Ecce Homo* into French. He concludes:

"I trust, dear Sir, that you will give this matter your kind consideration. It is something of extreme importance. For I am powerful enough to break the history of humanity into two parts."

Strindberg's answer runs as follows:

"It gave me great pleasure to receive a few words from your master hand with regard to my much misunderstood tragedy. I must tell you that I was forced to give the publisher the proceeds of the complete editions before he would agree to its publication. And then, in recompense for this, an old lady fell dead

---

[1] Nietzsche himself says that it is only the vain man who needs to see his worth acknowledged by other men, the proud man has himself. But the vain man is really modest.

during the performance at the theatre, another woman fainted and when the strait-jacket was produced on the stage, three-quarters of the audience rose like one man and ran from the theatre bellowing like mad bulls! . . . And with regard to your affair, I sometimes write directly in French (see the enclosed article with its 'boulevard' and yet somewhat picturesque style) —and at other times I translate my own works.

"It is almost impossible to find a French translator who would not try to 'improve' one's style according to the rules of the Normal School of Rhetoric and deprive one's expression of its fresh originality. . . . You will therefore be in a position to understand that I must regard the question of translating your book from a financial point of view, and inasmuch as I am only a poor devil (wife, three children, two servants, debts, and so forth) I could not afford to do it for less, especially since it is to be a piece of poet's work and not a mere hack's. . . .

"With regard to England I have really nothing to say, for there we have to do with a puritanical land delivered into the hands of women—which signifies the same thing as having fallen into a state of absolute decadence. . . ."

Strindberg, in his next letter, thanks Nietzsche for sending him his "magnificent" *Genealogy of Morals*.

Nietzsche's reply shows a sudden and tragic change; there was no doubt that that bold, dominating mind had commenced to waver in its course. To several of his correspondents at this time he wrote in a strange, cryptic, sinister style which was all the more perplexing since it sounded at one moment like real madness, the next, like the mocking laughter of some dionysiac god. Nietzsche, who during this whole period of correspondence was failing, now broke at last. He writes:

DEAR SIR: You will receive an answer to your story (*By the Open Sea*) in due course—it sounds like a rifle-shot. I have commanded a royal holiday at Rome—for I will shoot the young Kaiser.

Until we meet again! For we shall meet again. Une seule condition; Divorçons. . . .

NIETZSCHE CAESAR.

When Strindberg received this letter he thought that it was Nietzsche's pleasure to jest and therefore answered in the same vein—a letter in Greek and Latin:

DEAREST DOCTOR: I will, I will, I will be mad! Not without perturbation did I receive your letter and I thank you for it.

"More rightly wilt thou live, Licinius, if thou wilt not always steer forth upon the high seas, nor, cowering fearfully before the storm, cling too closely to the treacherous coast." (Horace)

In the meantime, all hail to madness! Adieu and keep in kind remembrance—

YOUR STRINDBERG.
(The best, the highest God.)

Nietzsche's answer in a single line was a terrible surprise to Strindberg. The cord had snapped. Nietzsche was henceforth to live on many years in the shadows. This last agonized cry before the lonely darkness settled around him read:

Herr Strindberg:—Eheu! No more! Divorçons!
The Crucified One.

Henceforth, Nietzsche suffered his miseries and his loneliness in silence and the man who had set all Europe ajar by ten years of terrific production, was heard of no more. A victim of paresis, he lingered on eleven and a half years in the "twilight of the gods," but even here perhaps his pride and his high courage persisted to the end.

During his detention at the Jena insane asylum, he wrote on request the following autograph:

"There are losses which exalt the soul, so that it forbears to whine, and walks silently under tall, black cypresses.—(Lonely Nietzsche 396)."

Strindberg, under Nietzsche's influence, also walked proudly, fought and forbore to whine, his martyrdom giving way to courage. Nietzsche's breakdown came to him as a profound shock. For months he worried over these last mad letters and finally he became afraid that he himself might be thought insane because he took them so seriously. A strange suspicion beset him. Frau Marholm (his sponsor) and Frau Förster Nietzsche would now contrive to put *him* in an asylum. When Strindberg wrote to Georg Brandes about Nietzsche's last ominous letters the latter replied: "I have expected it for a long time." But that Nietzsche was mad did not satisfy Strindberg. He himself had been thought mad and his tragedies taken as proof. Even Brandes, he felt, had his suspicions. Who, then, was sane? The majority? Public opinion? This raised a most interesting question to which Strindberg returns again and again in the succeeding years. Is not the charge of insanity merely a defence of society against men of genius and originality, those adders in its nest, who would destroy, transform it, and revaluate? Strindberg in his youth had been attracted by madness and courted it as an escape. During the period of his correspondence with Nietzsche he feared madness, but more especially he feared a calculated attack on his liberty, an insidious plot to incarcerate him forever in an asylum. His anxiety on this head continued intermittently for eight years, until his own breakdown in 1896, and even beyond this time, and often his fears reached the point of frenzy.

In the same year that Nietzsche collapsed, de Maupassant, who like Strindberg had sat at the feet of the masters and made himself one of the greatest naturalists, also lost hold and was sent to an asylum. And so the Anti-christ Nietzsche and "the melancholy bull" both strayed and were lost in the twilight— de-sceptered like Saturn.

> "Deep in the shady sadness of a vale
> Far sunken from the healthy breath of morn."

It is often said of Strindberg that he followed Nietzsche with anything but faithfulness, that he borrowed ideas when he had need of them, adapting them to his occasional purposes, but neglected those for which he had no use, and so changed and distorted them in the mirrors of his moods and preconceptions, that the likeness to the master was often lost. This criticism is no doubt true, though the spirit of Nietzsche's letters would seem to indicate that Strindberg was in tune with him at least on some points. But, if Strindberg was but a self-willed and wavering disciple in this case, it is no exception. Buckle, Darwin, Zola, Swedenborg, he also followed when he pleased, but in the main chose his own way. His departures from Nietzsche, his developments and additions, form a valuable variation of the master's doctrine.

In the first place it was Strindberg, not Nietzsche, who elaborated Schopenhauer's conception of the strife of the sexes as a conflict between noble strength and crafty, unscrupulous weakness. Nietzsche is so delighted with this conception that he ascribes it to himself. He is ever so much pleased, he says, to find developed in *The Father,* his own conception of love as the deathly war of the sexes. But there is very little in his writings to this effect. In *Zarathustra,* to be sure, he does say that: "Too sweet fruits—these the warrior liketh not. Therefore liketh he woman" and "Let man fear woman when she hateth: for man in his innermost soul is merely evil; woman, however, is mean," and "Thou goest to women? Remember thy whip!" But this is but the germ of the theme which Strindberg develops, varies, and repeats throughout the whole gamut of his works.

Again, Nietzsche's superman is a blond beast and he is Nordic, while Strindberg's hero is usually a delicate, cultured, sensitive man, often small and nervous, usually full of doubts and scruples, —he is scarcely a match for a determined woman. Nietzsche would not have allowed such a man to reproduce. Nietzsche's superman is a visionary being of remorseless and joyous power;

Strindberg's is a noble man of today, preferably a scientist or artist, or writer, and he does not look beyond. And it is partly for this reason that Strindberg's heroes are usually worsted, or win by a narrow margin with great hazard. Moreover, Strindberg looked upon Darwin's theory of the origin of species and the survival of the fittest as the finest support for the superman doctrine, and accepted it in detail, while Nietzsche admitted it only as a general law of development. In general, science, even occult science and psychology, plays a much more important part in the conception of the Swedish writer, for science becomes an instrument by means of which the heroic savant can outwill, hoodwink, baffle, or terrify his enemies, and by playing on their weakness or their ignorance and superstition, subdue and reduce them to his will. Hypnotism is one weapon of the cultured and heroic scientist, for his will is stronger than his enemies', and prestidigitation and sorcery (or what seems so to the ignorant dupes), is another resource which can bring even the beloved to terms, as in *By the Open Sea,* or destroy one's enemy who is physically stronger, as in *Tschandala,* by evoking the most terrifying images in his simple and suggestible mind.

Strindberg in the period which followed upon the above correspondence played so many variations on his master's theme that Georg Brandes grew alarmed and warned him against his uncritical application of Nietzsche's ideas which, he said, might lead, as well as not, to the right of brutal strength to suppress the world. But Strindberg had an irrepressible curiosity at this time and needed to assume new viewpoints in order to see things from all sides. "The contradictions in my system of writing," he says, "are consequent upon this." To Brandes he replied that he wished to continue indefinitely "my experiments with Nietzsche, whom," he adds, "I have in part anticipated." Brandes, however, despaired of these persistent experiments and maintained that it is our duty to fix upon a stopping place somewhere, that the unity of our life and thoughts may be preserved—perhaps he had darker thoughts. But, Strindberg, obsessed by the demons which govern world history, could not cease his deep and curious probings; he was destined to continue these experiments with men and things for many years, until his own psychosis in 1896, and even then, rising young again from this "dark night of the soul" with fresh experiences, to make new experiments and new discoveries in the strange and forbidden ways of the soul.

XXI

"I REALIZE NOW THAT I AM A GIANT"

SOME time ago a great German philosopher, Ueberweg, wrote a Logic in which he carried out his materialism with such thorough consistency that man's whole world became restricted to the limits of his skull. When, therefore, according to this doctrine, a man looks out on the trees and hills and sees the horizon in the distance he is but aware of events in his own brain. Beyond the distant horizon is the frontal bone of his skull, which, though he travels far, he can never reach. This bizarre conclusion was the direct consequence of the theory that everything is matter and of certain other principles of materialism. Thus the materialist became an extreme subjectivist and, oddly enough, a solipsist.

This is what happened to Strindberg. In the middle of the eighties he resolved to accept nothing which was at variance with the teachings of science, rejected God and the soul, occult and mysterious causes, and became, as his temper required, a very drastic naturalist. But hardly had he achieved this objectivity and fixed his mind upon the chemical and physical transactions which govern nature and human life, than doubtful ghosts, councilors of mystery and confusion, moved in closer to taunt his new-won faith, tempting him to subtleties and dangerous speculations, luring him with the wonderful and the weird, until lawful matter, the great realm of science, seemed to him but a wan and fading picture, extending from his cramped fingers to the stars, perhaps; yet, in the end, beyond its uttermost reaches was his skull and he became aware that the whole conception had its origin and spread in his brain.

Like his pietism, democracy, and other world views, Naturalism, too, had its hey-day and decline. In the retreats of his mind were many shrines, some long neglected, others smirched and dismantled, while others still flourished with many candles, but too brightly to endure. When Strindberg forswore his pietism and moved on to the cult of Naturalism, he cursed and desecrated the forsaken altar. When he recanted democracy and socialism to worship aristocracy and the superman he destroyed the shrine before leaving, for, like Julian, the Apostate, he could not bear the grin of false gods and needed to reassure himself in his new position. Thus he moved on from shrine to shrine, leaving behind him in defilement, the temples of former piety and devotion, and so crossed the allotted stations on the long road to Damascus.

In the middle of the eighties as a democrat and a naturalist he made little account of personalities and celebrities. The great figures of history, he proclaimed, were but chance products of circumstance, the vain and helpless organs of mass movements, for which reason, to worship them is only a form of idolatry or fetishism. His own idols, such as Spencer, were no better than the rest. Yet, for all his contempt for the great executive spirits of the past and present, he was far from belittling himself. In 1884, at the very height of his democracy and disrespect for heroes and sages, he himself was more vainglorious than ever before, indulging the most grandiose dreams in the Alps without a suspicion of his inconsistency. Even his self-depreciation, too abandoned and exaggerated to be quite sincere, failed to achieve modesty, hinting rather at the other grandeur of saint or scapegoat. In *The Son of a Servant* (1886) however, Naturalism and democracy conquered all pomp or vanity of person; Strindberg makes himself out there the product of heredity, environment, education, and spiritual forces, suppressing his sense of independent greatness to such a degree that his friend Heidenstam cried out at the misrepresentation.

When, in 1886, he came into contact with the monstrous ego of Nietzsche, his own caught the fire, expanding and soaring like a heated balloon, and now he knew himself to be "a giant" and there was no doubt about it. In speaking of Nietzsche, he says, "I believe he makes me blind, for my brain from over-exertion is like a wound, but he certainly makes me crazy, for the unheard-of egoism in his books has conveyed itself to me, . . . We will undoubtedly all meet in Gheel!" (A large sanitarium for the insane in Belgium.) To this sanctuary he turned more than once during these years with mixed feelings of longing and horror. Madness was, after all, the last defence of giants against the tyranny of external forces. Real madness or the feigned madness of Hamlet, the only alternative to prison or spiritual martyrdom.

A year later, Nietzsche, like a mystical hero after all his exploits, led the way into the shadows. As for Strindberg, the mental crisis which he fought with every weapon in his power a few years later, he now partly feared but half-encouraged. Nietzsche's doom, or that of the Father done to death by a woman, was not without its grandeur, and Hercules, after his infamies and madness, had been forgiven.

Another literary influence at this time, of a decidedly disruptive character, was that of Poe. Nietzsche had given Strindberg the sense of immense self-glory, but turned his mind by the infection of his own brooding greatness. Poe sharpened Strindberg's intelligence to the analysis of such hidden matters as the motives of criminals and the secrets of weird mysteries, but encouraged far too much those dangerous introspections which had already brought him, as he thought, to the abyss of unreason. Under Poe's guidance his love of these morbid investigations became an obsession, and he returned again and again to search in desperation those dim, illicit ranges of the soul. Where crimes are hatched, mysteries pondered, madness spun and treasured, where bats and monstrous fears spread unearthly horror, where the spirit staggers and creeps, fearful of its own weirdness and its own black depths, amid "shrieks and shapes and sights unholy," thither Poe led the way, and Strindberg followed his Vergil into these forbidden regions with all the partisan intensity and all the bitterness and asperity of Dante himself. So hot was his search for these monsters of the soul that he felt, as he says, like an over-charged Leyden flask, striking sparks and threatening to explode any moment. If so it should be, his last desire and testament is expressed by the one word "Gheel." There, if need be, he will give up his grievous responsibilities and return to that original helplessness, a thought which was perhaps anything but repulsive to Strindberg at this time.

Strindberg was so impressed with Poe and so struck with their many-sided resemblance that he ended by believing himself a reincarnation of the American poet. It was no accident, he thought, that Poe had died in 1849, the year he was born. His constellation of qualities had been transmitted by brain vibrations and thus Poe lived again in Strindberg. However this may be, the extraordinary resemblance of the two writers is undeniable, and appears more remarkable the more they are compared. In both we find the same love of the weird and the horrible, the same deep sense of sin and its manifold consequences in spiritual life, the crazed worship of purity in women, and a shrinking horror of the sexual or witch-like; the same quixotic interest in science, megalomania, and other agreements could be cited.

It was *The Gold Bug,* oddly enough, which took his fancy most, for he considered it a master stroke of analysis. From Poe's influence, Strindberg never entirely escaped. It can be traced even as far as the Blue Books. In 1888 he wrote a play in which the hypnotic power of suggestion and the weird infernal coloring have all the mood of Poe. Here a Bedouin maiden, whose hatred for the Franks, as she says "is boundless as the desert, burning as the sun, and stronger than my love," tortures a man to his death. Aided by the Simoon which withers the brains of Europeans, and fills them with a disgust of life, she so works upon the mind of a stray Frank soldier that he imagines he has been bitten by a mad dog, that he has rabies, that his wife has been unfaithful, and his child not his own, that he is himself a deserter and already dead under the headman's axe. Unable to bear these exquisite tortures, the Frank falls dead and the medallion-like little play comes to an end with the gruesome triumph of the Bedouin maid who is stronger, her love tells her, "stronger even than Simoon."

Another play written at this same time, also compact and re-resourceful, with many surprising turns of plot in the course of a few pages, shows the impact of both Nietzsche and Poe. *Pariah* is the compressed record of the mutual self-exposure of two criminals, one the Master nature, the other the slave or Pariah. The natural aristocrat admits having killed a man and does not repent the act, but he is horrified with the thought of stealing. The Pariah, on the other hand, has forged checks and suffered the penalty of a prison term. He has been punished for his theft while the other's murder went scot free. Yet Strindberg's sympathies are with the aristocrat, whose crime he thinks was not really a crime since it was not punishable (he had merely beaten a drunken cab-man), while the Pariah's offence was the more criminal in that he had stolen from motives of personal need.

This curious judgment is, of course, the direct opposite of what he maintained two years before as a democrat and socialist. Then, criminal laws were merely instruments in the hands of the upper class to maintain themselves in power and oppress the poor. Now, they express the instinct of the true aristocrat. Under Nietzsche's influence, but diverging in curious ways of his own, Strindberg came to believe that men are fundamentally and inherently of two sorts, aristocrats, and pariahs or slaves; that the pariahs are naturally criminals and naturally sympathize with slaves and criminals, and hence they are often to be detected even in the high places of kings and nobles. Thus the Swedish count, Snoilsky, was a pariah, as was proved by the mob sympathies of his parents and the slavish tendencies in his poetry, etc. In the application and variation of Nietzsche's principles, especially as here, to do in a literary rival, or in general to prove that all his enemies are pariahs and he an aristocrat, Strindberg's mind seems to be tottering for a fall and shows the last lengths of confusion and rage.

But in extreme contrast to his megalomania and gigantesque confusions is the precision and incisiveness of the dialogue in *Pariah* and the brilliance of Mr. X's detective work. In general, the star-clear intelligence and capacity and the splendor of phantasy, which he shows in most of the works of this period, prove without question that his turning away from reason, his retreat to the inner omnipotence of desire, was but episodic and partly perhaps a personal indulgence. Partly, too, it was motivated by the unhappy course of his love life. In 1886 he wrote *The Marodeure,* in which he delineated one aspect of his own marriage, the fiendish rivalry and oppression of a weak unscrupulous wife, with, however, the masculine triumph as a conclusion. In a later recasting, at a time when Strindberg's own affairs had taken a swift turn for the better, the conclusion is much softened. But later still his love turned to poison again, so that when the play was finally published (1888) under the title of *Comrades* the finale is far more brutal than before and more humiliating for the wife.

The Father (1897), in a more somber and terrible manner, recorded another strain in Strindberg's marriage and here the frenzied quickening malice of events overwhelms the worthy Captain (Strindberg) so that he succumbs, lost and raving in his straitjacket. But the bitterness and rancour had become a part

of his life, like poison of the vipers. He could not forget. Had not
Hercules cried out at the cruelty of Omphale and the burning
shirt of Nessus? Strindberg was only human. In 1886 the poison
of his memories poured out in a new play, *Creditors,* wherein he
portrays again the vampire woman who has sucked the best blood
of a young artist, her husband, while he labored for her and
spent his strength for her happiness. At the beginning of the
play the husband, Adolf, is discovered hard at work at his sculptur-
ing and conversing with his new friend, Gustav, who since his
wife's departure has nursed him back to health and roused him
to new confidence and new values by the hypnotic power of his
stronger will. As the conversation proceeds it transpires that when
Gustav found the poor husband, he was in a most pitiful state,
walking on crutches, reduced almost to imbecility by the cruelty
of his wife, who has, it appears, so insinuated herself into his
life that he is powerless without her, empty and helpless without
her cruelty. "The moment she leaves me," he says, "I begin to
long for her—long for her as for my arms or legs. It is queer that
sometimes I have a feeling that she is nothing in herself, but only
a part of myself—an organ that can take away with it my will,
my very desire to live. When she is smiling, I smile also. When
she is weeping, I weep. And when she—can you imagine anything
like it?—when she was giving birth to our child—I felt the birth
pangs within myself." Gustav points out that he is showing the
first symptoms of epilepsy, a suggestion which becomes a certainty as the play continues.

It now develops that Tekla, the artist's wife, has been married
before, that Adolph has won her for himself during her first
husband's absence, and that Tekla has written a novel, giving a
complete picture of the "idiot" to whom she had first been married. It seems that Adolph's and Tekla's child, when it was three
years old, began to look like the previous husband, who could
not possibly have been its father. Gustav explains that "the children of a widow who marries again often show a resemblance to

her dead husband," for which reason widows used to be burned in India. Adolph notices suddenly that Gustav resembles his wife, Tekla, and has the same mannerisms. The truth is that Gustav is the former husband traveling under an assumed name, and bent upon revenge. With this purpose in mind he first gains Adolph's confidence and then brings him to doubt his wife's fidelity, unveils her vampire nature by his artful "suggestions" and convinces his victim that he is on the verge of epilepsy and ruin. It is clear to the audience (though not to Adolph) that Tekla has taken her mannerisms and thoughts from Gustav, her first husband. When Adolph explains that Tekla has seemed to scorn his ideas and manners, just because they are his, Gustav tells him that that proves she has never loved him, for "a woman's love consists in taking, in receiving," and we cannot love more than once, for we cannot be deceived more than once. But having loved her first husband, how did she happen to desert him for Adolph? Adolph cannot say and Gustav in an almost humorous way, explains how it all came about. When the first husband (i. e. himself) went away, it left a void which Adolph filled. "For protection they played brother and sister. And the more their feelings smacked of the flesh, the more they tried to make their relationship appear spiritual." Gustav had "guessed it" and Adolph is much surprised. "They took a vow of chastity—and then played hide and seek—until they got into a dark corner— But they felt that there was someone whose eye reached them in the darkness—and they became frightened—and their fright raised the spectre of the absent one—which turned into a nightmare that disturbed their amorous slumbers, a creditor who knocked at all doors." His black hand was between theirs and they heard his voice at night. Suffering from their guilt they were obliged to find a scapegoat and so "the tyrant (the previous husband) had to be slaughtered." Adolph admits that this was what happened. As he now recollects, under the penetrating questions of Gustav, he has also given her everything, has sacrificed his

strength and enthusiasm, and belittled his own art, for the sake
of her career, her pride and happiness. He was, then, also her
creditor. Tekla was like "the savages who eat their enemies in
order to acquire their useful qualities. And this woman," continues Gustav, "has eaten your soul, your courage, your knowledge—" But Adolph, in spite of all, must have something to worship. Being a free-thinker, he must venerate a woman. "Slave!"
cries Gustav. "Your wife may seem incomprehensible, sphinx-like,
profound—it is sheer stupidity." What is a woman after all? "A
youth with over-developed busts, an under-developed man, a
child that has shot up to full height and there stopped growing in
other respects; one who is chronically anæmic. . . ." Gustav asks
Adolph for a picture of Tekla and then shows him what he had
never seen before, the cynical lines in her face, like that of an
affected coquette, with a low-cut dress to lure other men. If you
have told her she is too old to attract other men, beware of her
revenge, is Gustav's warning. When Tekla returns, Gustav
watches unseen from an adjoining room. After a long struggle,
Adolph all but accuses her of infidelity and vows hereafter to be
a real husband, whether she likes it or not. Whereupon she swears
that whatever happens he will never know it, though it is gossip
for the rest of the world. "And you'll suspect it, you'll believe it,
and you'll never have another moment's peace. You'll have the
feeling of being ridiculous, of being deceived, but you'll never
get any proof of it. For that's what married men never get."

There follows a long, masterly interlude of calm in which
Adolph recalls to her mind how, though now but a child, he had
once recalled her to life, defended and comforted her, and raised
her sun high,—even above his own. "Then," he says, "you admired me. Then I was the man—not the kind of athlete you had
just left, but the man of will-power, the mesmerist who instilled
new nervous energy into your flabby muscles and charged your
brain with a new store of electricity." When he has finished his
subtle, eloquent recital of wrongs, she has not understood a

word of it and seems incapable of making a distinction. "You mutilate my brain with your clumsy pincers—" he cries, "you put your claws into my thoughts and tear them to pieces!" He collapses and she makes him beg her pardon. Then, as has been prearranged between them, Adolph leaves the stage and takes up his post where Gustav had been in the adjoining room, and Gustav himself comes forward and, as if by accident, confronts his former wife. By flattery, he brings her to a very agreeable and reminiscent mood, reviews their past life, gets her to admit that he was a fine sort of husband, that her present husband is an idiot and a weakling. She, for her part, is warm in her recollections and very affectionate. It is a dream of hers, she says, for him and Adolph to shake hands in good friendship. Gustav notices that she is still wearing the earrings he gave her long ago. Their mood, warm with the recollections of their mutual pleasures, ripens to the point that Gustav puts his arm around her waist, which is observed by two ladies, i. e. by the world, and makes the improper proposal that they drown their memories in a farewell meeting, to which she accedes. Suddenly, she realizes that she has been trapped, that Gustav has planned the whole affair as a great revenge. When it dawns on her that her husband has been listening and has heard every word of infidelity and shamelessness, she is aware that the worst of all disasters has overtaken her. "When a man sees his own wraith he dies," she says. At that moment Adolph comes out of the room in an epileptic fit and falls dead. Her genuine grief gives evidence that she still loves him and the strong man, Gustav, as he departs expresses his pity, "Why, she must really have loved *him* too? Poor creature."

That this play is a recasting of *The Confession of a Fool*, another version of Strindberg's unhappy marriage, is evident down to the smallest details. Thus the name given to the former husband, Gustav, is the Baron Wrangel's, and his strong, confident, athletic nature is contrasted throughout with the rather sensitive, neurotic constitution of Adolph. Even the child, sent away because it resembled the former husband, has a certain parallel in Strindberg's experience. In 1888, he had begun to worry about his first daughter who had died when he had been married only a short time, for in dreams she appeared to him as alive. He made inquiries in Sweden for the grave number—all in vain. Sometimes it seemed to him that his wife, tormented with her shame, had hidden the child as the manifest reminder of it. Did this child resemble the Baron? Strindberg had had his suspicions before.

In this play we have again the struggle of master and slave. Gustav, by controlling his emotions and using his head, wins an easy victory over his enemies. He is cruel and ruthless, but this is necessary if one is to be strong. His keen, detective analysis of new situations marks the man of superior sagacity, and is reminiscent, too, of the manner of Poe. It is interesting to note that Strindberg in this play has apparently forgotten that he is, himself, a superman and gives his role to his enemy, the Baron. Himself, he portrays as the weak and neurotic Adolph, destroyed by the spiritual cannibalism of his wife. Strindberg's honesty or his sense of martyrdom often did him an injustice.

The three rather autobiographical plays *The Father, Comrades* and *Creditors* show the full power and peculiarity of Strindberg's delineation. Beginning with an abstract idea flaming with passion, he chose characters to exemplify its aspects. The result was that these characters were abstract, one-sided, exaggerated, like a gallery of wax-work horrors, yet their reality is proved in both cases by the effect on the audience. Dostoevsky's novels have been compared to various wards in a hospital and the analogy holds of Strindberg's plays, but the hospital at any rate was a real one, full of suffering people, or rather with the same people wandering hopelessly from ward to ward, analyzing and treating their own diseases.

Strindberg's shortest play with only two characters, and but one speaking character, is *The Stronger*. This cameo-like little piece which treats, oddly enough, of *female* jealousy, has perhaps some biographical roots in the occasional jealousy of Siri. The complexity and subtlety of the situation, with only one voice and a few gestures to tell the story, gives an excellent opportunity for Strindberg's craftmanship. In the end, we are in some doubt as to which of the two women is "The Stronger," the quiet sphinx-like vampire or the talkative and, at last, triumphant wife.

In the meantime, having written a number of first-rate plays, Strindberg, like every dramatist, desired to see them performed. But here he met the most crushing difficulties, some of which have already been described. To produce his plays and to make, as he thought, his fortune, he laid plans in 1888 to experiment with a new theatre, to travel through the provinces performing his shorter plays with a few actors and Siri, of course, in the leading role. For his own part he was to be stage director, costumer and manager. He was frightfully poor at the time. To Georg Brandes he complained that his children's shoes were torn and no money to repair them, that in the kitchen of the old castle at Holte they swarmed together, like flies. Yes, in that stifling "witches' kitchen" he lived in purgatory, plagued with sick children, unable to work. When his wife appeared suddenly in a bright dressing gown, he started in terror as with a quick intimation of magic and infernal spells. As she moved about the untidy, squalid kitchen bending to her tasks, she seemed at times an eerie, terrible woman performing illicit rites, hatching black plots of vengeance, and when she faced him and he glimpsed the line of her stooped shoulders and the frowzy hair and caught the inexplicable glint of her dark eyes, he believed her capable of anything. Why did he have such headaches? Was he being poisoned? How had the rumor gotten abroad that he was insane? Once, when a friend called for Strindberg, his wife said, "Why, didn't you know my husband is insane?" On one occasion, when Strindberg and his family were traveling in a crowded carriage, he was so struck with the ugly witch-like appearance of his wife, and so surprised and horrified that he had never been struck with it before, that he almost threw himself out of the coach, so great was his sudden loathing and disenchantment. Strindberg's miseries were too great to be borne. He bought a revolver and wrote to Heidenstam for directions as to where he was to put the shot. But of this we hear nothing further. Almost at the same time we find him rejoicing at the imprisonment of the terrible gypsy Tschandala, who had threatened him (and also his character the Magistrate) and reported him to justice for the rape of his daughter. For a long time Strindberg had quaked, most amusingly, in fear of the gypsy's vengeance, and carried about a gun with him night and day. Now that was over. "Hurrah!"

Again the scene changed, the trumpery world of spells and evil enchantment was whisked away by a tender smile, and things assumed their normal aspect, and again the little madonna came to life to bless him with a love dream as ardent, and as purple beyond the summit of any awakened hope, as in the first days of their passion. Now, he will forget his youth's madness in her arms, in the arms of his madonna so miraculously purified and restored, and live out his life in peace. "My God," he cries, "how tenacious is love." A month or two later he is raging again at the treachery of women and warning his friends against their designs. Yes, it is unsafe to live with them and fatal to be in their power. The law of vicissitudes, which Swedenborg maintained to be the necessary law in heaven as well as on earth, made a thrilling example and a test case of Strindberg.

Georg Brandes relates how, one day, he explained that being alone, he needed only bachelor's quarters, yet complained the next time that such provisions were absurd, for how, indeed, could a man with a wife and four children confine himself to such a space. He also tells how, one day, they came down to dinner in the same dining room, but separated, Strindberg at one table with a friend and Siri at another with the children, and neither would speak to the other. Also the brothers Brandes found a great deal of amusement in his waverings on the matter of religious faith, for one day he declared himself an outright atheist, a few days later, a deist.

Strindberg's marriage was the worst curse of all and gradually he came to see, though he fought and wavered in his dawning conviction, that "the ridiculous farce" was approaching an end. When Siri fled from his impetuous embraces, resisting the stormy entreaties of a love outlasting time, her own fading charms, and all the bitter memories of the past, his thoughts grew black and rancorous. His hatred of women sprang from his love of them and from the enforced celibacy in which he lived. This he confessed. Like his hero in the story *Corinna*, or the Baron in *The Link*, he has suffered, he feels, that ridiculous horror of celibacy in marriage enforced by a designing wife or, as it might be, by the fear of a larger family. What is worse, his family burdens have prevented him from courting gentlewomen, while his honor as an aristocrat has held him back from more unworthy connections. As for pederasty! It was not for him, and there was in fact no release or purgation of his passions save his violent hatred of women. Strindberg was as unhappy as Schopenhauer had ever been. With his friends at the café, to be sure, he could free himself, on occasion, from all the devils and rise to the wildest pitch of amiability, pledging them drink for drink, or more, with jests and songs accompanied on his own guitar. A true Viking, he loved the feast and the friendly debauch, but was also given to excess and trying originality on such occasions. One evening, for instance, when far from sober, he drew a revolver and fired above the heads of the guests to see, as he said, which would show the most fear. When everyone had taken to the open air to cool off a bit, he determined absolutely upon climbing to the top of the equestrian statue of King Christian V in the market-place, and would hear of no objections. While ascending, however, he was seized by the police, who on being told who he was, were all courtesy and good-nature, but forbade him to shoot on the streets. On leaving, Strindberg fired his revolver, whereupon the police thanked him, for now, they said, he could commit no further nuisance.

In 1889, Strindberg left Denmark and returned to Sweden after his long exile,—a prodigal son with no fatted calf and no other recognition of his rising fame than the increasing hate of his countrymen. In the modernized city of Stockholm, he felt alien and ill at ease and sat lonely and sad at his old café with his green absinthe and his memories. Once, however, he had retreated from the "sinking city" into the beloved desolation of the Stockholm islands, his mood became quite gay and he cultivated his Nietzschean ego, there in the loneliness, with more success. A consequence of his return to these gaunt and majestic scenes, and of his sojourn in Sweden, was the book *Swedish Nature,* 1890, celebrating the rugged beauty that from youth onward he had never ceased to love and long for when absent. In 1888, he had published another book on flowers and animals, judging the former with great affection and discrimination and commending certain animals, such as the nightingale, though less warmly than the flowers. Dogs and dog-enthusiasts, he condemned with unheard-of violence. Also, he had begun to paint again—nature, of course—the sky and the sun.

His winter in Stockholm was lonely and miserable. In the spring of 1890, he returned to the islands and was united for another brief period with his wife and children. But storms broke loose again, and then at last came the divorce. At this final episode, Strindberg's wife played a sad part. Shattered by the long conflict, her nerves twanging at the breaking point, she forgot all modesty, swaggered and gossiped, drank here, drank there, in all company, and appeared before the church-warden intoxicated. Moreover, a girl friend had appeared who consoled Siri far too much for Strindberg's endurance. Again, he raged with jealousy and bit the earth—for the last time. In January 1891, the divorce was granted and he was free. But, alas, the release which he had craved for so many years was not to his liking now. He felt empty and dispirited and had no courage for the new responsibilities which his freedom involved. He was plagued more than ever, it seemed, by the Nemesis of poverty which had followed him through so many years. He was divorced, to be sure, but his obligations to his family continued, duties shorn of rights and privileges.

Frau Hansson had arranged to translate his works into German and the Théâtre Libre would perform his plays, but though at times he soared high with the prospects and promised himself a large sum and happiness from these undertakings, he was at bottom a miserable man and gathered little consolation and less money, from either. His expectations as usual were pitifully dwarfed by the actual returns. Although at forty-two he had achieved the work of a long life-time, had written many books, histories, novels, stories, plays, had given Sweden a literature, introduced Naturalism and laid down the form of the modern drama, had won fame in his own country and distinction abroad, he was unable to muster the money for the most common necessities, was pursued by creditors, and held in constant fear that his beloved books would be distrained, or go, like the rest, to the pawn shop. Exhausted and disillusioned by these adversities, he dreamt, as in the troubled times of his youth, of forgoing a high destiny altogether, of accepting instead a job as hotel-porter, photographer, variety artist or journalist in Paris, and a few months after his divorce actually applied for a position as the keeper of a lighthouse. Unfortunately, this, too, was an illusion and he knew it. He had gone too far to turn back.

XXII

THE SECOND MARRIAGE

STRINDBERG'S divorce was not the overwhelming tragedy which the force of his love and hate, advancing with suffering and growing tension through the years, would lead us to expect. The real crisis in the marriage had occurred four years earlier in 1886-7 at the time of the writing of *The Father*. Since then, there had been a marked decline from the mood of high tragedy. The heroine had shown herself too much the witch and too little the madonna to balance the hero's passions. For him, the affair had become a downright misery with no catharsis. By 1891, his love had so far burned down that he felt only hatred and bitterness, and relief at her departure. But, what hindered it most from being a catastrophe in the grand style was that Strindberg, at the time, was much too distracted by other adversities to allow this great event its single and unique importance. Dismayed by the hatred and indifference of his countrymen, weak and dispirited by the lack of proper food and drink and by the state of beggary to which he was reduced, hopeless, seeing the shipwreck of all his literary works and plans, with no resources at home and no career abroad, it was little wonder that the drama of his unhappy marriage did not play itself out to a crashing climax. With the sorrows and loneliness of the separation were mixed other irrelevant sufferings which often took the upper hand, obscuring by their collateral insistence, the march of the principal theme. This frustration of a single-toned tragedy by the distraction of many minor despairs occurs frequently in Strindberg's novels, though rarely in the plays, for there he makes an abstraction, and much more often in real life than is commonly assumed. The tragic hero, according to the Greek tradition, must be a king, or a great man, for only as such can he take a great fall. Another requirement, which has received much less attention, is that such a hero must have leisure, poise, and enough freedom from economic and other troubles to give the tragic events the attention which they deserve. Had Œdipus been distracted by troubles such as Strindberg's, he had never pursued the straight course of his despair, nor blinded himself, nor pleased the logical Greeks *Œdipus Rex* would have become a naturalistic novel, circumstantial, full of inconsequences, with the scattering, soul-destroying effects which, since Strindberg, have become so familiar in modern literature. Strindberg was a great man, but he had little leisure to indulge a single tragedy.

Despairing of any recognition or even a living in his own country, frowned upon as he was by publishers and newspapers, Sweden's greatest writer planned to emigrate again, but for a long time he was prevented by the lack of money for his passage. In vain he cast about him for a few hundred crowns. They were not to be had and he remained a prisoner in an empty house, surrounded, as he thought, by hatred, suspicion, and evil plots, hemmed in and circumvented at every step. Hysterical longing for his children and occasional excess at the café added peaks to his unhappiness. The conviction that he was a giant gave it a deep ground tone. In his fancy he imagined himself a Prometheus, torn by the birds, with this difference, that not being a god, he could not suffer in silence, but must pour out his grievances in a manner which even he could not but think, at times, undignified.

Yet from his peers, those who understood him, there was no lack of recognition. About this time, a book about Strindberg was planned which was to show what the great men of the world thought about the writer so hated in his own country. Among the contributors were Brandes, Björnson, Lie and Hamsun. The book, which did not appear until 1894, received, however, little attention, and did not better his financial condition now or then. In the meantime, he had written frantic business letters to Ola Hansson, a friend he had met in Denmark, drawing a sad picture of his financial straits, of his continual fear of debts and distraint. Yes, he must fly the country to escape imprisonment, —must have the money. Could not the Free Theatre in Berlin assist him by the performance of his plays? Could not he open a photographer's shop in Berlin making a specialty of his own patent camera made out of a cigar box? In any case, he must raise money, by hook or crook, immediately. Ola Hansson and his wife Frau Marholm, with the greatest sympathy and concern, worked day and night to win him recognition. To facilitate his escape from Sweden they wrote a letter in *Zukunft* picturing the deplorable straits of the great writer and calling for assistance. Finally, their efforts succeeded and Strindberg in 1892 was able to leave for Berlin. The means which they had chosen to aid him were, however, highly displeasing to him and the Hanssons were rather cursed than praised for their good offices. His rage directed itself naturally against the woman. Frau Marholm's article in *Zukunft* requesting a subscription on his behalf was, he was sure, simply a begging letter and, what was more, she knew it and had planned it as a revenge upon the famous woman-hater. As a blue-stocking of parts her vanity had been gratified by this humiliation of a great writer. Strindberg was full of wrath but accepted the money. A few years later the degrading incident returned as a tragic development in *The Dance of Death*.

Frau Marholm, for all her sympathy and help, got no other reward than distrust and hatred. The more she busied herself in his affairs, the more alarmed he became. Finally, he became convinced that she was a dangerous woman, a sort of Dame Blue-beard, trying to hypnotize him, that she was a vampire who would creep into his life, since she had no life of her own, master him gradually, negate by her arts and insinuations his whole doctrine of women, steal his honors, and in the end commit him to an asylum—Strindberg, the old enemy of her sex. For a long time, he had watched her narrowly. He had noticed that, though unproductive herself, she possessed all the extraordinary imitative power of negroes, and now that he came to think of it, she even looked like one, a pale one, of course, and her maiden name was Mohr (Moor or negro). These facts were significant. She was the sort of woman who steals the life-seeds of a man and gives them out as her own. He determined to be on his guard, and when she discovered a lively interest in his last mad letters from Nietzsche and advised him to publish them, he grew more uneasy than ever. He came to fear that Frau Marholm, who was then in correspondence with Nietzsche's sister, Frau Förster Nietzsche, was plotting something dark and terrible—what, he did not know. Why should these two blue-stockings correspond? —that in itself was suspicious. By a curious circumlocution he imagined that Frau Marholm would think him insane, because he pondered seriously over those bedeviled letters of Nietzsche. In time, his suspicions of his benefactor became a certainty and he fled from her house before the net could tighten.

On her side, Frau Marholm found something sinister and threatening in Strindberg. "His voice was soft, discreet, commanding, his menacing glance prepared to frighten away any feminine pretension. Austere and reserved, his attention seemed fixed on some unseen shrine, searching its distant mystery raptly, with his strange elusive eyes." (The portraits of Strindberg at this period bear out this last detail to perfection.) No doubt Strindberg had his terrible moments which were enough to frighten any woman. He could be gay and cruel, miserable and raging, when wounded, reserved and mysterious, when suspicious, wildly revengeful, and when indebted to a friend he was insufferable. A friend who expects gratitude robs one of his life-blood, he held, for it is a debt that can never be paid. Now, it happened that Strindberg was greatly beholden to Ola Hansson and his wife, for they had rescued him from poverty and obscurity, and brought him to Berlin to produce his plays. This Strindberg could never forgive. Unable to repay the services or the money, he grew to hate them both. Frau Marholm's attempts to straighten out his affairs seemed to him like the most importunate meddling and smacked too much of the kindly care usually accorded to a lunatic. One day a doctor, a friend of Hansson's, asked him to go with him to inspect a lunatic asylum. This may have been an accident, thought Strindberg, yet if he were to disappear suddenly, it would be clear what had happened. Strindberg could not bear to be grateful. It was consequently his friends and benefactors that he most suspected at this time. His deep sense of sin, rooted in his earliest infancy, gave him no peace. His unrequited love of his mother, the exasperations and the frictions of his marriage, the recent desertion of his wife and children, the blasphemies, the shameful confessions, and all the accumulating overwrought splendors and miseries of a strident, overweening life rose up now to accuse him, driving him on to new sins and madnesses to pay for the old. A month after his divorce had been concluded, he was delighted with his copy of *The Confession of a Fool* (for the German edition had just been published). This terrible reckoning with the mother of his children was a great sin which eased his conscience and balanced justice. For the moment, he had an object for his inner guilt and his mood became quite gay and satanic. This persistent sense of sin made him fearful, yet desirous, of revengeful enemies. He longed for the absolution of punishment, sought suffering as a solace to his sin, yet wavered uncertainly, like a man in a jungle, trembling at each shadow or sound, trapped, persecuted, racked by fears in a world grown strange and hostile. When Strindberg accused a friend of persecuting him, of conspiring against his life or liberty, the friend was usually and obviously quite innocent. If he grew angry and left his company, Strindberg was a little gratified, for that seemed to him to be a corroboration of his suspicion. When, however, the friend remained quiet or proved his innocence, Strindberg was terribly disappointed, his suspicions multiplied, and his hate became boundless. One of these friends, Adolf Paul, was apparently quite embittered by his experiences, for he wrote a malicious book concerning Strindberg's life during this period in which all of his petty weaknesses are paraded with open delight. It was Strindberg's custom, when destitute and at his wit's end with worry, to write the most frantic letters to his friends for money. If they accorded it, he grew suspicious of their motives, but cursed them if they failed him. This made him a very hard man to get on with, and though he could be as lovable as any man alive when rightly disposed, the wonder is, after all, that he kept as many friends as he did, for he was the victim at this time of "delusions of persecution."

His solace during the five months in Berlin, whither he came to produce his plays, was liquor, comradeship, and light affairs. After a marriage of fourteen years, he felt his youth return and reveled in its pleasures. For ten years he had remained quite faithful. Only in that last desperate period, frantic with unrequited passion, had he wavered. Now he fell in good earnest. The scene of these revelries was a tavern called *The Cloister,* a picturesque place *Unter den Linden* with Gothic windows, chapels, and for hostess a pretty young blonde. Among the company who gathered at this resort were the physician-poet, Schleich, who wrote a sympathetic account of Strindberg's life during these years of his acquaintance; the German poet, Dehmel, who composed dithyrambic verse in his honor; Krogh, who painted his perhaps most celebrated portrait; Paul, who gave a hateful picture of Strindberg in his *Memoirs;* Ola Hansson, his patron; Hamsun, who held him in such high admiration; and the bizarre Pole, Prsybyszevski, who was to play such a terrible part in Strindberg's crisis a few years later. Here, where nine hundred kinds of strong drinks were served, the gatherings took on a tone that was often gay and riotous, but also nervous and uncertain as if a shriek lurked behind each jest. The company Strindberg found were a wild sort of men who sought madness and intoxication as an inspiration and a heightening of life, and who consequently made excess a principle. Under the Gothic windows of the little tavern, with all the air of a cloister or chapel about it, the carousals often appeared to him as a sort of blasphemy or black mass and the men around him, devils incarnate. At such times, it deserved more than ever the name with which he rechristened it, *Zum Schwartze Ferkel* (The Black Pig). But it was, in part, precisely the sinfulness of these orgies which intrigued him. The morning after, he would awake to consciousness of his wickedness, his inability to write, and the helpless children who depended on him, would shake his wild hair sadly and fetch a deep sigh, but in the evening he would be back again, playing his guitar, singing, with daring jests and contentions, welcoming forgetfulness and new sins.

Among the guests there was none who was more bizarre and extraordinary than the Pole, Prsybyszevski, called "the most melancholy alcoholist in the world." This man who, according to Erdmann, "studied with fanatical interest all morbid and abnormal phenomena . . . hallucinations, convulsions, hysteria, perverse drives, insanity, splitting of personality, etc.," who regarded existence as a "cult of the devil," and the life of the soul, mere "sexuality and heart-burn," was a fit companion for Strindberg's darker moods. Once he said to Strindberg, "Does anyone think we could ever be enemies? . . . No, you are my father"—the Pole here kissed Strindberg's hand and gave him his house key. "You shall go home with me and sleep with my Moschka (his first wife), you and no other, for she is very fond of you, and you will do me an honor thereby."

Zum Schwartze Ferkel was also visited by women, and Strindberg, clothed in white with a flower in his button-hole, debonaire and gallant, paid them court. On one occasion, a fascinating young creature having asked Strindberg to kiss her, the woman-hater removed his coat, climbed over the wine tables, and went about the matter in such a thorough-going fashion, that his friend drew his watch in astonishment. "Now it has lasted two minutes!" Another time, his gallantry toward a certain beauty offended an officer and a duel threatened from which, however, Strindberg hastily withdrew to Weimar. There he fared no better, for meeting a friend with a pretty wife, he promptly fell in love, and later fled from their house in groundless fear of a jealous husband. At this resort Strindberg had one affair after another, drank excessively and conversed endlessly with his friends. But though his external life sometimes wore an aspect of frivolity and joyous abandon, this was not the reality, but only a mask for his inner life, a defence against his isolation, his sufferings and growing anxiety. At heart a monogamist and a worshipper of women, he could find no real fulfillment in careless, brief caresses. What he needed was to justify himself and give his conviction of guilt some object. That much was achieved by his sinful affairs—but only for the moment.

In the meantime, the Free Theatre had performed several of his plays, *The Father,* 1890, (which was unfortunately censored), *Miss Julia,* 1892, (which was received with great favor though it had been banned in Denmark), and in 1893 *Creditors, Playing with Fire, Facing Death,* and *The First Warning.* The last three plays and four others, written during the years 1891–3, were highly autobiographical and most of them are echoes of his unhappy marriage. Strindberg had left his wife with anger and open hatred, but the longing for the children and a sense of the unnatural cruelty of the separation pursued him with avenging justice. A feeling of guilt but vaguely defined, yet exasperated by the loss of home and children and the social obloquy involved, aroused him to a defence of the father and the husband in cases similar to his own. In *Laokoon* (a poem), a woman-hater prays to the Gods, asking no mercy for himself but only for his children. In the one-act play *Facing Death,* a father kills himself for the sake of his ungrateful children who still cling to the fond memory of their weak deceitful mother. In *Mother-love,* the mother, a low parasitic creature, drags her talented daughter down to her level, allows her no freedom, and prevents her from escaping to the bright life to which she is invited. *The Link* portrays a divorce trial in which the passionate recriminations of the Baroness and the unavoidable replies of the Baron lose to them both the custody of the child. Strindberg's deep resentment against his wife, and his craving to exonerate himself are everywhere in evidence. The admirable Baron is defended at every point against the cruel and fatuous Baroness. It was she who had been unfaithful, who sold him her favors, corrupted the household, and perverted their child by treating him as a girl. It was she who had obliged him to celibacy in the marriage state and thereby forced him to unfaithfulness. Nor had he squandered her dowry as she maintained. That was a bagatelle. The little play is a cry out of *The Confession of a Fool* and the divorce trial, Strindberg's own. In *The First Warning,* the bitterness and self-defence continue. The husband makes another attempt to escape from the tortures of the woman he loves. As he packs his bag for the journey, a young girl and an older woman both reveal their love for him. This brings the wife to terms. She must now admit, however she has denied it in the past, that the husband is a man whom women love. Thus, the husband has a sure defence against his wife's accusation that he is too old or too dull, one that Strindberg himself had sometimes employed. He can demonstrate that he can be loved by other women. *Playing with Fire* repeats in a somewhat modified form the dangerous, guarded, ambiguous play of the old quadrangle of the Baron, the Baroness, Strindberg and the pretty cousin. The friend loves the wife, but is honorable and friendly toward the husband. The pretty, idle wife, being somewhat bored in her marriage, seeks the distraction of an affaire, whether it is a matter of love it is difficult to say. In one scene she pays court to him so furiously that he declares his passion, whereupon the husband takes his leave, warning them, however, that since they love each other, they must marry when it is possible. This quick retreat was more than they had expected. They had been playing with fire. The husband has been gone but a little while when the lovers fall into a desperate quarrel, and the friend departs, for, like Gustav in *Creditors,* he is strong enough to avoid the fire, however it tempts and lures him.

Debit and Credit is a little comedy, depicting the return of a great man to Sweden to establish himself in some secure and honorable post. No sooner has he landed, than he is surrounded by creditors, his brother, his previous mistress, etc., jealous threatening shadows from the past, until, unable to bear it longer, he makes his escape and so gives up his greatness and his prospects. Here, Strindberg is undoubtedly thinking of his own humiliating return to Sweden. *The Key of Heaven* is a bitter, satirical fairy play, which continues the travels of Lucky Pehr and leads the way to the wandering of the Stranger in *Toward Damascus.* The hero, a blacksmith, who, like Strindberg has lost his children whom he cherished above everything in the world, a prey to deep sadness and disillusion, prepares to take a long journey, in the company of a Dr. Allknowing. On the way he encounters St. Peter, an old and ridiculous person, and Sancho Panza, who, when the Smith becomes a king, heads a revolution against him. He meets with many curious adventures, but remains skeptical and disillusioned throughout, discontented with everything he sees. So with the other characters. Don Quixote dies, weary with life. The Smith does not produce the key of heaven and St. Peter despairs: "On earth I do not find heaven, only the gate—and that is death." *The Key of Heaven* shares a great deal with Ibsen's *Peer Gynt* but not, of course, its greatness.

Strindberg's half-year of light affairs was brought to an end by his acquaintance with a pretty little Austrian woman, Frieda Uhl, who was soon to become his wife. Of this second marriage Strindberg gave a belated account in *Fair Haven and Foul Strand*, 1902, nearly ten years after the events recorded occurred. He met her, it seems, at a party, when she was praised for her beauty but teased about her writing, and from the first she puzzled and bewitched him. In the matter of the proprieties she seemed too free, like a woman of the world, and Strindberg, who represents himself as perfectly respectable, was definitely shocked. But, chiefly, he was disturbed by her sudden transformations. As she walked along the street in a fur coat and slightly stooped, she looked like an old woman and there was something witch-like about her, but when she removed the coat the lines of a blooming girlish figure entranced him. There was "something weird and ominous" about it. "It was not the youthful beauty which is clothed in reflections from the paradise of innocence, but a dark, demoniac beauty which becomes a man's death, the grave of his virile will, and which leads to humiliation, ruin and disgraceful bargaining. But it was as inevitable and as inescapable as Fate."

At other times, she was the business woman and nothing more, serious, prosaic, talking only of editors and publishers, and her careless toilette showed that she had no desire to please as a woman. Now she was indifferent, cruel, blasé, then a melancholy, helpless child, and Strindberg hated the one as much as he loved the other. Her face, as he says, had a "flat forehead which looked as though it had been hammered smooth. . . . The eyes were large and well defined as with southerners. The nose seemed to have altered its mind while growing, for it looked a little bent in the middle and became Roman by degrees. This little unexpected joyful surprise lent a cameo-like charm to her profile."

An ominous feature of the courtship and one highly distasteful to Strindberg, the virile woman-hater, was that she took the upper-hand in everything and tried to play the part of the man. When she insisted on paying his bill at the restaurant, he was angry and dumbfounded, and when she gave him the first kiss, through her veil, he was mortified and fearful of the future, for it was a bad sign. Yes, and it was she who brought on the engagement and the marriage. He realized in the course of time that she was a strange woman with ideas, ambitions and a will of her own, that she was as anxious to preserve her personality against the encroachments of another as he, his.

What appeared to decide the question for Frieda was the picture he showed her of his eight-year-old son. She asked to keep it by her and an ominous silence followed in which he felt the net of her purposes drawing closer about him, with muttering and fateful presages for the future. After exacting a promise from him not to join his friends at *Zum Schwartze Ferkel* that night, she kissed him on the lips and the next day he wrote her a proposal of marriage. "Now the man lays his head in your lap," he wrote, "as a sign that the good in you overcomes the evil in him, but do not misuse your power." On receiving this letter she hesitated, and he broke off the affair. Then she, in her turn, stormed him with letters and telegrams, and finally drove to his house to demand that he accompany her on a trip that very night. He refused, explaining that, being indebted to certain people in the city, he could not indulge his caprices freely, and he gave other reasons. After using all the arts of a witch and an angel to persuade him, she gave way, a complete reconciliation took place, with chirruping and love-gambols. Strindberg returned to the famous wine room, somewhat relieved at her absence and there a half-hour after his engagement to Frieda, won the heart of a "sickly bluestocking," Aspasia (as she was called at the rendezvous), and took her away from his friend. During Frieda's absence they wandered the streets and drank, talking of literature and many things. Finally, realizing that she would desert him soon, he left her first and went home. A "telepathic feeling" told him he ought to be there that night, and sure enough it was a telegram from Frieda who was already back in town. Shortly afterwards, he fell ill and she came to his bedside, adorning his room with the flowers and green things he loved, and tended him altogether like an angel. They must become engaged, she told him, for the papers had announced it, and there would be a scandal if they didn't. Strindberg inquired about her father, a state councilor in Austria, a distinguished man, who had declared that he would rather shoot himself than have the notorious nihilist for a son-in-law. But the father had been brought to terms, it seemed, for he had finally seen that the thing had to be. The love episode thus advanced with all the variations of love and hate and all the intensity which could be expected. When Frieda showed him how certain she was of her power over him, he raged, as he is frank to say, like a lion in a cage, and shortly he went out to the café with his friends. He noticed that the power of love made them similar, obliterated the differences and frictions to such an extent, indeed, that they both grew fearful of losing their identity and set to quarreling simply to prove that they were separate individualities. Still, for all that this rivalry and infringement of personalities had its sad and prophetic moments, they were not doing so badly. As Strindberg told a friend acquainted with the tragedy of his first marriage, he was willing to try it again. There were, he could not deny it, certain elements of repetition, but on the whole the affair wore a happier face than the previous one, nor was he as deeply involved.

Finally, Frieda's parents in Odense became alarmed by a report that the couple had run away together and insisted on marriage, and Strindberg, his fortunes having recently improved, was only too willing. To facilitate the matter, for she was a Catholic, they set out for Helgoland, where a divorced man could marry a Catholic woman more easily. At the station he met the Baron, who was delighted to see him, but Strindberg was terrified, for it was a bad omen and a warning from the powers. On arriving at that island, to make the matter worse, they were obliged to wait six days for the necessary papers, and were in despair, for Frieda's sister who had accompanied them would be obliged to return. Strindberg was hoodooed as usual, with the vengeance of those unseen powers whose influence he felt more and more as time went on. Fortunately, the required papers came that evening, but the ceremony, which took place the next day, was ruined for Strindberg by the hysterical laughter of his betrothed, who was, it seemed to him, quite bent on proving to the court that they were both candidates for an asylum. Yet, after fourteen days of married life he was so completely enamored of it and so surprised and delighted to find himself so, that he cursed his bachelor existence and vowed never to return to it. They were, in fact, both so happy that they became fearful of Nemesis, for the old lore of envious gods stuck in the mind, and a deep uneasiness in the blood. It was perhaps to ease these feelings that Strindberg suddenly took it upon himself to warn all his friends of the evil and dangerous designs of "Aspasia," and his attack on her took the form of the crudest slander, fired off in every direction. He had been intimate with her in Berlin during Frieda's absence and then had broken it off. Now he decided against her definitely. She was a vampire, without question, spreading her Clytemnestra net for others. He would save his friends. Strindberg's letters, too, had consequence, for both Aspasia and a friend of his were obliged to leave Berlin.

Both Strindberg and his wife now feared more than anything else that discord might separate them, and the worst of it was that the fatal quarrel would be neither's fault. But, if not their fault, then some unseen other's! This thought frightened his pretty wife. They were further alarmed to find that their happiness destroyed their invention, that their natures were so harmonized as to completely neutralize each other. Falling silent, they lived like happy vegetables, which endured not long, however, before the inevitable discords and conflicts began. She cut up a work of his, clumsily, without reading it, and sent it off to the publisher in fragments, and he wished himself back in Berlin with his friends and, for the first time, deserted her for a solitary walk. Later she read his last book, *The Confession of a Fool,* and when he saw how her manner changed, her features becoming fixed in a new pattern, he knew that she was poisoned and would never be the same again. In reading the shameful account of his first wife she had no doubt recognized herself and sympathized with her much more than she could say. He trembled before the future. Yet her rather feline charms drew him back.

Strindberg now decided to go to London to found, as he naïvely hoped, a Strindberg theatre. Here, however, he was doomed to accomplish nothing, the English being perhaps by temperament unreceptive of Strindberg's type of genius. The countryside and towns were delightful enough, but he found the heat in London simply African and the poverty and wretchedness worse than anything he had ever seen. Incapable of literary invention, he turned with growing fondness to his "great work" on world history and buried himself in curious chemical studies, yet these brought in no money and soon they were destitute, obliged to live in one room with execrable food. Frieda now became "his pretty little jailer who stole into his soul and spied upon his thoughts," and there was no escape from her. One day, when he longed for privacy, she followed him on his walk, haunted him like an evil spirit. He chose the hot side of the street and walked on furiously. He led her along the water front into the most difficult, unsightly places, but could not lose her. She persisted with the strength of the wicked. Finally he wished her dead. Should he drown her? He would like to see her insulted, yes, or even overpowered by some workman. That night in bed they eyed each other fearfully, with the awareness of their mutual hate. She pretended to be asleep, but he could tell by her breathing that she wasn't. "Her cold threatening eyes" aroused the old thoughts of vampires and gadflies. Accursed, he thought. Accursed in thy coming in and in thy going out. Accursed! He was much relieved when she fell asleep, for then he could follow his thoughts and his ego could expand again. Strindberg's condition at this time was far from normal. Once, on London Bridge, he was much dismayed to see throngs of wretched men with their arms outstretched, like a pageant of the poor and needy. This is perhaps the first of Strindberg's hallucinations. Also he suffered, as usual, from megalomania. When his wife told him, in a fit of anger, that he greatly overvalued himself, Strindberg started as if he had heard a blasphemy, or the truth. He had now determined to leave her for a time, at any rate, and accordingly laid plans to sail for Rügen to seek financial assistance, while his little fury would remain to settle his affairs in England. The day before his departure he said to her: "You were beautiful as long as I loved you; perhaps my love made you so, not only in my opinion. Now, I find you the ugliest and meanest character which I have ever met in my life." To which she replied: "I know that I have never been so malicious toward anyone as toward you, without being able to give any reasons for it." "I can, though," he said, "you hate me because I am a man and your husband." The day of his departure, she changed face altogether, was all tenderness and love, and went so far as to kiss him on a crowded street of London. A criminal offence in England, he warned her, and shuddered. On arriving in Hamburg, he found his friends away and wired in all directions for money, but in vain. Then cholera threatened and he was quarantined in a strange city, penniless, desperate. From this dilemma he was rescued after a time by Paul, who sent him money to join him in Rügen. There we find him, presently, deep in his chemistry, conducting experiments in the blazing heat of the summer, in a curious mood of exaltation, nervousness and morbid fear. Once, he suspected that Paul would fling him down from a tower and fled in the utmost fright. "This insignificant, uncultured Finn, whom he had raised up from nothing, brought into his circle, boarded and lodged . . ." (which last was certainly false). Seeing he had nothing more to gain from his master, he rewarded him now with hatred and vengeance. Strindberg discovered, moreover, so he says, that an old lover of "Aspasia" was in the vicinity and was vastly uneasy on that account. In all, it was a terrible place he had gotten into.

"Had he come there to fulfill all his worst dreams?" he asks. It was hell. He, the blasphemer, tortured as in Dante's Inferno. For days he wandered in the endless sand of the island and cursed the horrible excess of it. It was a shifting, treacherous foundation, conserving the heat, hinting allegorically at ruin, self-made,—put there precisely to annoy him.

In the meantime, he received letters from his wife, one announcing her undying love, and representing them as Hero and Leander divided romantically by water, another full of reproaches of a man who had dared to desert his sick wife. In one letter she is on the point of founding a theatre in London, without capital, as he remarks, while in the next she has retired into a cloister, forsaking the hell of marriage and the evil of the world. Strindberg as he says, found it difficult to write a reasonable answer. When he sent a tender communication, he received a reproachful reply in answer to a previous one, and conversely; until, feeling that their correspondence was going the way of lunacy, they took to frantic telegrams. At the same time, she wrote to Paul, requesting him to watch over her husband who is, she declared, "the greatest genius that exists and the noblest man on God's green earth." But these well-intentioned letters to his friends, requesting them to take care of him, annoyed Strindberg more than anything else. They were artful manœuvers which could one day bring him to an asylum.

This "witches' kitchen" endured a month when suddenly he received an invitation from his mother-in-law to come for a visit to Odense at the villa of the father. His wife's parents had lived separately for some time, but now planned to come together again in honor of their daughter's homecoming and her new husband. Strindberg's experience gave him little confidence in reconciliations of this kind, for which and many other reasons he was full of uneasy forebodings as he at last drew near the villa. Here, however, he was met by a white-haired woman who took him in her arms as her son. "I have known you long before you saw my daughter," said the old woman with the quivering voice of a religious fanatic. "And I have likewise expected you. In your writing there is much evil, but your immorality is childish, your views concerning women are correct and your godlessness is not your fault. . . . You have married with a child of the world, but you will not endure her long when you see how she draws you down with the commonplaces of life." Strindberg found her a very original sort of mother, and though no doubt comforted by her words, was shocked by the manner and source of them. He discovered his wife had not yet arrived, and no one knew her whereabouts, while his father-in-law would not come until the next day. He was oppressed with the sense of being watched, slept badly, dismayed and apprehensive. In the morning he awoke with the suspicion that Satan had lured him into a nest of snakes. The distinguished man, his father-in-law, when he arrived paid him great respect, praised his works and assented to his view of women. "You have written everything that I would like to write," he said. He was much touched when Strindberg implored him to use the informal address (du) as became their close relation. "You are a good fellow," cried the old man, taking him into his arms. Once more, Strindberg found himself deep in a family; the father of four children, he was forced to become a child again himself. That afternoon he was scolded for his maladroitness at fishing and that night the old mother comforted him, explaining that now the worst was past.

When Frieda received letters praising her husband, so great was her love of power that she grew fearful of losing it and jealous of Strindberg's success with her parents. Since he preferred them to her, she wrote, he would never see her again. Thereupon, her father fell into a great rage and Strindberg wrote to his wife that if she did not join him at once he would divorce her. Next, a telegram arrived assuring him that she would meet him, but whether in Odense or Berlin was not clear, and for three days they tried in vain to decipher it. The tension became

unbearable. The old man in his anger fell out with Strindberg on
the financial question and the latter, made to feel like a vagabond
and a beggar, determined to live by song and guitar rather than
sell his soul to the nearest publisher. The presence of the husband
and the absence of his wife caused a scandal in the vicinity, the
people began to murmur, and the old man felt that his own honor
as well as Strindberg's was threatened. The deserted bride-groom
must leave the house at once, he said. Strindberg left. He did
not wait for the train, did not bid goodby to his father-in-law,
and though he heard him calling in a caressing, heart-breaking
voice, would not look back. With staff in hand, and no possessions in the world, like a vagabond, he set out on the road to
Odense, and now his mood was light-hearted, now sad and sentimental. On arriving, he took the train for Berlin, where he
found that his wife had traveled on to meet him in another place.
The farce, it seemed to him, was becoming a tragedy. If his wife
went home, her father would beat her. There seemed no chance
of her finding him.

He had need to unburden his heart, to tell his friends of the
fabulous confusions of his marriage trip, but they looked at him
with a sharp glance that made him stop short in his story. He had
now retired with friends to a distant town. As he walked the
streets, he was amazed to see the inhabitants stare at him from
the windows with wild distorted faces. Was a false report of his
insanity responsible for this curiosity? His friend looked at him
doubtfully. "Don't you know where you are?" he asked. The
town was a colony of lunatics (Gheel). In every house they raved,
or glimmered in their corners. Strindberg had a terrible suspicion! Had he been brought there for inspection? He determined
to give no occasion for suspicion and scrupulously avoided the
subject of his marriage trip. From Austria came the report that
the father-in-law, knowing the sorrow he had brought upon an
unhappy man, now thought of suicide and had wept aloud.
Strindberg pitied him deeply. To while away the time he oc-

cupied himself with botanical studies. One day, when he had finally concluded that plants have nerves because they react to morphium, an apple fell beside him and a man with a large stick accused him of stealing his fruit—i. e. until he decided that the stranger must be one of the lunatics. For the accused this was a terrible moment.

On arriving home he found his wife there, waiting for him as if she had dropped from the blue. Yet it all seemed quite natural. She was in her girlish phase, charming, happy, and with a purse of money for a celebration. Strindberg was completely reconciled and lived for two months, full of gold and happiness. During this time she gave him no occasion for jealousy and gratified him, in fact, by being jealous herself. Then there arose mysterious discords, the serpent hatred between inseparable lovers, which, thought Strindberg, only Swedenborg had properly explained. Finally, she swore to return to her parents. In the early morning, before he had arisen, he saw a white form beside his bed, intreating him mutely for mercy and kindness, but though a weak man, as he says, especially in such matters, he would not stir, but went to sleep again, while she traveled away from him forever, as he thought, back to that viper's nest in Odense. The worst of it was that she was pregnant, and would now have to bear his child in loneliness, shamed and taunted by her parents, miserable and helpless. This was an ugly circumstance and weighed heavily on Strindberg's conscience. Moreover, she had become a necessity to him. Prometheus, long used to the gnawing birds, grew unhappy when they flew away. Strindberg wept for his little sorceress, and could not do without her. Even her worst arts, her mind-reading, her anthropophagy, her terrible insidiousness, he would gladly endure again. Without her his hopes collapsed and his mind, stunned and exhausted, unwound and rattled back to emptiness. As he toyed with his revolver, like a spectre in a vague world from which all the spans and vortices had been removed, the question why he should live or what do, left him no peace. Things had come to a sad pass with him. In a paper he read a report that he was dead, to which he wrote a reply with the salt of gallows' humor in it. A few days later he was obliged to prove his existence by running about to borrow money. What he now needed the money for, oddly enough, was to travel back to Dornach to join his wife. His mother-in-law had invited him to come, to spend the winter there, in fact, in a town sufficiently close so the parents could look in on them from time to time. There, his wife wrote to add, he could finish his great work (*Antibarbarus*), on which his future depended, in peace, for she would do anything in her power to aid him, for—yes, she loved him as much as she had ever done. He must face the future with courage and, for the rest, return to her instantly. Once in the little town, they settled down in two rooms. Frieda cooked and kept house, Strindberg labored on his scientific works, and they lived quietly and happily enough, though oppressed, as usual, with poverty and the excessive confinement of their relation. She, for her part, bore these troubles with great sweetness of temper, treated her husband with consideration and kindness, even tried to believe that his scientific works might some day bring in some money. This change of heart Strindberg ascribed to the awakening of her maternal instinct. For himself, he was full of apprehension. "Now, when he would soon have two families to provide for, he trembled before the future with its increased duties, for a growing dislike to exercise his calling as an author had finally culminated in disgust."

"What an occupation—to flay his fellow-creatures and offer their skins for sale. Like a hunter who, when pressed hard by hunger, cuts off his dog's tail, eats the flesh, and gives the bone —its own bone, to the dog. What an occupation, to spy out people's secrets, expose the birthmarks of his best friend, dissect his wife like a rabbit for vivisection, and act like a croat, cutting down, violating, burning and selling. Fie!" Also a recent event had frightened the publishers and producers. A German translation of *The Confession of a Fool* had been denounced for immorality. This was an additional discouragement, but the worst was, he could no longer write. Gradually, hunger and need crept closer about their two rooms, where the atmosphere became stifling and unbearable. The children of his first marriage cried for food and assistance, and Strindberg was at his wit's end to help himself. Then came an invitation to spend the season on the estate of the mother's parents in Ardagger. Accordingly, they were soon ensconced in a huge white ghostly house, where lived the mother, and her aged parents, where reigned the tranquillity and the good peace of old age. Strindberg was lavished with food and attention, took to bed early and flourished much in consequence. But finally the grandfather, who was an advocate, pried into Strindberg's secrets, learned that he was interested in the transmutation of metals, and answering from the textbooks, denounced the project as wild and unfeasible. Strindberg answered mildly, was modest and good to a degree that surprised and delighted his wife. But he knew that now a break was inevitable. One day the gendarmes came (according to Strindberg's account) to summon him to the nearest court to answer the charges of immorality in connection with the translation of *The Confession of a Fool*. Strindberg refused to defend himself in such a matter, but the old man, who did not like the gendarmes about the place, insisted, and then it came to a falling out between them. It was decided that he and his wife should leave the grandfather's house and live by themselves in a little cottage near by. Here, then, they set up house again, planted flowers and a garden, and Strindberg himself painted pictures to cover the white walls. They were preparing for the reception of their child and in the end were full of wonder at their handicraft. "How overjoyed he will be to see so many paintings the first day!" said the prospective father. When the baby came, it was unfortunately not a boy but a girl, it cried from morning 'til night in an entirely abnormal fashion, and rather separated the parents than united them. Strindberg did not love the child enough, was Frieda's complaint. Also, at the bottom of her heart, she knew that Strindberg would leave her before long and that she could not follow him back into the world as she desired because of her responsibilities.

The child in the meantime continued to cry. Five women tended it. The old folks were alarmed and among the people in the vicinity evil rumors spread. The child had not been baptized. The foreign gentleman was an atheist. A woman had seen the devil, quite clearly, in the Strindberg garden. At last the old man pronounced an ultimatum. Either the child must be baptized in the Catholic faith, or they must leave. After a time, this was done, though Strindberg protested in the name of Protestantism, in which faith, however, he was not a believer. The child recovered.

Strindberg's belief at this time, that his enemies were spreading reports of his insanity, drove him to the greatest extremes of folly and madness. To doctors he wrote for a certificate of sanity and to his friends he appealed for sympathy and aid in vengeance. Against certain former friends he was unappeasable. "Aspasia," he will tear limb from limb. Paul will never enjoy another day of peace. For, though persecuted by a host of cowardly enemies, he has the power to withstand them all. Had not all his great enemies, the gyneolaters and blue-stockings, ended in death or confusion, one cutting her throat, another poisoned or insane? Some time after writing a thundering letter demanding that his plays be produced in Paris, instead of the twaddle of Ibsen or Björnson, he was gratified, yet frightened, to hear that this had been done, for he felt like a necromancer whose brain coerced and had its way with others, from afar. The humiliation and dependence of his life among relatives had rather strengthened, than not, the sense of his own overwhelming powers.

His heart warmed by a theatrical success in Paris, he now longed to return to the world, to converse with his own kind again, to gather the fruits of his genius, to be free from his little

jailer. She, sensing this dawning resolution, and envying his triumphs, which she could now neither share nor hope to equal,
became a fury and a vampire in good earnest, so that all that had
gone before seemed mere child's play to what followed. Out of
pure malice she required him to live in filth and noise, with dirty
milk-bottles and children's clothes. His room, strewn with deliberate disorder, came to look like the housekeeping of demons. She
served him execrable food. One day, she put before him a dish of
bones that dogs had apparently gnawed on. It was clear that she
rated him lower than the servants, lower even than the dogs. When
he fell sick, she refused to call a doctor, on account of the expense,
and she taunted him cruelly with his beggary. Living in such filth
and malice it is little wonder that he felt bewitched and desolate.
Later he realized that he had been passing through the Swedenborgian petty hells—an atonement imposed upon great souls, and
this heartened him and made his memories easier to bear.

The worst of his penances, a horror more personal and stifling
than any of the rest, was her curious probing and prying into his
secret thoughts. Due to the excessive familiarity in the marriage
relation, thought Strindberg, the wife acquires a terrible power of
reading her husband's mind, and invariably employs it to some
sinister end. When a mood seized him, or a new idea,—a solution of some old riddle of nature, a botanical theory or classifica-
tion, or a plan for a startling experiment in chemistry,—he guarded
and treasured it joyfully, but always fearful that some chance
gesture or remark might betray it to the prying curiosity of his
wife. In the end, in some forbidden way, she got it out of him,
stealing into his soul softly and treacherously, gaining power there
by degrees, that she might later scatter, burn, and plunder. He
felt her creepers on his inmost thoughts and was afraid. All day
long, her dark eyes watched his thoughts, her face immobile to
conceal from him her secret knowledge. Like an octopus, she
closed him in with her prying divinations, cutting him off from
the world, weakening his purposes and resolutions, the better to

destroy him. Often he fled from the cottage out into a solitary
place where the country closed him in, for there where she had
never been, his thoughts were his own. He had found her out.
She was an empusa, the kind of vampire so much dreaded in ancient times. If she humored him, he would no longer be deceived.
It was merely to the end that she might finally eat his flesh and
lap up his blood. If only his money would come, he could escape.
As it was, he was like a man in a dream who sees the vampire
approaching with her white distorted face, but cannot move. As
letters arrived for him from Paris, acclaiming his scientific discoveries, she was frantic with curiosity. When these letters ceased
coming, he knew what had happened.

Finally, after many trials of this kind, his money came and he
traveled away from the prison and his little jailer, back into the
world. But, as he looked back from the steamer, he felt "only
gratitude and melancholy. One moment the tie which linked
him to wife and child drew him so powerfully that he felt he
must fling himself into the water. Then, however, the paddle
wheels of the steamer turned powerfully forward a few times and
the tie tightened, stretched—and broke!"

So closes Strindberg's story of his second marriage, *Fair Haven
and Foul Strand,* but the facts are otherwise. Strindberg weakened
to the entreaties of his little fury and took her with him. A new
reconciliation followed. Frieda, frantic to get back to the world,
did not scruple to leave her child behind. She behaved like an
angel. Once back in Paris, the discords began again. The expected triumphs were tragically dim and short-lived, and the
money meager. They were both soon exhausted. Strindberg continued his fanatical experiments, though his work had been dis-
allowed by specialists of rank, while his wife, seeing their resources at an end, and despairing of any financial return from
his daring investigations, brooded and watched, her heart sinking
at the very thought of the oven, the retorts, the sulphur fumes
in which she saw an end of hopes and reason. She was desperate

and could be at times, no doubt with some justification, a little fiendish. Her husband, at least, found her so, unmistakably, and was delighted when in November, 1894, the sickness of their child called her back to Austria. "With a feeling of wild joy I returned from the Gare du Nord where I had left my dear wife." He had told her that they would see each other again *soon,* but these words now rang in his ears like a broken bell and a deep suspicion told him that they would *never* meet again. This turned out to be the truth. Strindberg returned with greater zeal to his chemical experiments and as he went to bed that night he felt blessed and happy. "A feeling of spiritual purity, masculine virginity, made the past marriage appear as something unclean." He regretted only that, his wife having left, he had no one to thank for his deliverance. It was not long before he wrote her a love-letter, to which, however, she replied with great coldness, warning him that the scientific triumph he had boasted was an illusion, calculated neither to preserve his reason or nourish his family. Love or Science! Once more he was faced with a Kierkegaardian alternative, and this time did not hesitate to choose the latter. He wrote her that everything was over, pretending another affair of the heart. When he had written the farewell letter, he smiled like a murderer whose job is finished. Then his conscience awoke to torture him and in his loneliness he prayed for her return. The divorce proceedings were broken from time to time by wild notes of longing and frantic reconciliations, for they loved each other and hated each other "with the wild hate of a love which was heightened by separation." To free himself from these bonds he now made good his lie, and pursued an affair with an Englishwoman, which ended, however, in nothing but shame and frustration. And now, midway in life, he determined never to love again, for the powers which had come to direct his life, and order even the smallest events therein, had absolved him from the thralldom of desire and reserved him, there was no doubt in his mind, for some higher purpose.

XXIII

INFERNO

STRINDBERG'S great relief at his wife's departure was largely due to her attitude toward his scientific researches. "His pretty little jailer," as he often called her, despaired of these investigations which carried his mind so far away from hers and became, as time went on, as jealous of the stars and atoms, of minerals and "the nervous systems of plants," as previously of women, or her husband's men friends. Atoms or women or absorbing friends. It didn't matter. They stole him away from her. She was determined, he thought, to weave a spell about him, to get him in her power in spite of everything, and he was quite as determined she shouldn't.

When she left, he returned in an exalted state to his student's room in the Latin Quarter, took out six porcelain crucibles, which he had bought at the expense of the family budget, tongs and a package of sulphur. Then he lit a smelting oven, locked the door, and pulled down the blinds, for at this time, "it is not wise to make use of chemical apparatus in Paris." With these simple preparations he commenced an experiment which he had performed many times before. It was an experiment which, if successful, would solve the great problem, disprove the reigning chemistry, and settle his future forever. The fire swirled about the crucible, "the sulphur burnt with hellish flames," the air was filled with its fumes. Outside on the street there was an ominous silence.

341

Strindberg watched the endless burning with his wild eyes, intently, and dreamed and waited. In the course of the night his hands, burned by the strong flames, became black and bleeding and the skin scaled off with dreadful pain. Yet he persisted and toward morning, had solved, as he thought, one of the greatest problems of chemistry. He had discovered a trace of carbon in the bottom of the crucible. He had therefore extracted carbon from pure sulphur, a thing long deemed impossible. He had demonstrated that sulphur is not a simple element, but composite. At last, the great triumph which he had dreamed of so long. Heretofore his experiments had yielded no result. He had suffered ridicule from his friends, from scientists, from his wife, his wife's grandfather, and many others. He had persisted, for he knew that in the end, as Haeckel had said, there can be but one ground stuff, that the complex must therefore be composed of the simple. Now he had succeeded in demonstrating this principle in the special case of sulphur. He had triumphed, but the jealous "powers" exacted a heavy toll, made him pay an equal penalty. For his burnt hands left him helpless, and the lack of funds made further experiments impossible. In his heart he dreamed of other triumphs. He would now extract hydrogen and oxygen from sulphur. This was forbidden.

Jealous of his discovery, he made no effort to publish it. He retired more and more from company and avoided his friends. "Silence and loneliness spread around me," he wrote. "It is the solemn and terrible stillness of the wilderness in which I challenge the Invisible One out of spite, in order to wrestle with him body to body, soul to soul."

Knut Hamsun, who knew him at this time, relates that he lived in the uttermost poverty and insecurity, slept and worked in one small room, lived on credit, borrowed where he could, wrote articles for a pitiful compensation, and in all, was more put upon by mean distresses than any famous man alive. Even clothes were wanting and the man who had been a dandy in Berlin and lived

Strindberg in the Inferno Period

high in Paris, after his dramatic triumph, became at forty-eight a disheveled, threadbare hobo. At the same period he was supposed to have received three hundred kronen a month from a patron. Did this money go for absinthe and experiments, or was it sent to one of the two families?

One of Strindberg's friends tells of meeting him one day in a cheap restaurant in the Latin Quarter, in a dilapidated condition, his grizzled head bowed low over the table. The students around him were hilarious, and the little waitress, to cheer this one lonely man, threw her arms about him and kissed him. In the same moment Strindberg was on his feet, looking, as only he had the art to do, like a man from Hell. Pushing the waitress aside he left the place in a condition far from sobriety.

Through the winter he continued his lonely experiments, but as Christmas approached he accepted an invitation from a Scandinavian family. But in the midst of the Christmas celebration, he was dismayed by the irregularity of this establishment, by the unrestrained manners and liberties of the artists who resorted there. Presently another picture arose in his mind. He thought of his little daughter and his forsaken wife and of a Christmas tree at Ardagger. With a word of apology he fled into the street, tortured by conscience, desperate, hunted. As he passed along the "horrible Rue de la Gaieté," the festive painted happiness of the people offended him. Finally he sank down on a terrace of a Brasserie on the Boulevarde Montparnasse, and consoled himself for a moment with a good glass of absinthe. Then a gay band of students and coquettes overwhelmed him, striking his face with switches. Again he fled as if "driven by furies" to a café on Saint-Michel and ordered another absinthe, and again he was driven away by another troop. "Whipped by the Eumenides" he made his way like Orestes, through the terrible gaiety and the mocking merriment of the crowds, back to his lonely room. There he breathed at last and took council with himself. Surely "the powers" which opposed his experiments, which punished his high ambition, must be overcome before his victory was complete. That night he was awakened several times by cold draughts on his face and by the intrusive tones of a mouth organ. All this looked very bad.

A few days later, a woman whom he hated took pity on him, raised a subscription on his behalf in the Scandinavian colony and took him off to a hospital, for his burnt hands had grown worse and bade fair to give him much trouble. There he found himself in a terrible company. "Heads of the dead and the dying: here a nose was missing, there a lip hung down, here a cheek had begun to rot." To make matters worse a frightful odor of iodine pervaded the place and the comforts and provisions were hateful. Yet for this, one must be grateful. Strindberg raged at the very thought of it.

Happily, however, a kind sister did much to lighten his misery, tended him with great cheerfulness and goodness, made it possible for him to use a library and a laboratory, and indeed, won his heart so completely that the dearest word of all came to his lips. He called her "my mother." She called him "my child." When, in February, he left the hospital, he would have loved to kiss the hand of this little "mother," who had shown him so beautifully the way to the cross, but was held back by a feeling of reverence.

In the meantime, Strindberg had not been idle. In a chemical book he found a passage relating how Lockyer had shown by spectral-analysis that phosphorous is not a simple substance; from his apothecary he received the report that his sample of burnt sulphur contained carbon. His victory was now complete; his reputation and sanity preserved. A year before he had been treated like a charlatan, a Cagliostro, his integrity suspected, his reason despaired of, even in his own family. Now he was on top, and had the power to shame the professors and tear down the university if he chose. He announced his discovery in an article which won him many opponents and a few disciples.

Yet his new triumph made him fearful, as though he had sold his soul for the glory of it; his loneliness was oppressive and the shadow of some unknown power walked beside him with threats and presages and mysterious signs. As he wandered through Paris each street name seemed to him to bear a meaning and a personal warning. Rue Alibert. Was not Alibert the name of the apothecary who had analyzed his sulphur? Then Rue Dieu (God). This name shocked him and he walked on with an uneasy conscience and a disquieting sense of a mystery unsolved. Then Rue Beurepaire—"a beautiful resort for wrong-doers," etc. Was he pursued by demons? He avoided the street names and fled, without knowing where, first into a region which reeked with the odor of raw flesh, then into a street of wickedness and crime where the prostitutes blocked his way and the street boys hooted. The knowledge that he was under the direction of unseen powers whose purposes he did not know, made the world appear a strange and ominous pageant. He withdrew more and more from the company of men and lost himself in spectral loneliness and fears.

One day, as he passed by a dyer's shop, he saw the initials of his name, A. S., painted there with a rainbow above and took it as a favorable sign, for had not God placed His bow in the heavens as a sign of His mercy? Directly afterward he picked up a book which asserted that sulphur had been found to contain oxygen and hydrogen and an unknown substance. This he took as a great confirmation of his own work. Another symbol, which confronted him with strange persistence, was the name of Orfila, the great chemist and toxicologist, who had led him through the labyrinth of his chemical investigations. Everywhere he saw that name inscribed and later on with a feeling of unavoidable destiny went to live in the Hotel Orfila.

It was at this time that he was tempted twice by the devil, tempted with love and with worldly ambition. One night at the Crémerie a captivating Englishwoman took a fancy to him and signed for him to leave with her. He rose to follow amid spiteful laughter. Out in the street they were mocked by cadets and prostitutes. It began to rain. They retreated to a café on the Boulevard Raspail. Then Strindberg discovered that he had no money. It was a terrible night and there was no doubt in his mind that "the powers" were opposed to this affair. He, a beggar, who had left his family without support, had no right to a new love. He tried his best to avoid her but in vain. On meeting her one night at the Crémerie, he was completely enthralled by her beauty, and, using his arts to great advantage, had almost succeeded, when suddenly a little girl, half model, half sweetheart, ran in and flung her arms around his neck and kissed him. That was the end. The Englishwoman rose up and left. Again the powers had interceded and Strindberg knew that he was released from love, forever.

After his success with sulphur Strindberg now began a set of experiments with the object of proving that iodine can be derived from benzine. In some manner, as he relates, these studies became known, and a gentleman representing the iodine interest of Europe appeared before him, offering him a hundred thousand francs if he would go to Berlin with him to make known his secret. He refused with some nobility and some trepidation. His discovery, he said, was not a commercial one. A few days later, on Whitsuntide, he remembered his childhood, the celebration of that blessed festival with tulips and lilies and young girls as white as angels, and was stricken with shame. Never would he attempt to make a fortune from his chemical studies. "O crux ave spes unica. No more of love! No more of money! No more of honor! The way of the cross, the only one which leads to wisdom."

In the fall of 1895 came good fortune again, friends and money to buy scientific equipment. For a time he lived quietly in lonely guarded happiness. Then the pendulum of fortune swung back and the paradise was lost again. More and more absorbed in a world in which no one could follow him, he broke with his friends, and stood alone with his great ego which now spread and swelled with unheard-of powers. From youth onwards, he asserts, he has been a medium, has been able to influence, to bewitch his friends, from a distance, telepathically. Now he feels capable of a real miracle. Though the divorce is in process he longs for his child. What if a catastrophe should occur! What if his child should fall sick! A telegram would come and he would return. Could his thoughts bring about such a wonder? He took her dear portrait and performed the deadly rite, then set to work with an indescribable feeling of uneasiness. That same evening he read a warning in the cryptograms of nature. As he turned his microscope on a budding walnut he saw "two hands white as alabaster, raised and folded as in prayer." Was it an hallucination? A friend corroborated it. From this moment on, the invisible god declared against him and the blows fell thick about his head.

When he received from the printer the proof of *Sylva Sylvarum,* he found the text confused like a mixed deck of cards. When the book was finally published, the printer sent him such a bill, that to pay it he was obliged to pawn his microscope and all his other valuables. Yet, it was worth it. "For the first time in my life," he wrote, "I am certain of having said something new, great and beautiful." With "proud and scornful gestures" he defied the hostile powers. "Hear you, Sphinx, I have solved your riddle, and I challenge you." After that his troubles came fast and thick. Three women played on three pianos in the rooms next to his, made disturbing unearthly noises overhead and through the walls, while his host sent him his bill which he could not pay nor leave until he had paid. At the same time his friends at the Crémerie turned enemies to the man and he fled from this resort and from his hotel, leaving books and possessions behind.

It was now that he entered the Hotel Orfila, an old religious house, in whose mystical mediaeval atmosphere he laid his plans for the last and greatest research. The chemists, the specialists, had not accepted his analysis of sulphur. They were jealous, thought Strindberg, and blinded by authority. He would not retract but, like a man whom the furies allow no pause or return, he continued his experiments, ruining his health, squandering his slender means for equipment. His claims became more grandiose than ever. He would make gold. Gold, like sulphur, cannot be a simple element. It must be compounded of the one ground stuff. Strindberg argues here rather from the materialistic monism of Haeckel than from the facts of chemical reaction. Later he wrote to Haeckel concerning his scientific discoveries and cherished the latter's letter, though it was somewhat non-commital, as a proof of his own sanity.

One day, in a narrow street, a Roman knight appeared before him suddenly, staring at a wall. As Strindberg followed his eyes he saw the letters F and S. The initials of his wife's name! "Then she loves me still," he concluded. Then the F changed to Fe and he had solved the riddle of the ages. Iron (Fe) and sulphur (S) were the components of gold. He set to work, but was troubled from time to time by inexplicable events. First, a mysterious stranger appeared who looked so much like his wife that he would have sworn he was her brother, had she had one. Why this gentleman wrote him and shadowed him, why he meddled in his life and looked so much like his wife, Strindberg never discovered.

At this time, a curious stranger appeared at the Crémerie, an American artist, who did much to heighten the tone of the company there. Confident and dashing, full of ideas, he made an excellent companion. One night he appeared in Strindberg's room and revealed himself as a lost man. The Patron had thrown him out of his room, his sweetheart had left him, his creditors pursued him on the streets, the unpaid models reviling him. Worse than everything else, he had lost his credit at the Crémerie and was therefore literally on the street. Strindberg considered the matter for a while and then decided to move on to another district and take a room with him. For two months he joined his lot with this miserable man, who confessed to him daily all his sorrows and misfortunes, yet concealed his past in a most suspicious fashion. To lighten the misery of his friend Strindberg was obliged to hide his greatness, to conceal his reputation and prospects, and to live through the sufferings and struggles of the young artist. He, the famous dramatist, the great original chemist, soon fancied himself a mere beginner. Also his friend disquieted him by his strange moods. On one occasion he sat tranquilly for days and refused to eat. He was examining the sensations of hunger, he said.

One day, Strindberg saw in the *Review of Reviews* a picture of the American prophet and physician Francis Schlotter, "who in 1895 had cured five thousand sick and then disappeared forever from the earth." Strindberg was astounded at the resemblance of this man to his friend, the poor artist. Their features were exactly alike and their histories, so far as he knew them, agreed point for point. Could it be that this wonder-healer, Francis Schlotter, was the Doppelgänger (double) of his comrade, the artist? Strindberg hurried to the Café de Versailles to ask the opinion of his friend, the sculptor, who on hearing the facts and seeing the picture, opened his eyes in amazement, and pointed out that their man had certainly two lodgings, one on the Left Bank, one on the Right, and that while he spent the evening in philosophical discussion with Strindberg, he was repeatedly met at the Ball Bullier. Was Francis Schlotter then really a Doppelgänger? Did Strindberg's room-mate lead this double life? On comparing the facsimile of Francis Schlotter's last letter with their friend's handwriting, they found a perfect agreement. When Strindberg confronted his friend with the evidence, he laughed with quiet indifference. But Strindberg was not to be deceived. When the artist related how he had slept all day without knowing why, Strindberg exclaimed, "Naturally; the astral body went walking, n'est-ce pas, in America . . ." After this remark a certain coldness was noticed on his side. (Later on, the friendship was concluded with mutual consent.)

One day, when Strindberg and his mysterious friend were having an absinthe at the café, an enraged laborer seized upon the latter with many loud oaths and demanded the thirty francs for the cross he had made. The waiters came and the gendarmes came and the man was put out. The artist bowed his head in shame. "What cross?" whispered Strindberg, dismayed at the scene. His friend explained that he had ordered a cross as a model for his painting, "The Crucified Women," but could not pay the workman. "The thirty pieces of silver!" said Strindberg. "Enough. Enough," cried his friend who had sickened. One night when they went home together Strindberg saw a great head of Zeus at the top of his bed and was frightened at the ghostly affair. It turned out to be his pillow, which, on another night, became the Devil himself. Strindberg's clairvoyance was increasing. He was improving every day. He saw not only Zeus and the Devil in a pillow, he saw human faces in pansies and above the Pantheon floated Napoleon and all his marshals.

At the same time he was oppressed by a terrible fear. While in Berlin he had had an affair with "Aspasia" who had subsequently married the Pole, who now hated him, he thought, to the death. On hearing that the Pole was back in Paris he shuddered, for he knew that he had come back to murder him in hot revenge. As he listened in his room he heard the strains of Schumann's *Aufschwung* and collapsed with fear, for that was the Pole's favorite piece. Again and again it was played over as only *he* could play it. Did his enemy wish to warn him of his murderous plans? Everything was mystery. Yet he felt the net tighten about him in dreadful, certain doom. On questioning a mutual friend, he was informed that the Pole would soon be in Paris. "To murder me," added Strindberg. "Of course. Be on your guard!" was the answer. Suddenly on the ground he saw several dried twigs arranged in the form P—Y and this hinted at the name Prsybyszevski. It was a warning from the powers—a favorable portent that made him more uneasy than ever. That night he prayed the

Old Testament God for help against his enemy and comforted himself with the psalms of David. Finally, his terror getting the better of his scruples, he stuck needles through the eyes in the portrait of his enemy. He could not afford to take chances with such a man.

The powers warned him again. For a long time, his one great solace had been absinthe. Through the cold green of that treacherous drink he could remove himself at will from all the ominous annoyances and the great frustrations, and all the hot passions on earth, withdrawing himself in a detachment aloof and sad, with Van Gogh's strained stillness about him, a frozen, mystical world. Yet it was dangerous and he knew it. Siri, his first wife, had warned him. Frieda, his second wife, had admonished him repeatedly. Now the powers declared their displeasure. One day while enjoying his glass at the café a drunken man stared at him insolently, another day a fire broke out in the chimney, and so on. A family party over-ran his table, a man put a coin on his table as if he had been a beggar, a stench broke out which drove him away. No doubt the powers were befriending him, thought Strindberg. Their interference was saving him from an asylum. It is interesting, in this connection, that Strindberg's supposed enemy, the Pole Prsybyszevski, once declared that most of the troubles of his great wild friend were due to the excessive quantity of absinthe and alcohol he consumed, and others concurred in the opinion.

For a time he continued to hear the tell-tale music of the *Aufschwung* and lived in ceaseless dread of the subtle Pole. One day he went to the house of Prsybyszevski's friend, which was usually guarded by a large, ugly dog. As they stepped out he threw his cloak about the shoulders of this friend, who immediately confessed all that Strindberg desired to know; that the Pole was his enemy and that all his troubles had been brought about by him, that he planned to do him to death. After a time the friend became uneasy, threw off Strindberg's coat, and with an oath, left his company. Had the fluid in his coat passed over into the body of this man who stood so close to the Pole, his enemy? "Was I a magician without knowing it?" Strindberg wondered. Shortly afterwards he learned that the Pole had been imprisoned on the suspicion of having incited his first wife to suicide and the murder of her children. For a time he was greatly relieved and breathed in peace. Then his delusion of persecution changed to one of guilt. He soon believed that through his hostile thoughts he had "influenced" the Pole and brought upon him this tragedy. He is all solicitude and remorse. If he had been a black magician, it was horrible, of course, but quite unintended. For many years, as he confesses, he had influenced his friends and enemies from afar, but never with such mortal effect. For the future he must be careful. Not long afterwards, however, he made a proposal that Georg Brandes found very amusing. He offered to ruin Brandes' enemies by sticking pins through the eyes in their portraits and dispose of them in whatever way that gentleman chose.

Strindberg's stay in Paris was broken in the summer of 1896 by a trip to Sweden, whither he went to undertake a cure at the house of his friend, Dr. Eliasson. There he was given the best of care and the famous physician did everything in his power to bring Strindberg back to reason. For one thing, he attempted to dissuade him from his fabulous scientific enterprises and warned him seriously against the dangers of the occult. If Strindberg continued his interests in the occult, he was lost, thought the doctor. But Strindberg, for all the care and council he was given, did not improve. His condition grew worse. He came to suspect that the doctor was jealous of his chemical successes, wished to steal his secret of gold-making, and murder him to cover up the theft. One night when visited with nightmares and horrors worse than usual, and convinced that the doctor designed to murder him before morning, he fled to another doctor in the town and refused to return to his death. Fortunately, this doctor was a theosophist to whom he could open his heart, without being thought insane.

When he returned home, his good friend Dr. Eliasson looked so sad and genuinely grieved on his account, that Strindberg determined never again to hold him in suspicion.

In the middle of the Polish horror, Strindberg fell under the tyrannical influence of a mysterious theosophist. After the publication of his *Antibarbarus* he received a letter from a distinguished gentleman praising that work and calling attention to its agreement at many points with the doctrines of theosophy. Naturally pleased with this commendation, Strindberg replied in a friendly way, with confidences and confessions. As their correspondence continued, however, the theosophist grew vastly displeased with Strindberg's want of modesty, and he, with the theosophist's presumption and tyranny. Modesty, indeed! "Before whom should *I* bow? Before the theosophists? Never." Strindberg raged at the thought of accepting the wisdom of the priestess, Mme. Blavatsky. It was his duty to preserve the integrity of his self against all such parties or sects. Only to the Eternal, to the powers, would he yield an inch. At their behest he will chasten his spirit and suppress his evil instincts, but that is all. He will not deny his ego, for that would be suicide. For him, the soaring distinction of the self is the last and highest end of existence. To suppress that principle would be madness. Strindberg also differed from the theosophist in another very central issue. He held that the moving powers in the world which order the sins and punishments and blessings are concrete living personalities. (Strindberg could never bear the abstract.)

These personal and metaphysical differences naturally led to trouble. The theosophist finally became so overbearing that Strindberg was afraid he held him for insane. "He called me Simon Magus, black magician, and recommended Mme. Blavatsky." Strindberg rejected Mme. Blavatsky. *"No one has anything to teach me,"* he wrote. Then the theosophist threatened him with the wrath of the powers, withdrew the stipend he had sent for some time, and Strindberg put his confidence in Providence.

Strindberg's gold synthesis won little recognition from chemists but the French alchemists accepted it with great applause. Tiffereau, in particular, was quite persuaded, but regretted that the amounts produced were so small that they frequently escaped detection. Strindberg was elected honorary member of the Société Alchimique de la France and became a contributor to *l'Initiation*, the official organ of occultists. . . . Yes, and the famous Papus of *l'Initiation* praised his investigations. Strindberg was much flattered and emboldened. In his heart he imagined that he had solved the riddle of the Sphinx and, like Orpheus, brought life back into nature, left cold and dead by the specialists. So far did he go that he lost, as he says, every trace of modesty. He had gone much too far, for he knew that the sin of pride, hubris, is the one crime which the gods never forgive.

Elevated by his brooding sense of sin and illicit power, Strindberg stood more and more alone, for the sublime man, as Nietzsche had taught him, is, of necessity, lonely and apart. Gradually he withdrew from the blessing of comradeship. The amiable faces of men had become but wooden symbols, white, portentous, like the startling, tell-tale painted visages in French primitifs. They had become symbolical masks and warnings on the long journey toward Damascus. He absented himself so much from company, indeed, that he lost by disuse, as he says, the power of speech.

The mystical blue dome of heaven closed down upon him and the silver stars burned, eternally fixed, overhead. He bought a rosary, frightened sparrows with a wax-work of the devil, fell full of wonderment at a madonna in a Catholic procession. He noticed that when a friend tried to destroy him by "influence," he was visited with an overwhelming grief. One man who had conspired against him had lost two brothers by madness and one by suicide. The day after he published an article attacking the modern system of Astronomy, Tisserand, the director of the Parisian laboratory, died, and in the course of a month, five more or less distinguished astronomers followed. Strindberg conceived a horror of himself. He was a sorcerer. There was no doubt of it. There was no end to his power or his wickedness. Without him the Eternal would be helpless for only through him could its purposes be realized. When under this conviction, Strindberg pitied his enemies, who walked behind his back, reviled or thwarted him. They were but tools of the powers and would be struck down when the time came.

His sense of sin remained to torture him. Throughout those long and painful processes of chemical transformation Strindberg was both horrified and tempted by the suspicion that alchemy is impious and forbidden. If he should succeed, or, succeeding, reveal his secret, the whole civilized world would be reduced to chaos. Strindberg is tempted by this greatest, this most unpardonable sin, for it would be an expiation, however paradoxical it may seem; in committing the greatest sin he would become the greatest martyr. Strindberg is, of course, no exception in this matter. The notion of committing a great sin to wipe out the vague culpabilities of the past and so clarify conscience and purify the soul, has deep roots in human nature and is to be seen most simply and distinctly in the religious beliefs of savage peoples. At times he fancied himself a saint, sometimes a sort of devil, now a scapegoat, suffering for mankind, now a Napoleon with ruthless sins.

Suddenly it is reported that Prsybyszevski has been released from jail and the old fear creeps back into Strindberg's heart. And now begins the great period of sleeplessness and horrors. If he burns sulphur in the daytime, like a necromancer, and, like a devil, dabbles in black magic to destroy his supposed enemies, he is himself a victim at night—pursued by his friends grown murderous through jealousy, by hostile strangers, by demons and powers. The moment he is settled in bed, the furniture is stealthily moved in the room above, and secret voices are heard plotting his death. He smells gas (Prsybyszevski, he believed, had murdered his family by gas), he hears an engine and a wheel whir-

ring above his head, he suffers electrical shocks, his chest con-
tracts and he suffocates—a horrible nightmare. He wakes just in
time to escape. At the next hotel, or perhaps it is at the house of
a friend, the same experience is repeated and again he flees in the
uttermost terror. For his feeling of guilt has grown beyond all
bounds and hence his fear of retributive justice. Thus, his friends,
and his closest friends, must become instruments of avenging
justice, that his delusive sense of guilt may be confirmed.

While visiting with friends at Dieppe, Strindberg lived through
a terrible night in the greatest peril. The electrical streams directed against him were unbearable. He grew weak and powerless. Hoarse whispers, rustling sounds, then an ominous silence.
Engines of death were set against him. He fled to the garden in
his night-shirt, where his host found him in the morning, shiver-
ing with the cold and mortally nervous. He had fled from his
room to escape certain death. This explanation did not satisfy
his friends and he left behind him a distinct impression of insanity. When he told a doctor about the electrical attacks, the voices,
the cramping of his chest, the latter shook his head. That sort of
thing was too common in insane asylums.

Strindberg himself was not unaware of the black abyss to
which his thoughts were hurrying, and never ceased to sift his
mind, and dissect with gruesome curiosity those twisted strands
of madness. To his old friend Heidenstam he wrote that he had
read through a whole library on insanity which had left him no
other conclusion than that everyone is mad except the doctors.
Were the nightly horrors he suffered the hallucinations of a
diseased brain? He was interested to find that, while racked with
the supposed streams of electricity, the magnetic needle was not
deflected, yet could not, on that account, deny his pains. Was he
a victim of illusions? He called upon his friends to corroborate
his perceptions. And in some cases they did. Others had seen the
pleading hands in the budding walnut and Napoleon in the
clouds above the Pantheon. Moreover, if others failed to reach

his clairvoyance was it not that their nervous systems were less developed than his? The great men of history, Napoleon, Caesar, etc., had had visions. The great Nietzsche had been taken off to an asylum. What was insanity? Why was it that he felt so sinful, when he knew himself to be innocent? Only his impious solution of the forbidden problem could account for this feeling. He flirted with the idea that his gold-making was a crime and a swindle and suffered lonely shame and remorse. Was he a victim of a persecution mania?

Gradually a new conviction stole over him. The men, whose intrigues and nightly attacks he feared, were not self-willed or conscious of what they did; they were servants of unseen powers, whose purposes they darkly fulfilled. He gazed out the window unconcernedly as if to forget he had had that terrible thought. Yet small events persuaded him. A towel fell down from the rack. He put it back. It fell again and this time he replaced it so securely that there was no chance of its falling. Again it fell. This could not have been the work of human vengeance. At times it occurred to him that the powers which persecuted him were creatures of his imagination, conjured up to torture him with merited punishments. Once he read in a northern mythology how Bhrigu, out of pride, imagined himself to be greater than his master, who therefore sent him to the underworld to suffer a thousand miseries. Strindberg saw the parallel at once. He was in Hell. Only who was *his* master? Swedenborg?

The horrors multiply. A mouse disturbed his sleep again and again as in a delirium. A wheel turned ceaselessly above his head and whirred mysteriously. He was awakened with the cry of "Alp! Alp!" (The German word for nightmare.) He saw a large company of people in whispered conspiracy, pointing to his room. As in the flashes of heat-lightning he glimpsed crouching, threatening forms, he felt himself in the grip of some dark power. His haggard, unshaved face, his wild, fixed eyes, excited fear and compassion in his friends. "I have come from Hell," he explained.

"I can well believe that," they replied. "You look like a corpse."
Damned! thought Strindberg. Damned to endless misery!

Suddenly Strindberg's second wife wrote to invite him to visit
his mother-in-law and her sister in Austria. He left with a sense
of deliverance and joy for he would now be united again with his
beloved little daughter, who was to become his only comfort and
solace in an evil world. When her timidity was overcome she put
her arms around his neck. "This is Faust's awakening to earthly
love," he wrote, "but lovelier and purer: I take the little one in my
arms ever again and feel its heart beat against my own. To love
a child is for a man to become a woman, to lay aside the masculine, to experience the sexless love of the Angels, as Swedenborg
calls it. Hereupon begins my education for heaven. But first,
sins!"

Yet, even here, joy was mixed with frightfulness. He seizes the
child's arm to caress her. She cries out with pain and terror. One
quiet evening as they sat by the fire, a sudden gust of wind blew
up and raged and shrieked against the house. The mother-in-law
threw him a glance full of terror and pressed the child in her
arms. Strindberg understood her meaning. "Leave us, you damned
one, and do not draw down the wrath of the revengeful demons
on the innocent."

XXIV

SCIENTIST OR SAINT?

STRINDBERG'S manifold scientific interests led him into a great variety of subjects: chemistry, astronomy, plant physiology, mineralogy, and psychology; and like Faust, there was no end to his curiosity, nor to his dreams of power. As a boy he had been enthralled by chemistry and set up many experiments for his own amusement. As a doctor's apprentice he had rebelled at the drudgery and discipline of the laboratory, yet marveled at its mysteries and his own private discoveries. In the 80's he had carried over the pageant of science into literature and founded Swedish Naturalism. Gradually his heroes became scientists and then, nature imitating art in the Wildean fashion, he gave up his career of a playwright to become one himself. In 1891 he sustained an overwhelming loss—first his wife and children left him in an empty house, then the literary impulse died and the man who had astounded his countrymen by unheard-of production covering a period of 20 years, could write no more. In the desolation and disorder which now surrounded him, he was more than ever tempted by the Faustian dream of unriddling the Sphinx, of solving her age-long mysteries in some high, sudden way. His sense of sin, his recurrent need to justify his rash existence, drove him on to new exploits. New sins and triumphs and sufferings! His mind had become a shrieking emptiness in which the old unbearable memories walked in and out like ghosts. He determined to devote himself to science. Like Goethe he will now have no other love than nature.

But if Strindberg longed to solve the secrets of nature, he was also motivated in his new career by his old hatred of authorities. Almost all of his theories were in open contradiction to the prevailing science of his day. Thus in Astronomy he maintained that the earth is not a sphere, that the stars do not shine by their own light. In Berlin one night, before a circle of skeptical friends, he maintained the very original doctrine that the moon is not a sphere but a disk thrown off from the earth while the man in the moon is the reflected image of America. When his friends objected that if they saw any image at all it would be the image of Europe while only people in America could see the reflection of America, Strindberg drew himself up with the remark: "When one puts forward hypotheses, one must not be petty."

Other hypotheses of his were quite as astounding. Thus on one occasion he maintained that it is the man who lays the egg while the woman is merely the "bird's nest" which incubates it. Thus if the egg in the semen could be preserved in constant temperature of 37° Centigrade, men might free themselves from women altogether. In this instance, as in many others, Strindberg's scientific inquiries and conclusions approached pure absurdity. "There were those days," as Smit relates, "in which Strindberg watches the pictures on the wall to see whether the whistling rotation of the earth might not shove them a bit awry, in which he believes he had constructed a psycho-magnet by embracing with his arms an iron lamp-post, in which he sees the elasticity of the vaulting of a house radiate like the Northern lights."

These fanciful extremes of untrained imagination were common with Strindberg. They show to what a degree he was removed from the cautions and precedents of science, how at heart he was a romanticist, alien to the patient drudging investigations of the laboratory. True scientists often go wild in fields not their own. Strindberg went wild in every field. Was he always serious in his contentions? It is interesting to remember that he once told Brandes that he was merely experimenting with Nietzsche's ideas, that he only half believed them himself. Beneath the surface gravity, and the fanatical ardor of Strindberg's contentions was a strain of irony and bitter laughter. Were his revolutionary discoveries true or was he a charlatan, a madman? When Lidfross objected to his methodology, he accused him of envy and malice. Also, Lidfross was undoubtedly in love with "Aspasia" and had opposed him for her sake, or out of vengeance. Strindberg could endure no criticism, for in his mind the alternative was clear. Either his grandiose theories must be accepted or he was a quack or a lunatic. Strindberg was fighting for his reputation and his sanity. Already the report had circulated in Sweden that he was a prevaricator, a conscious sham, and that he had finally gone mad. A damning review of his great work *Sylva Sylvarum* had appeared in one of the leading Stockholm papers. He felt the net of vengeance tighten about him. He felt the approach of madness, the glimmering out of his true self. It was clear to him that "the powers," unable to kill him outright, had chosen to drive him insane. From this doom there was no escape save in the vindication of his scientific work.

Fortunately, his theories were not all as fantastic as those cited above. In botany, for instance, his work is rich with ideas and stimulating, and in this realm he is credited with real discoveries. Principally, he was concerned here to break down the dead, mummified classifications and to bring life back into the world of plants and flowers by a declaration of vivid similarities and differences. He was also interested in the role of the inorganic substances in the life of plants, and maintained, without much proof to be sure, that plants can generate inorganic substances which they have not received from outside. This theory, it is worth noticing, was largely an inference from his principle of monism. Since there is but one ground stuff and all is in all, plants must contain minerals and yield them. It was also, in part, this principle which led him to assert the curious doctrine that plants have nerves. If matter is one, perhaps all matter is sentient. When Strindberg found that plants react to morphium, a specific stimulus to the nervous system, and considered their active love of the sun-light, their responses in some cases to insects, their sensitivity, their intelligence, his mind was made up. He was the more inclined to this view, of course, in that he loved flowers to distraction. That he should invest them with life was only natural. For him they breathed and suffered and sensed their surroundings. In Strindberg's plays the flowers wither and die in the presence of hate or evil thoughts and flourish wistfully and courageously in the environment of innocence.

Strindberg's chief scientific interest at this time was chemistry. Guided again by Haeckel's monism, he attempted to prove that sulphur is composed of carbon, hydrogen and oxygen. His experiments, of course, were all failures, his method and apparatus being far too simple and untutored to succeed in such a task. When specialists objected to his conclusions, he charged them with inconsistency. They were monists, he said, but would not accept the necessary consequence that, namely, the complex elements can therefore be broken down into some simpler stuff. To secure confirmation of his discoveries, Strindberg sent off letters in every direction. He wrote to Haeckel. He wrote to Brandes. The latter put the chemical works of the great Swedish dramatist in the hands of a Danish expert, who pronounced it the flimsy dabbling of a dilettante. Strindberg's method of transmuting one element into another seemed to him rather that of the alchemist than the chemist. He allowed, however, that Strindberg had made some discoveries, such as the combination of ammonium and water, which he said, he had in some remarkable way carried out, but called attention to the fact that these discoveries were not new and had already been made. Strindberg's gold-making, like his analysis of sulphur, was not accepted by the specialists. His analyst in Paris returned always the same answer: "No, not gold." The sci-

entists frowned. One, however, went so far as to say that were
he to devote two years to preparation in the laboratories he might
render to chemistry many discoveries, by dint of the extraordinary
combining power of his mind. His friend Schleich saw in Strindberg a new Goethe with the same intuitive powers and the same
universality.

There is, indeed, some similarity between the two men. Both
opposed the narrowness and stubbornness of specialists and suffered their taunts. Both stressed the importance of intuition, the
sixth sense as Goethe put it, and took as their province the vast
system of science encompassing the universe. Also Goethe, like
Strindberg, was opposed to transcendentalism and a priori philosophy. But here their agreement ends. Goethe's scientific interest
was broad and reflective with no practical motivation, while the
Swedish writer dreamed, no doubt too much, of gold and fame.
Moreover, Goethe, it must be said, was never half as wild as
Strindberg. He rejected Newton's theory of the composition of
white light but would never have contested such an orthodox
and obvious doctrine as the chemical analysis of air. Indeed, were
the comparison carried further, it would be apparent how dissim-
ilar they really are. The sage of Weimar was a reflective, balanced, disciplined mind in which all the diversities and conflicts
of the world found a place, and harmony and unity were preserved by compromise and qualification. Strindberg, always the
disciple of Kierkegaard, could never tolerate a compromise or a
smug harmony. His nature was too stormy, one-sided, passionate.
While Goethe's genius was reflective or discursive, Strindberg's
was linear and melodramatic.

His condition had now become quite serious. During his residence in Sweden with Dr. Eliasson the electrical attacks, the suffocation, the nightmares, the ceaseless anxiety had made his life
a misery. In Austria, though his little daughter was a great comfort to him, the same thing was repeated. Under the influence of
the two Catholic sisters, who were devotees of the occult, his

superstitious fears increased and he immersed himself more deeply than ever in the lore of witches and demons and Doppelgänger (doubles). Signs and portents appeared to him now on every side and the most trivial circumstance of ordinary life was taken as proof of ghostly intervention. Moreover, the failure of his scientific theories to win the recognition he had expected was but a challenge to more reckless speculations. What he had formerly advanced with some show of skepticism and only half-belief, he now maintained, it would seem, in full earnestness. These were alarming signs. Strindberg was moving slowly toward the more advanced stages of schizophrenia. He was losing his grip on reality, forgetting and misconstruing the course of human motivation, misreading the march of cause and effect in the outer world, withdrawing by degrees to a private (autistic) world built of his fears and longings. There, in that latter world, all his deep desires, anxieties, his sense of sin and persecution, his omnipotence, could be realized far better than in the daylight world of reason. There, he could be his true self, or his new self, at last. Like the main process of schizophrenia, the paranoid trends, i. e., the persecution feelings, the grandiose egoism, and the morbid sense of sin, were also, as we have had many opportunities to observe, on the wing. Scientific success might perhaps have saved him, but this was now hopeless.

It was at this time that Strindberg's mother-in-law handed him a book, telling him to read it but not to be afraid. There he found a most vivid and convincing description of hell. It was a simple straightforward account, full of detail and circumstance, such as a man might write who had actually been there and didn't mind telling about it. Strindberg was profoundly shocked, and what made the matter worse was that this description corresponded point for point with his own environment. When he had first come to the estate where he now lived, he had been surprised to find that the valley in which it lay was the exact reproduction of one he had seen long ago in the zinc bowl of his experiments.

Now he found the same scene described as hell. "The same cauldron-shaped valley, the hills covered with pines, the gloomy woods, the ravine with the brook, the town, the church, the poor house, the dunghill, foul water, the swine stall, all is there." It came over him suddenly, though he had previously scoffed at any such conception, that "the earth itself is hell, a jail built by a higher reason." The fire of hell, he learned, is the wish to rise. The powers awaken the desire, gratify it, and then turn their gifts to dust and nothingness. Thus, the damned soul suffers eternally the vanity and worthlessness of what it most desires. This was Swedenborg's account of hell. On comparing it with other descriptions of the same place in German mythology and elsewhere, he could no longer doubt his mind: he was in hell and damned. Yet the recognition of this fact did not seem to evoke a proportionable horror—rather a certain satisfaction. It was, perhaps, something for him to know, however unattractive the place and dismal the prospects, just where he was. Moreover, he soon learned from Swedenborg that only the higher souls are obliged to suffer the worst of hells, these souls alone being destined to a great career. The dawning consciousness of this new wonder increased his sense of the propriety of things. He was in the hell of great men and saints. Like Flaubert's Saint Anthony, he had been cursed and haunted, and tempted, and put upon by such a variety of dreams and mocking devils, that only a superior soul could be expected to endure them. It became clear to him that the powers had chosen a man worthy of all their tortures. Once Strindberg accepted the Swedenborgian scheme of heaven and hell, the meaning of his sufferings and sinful feelings became apparent. They constituted the purgatory through which the superior soul must pass. They were part of a divine plan, and he a chosen sacrifice, or rather, a hero to be purified in the sacred fires. It now pleased him to reflect that his tortures and conviction of sin were not, as he had supposed, an isolated insult in a meaningless, mechanical world. They were the necessary consequences of a divine intention. He had been hunted across the face of the earth and every man had thrown a stone. Innocent children had screamed and hidden their faces from such misery and wickedness. Demons and wives had enchained him; his reason had wavered. These evils, he soon realized, were but proportionate to his pride and sin, a fitting preparation for the high destiny to which he now felt himself mysteriously called. He was in hell without a doubt, yet there was justice in it and many compensations. He knew his place.

Strindberg was not altogether unprepared for the strange teachings of Swedenborg. His colossal dreams, his frustrations, his inexplicable sufferings, his conviction of sin had paved the way. For some time, too, he had devoted himself to mystical, theosophical lore and immersed himself in the books of the Buddhists. Moreover, he had derived much melancholy comfort from the Book of Job and the sad complaints of Jeremiah. In reviewing the fate of these classical sufferers, and reciting sadly and sonorously their great laments, he had come more and more to identify his own case with theirs, and to see his destiny from that high dramatic, impersonal altitude, from which human suffering appears a spectacle, sin or private woe a distinction, hell itself a pilgrimage with triumph ahead. While absorbed in these passionless pictures from the past, the misery of his long career became to him an epic, a pageant, a journey to the cross. Then, something like a smile came over his face, long unaccustomed to joy, and his eyes lighted up with a curious expectancy and wonder. The burden of narrow, ignominious pain was much lightened, for he had seen the principle and cause of his sufferings and that was everything.

Yet, it was impossible to accept all this without criticism. Strindberg was not satisfied with Job's submission, nor with the justice of Jehovah, which seemed to him only the tyranny of brute force. Better to wrestle with such a God, like Jacob with the angel. *He* would not yield up his self for any price, for that was suicide and nothingness. At the end of the *Inferno,* when Strindberg had all but decided to enter a Belgian Catholic monastery and to bury forever his worldly desires, a new skepticism seized him. He had been a prophet of democracy, of nature, of atheism, superman and aristocracy. He had espoused many causes but they had ended, every one of them, in emptiness and absurdity. Throughout his life, as he once said, he had sought God and found only the Devil. Yet, now, he had returned to religion again. Had he not been deceived once more? Would not religion also prove illusion and mockery? He awaited with great anxiety the appearance of his book *Inferno,* for he hated ridicule and feared the worst from its publication. At the conclusion of this most intimate confession of madness and conversion, he mistrusted his new religion. When the book appeared, what would follow? The reason? "A new jest of the gods, who laugh aloud when we weep hot tears."

Yet Strindberg was much strengthened and confirmed by Swedenborg. Oddly enough, it was a woman, Balzac's heroine, Séraphita, who first brought him round to see the virtues of this mystical writer. From her he learned the secret wisdom of Swedenborg, how superior souls wander through the purgatory of earthly life, amid unbearable afflictions, passing gradually through the three stages of love to oneself, love to one's neighbor, and love of heaven, but finally released at death to a spiritual life. Suffering, he learned, is a blessed saving grace shining through the world, and the greatest suffering is conscience, the one way to blessedness, repentance. Strindberg swore to repent. He was uplifted and heartened, for the world was now a rational order and the gods, his friends. Séraphita became his favorite heroine, which shows, incidentally, how much religion, at this time, overshadowed his hatred of emancipated women. For Seraphita was a *celestial* blue-stocking, as priggish in her way, as any of the women he had hated, and like her kind, she had gladly deserted her lover for a career—in heaven.

Swedenborg was indeed a revelation. Strindberg had never read such astounding things before. Here was a man who had walked the streets of heaven and talked to angels in their own gilded, bejewelled, but altogether comfortable apartments, who had conversed with celestial spirits and infernal spirits and knew to a nicety the peculiarities of each. Strindberg was shocked. This visionary had been a distinguished scientist, a shrewd business man, a favorite of the King. Later, he had investigated the realms of heaven and hell with the same assurance and composure he had shown on earth. Oddly enough, his account of these places was quite convincing.

Once when Swedenborg was lecturing on the soul, as he relates, a curious spirit of a young man who had died some time before approached him to inquire further about his conception of soul or spirit. Swedenborg explained to this young man that he was a spirit himself, for he explained, you are above the earth and only spirits can remain above the earth without support. The spirit, who hadn't noticed this before, fled away, crying, "Alas, I am a spirit, I am a spirit"! On another occasion, Swedenborg attended the execution of a Swedish lord and shortly after talked to the same man in the world of spirits. He was not at all conscious that he had died, explained Swedenborg, but was still in a great anxiety lest he should be executed. These instances of Swedenborg's clairvoyance are typical. That Strindberg should have been persuaded by them shows how far he had travelled since the days of his naturalistic experiments and hard-headed atheism.

When Strindberg learned that Swedenborg had experienced the same nightly horrors as himself, had been racked with electricity, choked by gas and stifling air, tortured by dirt, evil odors, and other such afflictions, he was most especially pleased. It was perhaps, after all, simply the fate of great men, which he could bear as well as another.

An interesting explanation of the similarity of their experiences is given by Jaspers in his book on *Strindberg and Van Gogh*. There he points out that Strindberg and Swedenborg were both schizophrenics and that their retreat to a mystical world, their occasional complete detachment from reality, their nightmares, electrical attacks and anxieties, their inflated sense of greatness, were but the consequences of the progress of a mental disease, often thought incurable. That Strindberg should have been attracted by the writings of this fellow-schizophrenic was perhaps only natural. He became, as Strindberg says, his bible, giving an answer to every question he raised. Still Strindberg would admit no master, not even Swedenborg. He had not accepted Nietzsche before. He would accept no others now. Fortunately, Strindberg did not become a disciple. Happily, he did not follow the steps of his great preceptor. While Strindberg made a very remarkable recovery from his mental sickness, Swedenborg progressed slowly toward the more advanced stages. In the end, his visions became more wild and irresponsible than ever; he was heard to mutter and converse with himself (or with spirits) at all times and through the night his voice was heard exclaiming and contesting. Toward the close of his life (1772) his associates, or many of them, could not but conclude that he was insane.

Strindberg's great sins, as he saw them, had been first, his impious inquiry into the secrets of heaven, his discovery of the transmutation of the elements, his forbidden quest of the philosopher's stone, and second, the Epilogue to *Master Olaf,* written many years before, in which he had represented God as an evil power, who scourged and tortured his creatures, men, into submission and reverence. He, therefore, regarded his punishments as justly merited, and praised God for his grace and goodness in sending him the anxiety, heart attacks, nightmares, and the petty hells of dirt and filth. It was a sign that God blessed him and desired him. The evil spirits who carried out God's will, scourging the superior souls to the cross, were not evil by nature, but only at His behest. In Swedenborg's scheme, the planes of existence showed men at all stages of perfection, rising from the lowest to the supermen. If men are to ascend to a higher plane "demons are a necessary consequence." Strindberg blessed them. At great moments he posed as Prometheus, the light-bringer, who was punished for stealing the secrets of heaven for men. He bowed his head before the sacred wrath. Once, like Job, he heard God speak to him out of a burning bush. At the first peal of thunder he stood his ground, at the second, he fell on his knees, humbling himself before God, for he longed to be defeated by God, but only after a struggle and with honor.

A religious tone prevails in the *Inferno* and even more so in the *Legends,* written shortly after, in 1897. But, from time to time, Strindberg is a prey to the old doubts. Perhaps, after all, faith is treacherous and God an evil power bent on murder and vengeance, as the Epilogue to *Master Olaf* had declared. At moments Strindberg seemed to abandon religion altogether and to regard conversion as a weakness and cowardice which great men will resist. Once, he raised the question whether Christ was not a demon in a previous world-order, who destroyed all beauty and joyfulness and murdered humanity. Certainly He had a double nature. When His anger was aroused, according to an old story, His face was frightful and hideous, full of wickedness. At other times He overdid his loving-kindness, forgiving the adulteress, preaching the non-resistance to evil, and thereby encouraging the worst of offences. In this mood, Strindberg will not humiliate himself before God, for this would be to treat Him like a tyrant, a slave-driver. Yet these doubts and disaffections were but minor episodes. The main sweep of his mind is toward Swedenborg and Catholicism and his own conversion.

When Strindberg's anxieties and torments on the estate in Austria became unbearable and money arrived, which permitted him to travel, he set out for Sweden, pursued as usual by the malice of "the powers." "Depart, my child," his mother-in-law had said, "I have had enough of this odor of hell." Strindberg departed, and the curse went with him, northward on his pilgrimage, to a new "sin-station," a new place of repentance. No sooner had he commenced to write, than hell broke loose over his head, furniture was moved, the confused thunder of heavy steps was heard. He changed his room. He changed his hotel. The moment he commenced to write, or to eat at the restaurant, the same rumbling mysterious noise began. In November, 1896, he explained to Georg Brandes that "the light," which Balzac has his Séraphita say, "will again come out of the ·north," meant him. Swedenborg had been the first illumination and he would be the second. Somewhat later, he settled down to a quiet life in Lund (Sweden) where in the company of a number of loyal friends who provided him with money and every tactful care, he made great steps toward his recovery. Good food, kindness, sleep, billiards, and the café, softened the desperate tensions of·his mind and restored his health. The youth paid allegiance and honored him as a hero after all his wars. Though the powers of Upsala regarded him, he thought, as the very principle of evil, the betrayer of the youth, the Devil himself, yet the students, as they proved fifteen years later on his 63rd birthday, were high in their enthusiasm. For the man who had exposed the vanity and uselessness of the University, betrayed the vicious life of the students, and had lately ridiculed the pretensions of youth in general, remained a youth himself, a stormy one, and held to the independent rebellious spirit of the student.

Strindberg's friends with whom he consorted in Lund found him a changed man. The reckless, strident, indomitable alchemist of Paris, was now a gray-haired, emaciated old man, a tottering, miserable old man who did penance for his sins. His long fight with demons, which had not yet ended, his anxieties, his electric girdle, etc., had robbed him of his youthful energy, his long contest with the magician, the theosophist, the electricians, had only been won at a fearful cost. When his friends saw him, their eyes alone expressed their sad astonishment. In his face was a gloom and weariness which they had not seen before. He walked slowly and solemnly, with measured steps as in a procession. When he spoke, his voice was pathetic and monotonous, and so slow and soft as to be almost inaudible. He was also shy of company and suspicious, fearing intrigues and evil omens, watchful of "the powers." At times, he seemed anxious to escape observation and hid himself safely in loneliness with slippers, bathrobe, flowers and books. On other occasions his fears relaxed and a bright roguish smile, a bold glint in his elusive eyes conveyed a sort of spiteful expectation and wonder. Evidently the celebrated fire of "the eagle" was not yet extinguished. At the café he could be all amiability and goodness, and usually protracted his stay there until one o'clock, returning home with a friend or admirer deep in conversation. At times, however, his good humor gave way to irritability and spitefulness. Small matters disturbed him. A bad cup of coffee or an unpleasant letter could ruin a whole day, but his good humor was as quickly restored. In more important matters, he was likewise volatile, full of violent shifts of mood. One day a friend found him bending over a cauldron, deep in his gold-making. He spoke, now, of the mysterious wisdom of Thibet, of the Caballa applied to chemistry, of daring experiments, of stripping the Sphinx of all her secrets, at last. Not long afterwards he is repentant, swears that he must give up his impious studies, since his religion forbids him any further concern with the occult.

To a questionnaire handed to Strindberg in the summer of 1897, he made the following answers:

What is the main feature of your character?

A curious mixture of the deepest melancholy and unheard-of levity.

What is your favorite pursuit?

Dramatics.

What is the greatest happiness you can imagine?

To have no enemies.

What do you hold to be the greatest misfortune?

To be without tranquillity and peace of conscience.

What books do you like best?

The Bible; Chateaubriand: *Genie du Christianisme;* Sweden-borg: *Arcana Coelestina;* Victor Hugo: *Les Misérables;* Dickens: *Little Dorrit;* Andersen's *Fairy Stories;* Bernardin de St. Pierre: *Harmonies.*

What paintings do you like best?

Th. Rousseau: *Paysages Intimes;* Brocklin: *The Island of Death.*

What heroines of fiction do you like best?

Marguerite in *Faust* and Séraphita of Balzac.

What historical characters do you hate most?

One has no right to hate anyone.

For the rest, Strindberg prized motherliness as the highest quality in women and a lack of pettiness as the distinction of men. His favorite music is Beethoven's Sonatas, his favorite English writer, Dickens, his favorite English painter, Turner.

These questions are well chosen and the answers throw many sudden lights on Strindberg's spiritual state at this time. The love of motherliness in women and hatred of pettiness in men are, of course, fixed features in his character, but the religious turn to some of the answers is new and significant, as is also his preference for the career of dramatist. His returning appreciation for Dickens is also illuminating. Strindberg had now given up his old masters, who taught that men are evil by nature with too much heart and too little head, and had turned about, full of warm admiration for the opposite views of Dickens. In his selection of favorite paintings, Strindberg also reveals a very important feature in his character, for the *Island of the Death* represents clearly the craving for death or for a return to the womb. (Kempf has connected this painting with the intra-uterine phantasy.) Strindberg's thoughts were turning more and more to death and guilt and punishment. The process of his conversion was the method of his cure. It is interesting to observe that the more he believed in demons and mysterious powers with the advance of his delusions, the more he approached an understanding of Sweden borg's supernaturalism and mystical doctrine of sin, terror and suffering. The advance of his madness was, thus, the approach to his conversion and cure. Within a year of this date, his religious ideas took poetic form and he wrote a series of his finest plays.

When the *Inferno* appeared (1897) it was met with opposition on one side and coldness on the other. Religious people were not particularly pleased, for though the atheist had been converted, there was some question as to whether he was not still insane. The radicals of course revolted, and many were shocked at Strindberg's conception that there are hells for everyone, the innocent as well as the wicked, and that superior souls are required to suffer most. It brought the matter far too close to home. When Strindberg had finished this astounding confession, and realized with joy that he would not be clapped in an insane asylum for his trouble, he fell to brooding on new experiences and finally wrote a continuation, the *Legends*. This book which recounts the wonders and developments in Strindberg's life during a few months (1897-8), part of which time he spent in Lund (Sweden) and part in Paris, is much quieter in tone than the *Inferno*, and shows greater progress in his religious conversion.

One amusing feature of this book is Strindberg's pretended discovery that all of his friends in Lund are in the same boat with him, that they suffer the same sleeplessness, nightmares, and electrical attacks, and that they are all reaching for God and approaching, through horror and repentance, the goal of conversion. His delineation of his friends' sufferings is often quite minute and their characters are drawn so realistically as to leave no doubt of their identity. Yet, whenever it pleased him to distort the picture, to make an ardent atheist religious, or a creditor a debtor, he did so without scruple. These friends were surprised and indignant to read that they had challenged "the powers" and suffered the same nightly tortures as Strindberg, that they had turned to Swedenborg for guidance, that they had repeatedly borrowed money from him. The truth was that Strindberg had come to

Lund without a cent and lived there on his friends. When kindly questioned about this misrepresentation Strindberg replied, "My dear fellow, you know that when I take a pen in hand, I am possessed of the devil."

Of particular interest is the development of Strindberg's conception of Doppelgänger. Cases like that of Francis Schlotter had ripened his interest in this curious phenomenon, which is discussed more fully in the *Legends* than elsewhere. He came to believe that a strong desire may tear the double loose from the body and carry it off whither it will. Experience had taught him that when he thought very hard about an absent friend, his image appeared before that friend. The image, of course, was something which could not be laughed away. It was his double. The bond between husband and wife in marriage was so strong, it seemed to him, and the man lays down so much of his soul in the woman, that it more than likely happens that his wife becomes his Doppelgänger, whom he loves vainly as his creation. In the Blue Books the Doppelgänger motif is taken up again in connection with witches. Strindberg there holds that an evil woman can actually transport herself and appear to a man in his dreams, personally, in order to tempt and torture him.

These speculations were, of course, only one aspect of his deep passion for magic and the occult. When Strindberg learned that the poet Huysmans had accused the Marquis Stanislaus de Guaita of bewitching him by black magic, causing him to have nightly pains in his breast, Strindberg was highly excited and indignant, the more so because he had had, as he said, just such pains himself. No doubt he had been a victim, too. He raged against the use of magic by evil men and regretted the time had passed when witches and enchanters were burned. He particularly sympathized with Huysmans because, as he learned from *En Route,* this writer had passed through just such a hell as his.

In the French playwright, Peladan, however, he found his prophet. From him, he learned that the magician may be a lofty soul, a superior man, a superman; he learned also to distrust science and to love religion, especially Catholicism. It was in Europe a great day of conversions—a resurrection of the gods. The spirit was turning from science, which Brunetière had declared bankrupt, back to religion, the deepest source of goodness. Strindberg felt greatly drawn to Catholicism and thought more than once of entering a Belgian monastery. When, however, on coming to Paris, he read in the paper that the Prior of a monastery he had thought of entering had been charged with immorality, he peacefully gave up all thought of it. Protestantism he had condemned and ridiculed as the "barbarism of the north," but gradually he made his peace with it, and maintained for the rest of his life a quiet, "compromise Christianity" built on Swedenborg.

When the *Legends* was published it was clear to many that the literary powers of the author, so long submerged by alchemy and madness, were coming to life again for a new fruition. Already he had begun to busy himself with a great play, portraying his long wandering to the cross. The year before (1897) he had travelled through his beloved Sweden gathering material for his book *Swedish Nature*. No doubt the breath of the sea and the ragged old islands did him a world of good, for had it not been for the rumbling noises and pursuing "powers," he would have been happy and sound.

XXV

TOWARD DAMASCUS

STRINDBERG'S conversion, which came about gradually during his Inferno period, follows the usual pattern and the internal conflict and final triumph of the religious self appears plainly in his own confession. The peculiar extremity of this conflict, in his case, was due to the polar, irreconcilable opposition of the two selves and the extraordinary "emotional reinforcement" which each enjoyed. It was a fight to the death and the contenders were strong and equally matched. It is little wonder that Strindberg cried out in horror at his own thoughts, that he alternately cursed himself out as the devil and celebrated himself as a god, that his consternation increased in the course of the most unusual happenings, with the thought that, with everything else, he had lost his self and did not any longer know who he was. To redeem itself, his wicked, atheistic self went to great lengths. It determined to make gold, to destroy the world, to drown the pretty little wife and injure the beloved daughter by magic. To preserve itself in power, it sacrificed love, friendship, even reason. It is well known, of course, that the drastic division and continued conflicts of opposing selves has its pathological side and figures in various types of insanity.

Strindberg's conversion began, perhaps, with the discovery that he was damned and in hell. This was a great solace, for there were worse places than hell, and those more miserable than the damned.

377

There are those who wander raving and lost on the verge, and cannot enter, who suffer a thousand meaningless afflictions every day, uncomforted by the wrath of the gods. Terrified by their moral aloneness and the dark impenetrable malice which surrounds them, lonely, without the solace of fellow-suffering or of precedents or institutions, they fall into a worse despair. They crave the vested legality of hell, the traditions and meaningfulness of that resort, for they would submit to any institution which would give some rationality to the miseries and appointments of human life. It is Hegel, of course, more than any other philosopher, who has shown the importance of continuous institutions in determining the significance of individual lives. Strindberg hated institutions and fought them all his life, yet like others, he longed for their shelter, for he could not stand alone. Meaningless sufferings he could never endure, but punishment for sin was acceptable.

The cure of Strindberg's mental disturbance began in Lund, under the care of his friend, Dr. Eliasson. It was completed by the return of his literary powers. In the same year in which he wrote the *Legends* (1897) he commenced a new confession in dramatic form, *Toward Damascus,* in which he recounted his painful journey to the cross. To have repeated this journey, in fact, would have been the greatest of penances for Strindberg, repetition being for him the most insulting adversity, but to repeat his steps in dramatic form was a solace, a deliverance, and a great factor in his cure. This is the power of art—to transform a narrow, tortured, futile existence into something beautiful, rational, and inevitable. As Strindberg wrote, his wasted frantic years became an epic and he an epic hero.

The *Damascus* drama begins with the departure of his second wife, traces the course of his gold-making, spiritual adventures, his nightly horrors, pursuit by the powers through the Swedenborgian hells, concluding at last with his conversion and retreat to a monastery. So deep and persistent is the moral intent of this chronicle, that each casual circumstance reveals a deeper meaning, becomes a warning or a fateful presage. Nature, herself, is now only a theatre of a long and weary pilgrimage and all her accidents and occasions are but symbols on the way to hell or heaven. In the first scene of this drama a funeral procession moves by and the dirge plays at a most inopportune time with a disquieting effect. Why should such a thing happen at that particular time? It was an accident, says the scientist, a coincidence. But such an answer is an evasion and no explanation at all. Why should the Stranger (Strindberg) be made to suffer so much more than other men? Science has no answer. Why should one billiard ball move when another hits it? The Scientist answers: Because all physical bodies behave in this way. But this is no answer and science is powerless before such a question, as Hume long ago discovered. Science is bankrupt, as Brunetière had just said, and Strindberg turned to the occult for an explanation of his strange experiences.

Toward Damascus is in many respects the most remarkable of Strindberg's plays and contains dramatic innovations of first importance. Being a chronicle of the author's own crisis, his damnation, expiation, and conversion, it is certainly the most personal and autobiographical of his plays, yet over and above the psychological and psychiatric interest is the moral, metaphysical, and religious significance which has the widest sweep, applying not to one but to every man. On the one hand, it is only a diary of a mad, unhappy genius, on the other, a Morality Play depicting the struggles of man for blessedness against his own sins and the temptations of the world. The very name of the hero, The Stranger, reminds us of "Everyman" and shows the generality that Strindberg intended. The heroine's name is also abstract: The Lady, and the Stranger calls her Eve, by which it is seen that he values her more as symbol of womanhood than as any particular woman. The other characters are named in a similar fashion and are: The Beggar, The Doctor, The Sister, The Old Man, The

Mother, The Abbess, The Dominican, etc. When, in the third part of the Trilogy, two new characters, The Tempter and The Confessor, are added, the resemblance to a morality play becomes more striking, for now we have the Tempter, representing the Devil, and the Confessor, an intercessor for God, both struggling for the soul of the Stranger, just as in *Everyman* and other plays of that kind. The Tempter in *Toward Damascus,* like the Devil in *Everyman,* is really quite an artful and charming fellow who seems to have a great deal of truth on his side. *Toward Damascus* has a great deal in common with the morality plays but also agrees in general theme with the great works which arose from them: *Pilgrim's Progress, Dr. Faustus,* and Goethe's *Faust.* The great, the unpardonable Sin of the Stranger, like that of Pilgrim and Faust, was sensuality, pride, and the desire for forbidden knowledge, and salvation consisted in overcoming this sin by the grace of God.

Though the theme of this play is old and well tried, with famous precedents, the novelties in dramatic technique are the strangest in the world and had never been employed before in modern drama. In the list of characters for the second part of this trilogy we find that The Beggar, The Dominican, and The Confessor are all one person, in, of course, different attire. The Beggar moreover, turns out to have a striking resemblance to the Stranger, possessing the same features and the same fateful scar on his forehead. All three, in their thoughts and emotions, seem to agree with certain sections of the Stranger's mind, so that when he argues with them he appears to be contending with himself, and their words have an odd disquieting effect on him, as when a man hears his own voice expressing ideas which he had long since forgotten. There is still another character who has a curious likeness to the Stranger, namely, the madman, Caesar, who, like the Beggar, is always appearing and reappearing at crucial turns of the plot and usually with a startling ghostly effect. Whether these four characters, The Beggar, The Dominican, The Confes-

sor, and Caesar are merely Doppelgänger, i. e. doubles of the
Stranger, or real men interested in his fate, it is difficult to decide, but in this uncertainty lies the great power of the work. In
The Dream Play with its capricious transitions and bizarre shifts
in time and space we have only phantasmagoria, and the action,
therefore, loses the force of reality. *Toward Damascus,* on the
contrary, for all its apparitions and ghostly figures, sustains the
illusion of the real world and the loves and sins and sufferings of
its characters are actualities. Here then, Strindberg has united the
intense subjectivity, the freedom and economy of action which
appeared later on in *The Dream Play,* with the bitter tang of
immediate reality which distinguished so importantly his naturalistic plays, and the combination has proved a very fruitful
one in modern drama.

In the first scene the Stranger meets the Lady on a street
corner and in his loneliness and misery entreats her not to leave
him. Aroused to pity, she remains while he recounts the terrible
pass he had come to and the desperate hopeless state of his soul.
For forty years he has waited for happiness, which never came
and though he has had everything in life he wished for, love,
children, literary success, it has all turned to poison. Wife and
children he has deserted and now suffers shame and remorse.
Success has also gone awry and left him with poverty, beggary,
exile, loneliness, so that he wanders from place to place, accursed
and hated as no other man, and now at last he asks the Lady the
fearful question: Do you think I am insane? He has lost faith in
everything, plays with poetry and with life, and his only religion
is that suicide is the escape. So uniformly crossed and adverse has
been his fate, that he is ready to believe that he is a monster, a
changeling, whom the elves, those unholy creatures, have put in
the place of a human child when it was born, and to this pro-
fane origin he now traces all the miseries and frustrations of his
life. That is the mystery of the curse which has settled upon him.
"As a child," he says, "I cried continually and seemed not to

thrive in life; hated my parents as they hated me; tolerated no compulsion, no convention, no laws, and my only longing was for the woods and the sea. . . . Often I seemed to notice that two very different beings directed my destiny: the one gave me all I desired, but the other stood beside and vilified the gift, so that it became worthless. . . . My mother never caressed me, but I remember that she struck me. Yes, you see, I was raised in Hate, Hate! Hardness against hardness. An eye for an eye! See this scar on my forehead; that is from an axe wielded by my brother, whose missing front tooth I knocked out with a stone." The Lady is deeply touched by this recital. Never in her life has she seen a man who aroused so much pity, whose mere appearance made her weep. The Stranger, for his part, feels himself bound to her irretrievably, for she answers to his ideal of the mother, but the Lady cannot remain with him; she must return to her husband, whom she calls the Werewolf.

Left alone, the Stranger glimpses for the first time the curious beggar who is henceforth to pursue him constantly on his long pilgrimage, showing an inexplicable interest in his fate. The Beggar is not an ordinary beggar for though he picks up cigar stubs out of the gutter he also speaks Latin. The Stranger is surprised to see a scar similar to his own on the Beggar's forehead, and when he learns that it has been caused by a relative he is frightened, feels the Beggar's arm to see if he is a real man, and finally sends him away with a gift of money. The Beggar thanks his patron for his kindly help and assures him he will be his friend. But the Stranger, who finds the Beggar's resemblance to himself a bit insulting, shakes him off with disgust. After a short interlude the Beggar returns and orders wine at the café where the Stranger is drinking away his sorrows. When the host refuses to serve him, an altercation occurs which annoys the Stranger but later he befriends the Beggar. The host then attacks him and when he declares himself to be a famous man, reads off his record as follows: Thirty-eight years old, brown hair, blue eyes; no regular position; income unknown; married but has deserted wife and children; known for subversive views on social questions; gives the impression of failing in the full use of his reason. The host seems to feel this description quite accurate and the Stranger is sent off with the Beggar in disgrace. Then the Lady returns and the Stranger complains of the terrible beggar who frightens him, he says, more than death. "Is it true," he asks, "that he looks like me?" "Yes, when you are in your cups," answers the Lady. She, like the Stranger, is oppressed by the evil in the world and the cloud of anxiety never lifts. "At this moment I feel as if the higher powers are holding a council over us and have come to a decision." "You also!" said the Stranger. "Do you know that I just now heard how the hammer fell, the chairs were pushed back from the table and the servant sent out. . . . O, this anxiety!" One way to overcome it is to do something decisive, so the Stranger agrees to accompany the Lady home and so free the princess from her Werewolf husband. "Come, my deliverer," says the Lady, and letting down her veil, kisses him hastily on the mouth. The Stranger is astounded at her initiative, and evil omens declare themselves all around him. From the church comes the loud cry of many women, the lighted rosette window darkens suddenly, a tree quivers and people look up at the sky as if they saw something terrifying there.

At the Doctor's house, for the Lady's husband is a doctor, the Stranger's troubles, if anything, increase. In the first place, he recognizes in the Doctor an old schoolmate who was once punished in his stead, while the Stranger, the guilty one, escaped. And there are other ominous depressing circumstances. He hears Mendelssohn's Funeral March, which has been haunting him so long that he thinks it an illusion, but he is relieved when he finds who is playing. The Doctor pulls out an arm and a leg of a corpse and tells of an idiot living in the house. Yes, it is a spooky house and the Stranger's uneasiness increases. While the Doctor is still visible, he and the Lady discuss their elopement, for the

Doctor, as his wife explains, is a bit deaf. Then comes the lunatic Caesar, who like the Beggar, bears a curious resemblance to the Stranger. Even his name Caesar was in school-days a nickname for the Stranger. (It will be remembered that one of Nietzsche's letters to Strindberg was signed Caesar and it is interesting to note that the madman here is represented as having lost his reason by reading a writer [Strindberg] who was greater than himself. Did Strindberg really think his play, *The Father,* or his novel, *By the Open Sea,* had driven Nietzsche insane?) This circumstance, together with the familiar, overbearing manner of the lunatic, has a devastating effect on the Stranger who straightway makes his escape from that house of horrors—to be followed by the Lady, and they begin their sorrowful wanderings.

They are next discovered in a hotel room penniless and in uttermost misery. They have been driven away from other hotels because they were not respectable and now they expect the host to return any moment to throw them out in the street. By an odd chance the room is not new to either of them. Each remembers to have stayed in this same room before, and probably not alone. The irony of this circumstance, his sudden poverty, the accumulation of apparently accidental evils, convinces the Stranger that someone, perhaps a higher power, is fighting against him. They flee out in the fields and are next seen in a cottage in the mountains. Here, everything is completely changed, for in this retreat they have enjoyed three days of blessed happiness which still continues. Yet they are fearful of this new joyfulness, expecting at every moment some terrible reverse. The Stranger, to forestall such an event, would like to die, but the Lady feels she has left something undone, that more suffering is allotted to her which she must needs accomplish, for that is the meaning of life. But the Stranger, warmed by his happiness, rises to a high mood, becomes a Superman, storming and challenging heaven. "Yes," he says, "now I live, at this moment: and I feel my ego swell and extend itself, becoming thin and infinite: I am everywhere, in the Sea that is my blood, in the rocks that are my skeleton, in the trees, in the flowers; and my head reaches up to the sky, I see out over the universe that is I, and I feel the whole power of the Creator in me, for that I am. I would like to take the whole mass in my hand and remould it into something more perfect, more enduring, more beautiful—would like to see all creation and all created beings happy: born without pain, live without suffering and die in quiet peace." The Lady is shocked by this blasphemy and complains that when he compares himself to the Creator he reminds her too much of Caesar. The Stranger is alarmed and inquires whether that is the only respect in which he resembles Caesar. Then their troubles begin again and their momentary peace is destroyed. The letter from the publisher, which was to contain money, informs him that there is nothing due him and the Stranger breaks out in a Promethean revolt against the powers.

"Now the gauntlet has been thrown down, and presently you will see the hand-to-hand fight of the Great. Come, strike me down with Your lightning, if You dare. Frighten me with Your storm, if You can." "No! No! Not that way," cries the Lady, horrified. "Who dares to disturb my love dream? Who tears the cup from my mouth and the woman from my arms? Envious gods or devils!" continues the Stranger and he curses the jealous heavens. "Principalities, Powers, Dominions, pfui!" "May heaven not chasten—" exclaims the Lady, who is a good Catholic.

Being without money or prospects, they are now obliged to travel the long road to the home of the Lady's parents. As they arrive, like beggars, with torn clothes at the end of the journey, everything conspires to alarm the Stranger and to arouse new suspicions. "How strange nature is, here," he says, "how everything has been united to arouse disquiet. Why is the broom here and the ointment horn there? Probably because it is their customary place, but still my thoughts turn to witches. Why is the smithy black and the mill white? Because the one is sooty and the other mealy, and still . . . But see the Giants up there—no, now this is more than can be borne—don't you see the Werewolf from whom I saved you?" The Lady sees the resemblance but after all it is only the cliff. Once in the kitchen they find the beggars' table prepared for them and the Stranger suffers such abuse and insults from the Mother (i. e. the Lady's mother) that he feels he can bear it longer. Instead of the quiet haven which his wife, (the Lady) had led him to expect, he finds himself in a witches' kitchen, with the evilest of women. When she suggests that he has planned, like a magician, to destroy the whole race of women, by his self-created image of one, the Stranger cannot but say, "That was Satan." He is full of wonder at a woman who can be so religious and yet so wicked. Evils follow in the wake of the Stranger. A letter comes, warning the Mother of this man and shame is brought on the house. The Old One (the Lady's Grandfather) cannot bear the sight of him. He hears the people talk of how a horse shied at the Stranger and a dog went wild, and the ferryman insisted that the boat was lightened as he boarded it. It was superstition of course,—and still— The Mother now persuades the Lady to read her husband's last frightful book (Strindberg's *The Confession of a Fool*) which she had promised him never to touch. The result is what the Stranger feared, for henceforth her eyes are opened to good and evil and it is as if she had eaten of the first deadly fruit. No longer his good angel, she becomes his fury and scourge. The Stranger, foreseeing the worst, departs from her suddenly while she drops to her knees in despair.

The next scene occurs in an asylum into which the Stranger has strayed, and the whole episode is but a fever phantasy of a man obsessed with anxiety and guilt and the fear of vindictive justice. At a long dining table the Stranger sits alone. On the other side are the Beggar, a woman who looks like the Lady, but is not, a man who looks like the Doctor, but isn't, the images, or "doubles" of the lunatic, Caesar, of the Father, the Mother, etc. It develops that the Stranger has been at this asylum for months, in bed, deathly sick with the fever, during which time he has confessed all the sins in the decalogue and made himself out as black as Satan. In the course of this scene the Confessor (for it is a Catholic asylum) reads out a long curse upon those who do not obey God's word, which the Stranger, of course, immediately applies to himself. "Accursed shalt thou be in city and in field; accursed will be thy basket and thy trough; accursed shalt thou be in thy coming in and in thy going out!"

The Whole Company (half aloud): "Accursed!"

The Confessor: "The Almighty will afflict thee with sorrow and need in all that thou touchest hand to, and in all that thou undertakest," etc. This long terrible anathema is the last cruelty and each word burns in the Stranger's heart. Unable to bear it longer, he flees from the curses and from his own salvation, back to the arms of his wife, for mercy. On his return he finds the Mother alone, the Old Man dead, and his wife away, no one knows where, in search of him. The Stranger tells the Mother that he is more than ever conscious of powers and forces which he has previously not believed in, and these, it seems, thwart his way, and visit him at night with horrors and preternatural experiences. He is now afraid to die and has developed an abhorrence of himself. The Mother seems to sympathize and to think him on the right way at last. But, suddenly, she changes color again and advises him to sleep in the garret, for no one, she says, has been able to sleep there a whole night, let him be who he will. "You are the most wicked person that I have ever met in my life," said the Stranger, "but that is because you are religious." The Stranger does not remain in his room long but returns to the kitchen where he meets the Mother again. He cannot sleep. The moonlight streams into the room, a horse stamps in the stable, (probably himself a victim of nightmares, as the Stranger suggests), and a cold draught of air freezes his heart. Even as he speaks he feels himself in the clutch of some power who wrestles with him wrathfully. "Almighty God," he cries, but cannot bend his knee. Suddenly he gives way. "Help me, Almighty God," and rises comforted—yet it was annihilation there on the floor. "My son," said the Mother, "you have forsaken Jerusalem, and are on the way to Damascus. Go thither! the same way you came, and plant a cross at every station." So the Stranger sets forth in search of the Lady and with a longing for light which gladdens the hearts of children and men. On the road, he meets again the strange beggar who shows him the foot-prints of the Lady, but the Stranger can no longer believe anyone. Then says the Beggar: "You believe only evil and therefore receive only evil. Try for once to believe in goodness, try!" "Why do you pursue me?" asks the Stranger. "Why do you pursue me, Saul?" answers the Beggar. Finally, the Stranger and the Lady meet in the mountain cottage by the sea where they have been so happy, but now it is winter, with snow and cold, and sorrow and remorse in their hearts. "There are moments," says the Stranger, "when it seems as if I bore in me all the sins, and all the sorrows, and all the filth, and all the ignominy of the World; there are hours when I believe that wrong acts, that crime itself is a penalty we must pay for previous sins." The Stranger takes the Lady's sins on himself, and with the spars of a sunken ship showing three white crosses as an omen, they set out again, retracing their steps, back to the hotel room, back to the Werewolf, back to the street corner where first they met, and so completing their weary pilgrimage back to the point where in the beginning they erred from the way. When the Doctor has his enemy in his hands, he considers that perhaps it would be better to avenge himself a bit, in order to lighten the conscience of the Stranger, who suffers too much from his guilt. Back on the street corner, the two wanderers find themselves talking very much as before and now, once more, they will flee to the mountains, to hide their misery. Before leaving, the Lady induces the Stranger to enter the church, but he will not remain. He will still not have it that Christ suffered and died for him; so must suffer himself.

The second part of the Trilogy continues the purgatorial wan-

dering of the Stranger with many repetitions of moods and episodes from the first part, and from other works of Strindberg.
Yet the two plays have a unity and a contrapuntal relation. In
the first the Stranger is a superman storming the heavens, defiant
of the powers and proud of his forbidden discoveries. He is accompanied by his deliverer, Eve, who has undertaken the mission
of restoring his peace and sanity and his ability to work. In the
second play, his good angel becomes an *Erdgeist,* a Caliban. All
his wickedness seems to have passed over to her. The Stranger
suffers every torment of marriage. Also his high ambition and
pride come to nothing. He is exposed in the most shameful
fashion. Indeed, the Nietzschean superman becomes in this play,
a nerveless, pitiful scapegoat.

When the Lady bears the Stranger's child, the bond between
them should have been strengthened. Instead, she becomes his
fury and curse, opens his mail, isolates him from the world, surrounds him with filth, and plagues him most demonically. The
child, she makes it clear, is not his, but hers. It will be her avenger.
Before the child arrives, the Lady's previous husband, the Werewolf, appears across the plain, raving-mad, and cursing the supposed happiness of the Lady and the Stranger. "Our house, our
roses, our clothes, with the bed-clothes included, and our child,"
he cries. The lunatic Caesar, suddenly restored to his wits, follows
close behind to take care of his doctor, now a lunatic himself. The
Stranger who now hates the Lady, and fears to await the coming
of the child, leaves for the great world to reap the rewards of his
scientific discoveries. Letters have come acknowledging the success of his gold-making and announcing great honors which await
him. At the end of his journey he finds himself in the midst of a
magnificent banquet and is presented with an order, as the man
who had done what all others had failed to do, as the discoverer
of the art of making gold. The banquet is not, however, what it
seems to be. The Werewolf, Caesar, the father-in-law of the
Werewolf (and the Stranger) are present and behind them are

other guests of curious and motley appearance. Like the scene in the cloister, the affair of the banquet is a fever phantasy, evoked by the Stranger's frantic fear and guilty conscience. Having received his order, the Stranger rises to explain that this is the happiest moment of his life, since he has won back his faith in himself. Immediately the scene shifts. Tramps steal in to take the places of the guests, and prostitutes sit down beside him and talk with insulting freedom. He is told that he has received, not a scientific order, but an order of drinkers. Gradually derision and hatred spread about him and everyone, he comes to realize, is his enemy. He is asked to pay the bill. When he is unable, the cry goes up: "The gold-maker cannot pay," and great joy is expressed that now the humbug will be jailed. He is, in fact, put in jail and when released is more desperate than ever. His only comfort is to drink in the low company of disreputable women, yet even they, he feels, are higher than he is. On returning to the Lady, he realizes that everything is over between them. They decide that the only reason they meet is to torture one another. The Stranger, the Lady explains, delivered her from a Werewolf, who was not one, and so became one himself. She, the Lady, took over all his wickedness, but with the result that he became more wicked than ever. The Lady now has her child. The Stranger has nothing. He decides to follow the Dominican (really the Beggar in disguise) and forsake the world and its vanities forever.

In 1904, six years later, Strindberg wrote another play to complete the Trilogy, a play which is, in some respects, the most interesting of all. Here we see the Stranger's last stand against the lure of the monastery. The Confessor (really the Beggar in disguise) leads him gradually through repentance and self-abnegation to the peace and blessedness of a spiritual brotherhood, remote in the mountains, but on the way they meet the Tempter who fastens upon the Stranger's soul and fascinates him. As a man of the world who has traveled much, doubted deeply, and pursued affairs with many women, he makes a deep impression on the Stranger, whose interest in life is much quickened by the daring speculations and by the free, alluring discourse on women. As he listens, all the old riddles which have tortured him seem solved. This Tempter, it occurs to him, is perhaps the Deliverer. And the Tempter, like the artful devil that he is, knows well how to treat the Stranger with gracious kindly humor, like a brother who has gone astray. He urges him to shake off his morbid fears and scruples, and bids him return to the pleasures of love and his old, bold wisdom. The Stranger is tempted. To amuse him and to carry out his own quizzicality, the Tempter interferes with a trial in the neighborhood and reduces justice there to a travesty. As they arrive at the court a young fellow is about to be sentenced for the murder of the betrothed of another man. The Tempter at once steps forth as the attorney for the defence, and explains how the dead girl had sadly betrayed the young fellow, her lover, had led him on, then deserted him for another. The accused, he asserts, had killed his sweetheart out of jealousy, which is a feeling of purity, a horror of strange admixture. "The dead girl is guilty," cry the people. Then the father of the girl rises to recount how years before a man had won his daughter's heart without, however, satisfying it, and so left her bitter and relentless toward the whole male sex. The man, he explains, is the Tempter himself. Immediately the whole court turns against the Tempter, who, however, defends himself in a long capable speech, explaining how, when quite young, he had been seduced by a woman, who was, he says, the beginning and source of *his* perversity. Then the woman who had seduced the Tempter rises to defend herself, whereupon the Judge calls a halt, for otherwise, as he says, "we will soon be back to Adam and Eve in Paradise." The Tempter, who thinks this a splendid idea, immediately calls forth Eve in her modesty and fig leaves, "Now, Eve, Mother, you have betrayed our Father," says the Tempter. "What have you to say in your defence?" Eve replies simply that the serpent deceived her. Whereupon the serpent is called forth. But when the Tempter asks the serpent who betrayed her, a thunderbolt strikes him and he falls to the ground. The Stranger is dismayed at the Tempter's boldness and the Tempter himself is quite put out. If only the serpent were guilty, then all men could be proved innocent, yet this ultimate guilt was impossible to determine.

This episode has considerable importance in the spiritual life of the Stranger, for the problem of guilt had been much on his mind, and the Confessor had reproved him for inculcating the doctrine that men are not morally responsible for their actions. The stern Confessor wins him away from the Tempter and the Lady wins him away. The Tempter is left behind. Another milestone has been crossed on the weary road to Damascus. The Lady appears one last time to call him back to life. She entreats him as a mother, she caresses him as a helpless erring child, and promises to make up for all the misery she has cost him. During her speech, her mantle falls, revealing the form of the eternal woman, "with loose hair and luxuriant motherly breasts." With the power of love of a mother, she says, "Mother—mother, for so I have loved you, you erring child." The Stranger breaks into violent sobs. Yet, from her also he breaks away. In his heart he has overcome the love of women and is ready now for the walls of the monastery.

Before that final step he craves one boon from the Confessor. He would talk once more with his first wife and with his daughter. The request is granted but ends in disillusion. The first wife is quite as she had been and his daughter shows herself sophisticated, impudent, and ungrateful, a modern child. And now that the last tie which bound him to the world has snapped, the Stranger retreats to the sequestration of the spiritual brotherhood, who have been following his career from afar and have long expected him. There he enters without name or reputation. There he makes the great sacrifice of his rebellious, ever-searching self.

The theme of this trilogy, like that of *Faust,* is love and illicit knowledge. The mood resembles that of morality and mystery plays. Throughout, the influence of Swedenborg is apparent. For example, the picture of hell as a place where the damned attain all their desires, only to find them dross and misery, is derived directly from the Swedish mystic. Again, the Confessor, who pursues the Stranger, taking the forms of the Beggar and the Dominican, in order to save his soul and scourge him to the cross, is also a Swedenborgian figure. In its magnificence and breadth, its high theme of the sin of pride and illicit knowledge, with the ground tone of retribution and the avenging fates, this play ranks with the great trilogies of the Greeks, with *Pilgrim's Progress* and *Faust*. In its weird transitions from the world of omens and avenging spirits to the natural irritations of poverty and domestic rancor, blending the highest with the lowest, the great tragedy of moral man with his pettiest desperations, it stands alone. The twin-motif of the pain of love and the loneliness of high striving are, of course, the grand themes of Strindberg's life, and a comparison of this play with the account of Strindberg's life in the chapters on *The Second Marriage, Inferno* and *Scientist or Saint* will demonstrate to what a surprising degree he borrowed from the actual facts of his life, and will serve, therefore, as an illuminating study in "poetic imagination."

XXVI

BEYOND NATURALISM

IT was not alone Strindberg's madness, nor his mysterious afflictions, nor his final conversion which drove him beyond Naturalism into that realm of guilt, and punishment, and repentance, where the Eternal sits watchful in his swirling clouds, not so far away, judging and measuring the sins of men. It lay in the nature of Naturalism itself. For Naturalism seeks to identify science and literature, to make literature a mere exemplification or a deduction from the laws of nature. But Naturalism is a fleeting mood and seldom seen in its purity. When the naturalist seeks a personal and dramatic theme in the field of the sciences, he is more than likely to end in the quasi-science of the mind. He may talk, as did Zola, of the laws of mechanics and medicine. The laws he depends on, primarily, are those still unwritten laws of psychology. Zola's play, *Thérèse Raquin,* and all of Strindberg's naturalistic plays owe their chief interest, not to the pitiful reaction to physical laws, but to the quickening, tragic play of thought itself. To show man's bondage to physical, chemical, economic laws produces the mood and inculcates the lesson the naturalist desires. But the tragedy is much deepened, escape cut off, and the doctrine driven home to its bitterest degree, if the mind itself, the last fortress of freedom, is shown to be a slave to law. To display most pitifully the mind's subjection to law, the naturalist is strongly inclined to pathology and crime, to extreme

and sordid exemplifications. Moreover, in time, he is no longer
satisfied with the tyranny of abstract law. The dramatic requirements of the art, itself, suggest a more personal and vindictive oppression. There is, thus, a tendency for the laws of mind to become demons and furies and the laws of nature, powers and gods
and revengeful spirits.

When Strindberg's world of nature and mind became alive
with demons and spirits, when the plants began to breathe and
the skies gave out warnings, he commenced to write again. The
fate of his naturalism was the fate of Naturalism in general. In
Hardy's novels, for instance, the tragedies of mechanical chance
become more spiteful and malicious, until finally the presiding
spirits, who have only been hiding all the time, appear personally
on the stage. In Hauptmann's plays the transition to the supernatural occurs quickly and *Before Sunrise* is soon forgotten.
O'Neill's plays, in spite of their natural matter-of-fact sordidness,
at times grow thick with spooks and symbols. The naturalistic return to the primitive, itself, makes this requirement. In general,
the transition to the supernatural and the symbolical personalizes
the action, thus favoring empathy, and exalts the theme to effect
catharsis. It is, therefore, a frequent temptation to naturalists.

In the years 1888–1902 Strindberg made an astounding recovery
from a mental condition which might well have been fatal, regained his powers, and wrote fifteen plays, most of which reflect
plainly his long, frantic period of purgatory and conversion. Yet,
they show a remarkable variety: a miracle play, *Advent;* a passion play, *Easter;* two fairy plays, *Swanwhite* and *The Crown
Bride;* a curious phantasmagoria, *A Dream Play;* a naturalistic
drama in two parts, *The Dance of Death;* and six historical
plays.

In *Advent,* Strindberg follows in spirit Swedenborg's delineation of hell and the earthly government, though with the individual changes and deviations which always marked his disci-
pleship. It is a story of a wicked judge and his wicked wife who

have grown old and complacent in unrighteousness. The judge flatters himself that he has always stuck to the letter of law and promises himself a peaceful old age with the benediction of the church. Yet, it turns out that he is unable to bear the light of the sun and is haunted by a procession of shadows: Death with its scythe and hour glass, The Lady in White (a woman he has wronged), The Beheaded Sailor, The Auctioneer, The Chimney Sweep, The Fool, etc., which cause him, on occasion, no end of horror and consternation. Yet, he persists in his wickedness, even when warned by The Other One. The Other One is an old sinner who is now doing penance (in hell) by scourging other sinners to the cross. He is the Devil, yet how pious and changed! The old judge and his wife are definitely surprised. They soon find themselves in hell with the Other One as their official torturer. There, they are whipped and slapped and starved; their vanity first flattered, then changed to misery and ridicule. The old people have never dreamed of such indignities before, such horrible insults and impudence. They express an ardent desire to go home. The judge at first is quite adamant. He is asked to pass sentence on a wicked judge, and does so with the hard justice he has always employed on earth. He learns, that without realizing it, he has condemned himself. Gradually he weakens, as does the old lady. At the end of the play they are wistful and saddened and then, at last, comes the foreshadowing of that divine mercy and forgiveness which ever waits upon repentance.

Throughout this miracle play, the action is bizarre and capricious to the last degree. Scenes and characters follow the moral theme and change their aspect in a twinkling, while space and time relent as in a dream. Warnings and portents! A spot of light perturbs the wicked judge but becomes the playmate of innocent children. Forms rise up to accuse and spooks confound the living. We are in the mausoleum of the soul before the tribunal of conscience. The wicked old judge is Strindberg, the blasphemer, the scourge of humanity, and hell is the hell of his conscience.

In Strindberg's next play, *There are Crimes and Crimes,* the theme is still guilt and punishment, but the scene is now shifted from hell to a modern crémerie in Paris, the resort of a circle of artists. Maurice, a sober, hard-working dramatist, has finally achieved the great triumph for which he has waited so long. His play will be performed in Paris. It is, he feels, the high good time of his life. He feels how the printing press whirrs and the wires flash out the intelligence of his great success, to Europe and to the world. This is his reward for years of hard work and reverses. It delights him to think how dismayed his enemies will be. In this mood he bids goodby to his mistress, Jeanne, and his beloved little daughter, and promises to return to them the next day, never to be parted again. But another fate is reserved for him. He encounters for the first time the dangerous Henriette, and though with dark forebodings he does his best to escape, the net of fate is too strong. Both, in fact, feel drawn to each other by a centrifugal force which is stronger than old love or loyalty or any duty.

Henriette witnesses with Maurice the great success of his opening night, after which they fly from ovations and friends to a lonely elegant café. There they are to wait for Adolph, the lover of Henriette and the best friend of Maurice, but neither really wants him to come. His empty glass stands like a ghost between them until Maurice, in a high mood, strikes it off the table. His love, he says, will kill anything that stands in its way. Yet he is anything but gay and confident. He is troubled in conscience by his sinful desertion of Jeanne and the child, and by the betrayal of his dearest friend, Adolph. Oppressed by this double sin, his sudden triumph gives him little happiness, he is ready to weep.

The conversation between these lovers, swept off their feet by an irresistible passion and exalted by a recent victory, is truly Strindbergian. When Henriette asks Maurice what binds him to her, he makes the original reply: "If I only knew, I should be able to tear myself away. But I believe it must be those qualities which you have and I lack. I believe that the evil within you draws me with the irresistible lure of novelty." Their conversation turns with fateful insistence upon sins and killings, crimes and scaffolds. Their thoughts grow wicked. Then the ghosts walk and Maurice shivers. Henriette confesses her crime. Her father incurred the hatred of her mother and sisters, "and he melted away like wax." She now believes herself guilty of his death.

It transpires the next day that Maurice's little daughter has suddenly died, and that Maurice himself is held to be the murderer. The police have been apprised of his hasty words of the night before, his talk of killings and scaffolds. His remark: "My love would kill everything that stood in its way," has been reported. Suspicion turns strongly against him, yet his mistress and friends support him unwaveringly. When Maurice himself hears the accusation, he declares in great excitement that he is the murderer and behaves so strangely that his friends lose their confidence in him, as do the police. He is arrested and spends the night in jail.

In the morning he is released and the charges withdrawn for want of sufficient evidence, yet the public still accuse him, the people threaten his life, and the papers flaunt the pictures of the murderer, Maurice, and his mistress, Henriette. Moreover, the new play has been taken off the boards and Maurice's enemy set up in his place. In twenty-four hours he has fallen from the pinnacle of victory to the darkest terrace of the soul. The night in the cell has made him bad and suspicious. He has lost his faith in humanity. On meeting Henriette, who has also grown morbidly suspicious, they put their hands together and decide against everybody. Adolph, they argue, must have sent the police against them. Jeanne and her brother must have done the same, for revenge. After proving the treachery of everyone concerned, they turn against each other. Henriette builds up a case to prove that Maurice is the murderer; Maurice does the same for her. Then detectives begin to haunt them. Henriette is accused of being a prostitute, and the waiters refuse to serve such a man as Maurice.

The next frightful humiliation is that neither has the money to pay the bill. They come to realize that their sin has bound them together, that though they hate each other they will be obliged to marry and suffer mutual torture in narrow rooms the rest of their lives.

When the good Adolph hears their mutual accusations he warns them that they are on the borderline of insanity. Henriette, he persuades to do penance by going home to her mother, while Maurice is told that since he is cleared of guilt his play has been put on again and his talents applauded. He then asks the abbé why his punishment had to be so hard when he was innocent. "Hard?" replies the abbé. "Only two days! And you were not innocent. For we have to stand responsible for our thoughts and words and desires also. And in your thought you became a murderer when your evil self wished the life out of your child."

There are Crimes and Crimes is one of Strindberg's finest plays, both in point of structure and thought. In the first two acts, the hero breathes the bright air of an uneasy triumph, crossed by shadows and presentiments and darkened as by the tolling of distant bells. He deserts his wife and child; he betrays his friend. In the midst of the magic of a new love, he probes his soul and shivers. Then the moral theme, rising from the realistic setting in the crémerie, gathers force from the forebodings and the careless sins of thought, takes fire in the sensitive soul of the dramatist already tortured with guilt, and accumulates, urgent, manifold, overwhelming, to the pitch of frenzy and madness. A subtle sin, a self-inflicted punishment; then forgiveness. It would be difficult to find a play at once so theatrical and even melodramatic in the quick outward exchanges of its rising movement, which is nevertheless confined, to such a great degree, within the walls of the self.

The play, of course, is highly autobiographical. The moral theme, the setting, even the most incidental episodes are drawn from Strindberg's own experience. A few years before, while lonely and desperate in Paris, he had performed a magical rite to induce sickness in his absent daughter, which would thereby occasion his rejoining his wife in Austria. This recourse to black magic had perturbed his conscience not a little. He had killed and wounded at a distance before, but a similar attempt on his little daughter, "his one comfort in an evil world," was appalling. The case of his old enemy Prsybyszevski had also stuck deep in his mind. The Pole had deserted his wife and children for a new love, and left them without support. Later, he was arrested and jailed on the suspicion of having incited his first wife to suicide and the murder of her children. Like Maurice in the play, he had been released on insufficient evidence.

Advent and *There are Crimes and Crimes* gave expression to Strindberg's new religion and to that deep sense of a moral order which had grown up recently during the miseries and divinations of the Inferno period. The fifty-year-old dramatist now began to exploit with youthful, illimitable energy the age of the Swedish Reformation, and between the years 1899–1900 wrote three historical plays of decisive merit. In them, guilt and punishment, expiation of ancestral sin, sacrifice, and the inscrutable judgment of heaven impel the tragic action. The blood-guilt of a brother, of a son, of a mother, the unavoidable crime of a king against a subject and friend; blood-guilt, treason, fanatical hatred, and the lust for power, form the base motif which sounds at intervals with dark insistency. It is the warning of the *Erinys* against the old uncleanness and it bespeaks the certainty of shipwreck and the death of every hope. The horror of some forgotten crime or some new sin recurs, haunting the bright stirring scenes of history with a vague disquiet. Clairvoyants, seers, and unearthly messengers foretell disaster when too late to be avoided. Then comes death and desolation. In the burning faith and the religious wars, in the frantic energies of the Restoration, Strindberg felt himself at home. Among the men of this period, with their splendid intensity and their downright, cruel, uncertain devotions, men won too recently and too quickly to new faiths and hatreds, Strindberg found kindred.

These tragedies bear a resemblance in their strength and incisiveness, in the complexity of character and motivation, and in the realistic delineation of human passion, to the historical plays of Shakespeare, Marlowe, and Greene. In Shakespeare's great pageant of dynasties, beginning with *King John* and ending with *Henry VIII,* old kings grow cruel and wayward, and new kings with the favor of nobles and armies and every bright promise for the future rise up to depose them. Then the new kings grow old, and become as hateful and suspicious and oppressive as their predecessors. They are slain or dethroned in their turn. There are weak kings, such as Henry VI; there are wicked kings, such as Richard III; and there is one strong, good king who offends our moral sense. The path of kings and nobles is strewn with shipwrecks. The end of all empire and striving is disgrace, murder, or the tower, and this is the moral of these tragedies.

In Strindberg's plays, the moral is the same. Prison, death, and frustration close the scene of majesty. The pious king, Magnus, suffers every humiliation with the death of his children and political collapse. Erick XIV likewise loses everything and ends in prison. But while such fatalities in Shakespeare's histories are occasioned by the weakness and wickedness of the king, or by the enmity and ambition of his rivals, Strindberg seeks deeper causes. He brings into play the sociological, economic, and morbid psychological factors in all their intricacy and subtle relevance. While Shakespeare confines himself, for the most part, to the political parade of princes, Strindberg shows us the hidden, governing mind of the people. He introduces us proudly to the great Jewish money-lenders to whom the greatest kings must bow. He reveals the power of diseased motivations in a king like Erick XIV. His interpretation is thus subjective and consciously scientific, which marks, of course, the main distinction between modern and Elizabethan drama.

Strindberg remained, to some extent, a naturalist. Yet the resources of science and psychology proved, after all, insufficient. The laws of probability would not explain why a steady train of disasters should fall upon a single head—why a king, a family, or a nation should be cursed, in sequence to some ancient crime. No, and there were thousands of perturbing, fateful events which reason seemed powerless to fathom or predict. Strindberg had come to the conclusion, which he expressed in an essay in 1903, that world history is governed by demons, and guided by powers toward ends of which humanity must remain in ignorance. In the historical plays, the characters express this view in dark unwilling suspicions, and all their wisdom collapses before that fatality which overshadows their lives, dimming their certainties and subverting their plans. Only one thing is certain. Sin and punishment are the presiding principles, the demonic motivations, and the intricacy of their pattern in the world is endless.

The recourse to the fates, to guilt, sacrifice, and atonement, relate the plays of Strindberg much closer to Greek tragedies than to anything in Shakespeare. Indeed, so closely does Strindberg follow the Greek tradition that a chorus is introduced, and the heroes, in a way which is truly remarkable in a modern drama, suffer their mysterious afflictions and the quickening pursuit of the furies, shrinking from the light of the sun, as did Œdipus and Orestes.

In the first of Strindberg's historical plays, *The Saga of the Folkungs,* King Magnus inherits the guilt of the Folkungs and must pay the penalty of sorrow, frustration and maddening disgrace, for the fates require a scapegoat and the muttering, insatiate powers claim a forfeit for the blood that has been spilt. Brother-strife and murder must be appeased, and new wrongs and miseries fill the cup before the muttering wrath is quieted. *The Saga of the Folkungs* is the Passion Play of a suffering Christ. It opens in the court barber-shop where in casual discussion the general discontent with King Magnus is sounded, the

critical, ambiguous state of the court revealed, with hints of treason, shame and rebellion. The first court scene begins, as is proper
to a play of this kind, with triumph and rejoicing, but not with
the Aristotelian *hubris*. The meek, good king thanks God for his
victory over the Russians and with mild forgiveness, against the
cries of his son and the whole royal train, releases the prisoners,
allowing the weird, dangerous Tartars to wander out on the
streets and the fields. Hardly has this been done, when a letter
arrives announcing that the Swedish army has been completely
defeated. Then The Possessed appears, a woman mentally de-
ranged but with a vision of the future, and foretells many disasters.

The Possessed: "You have blood on your crown, King Magnus!
But you are without guilt that the lawful successor to the throne,
Magnus Bigersson, was beheaded. You *had* to climb over his dead
body to the throne. You have the blood of the Folkungs on your
purple! . . . Poor lamb, you live among wolves and dragons, but
the light of your innocence blinds you, so that you see only the reflection of your own purity. You see only love and friendship, faith
and virtue, where you are up to your neck in treachery and wickedness, and where all crimes bloom, even Sodom's. . . ." At this
point the bishop curses the "unclean spirit" and warns her away
authoritatively. She remains. "Comfort him" (the king), she cries,
"for now evil times approach. The Asgards-dance comes, the
pest-boy with his rake and the pest-girl with her broom, the
poisoned cup and the famine, defiance of taxation and secret
cohabitation." She continues her forebodings in broken sentences
and verse, while the whole court listens with the helpless fascination of horror.

This presage of evils as atonement for guilt, and the fixing of
the king as the lamb of God who will take all sins on himself, is
really the argument of the play. It is told by an idiot, yet all
her prophecies come true. The pest comes, famine and rebellion, and no one is hated so much as King Magnus. In the palace

there is shame and treachery. His wife, Blanche, has a lover, and his mother, Ingeborg, has a lover, Porse, a Danish knight with whom she plots against his crown and his life. The king's own son betrays him, though pitifully, without knowing what he does. The ladies of the court, feeling that the end of the world has come, wander off to enjoy their last moments with soldiers. The king, as a final humiliation, is cursed with the ban, and staggers beneath the heavy cross, blinding his eyes from the hatred of his subjects, as he makes his penitential rounds about the church. Disgrace, murder, lust, and treason! Yet still the furies are unassuaged. In the last act his daughter, and his son and heir are poisoned, and at the height of this greatest sorrow, a messenger announces that the enemy is at the walls of the city. Then the king realizes that the worst has come to pass, that the old guilt has finally been washed away. It is perhaps with a sense of vague relief that he speaks the concluding line: "It has been accomplished."

Gustavus Vasa, which deals with the later career of that romantic king who, after many adventures reminiscent of King Alfred, wrested the throne from the Danish tyrant, to become "the father of the Swedish people," is more complex and vivid in its noble delineation of contending passions, and more skilful and realistic than the previous play. The main development, despite the numerous collateral themes, is cumulative and exciting, while the dialogue is terse and pertinent like the rapid-fire of batteries. Often, to be sure, it descends to mere colorful invective, but even this has its effectiveness. Through the taut scenes of passion and danger the huge king walks, with menace and thunder, like Thor, with his war hammer. Had he killed his first wife with this hammer? her son, the crown prince Eric, asks himself. He has his suspicions and hates his father as a tyrant and murderer. Others share his feelings. The king has many enemies and many rebellious subjects. When treasonable plots come to light, heads must fall. Gustavus Vasa is a stern ruler and apparently cruel and ruthless in his moments of volcanic anger and revenge, yet at heart, as the play clearly shows, he is an unhappy man, torn with scruples and remorse and divided ever painfully between the claims of royal justice and human pity. Like King Magnus, he is a scapegoat, a lamb for the sacrifice. His kingship has forced him to bitter sins and inhuman sacrifices. Thus, an old friend who had helped him to the throne had later turned treasonable. The king had been obliged to take his head, though it rankled in his heart and cost him his peace forever. Not only his conscience! His friends turn away from him, and his wife shrinks from his kiss and stares at his hands as if there were blood on them. When, at the beginning of the play, we observe the outward enactments of the king, we shrink from his cruelty and dispatch. When later we learn of his scruples and the necessities of office, we pity him.

The first scene is a masterpiece of developing tension and crucial, ambiguous expectancy. The miners of Darlecarlia, who have fought for the king and helped him to his throne but subsequently conspired against him, await the royal approach, await death or high favor. One after another they are commanded to the presence, but those who go do not return, and uneasiness increases among the rest. Finally, only two Darlecarlians are left. They are shown the bloody coats of their friends, and are warned against treason. Being determined on vengeance, however, they set out for Stockholm where they are soon caught plotting the death of the king. He, for his part, sees no other course than to behead them, though he hesitates with pity and pain of conscience. In the meantime, other evils have accumulated; revolution threatens, there is no means of defence, the exchequer is empty, and the rich allies of Lübeck have returned home. At the end of the play the king is prepared for abdication and flight. He hears the approach of an army of Darlecarlians, counts on his fingers the Darlecarlians he has had to sacrifice, and knows that the end has come. At last a drunken soldier staggers on to the stage to announce that the Darlecarlians have come to fight the king's enemies. "You have punished me, O Lord," cries the king, "and I thank Thee."

Gustavas Vasa is of course a continuation of Strindberg's first great play, *Master Olaf,* and just as the subsequent versions of that play reflect the development of his conceptions and feelings, so *Gustavas Vasa* shows how Strindberg carries on a story interrupted almost thirty years before. Master Olaf, it will be remembered, was forgiven for his rash design upon the life of the king. In the Vasa play, he has become the king's strongest supporter, and more stern and relentless, more dogmatically royalistic than the king himself. He is, if anything, too strong and dominating. "Go and roar in your church," the king once said, "I thunder here." Of special interest also, is the outcome of Master Olaf's marriage and his faith in the Reformation. His marriage, which had been a romantic love affair, has degenerated into a relation of cold, cynical forbearance, in which a thousand irritations have banished love. Even the memories are poisoned. When Master Olaf asks his wife whether she has forgotten, she answers:

"Yes. I have forgotten every bit of that old tommy-rot! I have forgotten how you swore to love me. I have forgotten the noise made about the pope's beard, and the stealing of the church silver, and the humbug with the bells, and the *pure* faith, and roast ducks and cackling swans, and martyrs with a taste for fighting and the following of Christ with wine and women, and the scratching of eyes and the tearing of hair, until we have twenty-five brand-new faiths in place of a holy Catholic Church." Master Olaf's young son feels the same way. Not knowing any longer what he is to believe, he wants to die.

This disillusion had come to grow on Strindberg. He had come to see that the banner of freedom has another face which is almost worse than tyranny. Long but fitfully, he had felt himself drawn to the permanence and traditions of the one eternal faith. Often he had craved the oblivion of doubt and freedom.

Now, in his advancing years, new generations had overtaken him with their pillaging and destruction, and their new ideals. An old man on the edge of a tilting planet, his hair turning gray, and everything about him seething and passing, Strindberg felt insecure. Time was the great menace. Too long the bright runners of Time had crossed the skies unchallenged, making sport with the souls of men. There were moods in which Strindberg hated progress, evolution, freedom, and all the attendants of Time. But one way to defeat Time, a resource of all weary men, is to turn it back on itself, to break its back, to deny its irreversibility. So Strindberg, in his historical plays, made his escape from the hurrying change of the present to the timeless pictures of the past.

In *Eric XIV, Gustavus Adolphus, Engelbrecht, Gustavus III,* Strindberg carries on the theme of guilt and punishment with many subtle variations of character and destiny. Each in his own way is a divine scapegoat, a lamb of God, quite as much as King Magnus or Gustavus Vasa. Eric XIV, crazed and detested by everyone, suffers a heavy fate for, like King Magnus, he inherits the guilt of the Folkungs. In delineating the mad suspicions, the mistrust and morbid excitability, the pride and weakness of this unhappy king, Strindberg reveals himself. *Gustavus Adolphus* is painted across a great canvas on which appear the encampments and armies of Sweden, the glorious youthful officers and their Alexandrian king, the stirring world events of the Thirty Years' War. Indeed, so massive and splendid are the scenes that it is difficult to see how it could ever be performed, for the man who had reduced the drama to two characters and one speaking character had created a play which only an amphitheatre or a circus would hold. In many respects it resembles, it is interesting to note, Schiller's *Wallenstein,* a play treating of the events in the camp of the enemy.

In interpreting the character of Gustavus Adolphus, Strindberg was guided, as in other cases, by the necessities and privileges of dramatic invention, and by his own philosophy of character. He robbed his heroes of their lustre and greatness, the critics objected. He had torn aside the veil of prejudice and hero-worship which had long concealed their true characters, replied Strindberg. However this may be, it is truly surprising to see how every great hero turns pale and weak and human under his touch, how they grow scrupulous and anguished, and, Olympian only in words, how each superman, for all his starlight and splendor, shows himself a Christ with thorns and cross, or weighs his guilt eternally in some lonely constellation. No doubt this happened far too often to agree with the truth or to please the critics. Strindberg was also very often careless and disrespectful of historical facts and became more so as the years went by. But, now, in the midst of his historical plays, he turned aside to treat the theme of the child redeemer in a modern play.

In *Easter,* we are introduced to a family which is cursed by the debt and poverty to which Strindberg himself was subjected most of his life. Also, the old guilt of the father who has embezzled money and now suffers the penalty in prison, hangs heavy over the house, and the kleptomania and mental disturbance of the daughter Eleanora adds to the cup of bitterness. But, as the play proceeds, and evils rain thick about their heads, it is this mystical, flower-crazed, clairvoyant, loving Christ-child who spreads light through the house with the power to bear suffering, and saves them all from despair. At the end of the play the frightful creditor turns out to be a good giant who only frightens children for fun. After curing the hero of his pride and ill will, he cancels the debt. Pride has been his only fault, but pride, Strindberg's punishments had taught him, is the great crime, the mother of crimes.

In 1901, shortly before Strindberg's third marriage, all the poisoned memories of his earlier marriages seemed to return with a quiet vengeance, and all the old bitterness and rancor were expressed in a new play, the blackest and most extreme in its demonic energy and vindictiveness that he ever wrote. *The Dance of Death* is a continuation of the duel of the sexes as portrayed in *The Father, Creditors, Comrades,* etc., but much more deadly, protracted, and furious than any of these. In a close room, infected with hate, where even the wallpaper takes on the odor and the flowers wither, sit the Captain and his wife, Alice. They talk for hours of the poverty and the miseries of their marriage, of his pride and arrogance and her cruelty and malice, and beneath the surface of an ordinary conversation rage the furies of a cold, determined hatred. She inflicts the most ingenious torments on him, he replies with subtle devastating cruelty, for each has resolved to torture the other to death. It is a play of hate. That emotion which has been banished in these utilitarian times performs here the full gamut of its horrors, and Strindberg of course with Stendhal, is its modern expounder. When, at the end of the play, the Captain has a stroke and approaches death, his wife pulls his beard and slaps him while he, powerless to speak, spits in her face. "Away with the carcass!" she cries; "out with it, and let's open the doors! The place must be aired! Ugh!"

Curt: "You are going to desert him?"

Alice: "A wrecked ship is deserted, and the crew save their lives—I'll not act as undertaker to a rotting beast! Drainmen and dissectors may dispose of him! A garden bed would be too good for that barrowful of filth!"

The Dance of Death resembles *The Father* very closely, but it also differs in important respects. Thus, while the Father is a martyr who draws our sympathy, the Captain is a real vampire, who feeds upon the lives of other men, defeating their hopes and purposes while seeming to aid them, drawing them ever deeper into his net of shame and dependence, and he shows himself as much of a demon as his wife a witch. They are indeed, in cruelty and strength, an even match,—or almost so. The Captain must give up his whiskey to contend with her. Like the Father, he is defeated in the struggle, suffering confusion and death, but Alice does not triumph as Laura did. With her husband dead,

her life, which had been only hate, is gone, and the peace of
death reigns through the house. "He *was* a good and noble
man," she says at the end.

The Dance of Death, like the plays of the eighties, is naturalistic, yet overlaid with preternatural aspects which govern most
the works following the Inferno period. The vampire captain
walks through the later scenes like a ghost of wrath and vindictiveness. He is too full of subtle, contemplated villainy. For it is
not so much the laws of psychology which drive him to these
lengths as the furies and avenging spirits of a Swedenborgian hell.
The naturalism is also broken, at the end, by the childhood love
which arises from the corruption of this most terrible marriage,
radiant and strong.

Strindberg next turned, with his unprecedented versatility, to a
new form. He wrote a fairy play, *Swanwhite;* a colorful, romantic, local drama, *The Crown Bride;* and a phantasmagoria, *The
Dream Play.* Yet in all of them the theme of guilt and punishment and avenging fates play a principal part. In the first, a good
little fairy suffers the wickedness of a witch of a step-mother, but
is finally delivered by her father and joined to her lover. In *The
Crown Bride* a girl is separated from her lover by a family feud
like that in *Romeo and Juliet.* In order to wear the bridal crown
of purity she sacrifices their illegitimate child through the instiga-
tion of a witch, and is brought to trial for murder. But repentance
saves her from the scaffold. The play is remarkable for its local
songs and its beautiful, faithful portrayal of the land and customs of Darlecarlia.

The Dream Play is a review of human bondage and misery. It
is a hymn of world-pessimism and world-pity. The Daughter of
the god Indra, comes to earth to see if men have a right to complain. She finds that they have only too much. "Men are to be
pitied!" is her refrain. She staggers and falls under the load of
the shawl of humanity, weighted with misery. "I paste! I paste!"

cries the servant girl. She expresses thereby the settled despair of those who have ceased to hope, or smile.

In these plays Strindberg was under the influence of Maeterlinck whose poetic method and fluid dream-like world he had long been approaching independently. In Maeterlinck's plays, which might have been influenced by the metaphysics of Bergson, the characters wander beside limpid streams, to love or suicide, flowing toward one another or away, not through the thrust of external circumstance but by a freedom, a deep necessity, an unfolding of their souls. In these plays of Strindberg the same free movement prevails and the dialogue is illustrative. While in *Gustavus Vasa* the speeches meet with the fury and direction of charging bulls, in *The Crown Bride* they do not meet at all. They follow one another, not with logical, but poetic relevance. They express not the duel and counterplay of thought, but the wandering flow of feeling.

Strindberg's world was taking many forms and colors. In these days he walked alone, but in his heart was a deep guilt and behind him in the past burned in thousands the shames and tortures, the mad hopes and sins of a reckless life, and before him walked his many shadows—a wicked judge, a murderer, a mad king and a tortured saint, a harassed school-teacher, a weird vampire of a captain and many more besides. Strindberg in his loneliness kept his shadows.

XXVII

THE LAST MARRIAGE

AFTER the tumult and excess of the Inferno period Strind-berg rejected his black magic, the use of which had long distressed his conscience, but he still swore by his Faustian discoveries in the realm of science and, by 1899, was convinced that the mint at Washington was installing his new process for making gold out of sulphur and iron! He continued to regard the world about him as a forest of symbols in which sad men wander in tragic confusion with only a dim presentiment of the mystery and guilt and judgment which surround them. In Nature he found the same riddles and numbers and intrusive demons, cryptic leaves, inexplicable rock formations, secrets and sly winds through the trees. In this net of enchantment Strindberg wavered and sought, and brooded like Merlin. The most ordinary circumstances of life, a chance piece of paper, a bad cup of coffee, or the cough of a stranger, filled him with uneasiness, or answered, perhaps, some haunting doubt. Morbidly excited by the quiet and loneliness which, in these later years, had fallen about him, his sensitivity and his clairvoyance increased until he fancied that he sensed all the thoughts and suffered all the sorrows in his vicinity. In 1890 he declared himself a medium again. "I believe that I stand in telepathic rapport with all absent friends, relatives, and enemies." With them he carried on long, connected discussions and sometimes the scene widened, 'til the ghosts of nations walked before his mind, and throughout the world, amid strife and enmity, he heard how people talked of him and cursed. Then came a spectre army of cripples and beggars. He saw a wall of human faces, anguished, grieving, despairing, such as appears at the close of *The Dream Play,* and again and again came the forms of those he loved, usually in some aspect of sadness or misfortune. His unfortunate talent for sharing the pains of others from afar remained to curse his loneliness, filling it with those ghosts of human suffering from which he had tried to escape. If a woman was in labor, he suffered all the pangs of childbirth; if an unknown man in his vicinity fell into grief and trouble, he took up the vibration; if a friend died he suffered death.

In Lund, 1896-7, during his recovery, Strindberg had profited greatly from his friends and enjoyed merry times with them in the café, yet often he withdrew in fear from their company, from their protectiveness, their sympathy or laughter, for there were plots in the air, he was sure, and enemies with fair words, and vampires, and avenging spirits. Why did people laugh suddenly in the midst of a discussion? It made him fearfully uneasy. Why did they rejoice when he suffered? Were they planning some grand betrayal and were now confident of success? Why were they suddenly sad or absent-minded? Why did they pity him? What had they done? What were they plotting? After his return from Paris where he spent a few months, 1897-8, his nervous excitability, his fears and suspicions, drove him into a deeper isolation. Frightened or irritated in the company of friends, he would fly to his lodgings and lock the door. If a visitor knocked, it was like a summons of fate. He started with fear and listened breathlessly. "Now it has come!" A young admirer who called on him in 1899 relates how he waited for a long time after knocking before anyone appeared. Finally the door opened a little, slowly and cautiously, a lean hand appeared, and two strong eyes searched his with open suspicion. When the stranger explained his business, the door was slowly opened and he was graciously received.

When, in 1899, Strindberg returned, after his long exile, to his beloved Stockholm, he met many old friends, all about fifty years of age, with widely different careers behind them. (*Solitary*.) They soon formed a circle at a café where, reviewing together their early experiences, they for a time shook off their years and disappointments, and felt themselves young again. Yet it was clear they had all grown old. They had ceased to speak of the future. Their memories, moreover, were bad and often they misquoted themselves and others so much that the scene was reduced to bedlam. Another source of friction was the innocent inquiries about friends and relatives. On inquiring the health of a brother or wife, one learned amid general embarrassment, that he or she was dead, insane, or divorced. When Strindberg attempted to renew an old friendship in the home of a married man, the result was even more depressing. The wives, knowing his enmity toward women, gave him no quarter. They fled in tears to the nursery, and returning, made him feel "like a beggar and parasite, who had tried to entice their husbands from house and home, from duty and faithfulness."

Rebuked by such experiences, he gradually crept back in his shell, brooding on old injuries and new, reviewing the steady misfortunes that had trailed him, through life, with bitter despair of the past. Why had he been punished so inordinately? Was he suffering for others' sins? No, he sometimes decided; he had lived by the Old Testament rule of "an eye for an eye and a tooth for a tooth." For this he had been rightly punished and now the avenging powers still pursued him with malice. Was hell eternal? he asked himself. In *Advent* even the wicked judge was given hope of forgiveness, while in *Swanwhite* a witch is made white again. Strindberg apparently had some hopes for *himself*. To calm the wild voice of his conscience he turned with delight to music, especially Beethoven, but the piece he liked best was the D Minor Sonata which rang in his heart like a deep accusation. In his fifteen plays treating of sin, punishment, and repentance he also found catharsis from the pain of his fears and his lurid guilt. Like King Magnus, Gustavus Vasa, and a host of others, he was, as he saw it, a lamb of God, bled for the atonement of others' sins and for the good of the people. In creating these characters he had given himself illustrious companions in a romantic martyrdom, though, to be sure, at the expense of history. In *Legends,* it will be remembered, he had likewise found companions in misery, by painting all his friends in Lund as victims of nightmares and pursuing powers. Misery loves company and it sometimes makes it. Another solace to his conscience was the money he sent to his children in Finland. When unable to help them he was in despair. It was about this time, also, that he met one of Siri's children for the first time since the divorce in 1891. What an exhilaration and what a strange sadness to meet again after so many years the little creature into which "a part of his soul had passed!" Strindberg suffered her absence and that of his other children. He comforted himself with a Catholic Bible of the Seventeenth century, a Renaissance Bible and one which breathed the mysticism of Jacob Böhme, for each spoke to his heart in different moods. At times he remembered the words of Séraphita and gloried in suffering, which shines like a blessed light through the world, awakening the soul to its greatness.

Having retired for peace and quiet to the inner sanctuary of the self, Strindberg found it a commodious place, full of noise and tumult. The more he closed his eyes to the world, the more clairvoyant he became, and sensitive to its happenings. The merest clue was enough. He constructed the rest. He had never seen his next-door neighbors but only heard them moving about, yet he knew their histories to a nicety. When the wine-dealer around the corner failed, Strindberg knew and suffered all his protracted despair. Similarly, on his solitary walks he met certain men whom he knew at a glance to be his enemies and others whom he could have sworn were his friends. Their eyes met. That was all. Strindberg would not break the charm of these intimate friendships by words. He intuited all that was needed. He knew all their moods and changes, for these friendships had their vicissitudes, like others, and often ended in hate. It was for this reason that he had withdrawn from closer contacts. He prefered to peep in wistfully on the world of human love and passion rather than suffer its cruelties again. He consequently avoided company and spied in people's windows instead. On his walks he repeatedly passed by a certain wealthy home and saw how four men sat motionless at cards, listening, watching the clock, hoping vainly for some event, some interruption. He came away saddened, for a glance told him everything. He had been through it all himself. At night the famous dramatist discovered that by turning off the lights in his own house he could get a splendid view of other interiors and there he sat in the dark watching wistfully the slow painful scenes of the domestic tragedy. If ever it was his good fortune to catch a glimpse of human happiness, his case was only harder to bear. He saw himself then as an outcast sinner, one of the dispossessed. At times he shrank before his loneliness and once when he noticed that his voice, through disuse, had disappeared, he complained pathetically of his torments, for he had never hated men, he explained, but only feared them.

In the meantime, the solitary penitent had become a famous man. His plays, on the whole, had been well received. *Gustavus Vasa* had scored a great success in Stockholm in 1899 and *Eric XIV* and *The Saga of the Folkungs,* a little later, were also praised as they deserved. *There are Crimes and Crimes* and *Easter* triumphed despite their unprecedented strangeness, and even the fantastic scenery of the great penitential drama, *Damascus I,* was somehow managed with great effect. But the public were unprepared for *The Dance of Death*. Its endless, weary, vicious scenes of strife, its vampire hero and demonic heroine, were more than anyone had counted on,—even from Strindberg. To be asked to return a second night to watch the Captain and his wife torture each other to death in their subtle professional fashion was preposterous. The critic Levertin was particularly bitter against this play, which he described as "a clumsy, tedious wooden-dance," and others were of his opinion. Levertin was vastly displeased, in fact, with most of Strindberg's work which too often descended, he thought, to "a furious criminal indictment, in which all that is mean and petty is brought forth triumphantly, in which hate and jealousy carry the day. . . . In Strindberg's books, all the wild beasts of the human spirit bellow and scream behind their grating—and among them we find not only the majestic lion, and the enchanting tiger with its gold-flecked skin, but also the filthy ape." But such extreme disapproval, though it contains in point of fact much truth, did not express the public mind. Strindberg's star, after the long eclipse of the Inferno period, was in the ascendancy again.

By the fall of 1890 it was clear that something very unusual had happened to Strindberg and that his enchanted isolation had been disturbed. His plays had recently shown a tender lyrical strain and now music and poetry and the melody of new hopes drowned out the dissonance of guilt and distrust and spinning horrors. He became a youth again, mild and good, radiant and humble, and when he took his pen, lyrics flowed as had not been so for years before.

Strindberg had chosen for the Lady in *Toward Damascus I* a young Norwegian actress, Harriet Bosse, who had previously only played the parts of young girls. From the beginning he had been definitely impressed, had sent her flowers, and wished her good fortune on her journey through the thorns and rocks. Later, when she had played the role several times to his complete satisfaction, he sent her roses, "naturally with thorns—there are no others," and celebrated her future as "the greatest actress of the new century." Following her success in *Toward Damascus,* she studied the leading role, Eleanora, in *Easter* and here also she won Strindberg's applause and his heart. Eleanora, the angel-child, bringing light into the world with joy and compassion, and the Lady, the mysterious, bewitching woman who took the hand of the Stranger and loved him and led him quietly along the terrible road of redemption, were Strindberg's archetypal heroines. They were divine images which he sought to keep in heaven and to realize on earth. If at times, they lost that lustre of divinity, and fell like rebellious angels, to shame and turpitude, Strindberg raged and wept in blackness, and, like the Carthaginians, sold his soul to recover the lost veil of his goddess. Yet, in spite of all his pains, his angels fell, one after another. Siri, the first wife, fell; Frieda, the second, made a quick descent, for she had a much shorter distance to fall. So with the heroines of Strindberg's plays and novels. Their divinity disappears the moment they have won their husbands, if not before. The Lady, in *Toward Damascus I,* answers to all Strindberg's dreams. She is the redeemer who will follow the Stranger through all his torments, with love and comfort, leading him in the end to peace, atonement, and reconciliation with mankind. She is an angel from heaven, yet the principle of the earth, and her earthiness is a necessary counterpart to the feverish dreams and soaring discontent of the Stranger. The Lady, as the feminine principle, is also aloof from the passion of the male, according to Strindberg's ideal. Passive, like nature herself, with tender protests, she resists his excesses and ardors in the name of modesty and religion. In *Damascus II,* the redeemer becomes a scourge and a fury, a Swedenborgian demon, whipping the Stranger to the cross. But Eleanora, who was conceived in 1890, the same year that Strindberg became acquainted with Harriet Bosse, remains an angel throughout the play, and is perhaps the first of Strindberg's heroines to do this. For Strindberg required his heroines to keep aloof and pure, and high above him, yet to remain obedient to all his finical exactions. Often the goddess revolted.

In Harriet Bosse, Strindberg had apparently found a new realization of his Platonic Idea and it was as the Lady and as Eleanora that she appealed to him. When, in the role of the Lady,

she comforted the Stranger at the crossroads, wept at his tragic
aspect, and listened with quiet pity to his nightmare tale of the
heavy curse which had pursued him through life with unmerited
suffering, Strindberg must have been touched and ever so grateful to her. When, later, he saw how she clung to the Stranger in
love and, with a dark certainty that their fates were one, deserted
her werewolf husband to follow him amid mysterious evils and
miseries to the cross, Strindberg must have been inexpressibly
moved. As he watched the stage of the Dramatic Theatre, and
saw the fantastic destiny scenes of his own life-story unfold, and
saw how the beautiful actress walked beside *him* along the road
of crosses and toward the sea, where winter and summer lay together, toward the monastery which would be his final destination, he must have felt that the powers had once more linked his
life, for better or for worse, with another. At any rate he developed a lively interest in her career and in her heart. He encouraged her in her art, he instructed her, and he sent her Maeterlinck's
plays and Kipling's novels to show her the mood he liked best.
For she must perform in his other plays, he decided, and make a
name for herself. He advised her to study the terrible role of Alice
in *The Dance of Death* and wished her great success, it would
seem, in this fiendish part. Then came his declaration of love to
which she answered March 4, 1890, with a modest tentative and a
final consent.

"If the Lady in *Toward Damascus*," she wrote, "has the power
to bind the Stranger to life by showing him the goodness and
light which streams through the world, he would not be justified
in deserting her for the monastery in the mountains. But suppose
she failed in her high purpose! How disappointed he would be,
if afterwards he discovered that she was by no means as gifted,
as enlightened and wise, as he had thought! If he felt that her
mind was too small to follow his great, powerful spirit! Don't
you think that he would be disappointed and all his hopes collapse, . . . And she! She will suffer, suffer will she, if her great

end is not achieved; for her purpose is to lead him toward a reconciliation with men. . . . I can imagine, however, the exultant joy of the little woman, if the Stranger—in spite of all her presentiments—would put her hand very quietly in his and wander with her—toward the goal, and so forget the cloister." (Erdmann.)

Strindberg, though he had suffered many disappointments in the past, had the courage to face the future. He became a father to the Lady, and her little child. At times he saw himself an eagle who will draw the dove up to heaven on his powerful wings; at times a weary man who will bury his head in the lap of his little mother. As usual his plans miscarried and his happiness was threatened. The marriage could not take place until he had concluded his divorce with his second wife in Austria. Strindberg raged at this new frustration and presently decided to forego the benediction of the church altogether, write up a contract of his own and nail it to the church door in violence to society and religion. He remembered that his old hero, Master Olaf, had taken a wife in open violation of the laws of the church and was tempted to follow this drastic precedent. He hesitated. Master Olaf was a prophet, while he had been an enemy of society and God, an outcast who had scorned all laws and conventions, and was therefore rightly punished. But no! His bitterness spoke again. If the Christian church will not bless their union, they will walk out under the great heavens and fulfill the ceremony in the sight of God. Fortunately, the divorce was concluded shortly afterward and an orthodox ceremony took place in May, 1901. Then began the shimmering uniqueness of a new love and Strindberg saw the wistful sunlight fall tenderly on their little red house in Karlavägen and over all the blessed world, making witches merciful and demons apologetic, and conferring on punishment and suffering itself a mystical beauty. It was clear that the Lady had kept her word and, like the Christ-child, Eleanora, brought flowers and mercy with her, and the smiling at pain. In the spring of 1902 a daughter, Anne-Marie, was born.

To shunt off the excess of his new faith and wonder, and objectify his new world-view, Strindberg wrote three plays, *Swanwhite, The Crown Bride,* and *The Dream Play,* in which love shows itself invincible, triumphing over the wickedness of a stepmother, over child-murder, feudal hatred, and the scaffold, or, as in the last play, shining through all the miseries of an evil world, as its one brief gratuity. Of these plays, the first was directly inspired by the love of Harriet Bosse and is brimming with faith and goodness, while the second sounds a much more somber tone, with murder and the scaffold in the background as the penalty for illegal love. In *The Dream Play,* written some time after the marriage, love is only a momentary flickering in a world black with suffering. Here, too, domestic strife breaks out and shows itself inevitable, since even the Daughter of Indra begins to fret and hate her husband in their mean and suffocating room. She had taken the poor ugly lawyer, whom everyone else hates, as her husband. In his profession he has never heard anything but curses and rage and vengeance and his hands have grown black with the evil about him. The Daughter of Indra in divine pity, crowns him with a wreath of thorns and offers to be his wife. But the evils of marriage prove too great for her. Cold, hunger, cabbage, dirt, suffocation, and a complaining husband bring her to a crucial despair. There is one kind of beauty that costs nothing, explains the Lawyer, and that is the beauty of orderliness. The Daughter warns him of "short accents." Then the strife begins:

"Pardon me, Agnes!" says the Lawyer. "But I have suffered as much from your lack of orderliness as you have suffered from dirt. And I have not dared to set things right myself, for when I do so, you get as angry as if I were reproaching you—ugh! Hadn't we better quit now?"

The Daughter: "It is very difficult to be married—it is more difficult than anything else. One has to be an angel, I think."

The Lawyer: "I think so, too."

The Daughter: "I fear I shall begin to hate you after this!"

The Lawyer: "Woe to us then!—"

It is evident from *Richtfest,* an autobiographical sketch written in 1904, that Strindberg's fanatical sense for orderliness would have put a terrible strain on any marriage. If he came home and found the curtains askew, or a coat on the sofa, or a broken chair, or a squeaking door, his day was ruined. If he found his child looking out of the window, or his desk disturbed, he was beside himself. It soon occurred to him that his wife was impossible. The noise of her boots disturbed him grievously and woke the child. She borrowed books from him and loaned them to his enemy, and when he asked for them back, she flung herself into a rage of righteous indignation. Also, like his first wife, she found herself a lady-friend who soon corrupted her tastes, transformed her personality, and alienated her affection. Strindberg lay awake at night, if the fever phantasy of the hero of *Richtfest* can be trusted, more lonely and miserable than ever as a bachelor, cursing the twisted skein of his existence which had led him to such a prison of the soul. For, once more, the witches danced and horrors crept about him. He heard the front door slam shut with unearthly force. Then came a galloping along the corridor like the pattering of hundreds of bare-foot men, but though he tried, he was powerless to move from his bed. In the next room he heard his wife stir in her bed but she was also frozen with fear. Through the wall came the great wave of her hatred. "Why did you not tell me that the house was haunted?" she asked him, trembling with rage and terror. So she held him responsible for that, too? he reflected sadly, and he determined to leave her. "So you are thinking of leaving?" She had seen the Baedeker on his desk. "Yes, in order not to be murdered or thrown out on the dust heap," he replied. "And throw us out in the street?" By the time Strindberg wrote this account of his marriage, the bright flame had burnt down to dust and bitterness. The hero of the novel is tortured by fever and repeated operations, and his broken report is mixed with the brain spectres of which Strindberg had lately grown so fond. One cause of the failure of this marriage, according to this account, was Strindberg's own goodness of heart. Thus, on one occasion, when he was caught playing with young girls, his wife burned with jealousy, and he realized that he should have taken this occasion to show her how it feels to be supplanted. Instead he pitied her, who had deserted him, and went home with her. It was evident that Strindberg regarded himself as a scapegoat who suffers because of his very goodness, for it seemed to him that his virtues irritated people more than anything else, so that they felt it a sort of duty to plague him. Whether this was true or not, it was certainly not an idea calculated to prosper his marriage, which was foredoomed, like all his protracted relationships, to ruin.

He himself might have foreseen this outcome, were it not for the enchantment of the lovely young actress, who met his moods to such a nicety, and undertook, with such quiet beauty, the work of his redemption. He might have foreseen how he would hate to have his Buddha, or his Oriental effects disarranged, or his flowers, or his soul. Yet he was blind to what he knew so well. He had begun, indeed, by loving this actress in the role of the Lady and had encouraged her in this part, yet the Lady in *Toward Damascus* turns wicked and spiteful and plagues her husband with the cruelest ingenuity. The Lady was, in fact, a composite picture of his first two wives, with many of the worst qualities of each. When Strindberg wrote the Damascus plays his vengeance had required a sacrifice. He had, therefore, delineated his first two wives in the character of the Lady, in their unhappiest aspects. He had begun his courtship of Harriet Bosse by requiring her to perform this double part of angel and scourge to the Stranger, in which she first lures him with her goodness, then curses him with her wickedness. This was a bad beginning. What could he hope from her after such a precedent? To be sure, he warned her against reading his fatal *The Confession of a Fool,* the book that had turned his second wife and the Lady in the play, into wicked furies. In vain! The marriage crashed. Wife and child traveled away, leaving a lonely man in a haunted house gazing sadly at the baby carriage, the toys, the garments and fragments with a thousand sweetest memories, reviewing the shipwreck of what, to him, was the most precious thing on earth.

Hereafter, distance lending enchantment and some relief, he called from time to time on wife and child and took the liveliest interest in their future. Later on, when the divorce had been concluded (1904) and time had set a proper space between his love and ardor, he advised her to marry again and marry handsomely, for she was not suited, he felt, to an adventurous life. Sometimes, in the memory of this brief winter love, Strindberg could be quite mild and forgiving, sometimes bitter and rancorous. In *Toward Damascus III* (1903-4) both moods appear. In the beginning, we see the Lady and the Stranger blessedly happy on the sea and by the white house, with the great stars heavy with tears hanging low over the pines and with a prayer in the quiet air. There is no end to their love. Then the Stranger grows bad and suspicious and fearful again and the Lady wonders whether he has not swallowed her personality. The Stranger explains that, so far from doing this, he has allowed her to drink from a great reservoir of the world's culture. They separate. When the Lady has lost her child, however, she returns to the Stranger and begs to be taken back and forgiven. At the end then, it seems, Strindberg treats her quite favorably. He is good to his first wife, he is good to his second, and he is true to the finer moments of the third. About the same time, he wrote a set of fairy tales and other stories, graceful lyrical little pieces, which remain today almost unequalled in their *genre*. In all of them, the distinction between good and evil is very clear and important, and good triumphs over evil with mysterious certainty.

Strindberg had now achieved a great reputation among liberals and conservatives, socialists and students, and the whole Swedish nation was ready to accept him. But, having arrived at the summit he had sought all his life, he chose to write "the most libelous book in Swedish literature," a vicious personal attack on his old friend Geijerstam, and on the literary circle in Stockholm, which lost him his bright reputation overnight. What possessed him to do this, it is hard to say—whether the rancorous memories of unhappy marriages, of faithless friends, or of a vampire who had annoyed him for years, or whether he feared that too much approval might clip his wings and reduce him to bourgeois smugness. In any case, so he says, the book gave him little pleasure in the writing. It was a work of duty with "the starry heavens above him and the moral law within." It was black magic, he knew, and there was no doubt that he would be stoned for it. Yet to this he was accustomed. The book must be written as vengeance upon a man who had crept into his life and stolen his words, his thoughts, his honors, and his happiness. *Black Flags* was a masterpiece of invective and satire and Strindberg's greatest novel. When it was published cautiously in a small edition, the scandal grew alarmingly, and the remaining copies fetched fabulous prices. (Hedén.) The critics were vindictive. The author has "defiled everything like a dog," wrote one. "It should never have been written," said another. "August Strindberg, how did you dare to do it?" The critics were right. It *was* a terrible book.

For many years Strindberg and Geijerstam had been the closest friends. But Geijerstam's great fault, in Strindberg's eyes, was that he had once threatened to write up the story of his first marriage. Subsequently he had edited some of Strindberg's works and aided him in other ways, but always he had pressed too closely into Strindberg's life, he thought, assumed too much authority, and taken too much credit. Once he had stolen an idea for a play from him and then asked him to the performance. This was the last straw. In *Black Flags* Strindberg takes his revenge. Zachris, the hero, is represented as a sort of literary vampire, whose only talent in the world was the alarming capacity for burying his suckers in the inner life of literary men, and by flattery, insinuations, interference, plundering and treachery, in which arts he was a master, reducing them to his will and to his mercy. He wrote to Björnson. He wrote to Ibsen. He wrote to every great literary figure, addressing them always as an old friend, praising them here and blaming them there, and offering in kindness to take them under his protecting wing. When the great men resisted this interference and sent him about his business, Zachris cherished their letters and read them aloud to show how all his services were paid by ingratitude. Thus he won sympathy. When unmasked or defeated or disclosed in his treachery, he had always this resource. He could throw off the lion's skin to become a helpless little lamb, and in this posture he could wring pity even from those who knew themselves to be his victims. But once he had insinuated himself into the heart and confidence, appealing to pity, gratitude, old friendship and using whatever wedge came to hand, he became terrible again and wielded an irresistible power. He was wily and resourceful and there was no getting rid of him. When the front door was denied him, he crept in at the kitchen door. When thrown out he slid down the chimney. He intruded everywhere. When a profound remark was made in a company, he distracted attention by an anecdote. When he read a book he believed that he had written it himself, and soon began writing it over again with slight variations. In these arts he was a wizard.

The great writer Falkenström (i.e. Strindberg) was an easy victim, because unhappily he could not endure the charge of ingratitude. "Twenty years," he confesses, "I fled from this creature, but he pursued me." Zachris stole his friends, broke up his marriage, gave orders to his theatrical directors, appeared always in the newspapers as his protector and patron—yes, took charge of his affairs, published his books and pocketed more than half the profit. Often he pressed in upon his sympathies like a woman, so that Falkenström blushed within. But while posing as his

master and teacher, Zachris also fought his ideas and "every time
that I was killed, this corpse-worm crept out."

Zachris' friends forgave him a great deal when they thought of
the torments he had suffered at the hands of his wife, Jenny.
Jenny is a cruel, depraved, cynical creature, and Strindberg's description of her would be worthy of the contemporary Stern, or
Thomas Mann. Her elegant beauty having faded, she must throw
back her head continually to offset the effect of her fallen cheeks.
Her bitterness makes her terrible. In the presence of Zachris she
explains to her previous husband what a fool she had been to
leave him. But if Zachris should die— "I carry your ring," she
continues, "for you were my first love, and remain the only one.
. . . And with you I would gladly have had children, but not
with this lout here. The idea that I should have to bear the brat
of this ox! I should want to drown it, before it came into the
world with spectacles, paunch and a cigar in the corner of its
mouth."

Zachris, in the meantime chewed his cigar until his lips were
brown. He was not pleasant to see, for he was thinking how now
he would avenge himself by forcing her to pregnancy, and so
ruin her beauty. When the first child came it was a monster and
so hateful that the mother would not look at it. "At two years
he could curse and drink punch; had given up the words father
and mother, and addressed people always with: 'Heh, listen!'
The guests he received with abusive language; listened to the
conversation of his parents and betrayed their secrets." Then
another boy was born, as unattractive as the first. Jenny sank under the burden. She fought for her beauty and her life while her
husband, though he persisted in his vengeance, himself died
a spiritual death. To escape him, she flies to the house of a Lesbian blue-stocking and then Zachris feels her loss, as a boundless
pain of longing. For, as Strindberg says, "in every human soul
dwells something beautiful. And memory, to the honor of the
human race, has the power to cancel the hateful and transform

what is common-place into a thing of beauty." Jenny dies slowly, fighting, desperate and weak, and the scene closes in frustration, chaos, misery and grotesque futility.

The sketch of Zachris is the masterpiece of the book and can only be compared, in frightfulness, to Sologub's picture of the Little Demon. It is also, of course, a brilliant analysis of the vampire character. But the book contains other portraits, some of them personal, and many biting criticisms of society. One problem to which he returns here as in *The Gothic Room* and the Blue Books, and which worried him, in fact, all his life, was the question of sex and the modern emancipated woman, and here in bitter resentment and poisoned memories, he surpasses—even himself.

XXVIII

THE BEDEVILED VIKING

IN *Black Flags* Strindberg depicted his old friend Geijerstam as the lowest and most dangerous reptile in the kingdom. Toward the man who had threatened to write the story of his first marriage and interfered with the third, who had stolen his ideas, meddled with his finances, and crept stealthily, like a thief, into his inner life, Strindberg showed no mercy. His revenge was a brutal unprecedented attack, a hateful caricature, which many regarded as the devil's own work. Geijerstam sank into disgrace and obscurity while all Sweden buzzed at the shameful exposure. As for Strindberg he shuddered at what he had done and commenced to hate his vanquished enemy even more than before. Oppressed with his guilt, he swore that, before God, he was justified. If he had ruined his former friend, it was no fault of his, but a greivous penance that the powers had imposed for the chastening of a higher soul. Yes, he was to be pitied.

To justify himself and drown the loud voice of his conscience, always roaring at some imaginary or real misdeed, Strindberg set forth on a new novel in which the society of the nineties is racked and riddled, and denounced more spitefully than ever before. *The Gothic Room* (1904), which is a continuation of *The Red Room* (1879), is mainly concerned with the fortunes of Dr. Borg, the cynical scientist, and his brother, the conservative editor. Politics, sex, marriage, women's emancipation and women's wickedness provide the themes; brother-strife, sex-hatred, and dire contention within the family darken the plot, which culminates in women triumphant, tyrannous dogs, wise lunatics and chaos. From these sorry times Strindberg seeks escape through religion and the mystical wisdom of Swedenborg. Marriage, which he had formerly defended, despite all its horrors, must now be abolished. It is the home of evil thoughts, of treason and shame, where vampires plunder the soul and men are forced to suicide and the blackest despair. "In the marriage-bed one loses his personality, his self-respect, his manhood. . . . It is the grave in which a divine image is laid, and out of it comes a beast." So intimate is the bond between man and wife that each can read the other's mind. The wife can anticipate and therefore frustrate the thoughts of her husband, and he can know her mind and see how she deceives him at a distance. Defiled by this contact with "the lower sphere of another man," the husband loses all interest in home and children and seeks to hang himself. He has but one defence against her. He can withdraw his "aura," in which he had warmed and flattered her and invested her with all her wonder and beauty, for without his aura she freezes and dies.

Dr. Borg, the brilliant, disgraceful, rowdy, giant doctor of *The Red Room,* has now grown more vicious and cynical than ever. He has been married twice. The first wife was so inordinately vain of her person that she grew jealous of the doctor's privilege, and thought the honor of possessing her too great for him. She therefore withdrew from his love and remained jealous even in the nuptial embrace. Finding this unsatisfactory, however, she complained to her mother that she was not really married and so acted the part of a virgin. And she persisted in these complaints even when the child came. It was in vain that her mother warned her that her husband would surely kill her and the world draw the worst conclusion from her idiotic prattling. She continued to lament her virgin state. One day she explained to her husband that, as it seemed to her, he had had no part in the child. Then the "African nature of the doctor" broke loose and the marriage was dissolved. After a few months, however, he wedded again and once more he was obliged to lower himself and admit, following the teaching of Ibsen and Björnson, that woman is superior to man, for this marriage, though two children were successfully raised, likewise turned out badly. Why did they not separate? Because the children, their misery and mutual hatred, bound them together. "The occultists say that man and wife produce a semi-spiritual substrate in each other which possesses a sort of personal existence; others hold that their souls grow into one another like grafted roots and that they live in perpetual embrace; they feel with and through each other as twins do; therefore the one part suffers when the other does evil; he suffers even the sorrow that he has caused; therefore man is defenceless against her whom he loves, and love is suffering." Again, the children, though a bond between them, are still a source of contention. "Can't a mother educate her own children?" cried the wife. "By the devil, no," replied the doctor. "She shall not raise sodomites!"

Dr. Borg develops a healthy abhorrence of emancipated women, yet he confronts them everywhere and mostly in his profession. One day a well-dressed woman, the mother of two children, complained to him of her nervousness induced by celibacy within the marriage state. But the doctor will not prescribe a lover, as she apparently desires, and sends her away with a curse. Had this been an isolated incident, it had been amusing enough. It was not. It was a symbol of the gyneolatry and decadence of the times. Soon the doctor's sister-in-law, Britta, appeared and, as the representative of the women's party, condemned his rudeness and threatened to report him to the medical society. "The jig is up," thought the doctor. And so it was. His reputation was slandered in the papers and his practice fell away.

Britta, herself, was a most determined person, devoted to "the modern woman" before God or any other duty. In the pursuit of this cause, she opposed her husband, the conservative editor, tooth and nail. Finally, she decided that he must be sacrificed, must be shorn of his power, the love of his children and everything dear. Having accomplished her purpose, the unhappy man, crazed by his misfortunes, runs mad through the woods, bellowing like a bull. This procedure, in turn, strikes terror in the heart of Britta. She freezes at this mortal estrangement of her spouse. She freezes and dies.

In the meantime, her daughter, Esther, has led a strange life. Being homely and therefore handicapped as a woman, she determined to be a man and so went off to the medical school, where she worked and drank and caroused with the students so much that gradually she was accepted as one of them, and no one thought of her any longer as a woman. One night therefore when the students went off to a brothel, they took her along as a matter of course. There, however, she met a young count to whom she felt drawn as to something better than herself. The count, for his part, is surprised to find a girl of good family in such a place. He himself has only come there to avoid the offence of appearing better than his friends. He is curious about this strange, unhappy girl and their conversation plunges with the usual Strindbergian directness, straight to the springs and miseries of the soul. There follows a penetrating analysis of the character of the prostitute. Then, they witness together the death-bed confession of an old man in which we hear again the horrible story of *Asra,* the fatal conflict between the devil of desire and the cruel restraints of Pietism. Such is the inauspicious beginning of their love. In it there is much that is touching and wistful but also a strain of weariness and disillusion which reflects the mental tone of the author. Being modern, the lovers decide upon a trial marriage. Esther's mother, Britta, who sympathizes with their notion, permits the count and her daughter to live together in her own house. Here for a time they are happy enough, but in the end the experiment is a failure. Married or not, the inevitable strife breaks loose and Britta compels them to marry. Before this can be done, however, the count intuits mystically the infidelity of his trial wife, and withdraws his aura in the warmth of which she had grown happy and beautiful. Thereupon she freezes, like her mother, her life and movement gone.

The young count expresses, of course, Strindberg's own views, but Dr. Borg is a better representative. His experiences in marriage were Strindberg's own. In particular the wife's charge that her husband is too old, or unsatisfactory in the marriage relation, that his child is not his own, Strindberg suffered three times over, and of each of his wives he makes the same complaint. In a novel written three years later (1906), older wounds burn and bleed, for in *The Scapegoat,* he sees his whole life as the dismal pilgrimage of a doomed man, fated to suffer for the faults and offences of others. The hero of this story, Libotz, is a lawyer in a small town, and as honorable and virtuous, as soft-spoken and innocent, as could well be imagined. Yet his very virtues arouse suspicions. Either he is an angel, says the publican, Askanius, or the worst snake and the meanest hypocrite in the world. The fact is, he is too good to be true, so that people feel it their duty to plague and torment him. In the beginning, to be sure, with the strong aid of Askanius, he prospers, builds up a clientele in the town, saves money, and wins respect by his honesty and ability. Then his wretched old father appears on the scene and demands that his son free him from the charge of falsifying his accounts. The poor lawyer is obliged to defend his guilty father, to go to jail with him as a drunkard, to wait on him hand and foot and take over all his guilt. The townspeople are only too willing to believe evil of Libotz and rejoice in his disgrace or misfortune. In the shop windows his face is caricatured and no one is hated as much as the gentle innocent lawyer.

Everyone turns against him. His friend robs him of his sweetheart. Askanius, his patron, believes him a scoundrel and hates him in spite of his gentleness and gratitude. And people hate him instinctively without knowing why. Perhaps it is only because his name is Libotz which is a hard name to pronounce. The poor lawyer had begun his martyrdom early. Even as a child his father, a grocer, had forced him to sell damaged coffee and give short weight to the customers. Since then he had suffered meekly for the sins of others. Once to be sure, even his patience gave way, and climbing to the top of a hill, with his cylinder hat in his hand, he made a personal complaint to God.

The character of Libotz is carefully drawn. He is the scapegoat or the serum-animal who carries within him all the poisons of society and thereby purifies it. Askanius, the host, is likewise a very striking character and the picture of his defeat and death in the vast grandiose restaurant which was to have been his pride and fortune, ranks among Strindberg's finest. Night after night he sits all alone at the window of this immense establishment with its hundreds of white tables, like ghosts, and hundreds of lights, and plays the music box through the ghastly emptiness. The place, in the course of time, becomes the scandal of the town and people go out of their way to avoid the spectral old man in the window.

Following his third divorce, Strindberg became a lonely vicious old man once more and lived again in haunted isolation, brooding over old injuries with mixed moods of vengeance and remorse. Now he counted himself a divine scapegoat, now the very devil himself; now he prayed and fasted and forgave the world; now marauded the seas to kill any chance enemies that had escaped him. Once more common noises and spectacles confounded him. If a chair moved above his head, it was the day of judgment. If a stranger frowned, or smiled, it was a plot. Also, like his character, Libotz, he suffered from the malice of the merchants, who always tried to sell him misfit shoes and shapeless clothes. Yes, it took all the courage he could demand to go shopping. And when he bought clothes for his children in Finland, the case was hopeless, for then he was always cheated.

While writing novels he had also been busy with poems, stories, and plays. In a poem *The Dutchman,* and a subsequent play, he depicted the sad career of a man who has lived through six marriages and six disillusionments. The Dutchman has been cursed with too many wives. He has paid the greatest penalty of all and now as a white-haired old man he reviews with quickening ardor and returning bitterness the long vicissitudes of love and hate. Strindberg next wrote a great world-historical trilogy *Moses, Socrates, Christ* which turned out to be, however, not so great as he had expected. Also, he wrote a continuation of *Swedish Destinies and Adventures* and a fragment of a drama, *The Island of the Dead.*

Yet Strindberg was dissatisfied. For several years the Stockholm theatres had ceased to perform his plays and there were still twenty-five which had never been put on. Happily, therefore, in 1907, he realized his old dream of founding a Strindberg Theatre. *The Intime Theatre,* as it was called, was a little house with a small stage, simple decorations, with draperies, hints and symbols. It was designed for the performance of short crucial dramas with few characters and a concentrated action, and the audience were to maintain a most intimate relation to the players. Footlights, which annoyed Strindberg and estranged the audience, were to be abolished and subtle light effects substituted. Strindberg had apparently learned much from the Little Theatre movement with which he had come in contact in Germany.

Although shyness often kept him away from the theatre during performances, Strindberg took a lively sympathetic interest in his actors and gave them much advice. For one thing they must watch most carefully the cadence of their speech, for if that was right everything else would follow. Oddly enough he regarded them as martyrs, for the sufferings they depicted so realistically must have cost them no end of pain, night after night! He thanked them from his heart. So delighted was he with his new theatre that he wrote four plays in the same year, 1907, uniquely designed to meet its needs. They are terse, drastic little pieces, written closely, with the compact and summary cruelty of which Strindberg was an undisputed master. *Thunderstorm, After the Fire* and *The Pelican* have much in common with the short naturalistic plays of the eighties, but *The Spook Sonata,* which abounds in bizarre unearthly effects, is reminiscent rather of *The Dream Play.* To emphasize their character and their suitability to *The Intime Theatre,* he called them Chamber Dramas and numbered them by the opus. Indeed, they were a happy analogue to chamber music, for though only a few strings are heard, they sob and threaten and complain multifariously, and sound forth intricately the cruel tragedies of quiet houses. For an old man whose heart was still too young for forgiveness or submission, but still rang with aspirations and disillusions, they answered, answered for all his bitterness. They sang in brutal accents, with several dark refrains, a contrapuntal despair of life.

In *Thunderstorm* Strindberg portrays his own lonely life after his divorce from Harriet Bosse, his longing that he may see her and the child again, and his haunting fear that he shall. Although he had advised her to marry again, he was no doubt horrified to find that she had taken him at his word and wedded an actor, for the idea that his child should have a step-father was always more than he could bear. The Master in the play, like Strindberg, had married at fifty a young woman whom he dearly loved, and promised to leave her the moment his age became a burden to her youth. Since the child came in due course of time, everything should have prospered—but after a few years the young wife made him feel so superfluous that he departed abruptly, thus redeeming his promise and saving his honor. He then buried himself in a quiet, peaceful loneliness, obliterated from his mind all that was ugly in the marriage, remembering only the beautiful parts and keeping alive the love-flowers, determined to live out his old age fondly through the enhancement and magic of memory. But it turns out that the wife, who had intended to leave first, is quite mortified at his departure. She retorts by spreading rumors which blacken his name and destroy his reputation, and she turns his friends against him—even his devoted brother. In these arts she excelled, for while to him she had been only hateful and stupid, for others she could be beautiful and winsome.

For years the Master lived in quiet solitude, keeping the house exactly as it was, immersed in his memories, when gradually it develops that his wife and her new husband, a gambler, are living in the apartment above and that his daughter is used as a decoy bird at a night club. (A typical Strindberg nightmare.) Accidentally the Master meets his daughter on the stairs, but is terribly disappointed. She calls him Uncle, for such she has been taught to believe he is, and seems to be quite satisfied with her step-father. (An even more horrible nightmare.) He is quite angry with his wife for disturbing the peace of his old age. She has grown beautiful in his memories, but now his phantasy is poisoned, his one solace. Then, in fulfillment of symmetrical justice, the gambler runs away with a young girl and the thirty-year-old wife is left alone to suffer the same sorrow that she had brought upon the Master. He, in the meantime, is deeply sympathetic, but has grown too wise to take her back.

The Pelican is a domestic tragedy with the mood of the early naturalistic plays. The mother of the house compares herself to the pelican, which tears its own breast to feed its young, but resembles more the lioness which eats its cubs. She is one of Strindberg's vampire women. For years she has starved her children ingeniously, eating the gravy and meat and giving them only water and bones, and she has frozen them to save money for her lover. Moreover, she has betrayed her husband and brought him to his death. In the play, she marries her lover to her daughter to have him in the house. But here the trouble begins and all her shamefulness is brought to light suddenly by her clairvoyant son. He pities her because she is so wicked and finally sets fire to the house to wipe out so much impurity. The flames close about the son and the daughter, who at last are warm again, while the mother leaps to her death through a window.

In the two remaining chamber plays, Strindberg is concerned with that elaborate net of human destinies, intertwining and crucially linked, in which apparently chance events are woven, by the great world-weaver, into a moral pattern. Throughout his most variegated life, the Stranger in *After the Fire* has been aware of connections and repetitions. He sees in one situation the result of another, earlier one. On meeting *this* person he was always reminded of one he had met in the past. On meeting a man whom he but half recognizes, he inquires: "Did we ever fight each other as boys? . . . Have we never told lies about each other, or robbed each other, or got in each other's way, or seduced each other's sisters? . . . No, but my father was in the customs' service while yours was a smuggler." These dark connections of destiny the Stranger always finds.

In *The Spook Sonata* the tangle of lives is even more intricate and alarming. The old vampire, Hummel, sits out in front of a quiet house, warming his freezing hand in that of the student whose father he has ruined. He plans to marry the Student to the Colonel's daughter, who is really his own. He sees his fiancée, with whom he had sworn eternal love sixty years ago, but she does not recognize him. Then comes the janitress! "That Dark Lady," he explains, "is her daughter and the dead man's, and that's why her husband was made janitor. . . . But the Dark Lady has a lover . . . and this elegant lover is the son-in-law of the dead man, and you can see his bed-clothes being aired on the balcony up there. . . . That's a bit complicated, I should

say!" As the play proceeds, the quiet house shows itself a whorl
of evil destinies in which every petty circumstance has a meaning beyond itself.

Old Hummel is a first-rate vampire. An old man of eighty,
his life gone thin and cold, he seeks warmth and vitality in the
lives of others, and schemes and plots, and goes through key-
holes, to gain power over younger souls. Being possessed of
great wealth and all the tenacity of a boa, he usually has his way
with people, creeping about them with his clammy limbs and
strangling, and, though an invalid in a wheel-chair, he brings
chaos and calamity to many lives. In order to feed upon the
soul of the Colonel, he penetrates his secrets and buys up his
debts, and in one short interview strips him naked, takes away
his furniture and property, proves that he is neither a colonel
nor a nobleman, that he is not the father of his child nor any of
the things he pretends to be, and exposes him with shameful
cruelty, as Strindberg had his friend Geijerstam. Then, in an impressive scene, the old vampire lays bare the hypocrisy and rot-
tenness of all the Colonel's guests and commands them out of
the house. But, at this point, the Mummy interferes. The
Mummy is the wife of the Colonel and an erstwhile mistress
of Hummel, who for forty years has lived in a closet wor-
shipping her youthful image and talking to her parrot, whom
she has come to resemble very much. She turns the tables on
the vampire in a twinkling and it is proved that he is a greater
sinner and hypocrite than they, and less what he seems to be.
Old Hummel is now so shattered that the Mummy brings out
the death screen and makes him hang himself. Did Strindberg
think this *his* due for having exposed and libelled Geijerstam?
On rare occasions, perhaps. Like Hummel, certainly, he "was a
man who cannot forgive until he has punished." "To punish,"
the vampire admits, "has always seemed to me an imperative
duty. . . ."

After dealing Geijerstam his death-blow in *Black Flags,* Strindberg continued unappeasable. In the Blue Books, he portrays him again as a sort of classic vampire, and in *The Great Highway* (1909), he gives him the same black character. When, during the same year, Geijerstam died in sorrow and humiliation, a victim, it is said, to the open vindictiveness of *Black Flags,* Strindberg is still far from remorse or forgiveness, and there is some reason to believe that he was rather pleased, than not, at the astonishing success of his attack. To rejoice in the death of an enemy was not, of course, Christian manners, and Strindberg, who counted himself in these days both a Christian and a martyr, was somewhat uneasy,—still, on reflection, he found precedents in *The Old Testament* and so continued in his ways. Thus, when his literary enemy, Levertin, died, Strindberg, who had suffered the vicious attacks of his critic for years in silence, out of respect for the Christian principle of "turn the other cheek," now opened up his batteries on the grave and made the dead man pay. In general, he was of the belief that the misfortunes of his enemies, and even of his gentler critics, was the direct consequence of their opposition to him, and was usually quick to point this out. It was only natural, therefore, that he should rejoice on these occasions, for there was justice in the world and powers befriending him. But, sometimes though justice kept her balance, there was something crooked in her smile, and Strindberg knew that he himself must pay the penalty. In 1908, when *The Intime Theatre* was deep in financial troubles and Strindberg himself responsible to the extent of all his property and books, the cause could be no other, he thought, than his own past impiety. He promised to strike from his works all godless or immoral lines, a threat which brought his director to despair. In such moods, he likewise lamented his youthful wildness, his atheism, his Darwinism, and he regarded his gold-making as a diabolic temptation, a witches' brew with bats and night-shades.

In these years, Strindberg experienced a new conversion. He

fought to believe the Christian dogmas and sometimes regretted, with Sir Thomas Browne, that there were no more difficult ones to try his faith. At other times, he frankly admitted that three-gods-in-one was too much for him, and then, shifting to the old Patristic principle, would declare solemnly enough that he accepted the dogmas of the Church because of their intrinsic absurdity. His very uncertainties made him intolerant. Religion, he maintained, should be made compulsory in the schools, and all high officials should be passed by the Church. Also, in the direction of abstinence, he made great strides, banishing strong drinks, though retaining beer, and the Temperance societies made much of him. Whether for health or religion, he also denied himself complete satisfaction in the precious matter of coffee. Perhaps he remembered how Swedenborg had been interrupted by an angel in the midst of a most gratifying meal and sternly warned about the flesh. But abstinence was a trial for Strindberg, even as a man of sixty, and meekness was impossible. In him the Christian virtues duelled incessantly with the old pagan energies.

The Viking, Strindberg once said, is always half philosopher and half marauder. During the years 1907–09, he himself alternated between brooding and killings, and in his rage he cut down friends and enemies alike. Sometimes his victim was an almost unknown man; sometimes a critic, who years before had taken exception to one of his books; at other times simply the state, the atheist, the aristocrat, the woman, or better, the blue-stocking. Thus, Selma Lagerlöf suddenly appears in the libellous *Black Flags* under the name of Thekla Lagerlök, and Heidenstam, the man whom Strindberg once counted his only friend, was made to suffer his rage. His old enemy Wirsén, on the contrary, he handled with some respect. He even went so far as to admit that Wirsén had been right in opposing his naturalism and irreligion of the eighties. Yet, after all, Wirsén had not been pure in his motives. Strindberg's attacks were usually spiteful and personal. The issue may have been a matter of philosophy or literary style, but Strindberg was more than likely to bring in the color of his victim's hair, his face, his profession, his wife, if he didn't like them, thus making his polemic sweeping and general. When his devoted friend, the painter Carl Larsson, once objected to his pessimistic view of mankind, Strindberg darkened and, turning to the piano, played and sang a sepulchral song as a warning. Then, in a Blue Book, came an outrageous attack. Larsson is there described as a fox-faced, backbiting liar, who calls on Strindberg after a misfortune to see whether he is suffering properly, who, though he poses as a model husband and father, shames the wildest youth and accompanies them to the brothel. Then, after dissecting him and finding that his muscles, skin, beard, etc., are all of them false, Strindberg begins to wonder whether, after all, he is not merely describing himself!

In 1910, Strindberg moved into the Blue Tower on Drottingsgata to enjoy the company of the actress, Fanny Falkner, whom he had met at the theatre, and to profit by the care and the splendid cooking of her mother. At first, however, he was little pleased with either. The dishes she prepared for him he characterized as "swine and Esquimau food" and sometimes it came to him pathetically that he was being poisoned. Also, both mother and daughter he accused of fraud and embezzlement and once, in his rage, threw Miss Falkner quite out of his room. The next we hear is that he has fallen in love with her, writes plays in her honor, and boosts her for the leading roles at the theatre. In this matter, however, he is opposed by his manager, for, like his first wife, Miss Falkner is no great actress. Strindberg now shakes off his sixty years, assumes the costume and manners of youth, straightens his back, quickens his step, and renews his joy in life. In a verse drama, *Abu Casem's Slippers* (1908), in the mood of *The Thousand and One Nights* and undoubtedly inspired by his little elf, Strindberg portrays the feverish life and death devotion of a prince for a maid, Zulieka. Despairing of winning her, he wastes romantically, bound by fever and passion. Finally, he seeks his blue dove in the woods and roars like a lion at his deprivation, and roars again with love when he finds her. She, to do her credit, after all her excuses is quite impressed. They embrace like long-lost children. In the background always is the Ape, who imitates everybody unpleasantly, and represents, no doubt, the irony of fate or of the earth forces.

Miss Falkner became, in time, indispensable to Strindberg—the dear confidante of all his passing thoughts—and she could not but be flattered by the tender affection of such a distinguished man. Thus, the story went the rounds that he was engaged to this eighteen-year-old girl, an idea which Strindberg refuted mirthfully. He was much too old for that—and much too wise. Not long afterward, while looking at the heavens through a telescope, he proposed to her and she accepted. They would be married. But, before this could come about, Miss Falkner reflected, and changed her mind. Whether her reversal was a hesitation at the idea of wedding a man of sixty, or a sudden absolute terror of becoming the wife of the famous Strindberg, is not known. Certainly, on this latter ground, any woman had reason enough. Strindberg's sense of order had grown into a perfect passion for the immaculate, and, though he called it "a sense for beauty," this helped very little. To live beside a man who started at every knock on the wall or clatter of chairs, as at a thunder of warning or sign from the powers, was beyond her strength, and Miss Falkner knew it. She tells how one day, feeling himself pursued by a woman on the street, he stepped deftly aside, requiring her to walk ahead of him, and then stepped on her heels for revenge. This sort of thing made her consider.

Miss Falkner's refusal, though he knew it was for the best, broke Strindberg's much-tried heart, which, he found to his dismay, was still too young and ardent, too ready for love and pain. The world-worn lover suffered deeply this new infruition, and was precipitated again into rancor, hatred,—and a new conversion. In 1909, he wrote his last play, a new rendering of his Damascus journey to the cross. "The Wanderer" has broken with mankind to journey in the lonely snows of the Alps, yet he is forced back to society, like the Stranger in *Toward Damascus,* and made to cross the sin-stations of purgatory.

During this period, also, feeling that the end was approching, and having much bitterness in his heart and many disclosures to make, Strindberg reviewed his long career and wound up the frantic years in a great compilation, a synthesis, as he said, of his whole life. Even as early as 1906, he had commenced to turn over the leaves of the past, to recall those fateful moments of his existence, those luminous turns of argument which disclose, as by a stroke of lightning, the very pivot of the soul, to consider and sift a thousand circumstances, scientific, religious, common-place, personal, and he returned again and again to his curiosity shop, a big green box, in which for years he had collected wisdom and lore, personal grievances and idiosyncracies, vengeance, and all the odds and ends of the earth. In the Blue Books, as he called them, no attempt is made at plot or even continuity. They consist of single-page entries in which the teacher and the pupil, representing Strindberg's stronger and weaker self, expound their science, their wonders and riddles, agree in weird recollections of men and things, or castigate some well-known person or institution. Thus, Wagner's music is condemned and the resentment he arouses explained as the healthy hatred of that which is evil. Scientists, specialists, and particularly evolutionists, are roundly scored as pompous, sterile wind-bags. Darwinians, whom Strindberg always calls little apes (Æfflinge), may have descended from monkeys, but not Strindberg and other good Christians. Atheists, we learn, are either hypocrites or disciples of chaos. Here, also, we meet again many of Strindberg's old scientific theories, theories on every subject, and violent attacks on modern discoveries. Thus, the stars, he affirms, are not sources of light, for they appear smaller under the magnifying lens of the telescope, nor are they so very far away. The Frauen-höffer lines on the spectrum, which have advanced Physics and Chemistry so enormously, Strindberg describes as a monstrous absurdity, while the work on radium and the consequent "re-duction" of the elements, he seemed to believe had been stolen from him. It was unjust and ridiculous anyway, that a woman, Madame Curie, should be credited with the discovery. It was wicked! Strindberg is also loud in his ridicule of Cuneiform, the language of the Babylonians, then just recently discovered. He had studied Chinese in his youth and mastered all its difficulties, yet could make no sense of Cuneiform. It was therefore nonsense, he concluded, yet his discussion shows that he had made a seri-ous effort to interpret the strange symbols and his remarks are, as usual, spectacular and original. In the Blue Books, also, ap-pear accounts of Strindberg's many chemical studies and his truly important work in the physiology of plants.

Witches, vampires, mystical phenomena, receive, of course, a good share of attention and the influence of Swedenborg is apparent throughout. Nowhere does the text excel so much as in its wealth of psychological insights, though always underneath is seen the urgent motives of assault and self-defence. Thus the teacher goes on to many things. One moment he speaks of the irresistible dimple beside the knee of a virgin, while the next he speculates, perhaps, on the curious formations in the mountains of Colorado. In all, the four volumes of the Blue Books, which occupied Strindberg's last years, are a treasure house of wisdom and oddities, and one of the finest common-place books ever written.

Strindberg, at sixty-one, was still strong in opposition. So were his opponents. Against the explorer, Sven Hedin, he directed an unexpected attack and a controversy followed, at the conclusion of which Hedin drew a lurid picture of the envious Strindberg standing on the ruins of his own tragic life, and hurrying in the blackness toward hell, accompanied by bats and the shrill tones of flutes. He was a surprising mixture, thought Hedin, of "titan, sphinx, vampire, and parasite." Strindberg's old friend, Heidenstam, now conservative and aristocratic, also replied to his enmity, represented him as a barbarian, impatient of the truth, and he saw in his gray mistrustful glance the runaway slave. When also, in the same year, *The Intime Theatre* passed out of Strindberg's hands, an altercation ensued in which he rated and cursed his faithful colleagues in the undertaking, in the vicious manner which he had made all his own.

In 1910, to the astonishment of everyone, Strindberg blossomed out as a newspaper writer and composed a vast number of articles with the same feverish polemical intensity which had characterized his youthful apprenticeship. Stockholm had put Strindberg in his grave, but his surprises, it seemed, were endless. These radical, dangerous, often vicious articles, treating of religious, political, and social subjects were written in a bold style for the instruction of the Swedish nation, and he persisted in these writings as long as he could hold a pen—up to the time of his death. In the meantime, his fame had spread, his greatness, despite occasional dissent, was generally acknowledged, and there was no reason on earth, that anyone could see, for his bitterness and savage attacks. Had he joined hands with the liberals, he might have pleased his critics, made peace with society, won, perhaps, the Nobel prize. He refused and would have nothing to do, in fact, with any party. He refused to be reasonable. He refused to be common-place and followed, disconcertingly, the star of his genius. Against the Nobel prize and its judges he turned all his ridicule and when a large sum of money was to be collected for him, he declared roundly that he would accept nothing but an anti-Nobel prize.

In 1911, as Strindberg reached the peak of his fame and was celebrated as a great man and the nation's first poet, he commenced to weaken physically, and, taking to his bed in sickness, gave himself up to bitter indifference. His past career with its doubtful triumphs gave him little comfort now, and the thought of heaven, even less. His life-work was ended, he saw, and heaven, though certainly true, was far away. Though able to rise again, after a time, and write his articles and Blue Books, he was never again the same. During his illness, complicated by a severe inflamation of the lungs, he had felt the brush of the black wings on his face and knew that soon, for all his tumult and defiance, he must obey. While facing this weird end of all human hopes and striving, his triumph culminated until it made him fearful. In the newspapers he pronounced against the celebrations with which he was now continually threatened, refused honors and distinctions, and when he was given money, paid it out to the poor. The praise of men, it seemed, was hard to bear, worse than their hatred, and martyrdom safer than the summit of fortune. But Strindberg could not deny the people. On his sixty-third birthday, January 22, 1912, they paraded past his house with torches flaming, and the old poet, the son of a servant, so many years the enemy of his class, stepped out on his balcony to receive their acclamation. Students also honored him this day, students, artists, writers, organizations, great men from other countries, admirers everywhere, and testimonies were received even from America. In the city itself, Strindberg plays were performed and much wine consumed in commemoration.

After this, Strindberg continued in the worst of health and suffered greatly, for his illness, as he learned, was cancer, and incurable. When his condition permitted, however, all his old ardor seemed to return; he wrote accounts of his sick-bed experiences for the newspapers and planned numerous literary works. In April 1912, he received word that his first wife, Siri von Essen, had died, an event which threw him into great sorrow, mixed, perhaps, with remorse and the futile longing for a far-away, indissoluable love. Siri, who since the divorce in 1891 had worked and saved and fought for her children, was, after all, his one true love, and she held him still. After her death he dressed in black. When three weeks had gone by, he himself died in great pain. But toward the end came peace and a sense of deep requitement. The powers which had pursued him so long had apparently been assuaged. "Now, everything has been atoned for!" he said.

In the Blue Books, Strindberg illuminated with the shimmer of a thousand memories, his stormy, ill-starred, triumphant life, and in most of his works the theme is the same. Sometimes he painted himself better than he was, usually worse, but always heaven-bound and desperate. As the hot winds blew through his frantic hair, Strindberg grew wise, and, as he wrote, his characters took many forms, saints and vampires, martyrs, devils, and good men with frightful destinies, and often they grew so real and convincing that he himself was at a loss to know which was he. They nodded and led him strangely. In his youth, Strindberg created Master Olaf in his own image, and everything was as it should be. Then, Master Olaf, rejected, began to change in the new editions, to grow doubtful, and skeptical of his great mission in the world. In *Gustavus Vasa* he became a fervent royalist, the strongest arm of the king he had tried to assassinate. In the meantime, Strindberg changed with him. Was he, then, a slave and a tool of his own created characters? Were these men he had built out of phantasy, his masters? He feared habitually the intrusion of quiet, white-faced men and drew back his soul in terror. But in Strindberg's soul walked many men, of all complexions and virtues. They walked and talked, left him no peace or gentle distraction, and they horrified him by their obstinacy and vividness. To be free from them and alone with himself, he gave them life in his plays and novels. Each year he cast out his devils. Each year he drove his sheep out, over the cliff. There were many devils evicted, but little peace achieved, for there were many more, and some came back. In some of his characters he discovered his own thoughts, his words, his manners and passions. He discovered his own self in them and shuddered. Then, he went on and sought his soul elsewhere, and brought forth hundreds more, cast in his own likeness.

One of the truest of these characters was "Jubal Who Had No I," for in the story by this name, Strindberg's whole life may be seen in allegory. This story tells of a boy whose father denied his will to such an extent that he ceased to use the word "I" or to regard himself as a person. His father decides he shall be a tapster and he, of course, since he is deprived of his ego, has no will in this matter or in any other. The boy, whose name is Peal, therefore began his career as a tapster and sang so merrily at his work among the vats that many customers were attracted to the place. One day a theatrical manager passed by and, admiring his talents, advised him to develop his voice and make a figure in the world. Peal, at first astonished that anyone should treat him as an individual and somewhat frightened, agrees at last quite joyfully, and in the course of time becomes a great singer. He now travels abroad where he is so courted and applauded that he falls into wonderment at his own greatness and cannot think too highly of himself. He is told that his name—Peal—is unsuitable to a great singer, that he must take a foreign name that will impress his countrymen when he returns. He therefore abandons his own name, assumes the name of Jubal and begins to dress and act as a native Englishman. He wears English clothes and carries himself stiffly and will not turn around when his name is called in the street. When he meets his old friends a strong compulsion within him holds him back and a voice that is not his own denies the acquaintance. He is no longer himself, for the boy who had no ego has found a fine gilded one that is not his own.

At the height of his power and distinction, he falls in love with a little singer who steals away his name and grandeur and robs him of the borrowed lustre of his new self. Henceforth he is only the husband of the great Madame Jubal. Thereafter follows a long painful wandering in quest of his lost identity, during which time he plays many parts in the vain attempt to find himself. Once he hears himself referred to as "maestro" and straightway begins to compose music, thinking at last to recover what he had so carelessly lost. But this, too, proves an illusion and his elusive ego tempts him on to further wandering, till at last, despairing of the fruitless search, "like all weary men, he was seized with a longing for his life's origin, his mother." Far into the hills he sought her, and complained bitterly of the vampire who had stolen into his life and spirited away his soul. "Why was I taught as a child that I had no soul!" he cried. "It was your poor dead father's fault," said the mother, "for he thought that children were not supposed to have a will of their own." Then she called him by his real name—Peal—and suddenly "he was transformed into his former self. All his roles of kings, of demons, of maestros and models vanished in the air and he was only one thing—his mother's son." Kneeling before her and laying his head on her lap, he whispered, "I have had enough of life. Now I long to die."

THE END

BIBLIOGRAPHY AND MAIN SOURCES

A—STRINDBERG's PLAYS, NOVELS, STORIES; AUTOBIOGRAPHICAL, HISTORICAL AND SCIENTIFIC WORKS.

I. STRINDBERG WORKS IN GERMAN TRANSLATION

August Strindberg's Schriften. Deutsche Gesamtausgabe Emil Schering, translator, 33 volumes. Other translations have appeared in German—far more than in English. The English titles of the Strindberg works referred to in this book are marked by an asterisk in the Index.

II. STRINDBERG WORKS IN ENGLISH TRANSLATION.

Plays

The Outlaw (1871), Master Olaf (1872), Lucky Pehr (1883), The Father (1887), Comrades (1888), Miss Julia (1888), Creditors (1890), Pariah (1890), Simoon (1890), The Stronger (1890), The First Warning (1893), Debit and Credit (1893), Mother Love (1893), The Link (1893), Advent (1898), There are Crimes and Crimes (1899), Gustavus Vasa (1899), The Dance of Death I, II (1901), Easter (1901), The Crown Bride (1902), Swanwhite (1902), The Dream Play (1902), Storm (1907), After the Fire (1907), The Spook Sonata (1907).

Novels and Autobiography

The Red Room (1879), The Son of a Servant (1887), The Growth of a Soul (1887), The Confession of a Fool (1888), On the Seaboard (1890), Inferno (1897), Legends (1898), Fairhaven and Foulstrand (1902).

Stories and Miscellaneous Works

The German Lieutenant and Other Stories, Have Plants Nerves? Historical Miniatures, In Midsummer Days and Other Tales, Married I, II, Stories and Poems, Zones of the Spirit.

B—Important Books and Articles about Strindberg

Aster, Ernst von: Ibsen und Strindberg, Menschenschilderung und Weltanschauung; Diem, Eugen: August Strindberg. Ein Beitrag zur Krisis des modernen Europäers; Erdmann, Nils: August Strindberg, Die Geschichte einer kämpfenden und leidenden Seele, trs. by Henrich Goebel; Esswein, Hermann: August Strindberg; Hansson, Ola: Das Junge Skandinavien; Hedén, Erik: Strindberg, Leden und Dichtung; Helmecke, Carl Albert: Buckle's Influence on Strindberg; Jaspers, Karl: Strindberg und Van Gogh; Liebert, Arthur: A. Strindberg: Seine Weltanschauung und Seine Kunst; Lind-af-Hageby, Lizzy: A. Strindberg: The Spirit of Revolt; Neue Rundschau, Berlin, 1906, A. Strindberg und Georg Brandes, Ein Briefwechsel; Paul, Adolf: Strindberg. Erinnerungen und Briefe; Scheffauer, Herman: A Correspondence between Nietzsche and Strindberg in North American Review N. Y. C. 1913; Schmid, Günther, Strindberg's Naturwissenschaftliche Schriften, in Deutsche Rundschau, Berlin 1918; Strecker, K. M. W.: Neitzsche und Strindberg mit ihrem Briefwechsel; Uddgren, Carl Gustaf: Strindberg, the Man; Upvall, Axel, Johan: August Strindberg. A psychological study with special reference to the Œdipus complex.

INDEX

* The titles of Strindberg's writings are marked with an asterisk.

INDEX

Date Due